WEBSTER'S
NEW WORLD™

Law Dictionary

WEBSTER'S NEW WORLD™

Law Dictionary

by Susan Ellis Wild, Legal Editor

WILEY

Wiley Publishing, Inc.

Webster's New World® Law Dictionary

Copyright © 2006 by Wiley, Hoboken, NJ

Published by Wiley, Hoboken, NJ
Published simultaneously in Canada

For general information on our other products and services or to obtain technical support, please contact our Customer Care Department within the U.S. at 800-762-2974, outside the U.S. at 317-572-3993, or fax 317-572-4002.

Wiley also publishes its books in a variety of electronic formats. Some content that appears in print may not be available in electronic books. For more information about Wiley products, please visit our web site at www.wiley.com.

Library of Congress Cataloging-in-Publication data is available from the publisher upon request.

ISBN-13 978-0-7645-4210-7

ISBN-10 0-7645-4210-9

Manufactured in the United States of America

10 9 8 7 6 5 4 3 2 1

Dedication

To my mother, an original Webster, who gave me my love of words.

About the Author

Susan Ellis Wild has been a practicing lawyer since 1982, and currently is a fulltime litigator in Allentown, Pennsylvania. She is President of the 600+ member Bar Association of Lehigh County, Pennsylvania. Susan has litigated more than 100 cases and frequently writes and speaks to audiences about law-related topics. She has been appointed by courts on numerous occasions to act as an independent arbitrator/mediator of cases. Susan is admitted to the Bars of Pennsylvania, the District of Columbia, and Maryland, and has appeared in courts in a number of other states.

Table of Contents

Part I
DICTIONARY

A

AAA *abbr.* See **American Arbitration Association.**

AALS *abbr.* See **Association of American Law Schools.**

ABA *abbr.* See **American Bar Association.**

abandon *v.* **1** To intentionally give up for all time an assertion or a claim of an interest in property or in a right or privilege. **2** To repudiate, withdraw from, or otherwise disassociate oneself from a duty or responsibility. **3** To intentionally fail to complete.

abandoned property See **property.**

abandonee *n.* A person or party to whom property or a right has been abandoned or relinquished.

abandonment *n.* **1** The act of abandoning property or a right with no intent of reclaiming it or of later giving it away or selling it. See also **forfeiture, relinquishment, renunciation, surrender,** and **waiver. 2** The act of abandoning a person with the intent of terminating the duties or him or her. For example, the intentional failure by a parent to communicate with or to provide financial or other support to his children. See also **desertion.**

abate **1** *v.* To end, eliminate, do away with, or make null and void. **2** *v.* To diminish, decrease, or lessen in degree or amount. **3** *n.* The reduction of a bequest or devise made in a will because the combined value of all bequests and devises, and/or the debts owed by a testator, exceed the assets in the testator's estate. **4** *n.* The rebate or reduction of taxes already assessed and/or paid.

abatement *n.* **1** The act of abating. **2** The process of, or the state of, being abated. **3** The amount abated.

abatement clause *n.* A contractual provision releasing the tenant of a lease from the obligation to pay rent when an act of God prevents the occupancy of the premises.

abator *n.* A person who diminishes or eliminates a nuisance.

ABC test *n.* A rule of law that allows employers not to provide unemployment compensation to independent contractors. The test for whether an individual is an independent contractor as opposed to an employee is threefold: 1) does the individual work independently of the employer's control (A = alone); 2) does the individual maintain his own place of business (B = business); and 3) does the individual practice or work at an established trade, and exercise control over his own schedule and method of operation (C = control)? The name derives from the letters normally used to designate the three parts of the test. See **contractor.**

abdication *n.* The act of a person or branch of government renouncing or abandoning an office, trust, sovereignty, privileges, or duties to which he or she is entitled, holds, or possesses by law.

abduct *v.* **1** To carry or lead a person away from where he wants to be or wants to go by use of force, threats, or deception. **2** To restrain or conceal a person in order to prevent his escape or rescue. See also **kidnapping.**

abet *v.* To actively, knowingly, and/or intentionally aid, encourage, incite, instigate, or otherwise support the commission of an act.

abeyance *n.* **1** An indefinite or temporary state of inactivity or suspension. **2** An incomplete or undetermined state of existence. **3** The status of real property or of a position or title when its ownership or occupancy is not vested in any existing person or party.

abide *v.* **1** To await. **2** To accept or submit to. **3** To tolerate or withstand. **4** To adhere, execute, obey, perform, or otherwise act in conformity with. **5** To dwell, remain, reside, or stay.

abiding *adj.* Certain; indestructible; permanent; steadfast; unaltering; unfaltering; unshakeable.

ab initio *adv. Latin.* From the first act. From the beginning; back to one's creation or inception.

abnormally dangerous activity *n.* An undertaking so dangerous that, even if precautions and reasonable care are used, it cannot be safely performed and anyone who engages in it is strictly liable for any resulting injuries and damage, especially if 1) there is a risk of serious harm to people or property, 2) the activity cannot be performed in some other way that avoids those risks, and 3) the undertaking does not normally occur at the location where it is to take place. See also **liability.**

abode **1** *n.* A dwelling, home, or other fixed place where a person resides. **2** *v.* Past tense and past participle of **abide.**

abolish *v.* To abrogate, annul, cancel, eliminate, put an end to, recall, repeal, or revoke, especially things of a seemingly permanent nature, such as customs, institutions, and usages.

abolition *n.* **1** The act of abolishing. **2** The legal abolition and prohibition of slavery. **3** The abolition of slavery in the United States by the Thirteenth Amendment to the United States Constitution.

abortion *n.* **1** The premature termination of a pregnancy. **2** The intentional and artificial termination of a pregnancy that destroys an embryo or fetus. **3** The spontaneous expulsion of an embryo or fetus before it is capable of living outside the womb.

above *adv.* **1** Previously in the same chapter, document, or text. For example, a reference to a court case cited earlier in the same document. **2** Having the power to review the decisions regarding questions of fact and/or law made in a court. For example, appellate courts, such as the United States Supreme Court, are above, or can review, the decisions made by one or more trial courts. See **jurisdiction, question of fact,** and **question of law.**

abridge *v.* **1** To diminish, lessen, or restrict a legal right. **2** To condense or shorten the whole of something, such as a book, and not merely a portion of it.

abrogate *v.* **1** To annul, cancel, destroy, overturn, repeal, revoke, set aside, supercede, or otherwise do away with or put an end to. **2** To abolish a custom or law by some authoritative, formal, legislative, or other legally effective method.

abscond *v.* **1** To secretly or suddenly leave a place or to go into hiding, especially to avoid arrest, prosecution, the service of a summons or other legal process, or an action by a creditor. **2** To leave a location, often in a hurry, with money or property of another.

absent without leave *n.* The act of being away from one's military duties or post without permission but with no intent of deserting. Abbreviated as AWOL. See also **desertion.**

absentee *n.* A person who is not where he or she would normally be found, such as a place of residence or work.

absentee landlord *n.* A landlord who resides so far from the leased real property that his is not, or is not expected to be, readily available to personally address any problems concerning the property.

absentee voting See **voting.**

absentia See **in absentia.**

absolute *n.* **1** Without any conditions, encumbrance, qualification, or restriction. See also **discretion, divorce, immunity, privilege,** and **fee. 2** Not liable or subject to revisions; conclusive. **3** Free from any restraint or restriction in the exercise of government power.

absolute law See **natural law.**

absolute liability See **strict liability.**

absolve *v.* **1** To forgive misconduct. **2** To free from guilt or suspicion; for example, when evidence proves that a suspect is innocent of a crime. **3** To free from the penalties imposed as a result of misconduct. **4** To free from a debt, duty, obligation, or responsibility.

abstention *n.* **1** The act of voluntarily refraining from taking some action, such as casting a vote or participating in a decision or deliberation. **2** A federal court's act of declining to exercise its jurisdiction while awaiting or deferring to a decision by a state court. In doing so, the federal court retains jurisdiction of the legal issues at hand and may decide those issues if the plaintiff is not satisfied with the state court's decision. See also **comity** and **relinquishment.** Several rationales for a federal court's abstention are named for the United States Supreme Court decision in which the rationale was first applied. These include:

> *Burford abstention.* The refusal of a federal court to consider a challenge to a state's administrative regulations and proceedings or to review a

state court's decision involving those regulations and proceedings when they involve a substantial or sensitive area of state concern. *Burford v. Sun Oil Co.* (1943).

> *Colorado River abstention.* A federal court's act of declining to exercise its jurisdiction when there is underway a state court proceeding involving the same parties and questions. *Colorado River Water Conservation Dist. v. United States* (1976).

> *Pullman abstention.* A federal court's decision to await the interpretation of a state law by that state's court before deciding a federal constitutional question that is dependant upon how that law is interpreted. *Railroad Commission of Texas v. Pullman Co.* (1941).

> *Rooker–Feldman abstention.* A federal court's declining to consider the argument that a state court judge violates a party's federal rights for the reason that the proper venue to challenge that judge is that state's court system. *Rooker v. Fidelity Trust Co.* (1923) and *District of Columbia Court of Appeals v. Feldman* (1983).

> *Thibodaux abstention.* A federal court's act of declining to exercise its jurisdiction to allow a state court to decide difficult issues if importance in order to avoid unnecessary friction between federal and state authorities. *Louisiana Power & Light Co. v. City of Thibodaux* (1959).

> *Younger abstention.* **1** A federal court's decision to halt or interfere with a state court's criminal proceeding unless the prosecution has been brought in bad faith or harassment. **2** A federal court's decision to halt or interfere with a state court proceeding on the grounds that the arguments of the party seeking the federal courts involvement can be raised and fairly deter-

mined in the state court. *Younger v. Harris* (1971).

abstract *n.* A concise summary of a text. See also **abstract of judgment, abstract of record,** and **abstract of title.**

abstract of judgment *n.* A copy or summary of a court's judgment. When it is filed with the appropriate authorities, a lien is created on the judgment debtor's nonexempt property in favor of the judgment creditor.

abstract of record *n.* A summary of the record of a case advising an appellate court of the underlying facts, all the steps taken to-date in the case, the decision of the trial court, and the legal issues to be decided.

abstract of title *n.* A short history or summary of the ownership of a parcel of land. The abstract includes a list of all conveyances, transfers, and other evidence of title; all grants, conveyances, wills, records, and judicial proceedings that may affect title; and a list of encumbrances and liens of record on the land, along with a statement whether the encumbrances and liens still exist. A company whose business is to obtain such information from public records usually does such an abstract for the mortgagee or buyer of real property in connection with a proposed sale of land. See also **chain of title.**

abstraction *n.* **1** The act of separating, taking away, or withdrawing. **2** The act of taking with the intent to injure or defraud. **3** The unauthorized taking of financial statements or funds with the intent of misappropriating them.

abuse **1** *v.* To mistreat or neglect a person, particularly as to one for whom the actor has special responsibility by virtue of a relationship, e.g., spouse, child, elderly parent, or one for whom the actor has undertaken a duty of care,

e.g., nurse-patient; **2** *v.* to use an object in an illegal or unreasonable manner. **3** *n.* The mental or physical mistreatment of a person, frequently resulting in serious emotional, mental, physical, and/or sexual injury.

> *child abuse.* **1** The intentional or neglectful abuse, which includes sexual mistreatment, inflicted on a child. **2** A parent or caregiver's intentional or neglectful act or failure to act that results in a child's abuse, exploitation, or death. **3** An act or failure to act that results in a possibility of immediate and serious harm to a child. See also **battered person syndrome** and **child neglect.**

> *elder abuse.* The abuse of an elderly person by his or her child or caregiver, that may include battery, verbal abuse, isolation, and the denial or deprivation of food.

> *sexual abuse.* **1** An illegal sexual act. **2** Unlawful sexual activity or contact with a person without her consent. The activity or contact is usually imposed by the use of force or threats of violence. The application of the term varies, but it is usually applied to activities or contact that do not amount to **rape,** but sometimes the term includes rape. Also called carnal abuse and sex abuse.

> *spousal abuse.* The abuse inflicted on a person by his or her spouse. See also **battered person syndrome** and **cruelty.**

abuse excuse *n.* A courtroom tactic whereby a criminal defendant claims that mental or physical abuse either explains the defendant's conduct, especially in cases involving violence against the alleged abuser, or makes the defendant incapable of telling right from wrong. The phrase is almost exclusively used as a term of derision by those unsympathetic to such claims.

abuse of discretion   *n.* A trial court or administrative agency's ruling on a matter within its discretion that, in light of the relevant facts and law, is arbitrary, capricious, unconscionable, unfair, unreasonable, or illegal. An appellate court will not reverse a ruling that was within the discretion of the trial court or administrative agency merely because the appellate court would have reached a different decision. Instead, the trial court or administrative agency's decision must be wholly inconsistent with the facts and the law and with any reasonable deductions that can be made therefrom.

abuse of process   *n.* The tort of beginning or otherwise using the judicial civil or criminal process for an improper purpose. There may be a legitimate basis for instituting or using the judicial process, but the actual intent behind the action is improper. See also **malicious prosecution.**

abut   *v.* To adjoin; to border on; to cease at the point of contact; to connect or join at a border; to share a common border with.

abuttal   *n.* The border of a parcel of land in relation to adjoining lands.

academic freedom   *n.* **1** The right of a teacher or student, especially at the college or university level, to discuss or investigate any issue, or to express opinions, on any topic without interference or fear of penalty or other reprisal from either the school or the government.   **2** A school's freedom to control its own policies without government interference, penalty, or reprisal. The extent to which academic freedom exists depends on many facts, including whether the school is a private or public institution and whether it is a primary or secondary school or a college or university.

acceleration   *n.* **1** The shortening of the time, or the immediate creation or vesting, of a legal duty, interest, or right that was to arise or vest in the future. See also **acceleration clause.**   **2** The hastening of a real property owner's enjoyment, or the vesting, of his remainder interest in an estate because of the failure or premature termination of a preceding estate.

acceleration clause   *n.* A provision in a contract or in a testamentary or other legal document that, upon the occurrence of specific events, a party's future interest in certain property will prematurely vest. For example, in many loan or mortgage agreements, provision is made that if some specified event occurs, such as the debtor's failure to pay an installment, the creditor may declare the entire outstanding balance to be immediately due.

acceptance   **1** *n.* The act of voluntarily agreeing, expressly or by implication, to the terms of an offer, thereby creating a contract. However, if the act modifies or adds to the terms of the offer, it is not an acceptance, but a counteroffer. See also **offer.**   **2** *v.* To accept delivery of property or to otherwise agree, expressly or by implication, to become its owner, either in exchange for the performance of a contractual obligation or the completion of an inter vivos gift. See also **contract** and **gift.**   **3** *n.* The receipt of a check or other negotiable instrument by a bank or another drawee.

access   *n.* The ability, opportunity, permission, or right to approach, communicate, enter, pass to and from, or view without interference or obstruction. See also **easement** and **visitation rights.**

accession   *n.* **1** The act of acceding or agreeing, especially when it involves the yielding of part or all of one's own position.   **2** The act of acceding to, or coming into possession of, an office, right, or title.   **3** In international law, the formal assent by one county to a treaty between other countries. By doing so, the country becomes a party to the treaty. **4** The acquisition of title to personal property by applying labor that converts it into an entirely different thing (such as turning leather into shoes) or incorporates it into other property. **5** An artificial or natural addition or improvement to property. **6** A real property owner's right to all that the property produces and to all that is artificially or naturally added to it, such as land reclaimed by the use of dams or the construction of buildings and other improvements. See also **annexation.**

accessory *n.* **1** Additional; aiding the principal design; contributory; secondary; subordinate; supplemental. **2** One who aids or contributes to the commission or concealment of a crime or assists others in avoiding apprehension for the crime but not present when the crime was committed. Mere silence or approval of the crime is insufficient to make one an accessory; the person must take steps to facilitate the commission or concealment of the crime or the avoidance of the criminal's capture. See also **misprision of felony, accomplice, aid and abet, conspiracy,** and **principal.**

> *accessory after the fact.* One who was not at the scene of a crime but knowingly assists, comforts, or receives a person known to have committed a crime or to be sought for the commission or attempted commission of a crime, in an attempt to hinder or prevent the felon's arrest or punishment. Such a person is normally regarded as less culpable than the criminal and is subject to prosecution for **obstruction of justice.**

> *accessory before the fact.* One who assists, commands, counsels, encourages, or procures another to commit a crime, but is not present when the crime is committed. Such a person, known as an aider and abettor, is normally considered as culpable as the person who actually commits the crime and is normally treated by the law as an **accomplice.** See also **aid and abet.**

accident *n.* **1** An unintended, unforeseen, and undesirable event, especially one that causes harm, injury, damage, or loss. **2** An unintended and unexpected event, especially one that is undesirable or harmful, that does not occur in the usual course of events under the circumstances in which it occurred, or that would not be reasonably anticipated. **3** In equity, an unexpected and injurious event not caused by misconduct, mistake, or negligence. **4** In many automobile insurance policies, any unintentional event including those caused by misconduct, mistake, or negligence.

> *unavoidable accident.* An accident that is not caused by the negligence or other fault of anyone involved.

accidental death *n.* Death resulting from an accident from an unusual event that was unanticipated by everyone involved. A death may be considered "accidental" even if it was intentional or expected. For example, an insurance policy may provide that its accidental death benefit will be paid if the insured is murdered (although generally not if the beneficiary committed the murder).

accidental death and dismemberment insurance *n.* Insurance that pays the insured or his beneficiaries specified amounts, in addition to or in substitution for compensation for injuries suffered by the injured, for the loss of specific body parts, body functions, or death resulting from an accident.

accidental death benefit *n.* A payment, in addition to the compensation received by the beneficiaries of an accident insurance or life insurance policy, to be made paid if the insured suffers an accidental death. See also **double indemnity.**

accident insurance See **insurance** (*casualty insurance*).

accommodated party See **accommodation party.**

accommodating party See **accommodation party.**

accommodation *n.* **1** Something done, such as providing a loan or signing an accommodation paper as a surety for another, that is done as a favor without any direct or indirect benefit, compensation, or consideration. **2** The act of making a change or provision for someone or something.

accommodation maker See **accommodation party.**

accommodation paper *n.* A negotiable instrument that one co-signs as a surety as an accommodation to another party, who remains primarily liable without receiving any benefit, compensation, or consideration. See also **accommodation party.**

accommodation party *n.* A person who, without any direct or indirect benefit, compensation, or consideration, co-signs a negotiable instrument as a favor to the person who owes the money and, thus, becomes liable on it to all parties except the accommodated party who, by implication, agrees to pay the instrument and to indemnify the accommodation party for any losses incurred in paying it. This is frequently done when the creditworthiness of the accommodated party does not satisfy the person taking the negotiable instrument or extending the credit. Also called, in the case of a promissory note, an **accommodation maker.**

accomplice *n.* One who knowingly, voluntarily, or intentionally, and with common intent and criminal purpose shared with the principal offender, solicits or encourages another to commit a crime or assists or attempts to assist in its planning and execution. Normally, one's mere presence while knowing the crime is about to be committed, without any contribution to the commission of the crime, does not make a person an accomplice. However, in some situations, knowledge combined with the failure to make an attempt to prevent the crime will make one an accomplice. An accomplice is normally regarded as just as culpable as the person who actually commits the crime. See also **accessory, aid and abet,** and **conspiracy.**

accord *n.* **1** An agreement to satisfy a claim by some form of discharging the obligation other than what the obligee is, or considers himself, entitled to. See also **accord** and **satisfaction.** **2** In legal citation, the identification of one case that clearly supports the proposition for which another case is being quoted.

accord and satisfaction *n.* An accord that has been satisfied by the completion of the agreed upon payment or performance. The satisfaction (that is, completion) of the accord extinguishes the original obligation that the obligee was, or considered himself, entitled to. Once satisfied, the subject of the accord can never be raised in any future legal action. See also **novation** and **settlement.**

account *n.* **1** A detailed record of a financial transaction, indicating the debits and credits between the parties to a contract or a fiduciary relationship. **2** The debt remaining to be paid, or the credit to be refunded, as indicated in such a record. **3** A detailed record of the financial transactions, business dealings, and other relations for which records must be kept. **4** In the Uniform Commercial Code, a right to payment for goods whose sale or lease, or for services whose performance, are not evidenced by a negotiable instrument or **chattel** paper. **5** A business relationship involving the management of money or the availability and use of credit. **6** In the common law, a legal action to require a person to account for money or property. See also **accounting**. **7** A statement by which someone explains, or attempts to explain, an event. **8** In business, a particular client or customer. See also **joint account**.

accountant-client privilege See **privilege**.

account creditor *n.* One to whom the balance of an account is owed. See also **account debtor**.

account debtor *n.* **1** One who owes the balance of an account. **2** In the Uniform Commercial Code, one who owes an obligation on an account, chattel paper, or intangible property. See also **debtor** and **account creditor**.

account payable *n.* The balance owed to a creditor as indicated by an account. See also **account receivable**.

account receivable *n.* The balance owed by a debtor as indicated by an account. See also **account payable**.

accounting *n.* **1** The act or a system of establishing how the assets of a business, estate, trust, or other similar entity were managed and disposed of. **2** In equity, a legal action to require one, usually a fiduciary or a constructive trustee, to account for and pay over funds held by them but owed to another. See also **account**. **3** In equity, a legal action for the recovery of funds owed for services performed, property sold, money loaned, or for damage for the incomplete performance of minor contracts. See also **account**. **4** A legal action to complete or settle all of a partnership's affairs. Usually done in connection with the dissolution of the partnership or with allegations of a partner's misconduct. See also **winding up**.

accounting for profits See **accounting**.

accounting method *n.* The accepted method by which a person or business consistently determines his income and expenses and allocates them to an accounting period in order to determine his taxable income. See **accrual method, cash method,** and **contract**.

accounting period *n.* The regular span of time used for accounting purposes. For example, the period used by a taxpayer to calculate her income and to determine her tax liability.

accretion *n.* **1** In property law, the gradual increase in land through natural processes; for example, the creation of land caused by the deposit of sediment on a shoreline of a river or ocean. The new land becomes the property of the owner of the property to which it is attached. See also **alluvion, reliction,** and **avulsion**. **2** In succession law, the increase in an heir or legatee's interest in property when a co-heir or co-legatee dies before the property vests, rejects his inheritance or legacy, fails to comply with a condition to be met before vesting, or otherwise becomes incapable of taking the property.

accrual method *n.* An accounting method that records income and expenses when they are earned or incurred rather than when they are received or paid. See also **cash method** and **completed contract method**.

accrue *v.* **1** To come into existence or mature as an enforceable claim or right. For example, a cause of action may be sued upon once it is an enforceable claim. Likewise, the interest on a sum owed accrues on the date the interest becomes due. **2** To accumulate.

accumulated depreciation *n.* The total depreciation currently recorded against either a single or all productive assets.

accusation *n.* **1** A formal charge of criminal wrongdoing against a person or corporation. See also **indictment, information** and **presentment.** **2** An informal charge that one has committed an illegal, immoral, or otherwise wrongful act.

accusatorial system See **adversary system.**

accuse *v.* **1** To make an accusation against. **2** To prosecute. **3** To formally institute a legal action against a person or corporation wherein they are charged with committing a crime. **4** To judicially or publicly charge one with a criminal offense.

accused *n.* **1** A person who is blamed for a wrongdoing. **2** A person who has been arrested or formally charged by an indictment, information, or presentment with a crime.

acknowledgment *n.* **1** The recognition of a fact or the existence of an obligation and the acceptance of the accompanying legal responsibility. For example, a putative father may acknowledge a child as his during a paternity proceeding. **2** One's formal declaration in the presence of a notary public or other authorized individual that she has signed a deed or other document and that the signature is authentic.

ACLU *abbr.* See **American Civil Liberties Union.**

acquaintance rape See **rape.**

acquiescence *n.* Tacit or passive conduct that implies agreement or consent. For example, if one makes a statement and another is silent when an objection should be forthcoming, the second person's acquiescence to the statement may be inferred.

acquit *v.* **1** In criminal law, to clear a person, to release or set him free, or to discharge him from an accusation of committing a criminal offense after a judicial finding that he is not guilty of the crime or after the court or prosecution determines that the case should not continue after the criminal trial has started. See also **autrefois acquit** and **double jeopardy.** **2** In contract law, to pay or discharge a debt, duty, or a claim.

acquittal *n.* **1** In criminal law, the legal finding, by judge or jury, that an accused person is not guilty of the crime he is charged with. Once the acquittal is reached, the defendant may not be prosecuted again for the same criminal act or transaction. **2** In contract law, the release or discharge from a debt or other contractual obligation.

act **1** *n.* A statute. **2** *n.* Something done or performed. **3** *v.* The process of doing or performing. See also **actus reus, overt act** and **omission.**

action *n.* **1** Any behavior, conduct, or series of acts by a person. **2** A civil or criminal judicial proceeding intended to resolve a legal dispute, claim, or accusation.

> *civil action.* An action brought to enforce, protect, or redress a civil or private right or to compel a civil remedy; any action brought other than a criminal action.

> *class action.* **1** An action brought by a person or a group of people as representatives of a larger group

who have a common legal claim but are so numerous that it is impracticable for all of them to participate or be joined as individual parties in the case. **2** An action brought against a large group of people who have a common legal defense to a claim that they are all potentially liable for but are so numerous that it is impracticable for all of them to participate or be joined as individual parties in the case.

criminal action. An action initiated by the government to punish a person or entity for a crime.

damage action. An action seeking an award of money from the defendant for a wrong committed upon the plaintiff.

derivative action. **1** An action brought on behalf of a corporation by a shareholder when that corporation is entitled to bring an action and, deliberatively or otherwise, fails to do so. **2** An action that is based upon the injury suffered by someone other than the plaintiff. For example, a husband may sue for loss of consortium or services if the defendant injured his wife.

in personam action. See **in personam.**

in rem action. See **in rem.**

quasi in rem action. An action against an out-of-state defendant over whom the state lacks in personam jurisdiction that is commenced by the attachment, garnishment, or other seizure of property owned by the defendant that is located within the state and that is unrelated to the plaintiff's claim.

third-party action. An action initiated by a defendant in a civil case against a person or entity who is not a party to the proceeding that is against the defendant and against whom the defendant claims a right of contribution or indemnity, should the defendant be found liable to the plaintiff.

action in personam See **in personam.**

action in rem See **in rem.**

action quasi in rem See **action.**

actionable *n.* Wrongful conduct that provide grounds for a lawsuit or other legal proceeding.

actionable per quod *n.* Actions that require the allegation and proof of additional facts. For example, in libel or slander, the statement in question may not appear defamatory on its face (such as "Mr. Smith is a member of a particular club"), so the plaintiff has to prove additional facts to establish its defamatory nature ("Every member of that club is a sex offender"). In such actions, the plaintiff has to prove that he suffered damages in order to have a cause of action.

actionable per se *n.* Actions that do not require the allegation or proof of additional facts to constitute a cause of action nor any allegation or proof that damages were suffered. An example, in libel or slander, is a statement that obviously damages a person's reputation (such as "Mr. Smith is a sex offender") that does not require any reference to circumstances or facts to understand its defamatory meaning. In such actions, the plaintiff does not have to prove that he suffered any damages in order to have a cause of action.

act of Congress *n.* A statute formally enacted by Congress in accordance with the powers granted to it by the United States Constitution.

act of God *n.* An overwhelming natural event, often unpredictable or difficult to anticipate, that is uncontrolled and uninfluenced by the power of man and that could not be prevented or avoided by foresight or prudence.

actual   *adj.* Real or existing in fact as opposed to being assumed or deemed to have happened or exist. See also **apparent** and **constructive.**

actual authority   See **authority.**

actual cash value   *n.* A fair or reasonable price that can be obtained for an item or property in the ordinary course of business, not under duress or exigency. Synonymous with **fair market value.**

actuary   *n.* One who computes insurance and property costs, such as the cost of insurance premiums and risks.

actus reus   *n.* The voluntary and wrongful act or omission that constitutes the physical components of a crime. Because a person cannot be punished for bad thoughts alone, there can be no criminal liability without actus reus.

ADA   *abbr.* See **Americans with Disabilities Act.**

ad damnum   *n. Latin.* To the damage. The amount of money sought as damages by the plaintiff in a civil action.

ad damnum clause   *n.* A statement in the complaint in a civil action that specifies the amount of money sought by the plaintiff. See also **complaint** and **prayer.**

addendum   *n.* An addition to a document.

additur   *n. Latin.* It is added to. A trial court's order to increase the damages awarded by a jury. It is done to prevent the plaintiff from appealing on the grounds that inadequate damages were awarded, but the court cannot issue the order without the defendant's consent.

The term may also refer to the increase itself, the procedure by which it is done, and the court's power to issue the order.

adduce   *v.* To compile or offer, generally in the context of introducing evidence at trial.

ADEA   *abbr.* See **Age Discrimination in Employment Act.**

ademption   *n.* The reduction, extinction, or withdrawal of a devise or legacy by some act of the testator, before his or her death, that clearly indicates an intent to diminish or revoke it. See also **ademption by extinction, ademption by satisfaction, abatement, advancement,** and **lapse.**

ademption by extinction   *n.* An ademption of some specific or unique property that occurs when the property is destroyed, given away, or sold or does not otherwise exist at the time of the testator's death.

ademption by satisfaction   *n.* An ademption that occurs when the testator, while alive, gives the property that is the subject of a devise or legacy to the intended beneficiary in lieu of the testamentary gift.

adequate remedy at law   *n.* A legal remedy, usually an award of money, that provides sufficient compensation to the plaintiff, thereby making equitable relief, such as specific performance, unavailable.

ad hoc   *adj. Latin.* For this; for a particular purpose. For example, ad hoc committees are often created to accomplish a particular purpose.

ad hominem   *adj. Latin.* To the person. Appealing to personal prejudices instead of reason; attacking one's character rather than his arguments.

adjoining *adj.* Abutting; bordering upon; sharing a common boundary; touching. See also **contiguous** and **adjacent.**

adjourn *v.* To briefly delay, suspend, or postpone a court proceeding. See also **continuance.**

adjournment sine die See **sine die.**

adjacent *adj.* Laying near or close by, but not necessarily connected. See also **adjoining.**

adjudge *v.* To render a judicial decision or judgment concerning a disputed subject that is before the court. For example, a court may adjudge that a defendant is obligated to pay the damages sought by the plaintiff.

adjudication *n.* The process of hearing and resolving a dispute before a court or administrative agency. It implies a final judgment based on the evidence presented, as opposed to a proceeding where the merits of the case were not considered by the court or administrative agency. See also **default judgment.**

adjure *v.* **1** To earnestly and solemnly bind, charge, or command. Frequently, persons who are adjured are placed under oath or a threat of penalty. For example, juries are adjured to consider only the evidence presented at trial as they attempt to reach a verdict in an action. **2** To earnestly and solemnly entreat or request.

adjusted basis *n.* The value of a taxpayer's original investment in property, adjusted by the value of subsequent capital improvements and depreciation deductions. See also **basis.**

adjusted gross income *n.* A taxpayer's gross income minus the deductions, usually business deductions, they are allowed under the tax code. See **income.**

ad litem *adj. Latin.* For the suit. For the purposes of, or pending, the particular lawsuit. See also **administrator ad litem** and **guardian ad litem.**

administration *n.* **1** A court's management and distribution of property during a judicial proceeding. **2** The management and settlement of the estate of an intestate or of a testator who has no executor by a person appointed by the court.

administrative agency *n.* A governmental regulatory body that controls and supervises a particular activity or area of public interest and administers and enforces a particular body of law related to that activity or interest.

administrative law *n.* **1** The law covering the organization, duties, and operation of an administrative agency. **2** The law created by an administrative agency consisting of rules, regulations, orders, opinions, or reports containing findings of fact and administrative hearing decisions.

administrative law judge *n.* An official of an administrative agency who presides at an administrative hearing and has the power to administer oaths, issue subpoenas, and rule on the admissibility of evidence as well as hear, consider, and weigh testimony and other evidence and make or recommend factual or legal decisions.

Administrative Procedure Act *n.* A federal statute governing the rule-making and administrative proceedings of federal administrative agencies by providing guidelines for rule-making and adjudicative hearings, judicial review, and public access. Most states have similar statutes governing their state administrative agencies. Abbreviated APA.

administrator   *n.* A person appointed by the court to manage a part or all of the assets and liabilities of an intestate or of a testator who has no executor. In many states, the person can be a man or a woman, but in the others, the term refers to a male, while a female who is appointed to perform these duties is called an **administratrix.** See also **administrator ad litem** and **ancillary administrator.**

administrator ad litem   *n.* A person appointed by the court to represent the interests of an estate in an action. Such an appointment is usually made because the estate has no administrator or because the current administrator has interests in the action that conflict with those of the estate.

administratrix   See **administrator.**

admiralty and maritime   *n.* All things related to events occurring at sea and on inland waters.

admiralty courts   *n.* Federal courts exercising jurisdiction over admiralty and maritime matters. However, in some matters, the Congress has granted concurrent jurisdiction to the state courts.

admissible evidence   *n.* Evidence permitted by the law to be considered by a judge or jury in deciding the merits of an action. Only admissible evidence may be considered, but the judge has the discretion to exclude admissible evidence from his or the jury's consideration. For example, cumulative evidence, or evidence whose probative value is outweighed by the risk of confusing the issues to be decided, may be excluded.

admission   *n.* **1** Any act, assertion, or statement made by a party to an action that is offered as evidence against that party by the opponent.   **2** A defendant's failure to deny, or his voluntary acknowledgment of the truth, of an alle-gation in a complaint, counterclaim, or request for admissions.   **3** The acceptance by a judge of evidence for consideration by himself or the jury when determining the merits of the action.   **4** The granting or obtaining of a license from a state or an established licensing authority, such as a state bar association, or permission from a court, to practice law in that state or before that court. See also **admission pro hoc vice.**

admission pro hoc vice   *n.* The granting of special permission to an out-of-state attorney, or an attorney not admitted to practice in any state or before any court, to practice law as counsel for a party in a particular lawsuit.

admonition   *n.* A judge's advice, cautionary statement, direction, reprimand, or warning to a jury, lawyer, party, spectator, or witness regarding any matter that arises during a judicial proceeding.

adoption   *n.* **1** In family law, the legal process that establishes a parent/child relationship between individuals who are not related by blood. Once the adoption is completed, the adoptive child becomes entitled to all the privileges belonging to a natural child of the adoptive parents, and the adoptive parents acquire all the legal rights, duties, and obligations of the child's natural parents. Furthermore, all legal rights, duties, and obligations between the child and his or her natural parents (except, in some states, the obligation to pay delinquent child support payments) terminates upon the completion of the adoption.   **2** In contract law, the acceptance by a person or entity of the rights and responsibilities made for their benefit under a contract to which she is not a party.   **3** To accept legal responsibility for the act of another. See also **ratify.**

adoptive *adj.* **1** Related by virtue of an adoption. For example, an adult who adopts a child is that child's adoptive parent. (Although the adult is referred to as the adoptive parent, the minor is known as the adopted child.) **2** Pertaining to an adoption of any kind. For example, by adoptive works or conduct, one may accept legal responsibility for the act of another.

ADR *abbr.* See **alternative dispute resolution.**

adult *n.* A person who has attained the age of majority. See **age.**

ad testificandum *adv. Latin.* For testifying. See **subpoena** (*subpoena ad testificandum*). See also **habeas corpus.**

adultery *n.* The voluntary sexual intercourse by a married person with someone other than his or her spouse. The consent of both parties and penetration are required for adultery to exist. Under the common law, only a married woman could commit adultery, but most states now apply the term to married men as well. Also, in the states where adultery is still a crime, most statutes now provide that the unmarried sexual partner of a married person can also be charged with the offense. See also **criminal conversation, fornication,** and **rape.**

ad valorem tax See **tax.**

advance *n.* Monies paid before any consideration is received in exchange.

advance directive *n.* A durable power of attorney that becomes effective if and when one becomes incompetent, and that directs the limit to what medical procedures should be employed to prolong one's life.

advance sheets *n.* A paperback or looseleaf booklet or pamphlet containing recent decisions issued by a (usually appellate) court. Advance sheets are published between the announcement of the court's decision and the decision's incorporation in a bound volume of law reports. See also **reports** and **slip opinion.**

advancement *n.* An irrevocable gift to an heir during an intestate's life, given with the intention that it shall diminish or extinguish the heir's share of the intestate's estate under the laws of intestate succession. See also **satisfaction, ademption,** and **lapse.**

adventure *n.* Any commercial or financial venture involving speculation or risk. See also **joint venture.**

adversary *n.* An opponent, especially an opposing attorney or party in an action.

adversary procedure See **adversary system.**

adversary proceeding *n.* **1** A judicial hearing or other proceeding involving a real dispute between opposing parties. See also **controversy** and **ex parte.** **2** A proceeding before the Bankruptcy Court to settle disputes regarding the distribution of the assets of a bankrupt.

adversary system *n.* A method of adjudication in which active and unhindered parties, usually through their lawyers, contest with each other and present support in favor of their respective positions, usually through the examination and cross-examination of witnesses and the presentation of other evidence, to a neutral and independent decision-maker. In criminal cases, this is often called the accusatorial system.

adverse possession *n.* A method of acquiring title to real estate by actually, continuously, and openly occupying the property for an uninterrupted amount of time to the exclusion of all others and in defiance of the real owner's rights. The required period of occupancy, as well as other possible conditions, are set by statute.

adverse witness   See **hostile witness.**

advice and consent   *n.* Phrase found in Article II, Section 2, Clause 2 of the United States Constitution describing the Senate's role in confirming presidential appointments and ratifying treaties. The "consent" takes the form of a vote. Rarely does a president formally seek the Senate's advice (it has happened only twice; the last time was in 1848), but senators often advise the president informally as to which potential nominees and treaty provisions are acceptable.

advisory jury   *n.* Used in cases where there is no jury trial as a matter of right but the judge desires the non-binding input of a jury. Rarely used.

advisory opinion   *n.* A nonbinding opinion by a court, judge, or law officer on the interpretation or constitutionality of the law, a proposed statute, or a hypothetical legal question submitted to it by a legislative or executive body or an interested party. The United States Constitution prohibits federal courts from issuing advisory opinions.

advisory verdict   *n.* A decision, usually non-binding, of an **advisory jury**.

advocacy   *n.* Active support for a legal cause by argument and persuasion.

advocate   **1** *n.* One who actively assists, defends, pleads, prosecutes, speaks, writes, or otherwise supports the cause of another.   **2** *n.* A lawyer.   **3** *v.* To speak, write, or otherwise support a cause by argument.

aff'd   *abbr.* Affirmed.

aff'g   *abbr.* Affirming.

affiant   *n.* One who makes and subscribes to an affidavit.

affidavit   *n.* A voluntary and written ex parte statement of facts signed and the truth of its content affirmed or sworn to by the declarant before a notary public or another officer authorized to administer oaths. See also **affirmation.**

affidavit of service   *n.* An affidavit that certifies the service of a notice, process, summons, or writ by stating the time and manner in which the document was served.

affiliate   *n.* A corporation that is related to another corporation by one owning shares of the other, by common ownership, or by other means of control. See also **company** *(parent)* and **subsidiary.**

affinity   *n.* **1** A close agreement.   **2** The attraction between people.   **3** Any relationship created by marriage. See also **consanguinity.**   **4** A term used to describe the relationship that one has to the adopted or blood (and usually close) relatives of their spouse. For example, affinity exists between a woman and her husband's brother.

affirm   *v.* **1** To confirm, ratify, or otherwise approve a lower court's decision on appeal.   **2** To solemnly declare that certain statements are true or that one will testify truthfully.   **3** To make a solemn promise. See also **oath.**

affirmation   *n.* **1** The act of affirming the truth of one's statement. It serves the same purpose as an oath and is usually done when the declarant objects to making an oath on religious or ethical ground.   **2** A voluntary and written ex parte statement of facts. It is sometimes required that the document be signed and the truth of its content be affirmed by the declarant in the presence of a notary public or another officer authorized to administer oaths. See also **oath, affirm,** and **affidavit.**

affirmative action   *n.* Any acts by a private or public entity to eliminate discrimination, to correct or remedy the effects of past discrimination, or to prevent future discrimination. Such discrimination is usually based on the race, sex, national origin, or disability of the person being discriminated against. See also **reverse discrimination.**

affirmative defense   See **defense.**

affirmative easement   See **easement.**

affirmative relief   See **relief.**

affix   *v.* To permanently add to, attach, or fasten on.

affray   *n.* The voluntary and consensual fighting between two or more individuals in a public place to the terror of onlookers or the disturbance of the peace. There is no affray when a person is unlawfully attacked and resorts to self-defense instead of fleeing. See also **assembly.**

a fortiori   *v. Latin.* By the stronger (reason). To draw an inference that when one proposition is true, then a second proposition must also be true, especially if the second is included in the first. For example, if a 19 year old is legally an adult, then a 20 year old is, too.

aforethought   *adj.*   Considered in advance; deliberate; premeditated. See also **malice aforethought.**

after-acquired property   *n.* **1** In commercial law, property acquired by a debtor after the execution of a security agreement wherein property acquired by the debtor before the execution of the agreement has been pledged as collateral for a loan.   **2** In bankruptcy law, property acquired by a bankrupt after a petition for bankruptcy is filed.

after-acquired title   *n.* The title acquired by a buyer, who previously purchased property while unaware that the seller did not have complete title to it, after the seller, unbeknownst to the buyer, later acquires complete title to

the property. Title automatically vests in the buyer upon the completion of events that would otherwise give complete title to the seller.

after-born child   See **child.**

after-born heir   See **heir.**

A.G.   *abbr.* See **Attorney General.**

against the (manifest) (weight of the) evidence   *n.* An evidentiary standard allowing a trial judge to set aside a jury's judgment or verdict and order a new trial when it clearly appears to the judge that the jury's decision is unsupported by the credible evidence presented at trial; is based upon false evidence or some improper motive, bias, or feelings; or would result in a miscarriage of justice. However, this does not permit a judge to substitute the jury's decision with his own merely because he disagrees with the decision.

age   *n.* A period of time, especially one marking the time of existence or the duration of life.

age of capacity. The age, usually determined by statute, at which a person becomes legally capable of becoming a party to a contract, executing a testamentary document (such as a trust or will), initiate a lawsuit without a guardian, and so on. See **capacity.**

age of consent. **1** The age, usually determined by statute, below which a person may not marry without parental consent. See also **consent.** **2** The age, usually determined by statute, below which a person is legally incapable of consenting to sexual intercourse. See **consent** and **rape.**

age of majority. The age, usually determined by statute, at which a person attains full civil, legal, and political rights. See also **age of consent.**

age of reason. **1** The age, usually determined by statute, below which a child cannot be legally capable of committing a crime. **2** The age, usually determined by statute or case law, below which a child cannot be legally capable of committing a tort.

legal age. The age, usually determined by statute, at which a person becomes legally capable to exercise a specific right or privilege or to assume a specific responsibility. For example, in many states, a person may legally drive an automobile once she is 16 years of age, but has to wait until she is 21 to legally drink alcohol.

age discrimination *n.* The denial of privilege or other unfair treatment based on the age of the person who is discriminated against.

Age Discrimination in Employment Act *n.* Federal statute that protects most employees between 40 and 70 years of age from age discrimination in the workforce. Other federal and local laws provide other protections against age discrimination in such areas as housing. Abbreviated ADEA.

agency *n.* **1** A fiduciary relationship in which a person or entity act, by mutual consent, for the benefit of another and bind the other party by words or deeds. See **agent, authority, fiduciary** and **principal.** **2** A governmental body with the legal authority to administer and implement specific legislation.

agency couple with an interest *n.* A relationship between principal and agent in which the agent is given an interest in the subject matter of the agency.

agent *n.* One who by mutual consent is authorized to act for another. See **agency, authority,** and **principal.**

aggravated *adj.* In criminal and tort law, a crime or tort becoming worse or more serious due to certain circumstances (determined by a statute for aggravated crimes and usually by statute and case law for aggravated torts) that occur or are present during the commission of the crime or tort, such as the possession of a deadly weapon, the youthfulness or pregnancy of the victim, or the reckless disregard for the other people's safety. The perpetrator of an aggravated crime is usually subject to more severe penalties than for unaggravated forms of offense. The perpetrator of an aggravated tort is subject to punitive damages. See also **mitigating circumstance** and **simple.**

aggravating circumstances *n.* Circumstances, facts, or situations that increase the culpability, liability, or the measure of damages or punishment for a crime or a tort.

aggregate **1** *n.* The sum, total, or whole of all the parts. **2** *v.* To collect or combine.

aggregation doctrine *n.* The rule that prevents a party from combining the amounts in controversy in all of their claims in order to exceed the jurisdictional amount requirement in a federal diversity of citizenship case. See also **amount in controversy** and **jurisdiction** *(jurisdictional amount).*

aggrieved *adj.* To be adversely affected, or to perceive oneself as being so, by an act or situation or by a court's decision.

agreement *n.* **1** A mutual understanding between two or more legally competent individuals or entities about their rights and duties regarding their past or future performances and consideration. While an agreement usually leads to a contract, it could also be an executed sale, a gift or other transfer of property, or a promise without a legal obligation. **2** The understanding between two or more legally competent individuals or entities about the rights and duties regarding their past or future performances and consideration as manifested by their language (oral or written) or by implication from other circumstances such as the usage of trade and the course of performance. See also **contract.**

agreement to agree. A mutual understanding between two or more legally competent individuals or entities that they will later enter into a contract even though the contract's exact terms have not yet been decided; non-binding.

binding agreement. An enforceable agreement or contract.

collective bargaining agreement. A contract between an employer and a union or other representative, voluntarily selected by a majority of the employer's workers within a bargaining group, concerning the wages, hours, and other conditions of employment for that group.

divorce agreement. An agreement between spouses made during a divorce concerning child custody, child and spousal support, property distribution, and other matters. Such agreements are usually incorporated into the parties' divorce decree. See *separation agreement.*

gentlemen's agreement. An agreement not intended by the parties to be legally enforceable, but that is expected to be performed or followed as a matter of friendship or honor. May or may not involve illegal subject matter such as gambling bets.

postnuptial agreement. An agreement between spouses made during their marriage to determine the right to support and each other's property in case of death or divorce. Such agreements are not enforceable unless each party makes a full disclosure to the other of their assets and has consulted with their own attorneys. Even then, most such agreements are not enforceable unless made by spouses who are in the midst of a separation or divorce.

prenuptial agreement. An agreement between spouses made before their marriage to determine the right to support and each other's property in case of death or divorce. Generally, such agreements are enforceable, especially if both parties make a full disclosure of individual assets and have consulted with their own attorneys. See also *postnuptial agreement* and *separation agreement.*

property settlement agreement. See *separation agreement.*

separation agreement. An agreement between spouses made during a divorce or while obtaining a legal separation concerning child custody, child and spousal support, property distribution, and other matters. Such agreements are usually incorporated into the parties' divorce decree or into a judicial decree granting a separation to the parties. Frequently referred to as *property settlement agreement* (PSA).

simple agreement. An agreement for which nothing is legally required to make it enforceable other then some evidence that the agreement was made and the parties consent to it.

unconscionable agreement. Same as adhesion contract. See **contract.**

aid and abet *v.* To order, encourage, facilitate, or to actively, knowingly, intentionally, or purposefully assist, or otherwise promote or attempt to promote the commission of a crime or a tort. Affirmative conduct is regarded; aiding and abetting cannot be established by omission or negative acquiescence. The person who aids and abets is usually just as liable, and subject to the same measurement of damages and penalties, as the person who commits the crime or the tort. See also **accessory, accomplice** and **conspiracy.**

air piracy   See **hijack.**

air rights   *n.* The ownership or right to use any or all of the airspace above one's real property.

a.k.a.   *abbr.* "Also known as." See **alias.**

aleatory   *adj.* Dependant on the occurrence of an uncertain contingent event.

aleatory contract   *n.* A contract in which the performance of at least one party depends upon the occurrence of an uncertain future event.

Alford plea   *n.* A guilty plea entered as part of a plea bargain by a criminal defendant who denies committing the crime or who does not actually admit his guilt. In federal courts, such plea may be accepted as long as there is evidence that the defendant is actually guilty. Named after *North Carolina v. Alford* (1970).

ALI   *abbr.*   See   **American   Law Institute.**

alias   *n.* **1** An assumed or additional name used by a person, frequently to conceal her true identity, or such a name applied to a person by others. See **also known as.**   **2** An alias writ.

alias writ   See **writ.**

alibi   *n.* **1** In a criminal action, a defense that the defendant was somewhere other than the scene of the crime when the crime was committed.   **2** The fact or state of being somewhere other than the scene of the crime when the crime was committed.

alien   *n.* **1** One who is not a citizen, national, or subject of a particular country.   **2** One who is not a citizen, national, or subject of the country in which he resides.   **3** One who is born in or owes his allegiance to a foreign country.

deportable alien. An alien who may be deported because she was an inadmissible alien when she entered the United States or has violated the regulations (for example, by committing a serious crime) governing the conduct of aliens who are within the country.

illegal alien. **1** An alien who enters or remains in the United States without legal authorization or by fraud. **2** An alien who marries an American citizen, but with no intention of living with his or her spouse as husband and wife, for the purpose of improperly entering the United States or avoiding deportation.

inadmissible alien. An alien who cannot legally enter the United States. There are many reasons why an alien may be prohibited from entry, including a criminal record or poor health.

nonresident alien. An alien who permanently resides outside the United States.

resident alien. An alien who legally established permanent residency in the United States.

alienation   *n.* In real property law, the voluntary and absolute transfer of title of possession, by gift, sale, or testamentary instrument, of real property from one to another.

alienation of affections   *n.* In tort law, the willful or malicious interference with the relationship between a husband and wife by a third party without justification or excuse. The interference may be adultery or some other act that deprives one of the affection of a spouse.

It also includes mental pain and suffering such as anguish, humiliation, embarrassment, and loss of social position as well as actual financial losses caused by the disruption or destruction of the marital relationship. See **consortium.**

alienee   *n.* One to whom property is alienated.

alienor   *n.* One who alienates property to another person or entity.

alimony   *n.* Money paid after divorce to former spouse for support, usually for a specified period of time, by court order or written agreement. If paid during pendency of the divorce proceedings, referred to as alimony pendente lite. See **pendente lite.**

aliunde rule   *n.* The doctrine that a verdict may not be called into question by a juror's testimony without a foundation for that testimony being first established by competent evidence from another source. For example, a verdict may not be overturned on the testimony of a juror that he was bribed, unless there was first evidence from another source of the bribery.

ALJ   *n. abbr.* Administration law judge.

allegation   *n.* **1** An assertion of fact that one intends to prove at trial, especially one in a legal pleading such as a complaint, counterclaim, or indictment. **2** Any declaration of something to be true without giving any proof.

Allen charge   *n.* In criminal law, an instruction given by a judge to encourage a deadlocked jury to make a renewed effort to reach a verdict. Named after *Allen v. United States* (1896).

allocution   *n.* **1** The procedure during sentencing when a judge gives a convicted defendant the opportunity to make a personal statement on his own behalf to mitigate the punishment that is about to be imposed. The defendant does not have to be sworn before he makes his address, his comments are not subject to cross-examination, and the opportunity may include the right to offer evidence (such as an explanation for his conduct or a reason why severe sentence should not be imposed) beyond a request for mercy or an apology for his conduct.   **2** A similar procedure where the victim of a crime is given in some states the opportunity to personally speak, before punishment is imposed, about the pain and suffering suffered or about the convicted defendant.   **3** The procedure by which a guilty plea can be accepted in a criminal action. The process usually consists of a series of questions designed to assure the judge that the defendant understands the charges, is guilty of the crime he is accused of, understands the consequences of a guilty plea and that he is entitled to a trial, and is voluntarily entering the plea.

allodial   See **ownership** and **allodium.**

allodium   *n.* Real property owned absolutely and free of any obligation to another with a superior vested right.

allowance   *n.* **1** A portion or share, especially of money.   **2** A portion of a decedent's estate awarded by statute to the decedent's survivors for support during the administration of the estate, regardless of whether they have any rights to the estate or any testamentary disposition or competing claims to the estate. If statutorily available is only to the surviving spouse, it is known as a spousal (or widow's or widower's) allowance. If statutorily available is to surviving spouse, children, or parents, it is known as a family allowance. See also **elective share.**   **3** The court-ordered financial award to a fiduciary for services rendered.   **4** A deduction.

alluvion   *n.* The creation of land caused by the gradual depositing, either by artificial or natural forces, of earth, sand, gravel, and similar materials along the shoreline of a river or ocean by running water. The new land becomes the property of the owner of the property to which it is attached, provided the accumulation is so gradual that it cannot be visibly perceived from moment to moment. See also **accretion, reliction, alluvium,** and **avulsion.**

alluvium   *n.* The land created by alluvion.

alonge   *n.* A piece of paper occasionally attached to a negotiable instrument for the signing of endorsements once the original instrument is filled with endorsements.

also known as   *n.* Phrase used before a list of names used by a specific individual in order to avoid confusion about the person's true identity or by others when referring to the individual. See also **a.k.a.** and **alias.**

alteration   See **material alteration.**

alter ego   *n.* The other self. A doctrine allowing a court to ignore the limited personal liability of a person who acts in a corporate capacity and impose personal liability for the corporation's wrongful acts when it is shown that the individual was using the corporation to conduct personal business and that there was no real separation between the individual's and the corporation's identity. See also **corporate** *(corporate veil).*

a.k.a.   *abbr.* See **also known as.**

alternative dispute resolution   *n.* Formal methods of settling disputes other than by court action, collectively referred to as alternative dispute resolution or ADR. See also **arbitration, conciliation, mediation,** and **summary proceeding.**

alternative minimum tax   See **tax.**

alternative pleading   See **pleadings.**

alternative writ   See **writ.**

ambiguity   *n.* A confusion or uncertainty about the intention or meaning, especially of a provision in a contract or statute.

> *latent ambiguity.* An ambiguity that is not obvious and is unlikely to be found while using reasonable care. For example, a third party contract that provides for a payment to be made to a charity, but two charities exist with the same name. Extrinsic evidence, if allowed, may be required to determine the correct interpretation of the ambiguity. However, if each party, in good faith interprets the ambiguity differently, the meeting of the minds necessary to create a valid contract is not present.

> *patent ambiguity.* An ambiguity that is obvious or apparent upon reasonable inspection.

ameliorating waste   See **waste.**

amenable   *adj.* **1** Legally answerable; required to respond; responsible; subject to. **2** Capable of being tested, adjudged, or brought to judgment. **3** Susceptible to; disposed toward; capable of being persuaded.

amend   *v.* To add to, delete, correct, revise, or otherwise alter.

amendment   *n.* **1** The addition, deletion, correction, or other changes proposed or made to a document. The term is usually capitalized when referring to an amendment in the United States Constitution (for example, the Fifth Amendment). **2** The act or process or revising something. See also **emendation.**

a mensa et thoro   *adv. Latin.* From board and hearth. See also **divorce.**

amercement *n.* **1** The imposition of a discretionary fine or penalty in an amount not set by statute. **2** The fine or penalty so imposed.

American Arbitration Association *n.* A national organization that promotes the use of arbitration to resolve commercial and labor disputes. It also maintains a panel of arbitrators for those who wish to utilize their services. Abbreviated AAA.

American Bar Association *n.* The largest national organization of lawyers, it promotes improvements and reform in the administration of justice and in the provision of legal services to the public. Abbreviated ABA.

American Bar Foundation *n.* A subsidiary of the American Bar Association that funds and sponsors projects in law-related education, research, and social studies.

American Civil Liberties Union *n.* A national organization of lawyers and others who are interested in enforcing and preserving the individual rights and civil liberties guaranteed by the federal and state constitutions. Abbreviated ACLU.

American Law Institute *n.* A national organization of attorneys, judges, and legal scholars who seek to promote consistency, clarity, and simplification in the law through such projects as the Restatements of the Law and the Model Penal Code. Abbreviated ALI.

American Stock Exchange *n.* The second largest stock exchange in the United States. Located in New York City, it frequently engages in the trading of stock of small or new companies because of its less rigid listing requirements. Abbreviated as AMEX and ASE. See also **New York Stock Exchange.**

Americans with Disabilities Act *n.* Federal law enacted in 1990 to protect individuals with physical or mental disabilities from intentional or unintentional discrimination in housing, employment, education, access to public services, etc. Abbreviated ADA.

AMEX *abbr.* See **American Stock Exchange.**

amicus brief See **brief.**

amicus curiae *n. Latin.* Friend of the court. One who is not a party to an action but petitions the court or is invited by the court to provide information or submit her views because she has a strong interest in the case at hand or a perspective that may not be adequately presented by the parties.

amnesty *n.* A pardon for past criminal offenses for a class or group of individuals who are subject to trial but have not yet been convicted. Amnesty may be limited or conditional. For example, amnesty may be offered only to those who perform a certain act, such as community service, within a specific period of time. Also referred to as grant of amnesty.

amortize *v.* **1** To gradually extinguish a debt in advance of its maturity, usually by paying regular installments in excess of the accrued interest each time a periodic interest payment is due. See also **sinking fund.** **2** To arrange to gradually extinguish a debt. **3** To apportion the initial cost of an intangible asset each year over the course of the asset's useful life until the entire cost has been used up.

amount in controversy *n.* The monetary damages sought by a party in an action; the value of a claim even if not expressly stated in the **pleadings.** See **aggregation doctrine** and **jurisdiction** *(jurisdictional amount).*

AMT *abbr.* Alternative minimum tax. See **tax.**

ancestor *n.* **1** One, such as a parent, grandparent, great-grandparent, who precedes another in lineage. **2** Any relative from whom one inherits by intestate succession.

ancient document See **document.**

ancillary *adj.* Auxiliary; collateral; dependant; supplemental; subordinate.

ancillary administrator *n.* A person appointed by the court in a state where the descendant was not domiciled to manage the assets and liabilities and to oversee the distribution of decedent's estate in that state. Such an administrator usually works as an adjunct to the executor or administrator appointed in the state where the decedent was domiciled.

ancillary claim *n.* A claim that is auxiliary to, supplemental to, or dependant on another claim. For example, a claim against a physician who negligently prescribed an unsafe drug may be ancillary to a claim against the drug manufacturer who produced the medication. See **jurisdiction.**

ancillary jurisdiction See **jurisdiction.**

and his heirs See **heir.**

Anders brief *n.* A request filed by a court-appointed attorney to withdraw from the appeal of a criminal case because of his belief that the grounds for the appeal are frivolous. Named after *Anders v. California* (1967).

animus *adj. Latin.* Purposefully; intentionally. **1** Animosity; hostility; ill will; strong dislike; hate. **2** The animating thought, intention, or purpose of an act.

annex *v.* **1** To add, affix, or append as an additional or minor part to an already existing item, such as a document, building, or land. **2** To attach as an attribute, condition, or consequence.

annexation *n.* **1** The act of annexing; the state of being annexed. **2** The point in time when an addition or addendum becomes part of the thing to which it attached. **3** The formal act of a political unit, such as a nation, state, or municipality, annexing land to its' domain. **4** Annexed land.

annotation *n.* Comments that analyze, explain, or criticize, or a collection of brief summaries of appellate cases that have applied or interpreted, a particular statutory provision. These comments and summaries are appended to, and published with, the statute in a set of volumes. For example, the United States Code Annotated contains the statutes of the United States and, after each statutory provision are the comments and summaries pertaining to that provision.

annuitant *n.* One entitled to the periodical payments, but not the principal, of an annuity.

annuity *n.* A fixed sum paid out at regular intervals for a certain period of time and subject to limitations set by the grantor. For example, a person may be entitled to fixed and periodic payments for the rest of his life once he reaches a certain age. See also **life estate** and **trust.**

annul *v.* **1** To cancel, make ineffective, invalidate, nullify, void. **2** To judicially declare something to be void either from the date of decree or ab initio. **3** To make an ecclesiastical or judicial declaration that a marriage is void ab initio and never existed. See also **divorce.**

answer   **1** *v.* To respond to a pleading, discovery request, or other judicial process or procedural step.   **2** *v.* To address or counter allegations, account for one's actions, or otherwise put up a defense.   **3** *v.* To assume the liability or responsibility for another's actions.   **4** *v.* To pay a debt or other liability; to suffer the consequences for one's actions.   **5** *n.* A pleading that is a defendant's principal response to a plaintiff's complaint. It denies, admits, or otherwise addresses each of the allegations in the complaint. It also usually sets forth the defendant's affirmative defenses and counterclaims. See also **reply.**

ante   *adv. Latin.* Before. Before in time, order, or position; in front of. See also **post.**

antenuptial agreement   *n.* Same as prenuptial agreement, although less commonly used. See **agreement.**

anticipatory breach   See **breach of contract.**

anticipatory repudiation   Same as anticipatory breach. See **breach of contract.**

antidumping law   *n.* A federal statute authorizing the imposition of special duties on imported foreign goods when the manufacturers are attempting to sell the goods in the United States at less than fair value to the material detriment of American industry. See **dumping.**

antilapse statute   *n.* A statute enacted in most states allowing the heirs of a devisee or legatee who dies before the testator to take the testamentary gift intended for the devisee or legatee. Without the statute, the gift would fail and go to the residuary beneficiary (if any) or to the testator's intestate heirs. For example, without the statute, a bequest to a son who dies before his father would lapse, and the

grandchildren could receive nothing, but with it, the grandchildren would receive the gift that would have gone to the son. Often, these statutes apply only to the heirs of the testator's relatives who are named as devises and legatees in the testamentary document. See also **lapse.**

antitrust law   *n.* The body of law, primarily consisting of federal statutes, designed to promote free competition in trade and commerce by outlawing various practices that restrain the marketplace. See also **Clayton Act** and **Sherman Antitrust Act.**

APA   *abbr.*   See   **Administrative Procedure Act.**

a posteriori   *adv. Latin.* From what comes after. Inductive; empirical; reasoning or the ascertaining of truth by actual experience or observation. See also **a priori.**

apparent   *adj.*   **1** Readily perceived; manifest; obvious; visible.   **2** Seeming, but not actual or real. See also **actual** and **constructive.**

apparent authority   See **authority.**

appeal   *n.*   **1** The process to seek and obtain a review and reversal by a court of a lower court's decision.   **2** The process to seek and obtain a review and reversal of an administrative decision by a court or by a higher authority within the administrative agency. See also **certiorari, notice of appeal, trial** *(trial de novo),* and **writ of error.**

> *appeal (as of) (by) right.* An appeal in which a court or administrative agency must review the decision that is sought to be reversed.

> *appeal by permission.* An appeal in which a court or administrative agency's review of a decision is

within the court or agency's discretion. Also called discretionary appeal. See also **certiorari.**

consolidated appeal. An appeal in which the issues to be reviewed in two or more cases are similar enough that it is practical to unite the reviews into a single appeal. See also **joinder.**

cross appeal. An appeal by an appellee, usually considered at the same time as the appeal by the appellant.

direct appeal. An appeal of a trial court's decision made directly to the jurisdiction's highest appellate court without first seeking review by the intermediate appellate courts. For example, although a United States District Court decision is usually first reviewed by one of the Untied States Court of Appeals before the United States Supreme Court considers it, a direct appeal bypasses the Court of Appeals and sends the District Court decision directly to the Supreme Court.

interlocutory appeal. An appeal of a trial court's interim decision while the case is still pending in the trial court. Some interlocutory appeals involve legal questions whose resolution are necessary for the trial court to reach a proper decision in the action. Others involve issues that are entirely separate from the merits of the case. In most states, interlocutory appeals are permitted only in limited circumstances and are rarely granted.

appeal (as of) (by) right   See **appeal.**

appealable decision   Same as appealable order. See **order.**

appealable order   See **order.**

appeal bond   See **bond.**

appearance   *n.* **1** The coming into a court to participate in a court proceeding by a party who has been validly served process or by a party who is voluntarily submitting itself to the court's jurisdiction.   **2** The coming into a court to participate in a court proceeding by a witness or an interested person or by a lawyer acting on behalf of a party or interested person.

compulsory appearance. An appearance by one who is required to do so because he has been validly served with process.

entry of appearance. The formal act of an attorney notifying a court of his representation of a party to the proceedings, either by written document, or orally in open court.

general appearance. An appearance wherein a party consents to the court's jurisdiction and waives the ability to later contest the court's authority to reach a binding decision against her in the case.

initial appearance. A criminal defendant's first appearance in court. Usually, this is when the charges are read to the defendant or the defendant is given a copy of the charges, the defendant is advised of his rights and enters a plea, and the amount of bail (if bail is not denied) is determined. See also **arraignment** and **presentment.**

special appearance. An appearance made for the sole reason of contesting the court's jurisdiction over the defendant.

voluntary appearance. An appearance by one who has not yet been served with process in the case.

appellant   *n.* A party who appeals a court or administrative agency's decision. See also **appellee.**

appellate *adj.* Relating to a specific appeal or to appeals in general.

appellate court See **court.**

appellate jurisdiction See **jurisdiction.**

appellee *n.* The opponent of the party who appeals a court's or administrative agency's decision.

applicant *n.* One who applies for or requests something.

application *n.* **1** The act of applying or making a request. **2** An oral or written formal motion, request, or petition.

apply *v.* **1** To make a formal motion or request to a court. **2** To be relevant; to have bearing upon; to be instructive. **3** To devote, use, or assign for a particular purpose.

appointed counsel See **counsel** *(assigned counsel).*

appointee *n.* **1** One who is appointed or assigned to a position or a public or private office or to perform a task. **2** One who will receive property pursuant to a power of appointment. See also **power of appointment.**

appointment *n.* **1** The appointment, designation, or placement of an individual in a job, office, or position, or to perform a duty. **2** A job, office, position, or duty to which one has been appointed. **3** The act of designating who will receive property pursuant to a power of appointment. See also **power of appointment.**

apportionment *n.* **1** The allocation, distribution, or division of something into proportionate shares. **2** The drawing of the boundaries of legislative districts so that each district is approximately equal in population. See also **gerrymandering** and **reapportion-**

ment. **3** The allocation after every census of the seats in the United States House of Representatives among the states based on population.

apportionment of liability *n.* In tort law, the division of liability for the plaintiff's injuries among multiple tortfeasors. In some cases, some of the liability may be apportioned to the plaintiff as well. See **indemnity, liability,** and **settlement.**

appraisal rights *n.* The statutory right available in most states for a corporation's minority shareholders who object to certain extraordinary corporate actions (the nature of which varies state to state, but usually includes consolidations and mergers) to have a fair price of their stock determined in a judicial proceeding prior to the action and to require the corporation to repurchase their stock at that price. See also **fault.**

appraise *v.* To determine the fair price or market value of something. See also **market value** and **assess.**

appreciation *n.* **1** The incremental increase in an asset's value, usually because of inflation. Compare **depreciation.** **2** The awareness or understanding of the meaning, significance, value, or worth of something.

> *unrealized appreciation.* The appreciation in the value of property that has not yet been subject to tax. See also **realization.**

appropriation *n.* **1** The taking of control or possession of property, especially the government's taking of private property for a public purpose. **2** The act by a legislative body to designate or set aside public funds for a government expenditure. **3** In tort law, the taking of the name or likeness of one person by another for a commercial purpose. It is considered an invasion of privacy.

appurtenant *n.* A right or thing, such as an easement, attached to or associated with land, that benefits or burdens the use or enjoyment of the property by its owner and continues to do so when title passes to another.

APR *abbr.* Annual percentage rate.

a priori *n. Latin.* From what is before. Deductive reasoning or the ascertaining of truth by proceeding from an assumption to its logical conclusion rather than by actual experience or observation. For example, one who walks by a store when its alarm is sounding and sees that its window is broken can deduce that a burglary has occurred without having watched the burglars commit the actual crime.

arbiter *n.* One called upon to decide a legal dispute outside of a court. See also **arbitrator** and **conciliator.**

arbitrary *adj.* **1** Determined or founded on individual discretion, especially when based on one's opinion, judgment, or prejudice, rather than on fixed rules, procedures, or law. See also **abuse of discretion. 2** Absolute; despotic; completely unreasonable; lacking any rational basis. This type of decision is often called arbitrary and capricious.

arbitration *n.* A method of alternative dispute resolution whereby a dispute, with the consent of all the parties, is submitted to a neutral person or group for a decision, usually including full evidentiary hearing and presentations by attorneys for the parties. Often, arbitration is the only form of proceeding permitted under the terms of contracts; see *arbitration clause.* See also **conciliation, mediation,** and **summary proceeding.**

arbitration clause. A clause in a contract requiring the parties to submit all disputes arising from the contract to an arbitrator or group of arbitrators rather than to proceed with litigation. Usually, a breach or repudiation of a contract will not nullify the clause.

binding arbitration. Arbitration proceeding that is final and binding by prior agreement of the parties, or by legal rule or statute; no right of appeal or further proceedings. *compulsory arbitration.* Arbitration required by law rather than by the mutual agreement of the parties to a dispute.

nonbinding arbitration. Arbitration in which the parties to the dispute are not required to abide by the arbitrator or arbitrators' decision and may ignore the decision and submit the dispute to litigation.

arbitrator *n.* A neutral person who resolves disputes between parties. Usually, the parties to the dispute choose the arbitrator. See also **arbitration, arbiter,** and **conciliator.**

arguendo *adv. Latin.* In arguing. **1** Hypothetically; for the purpose or sake of argument. A term used to assume a fact without waiving the right to question it later on. For example, a defense attorney may state to the judge: "Assuming arguendo that the defendant committed the crime, the statute of limitations prevents the state from prosecuting him for it." **2** During the course of an argument or a conversation. For example, "Mr. Smith mentioned arguendo that his client had three prior convictions."

argument *n.* **1** The reason or reasons offered for or against something. **2** The formal oral or written presentation of such reasons intended to convince or persuade. **3** The section of an appellate or trial brief in which a party presents its interpretation of the law.

closing argument. At a trial, the final statement given by the parties or their attorneys to the judge or jury, before deliberation, in which they summarize the evidence and the applicable law, present their interpretation of the same, and ask that a judgment or verdict be reached in their or their clients' favors.

oral argument. **1** A party or his attorney's oral presentation to a court stating the factual and legal reasons why the court should decide a legal issue or take particular action in their favor. **2** The procedure by which such arguments from all parties are heard by the court.

reargument. The oral, and sometimes written, presentation of additional arguments to a court on a matter previously argued before the court, but on which no decision has yet been rendered, for the purpose of advising the court of some controlling appellate court decision or principle of law that was previously overlooked or of some misapprehension of facts. See also **reconsideration** and **rehearing.**

argumentative *adj.* Stating facts and suggesting that particular inferences and conclusions can be drawn from them.

armed robbery See **robbery.**

arm's length *adj.* Of or relating to the bargaining position or dealings of two or more unrelated parties of approximately equal bargaining power who are not connected, on close terms, or in a confidential relationship with each other and whose mutual dealings are influenced only by their own self-interest.

arraignment *n.* The first step in a criminal prosecution wherein the defendant is formally advised of the charges against him. This is done by reading the charges to the defendant or by giving them a copy of the charges. The defendant is also advised of his rights (for example, the right to plead not guilty and to have a jury trial) and enters a plea, and the amount of bail (if bail is not denied) is determined.

array **1** *n.* A group of people called into court at the same time for potential jury duty. From such a group the members of a jury or juries will be selected. **2** *n.* The members of such a group who are empaneled to be a jury. **3** *v.* To empanel a jury for a trial. **4** *n.* The list of empaneled jurors. **5** *v.* To call out the names of the jurors as each is empaneled.

arrear *n.* **1** The state of being late in the payment of a debt or the performance of an obligation. **2** An overdue or unpaid debt or unfinished duty. See also **arrearage.**

arrearage *n.* An overdue debt. See also **arrear.**

arrears See **arrear.**

arrest *n.* The intentional deprivation, whether actual or constructive, of a person's freedom by legal authorities using forcible restraint, seizure, or otherwise taking the individual into custody, especially in response to a warrant or a suspicion based on probable cause that the person being arrested has committed a crime. The person making the arrest must have the present power to control the person being arrested. Furthermore, the intent to make an arrest must be communicated to the individual who is being detained and that person must understand that the seizure or detention is an intentional arrest. See also **privilege** and **resisting arrest.**

citizen's arrest. An arrest made by a private individual rather than by a law enforcement officer. Such arrests are lawful only if 1) an offense was committed in the presence of the person making the arrest, or 2) the person making the arrest has reasonable cause to believe that the person arrested has committed a felony.

false arrest. An arrest made by a person who falsely claims to be a law enforcement officer or by a law enforcement officer who has no legal grounds for making an arrest. See also **false imprisonment.**

malicious arrest. **1** An arrest made without probable cause and for an improper purpose. **2** An arrest made with knowledge that the person arrested did not commit the crime he is charged with. See also **malicious prosecution.**

parol arrest. An arrest ordered by a judge or magistrate while presiding over a court proceeding. Such an arrest is done without a written complaint and is executed immediately, for example, an arrest of a person in a courtroom who has been found in contempt of court.

pretextual arrest. A valid arrest made for a minor offense with the intent to hold the person in custody while investigating his involvement in a more serious offense for which there is yet no lawful grounds to arrest the suspect.

warrantless arrest. An arrest made in a public place without a warrant that is based on either the probable cause that the person committed a felony or the person committing a misdemeanor in the law enforcement officer's presence.

arrest of judgment *n.* The court's refusal to render or enforce a judgment after a verdict has been reached because of some apparent defect or error in the proceedings or because the verdict is not supported by the evidence.

arrest record   See **criminal record.**

arrest warrant   See **warrant.**

arson *n.* **1** In common law, the willful and malicious burning of someone else's dwelling house. In some states, the term includes, under specific circumstances, the burning of a dwelling house by its owner. **2** Under modern statutes, the intentional causing of a dangerous fire or explosion for the purpose of destroying one's own or another's property.

art **1** *v.* To utilize knowledge or skill according to rules and principles to create something. **2** *n.* A business, occupation, or pursuit that depends upon a skill. **3** *n.* In patent law, the method, process, or technique for creating something or for achieving a useful result.

article *n.* **1** A separate and distinct part of a written instrument, such as a contract, statute, or constitution, that is often divided into sections. **2** A written instrument, containing a series of rules and stipulations that are each designated as an article.

Article I court   See **court.**

Article I judge   See **judge.**

Article III court   See **court.**

Article III judge   See **judge.**

articles of association *n.* A written agreement legally creating an association and sets forth the purpose and rules of the organization.

Articles of Confederation *n.* The first constitution of the United States, ratified in 1781 and replaced eight years later with the present Constitution of the United States.

articles of impeachment *n.* A formal statement of the reasons to remove a public official from office. See **impeachment.**

articles of incorporation *n.* A written agreement setting forth the basic structure of a corporation. The document normally includes the name, duration, and purpose of the corporation; the names and addresses of its initial board of directors; and the number and classes of shares of stock that it will be allowed to issue. Normally, the corporation is not legally created until the articles of incorporation are filed with a state government. See also **by-law** and **charter.**

artificial person See **person.**

as of right *adj.* Description of a court action that a party may take without permission of the court, as opposed to requiring **leave of court**.

ascendant See **ancestor.**

ascent *n.* The passing of an estate to an heir who is an ancestor of the intestate. See also **descent.**

ASE *abbr.* See **American Stock Exchange.**

as is *adj.* In the condition it presently exists or as found on inspection immediately prior to purchase, even if damaged or defective, without modification and without any express or implied warranties. When referring to a sale of goods that were sold as is, based on an inspection of a sample, the goods delivered must be of the same type and quality or better than the sample was immediately prior to its inspection.

asportation *n.* The carrying away or moving the personal property of another. It does not matter how short the distance or slight the movement as long as the person who carries away or moves the property is knowingly and intentionally exercising control of the property without the consent and to the exclusion of the rights of the owner. See also **caption, larceny, robbery,** and **trespass.**

assault *n.* **1** In criminal and tort law, an act, usually consisting of a threat or attempt to inflict bodily injury upon another person, coupled with the apparent present ability to succeed in carrying out the threat or the attempt if not prevented, that causes the person to have a reasonable fear or apprehension of immediate harmful or offensive contact. No intent to cause battery or the fear or apprehension is required so long as the victim is placed in reasonable apprehension or fear. No actual physical injury is needed to establish an assault, but if there is any physical contact, the act constitutes both an assault and a **battery.** **2** In criminal law, in some states, the term includes battery and attempted battery. **3** Any attack. **4** *v.* The act of inflicting bodily injury upon another. See also **mayhem.**

> *aggravated assault.* A criminal assault accompanied by circumstances that make it more severe, such as the victim's suffering serious bodily injury or an assault committed with a dangerous and deadly weapon. The additional circumstances that make the act an aggravated assault are set by statute.

> *sexual assault.* **1** Rape. **2** Any sexual contact with another person without the other's consent or when the other lacks the capacity to give legally effective consent.

assault and battery See **battery.**

assembly *n.* **1** A group of people gathering, coming together, or meeting, or already so assembled, for a common purpose. **2** A legislative body, especially, in many states, the lower house of the state legislature.

> *unlawful assembly.* Three or more individuals gathering, coming together, or meeting with the common intention of committing a violent crime or some act, lawful or

unlawful, that will breach the peace.

assess *v.* **1** To determine the value of something, especially of real estate for property tax purposes. See also **appraise.** **2** To establish the amount of, and then charge, a fine, taxes, or another payment. **3** To require stockholders and partners to fill the need for additional capital by making additional contributions to their corporation or partnership.

asset *n.* **1** Any property or right that is owned by a person or entity and has monetary value. See also **liability.** **2** All of the property of a person or entity or its total value; entries on a balance sheet listing such property.

> *capital asset.* For income tax purposes, most property of the taxpayer except for a few certain business assets (for example, inventory and stock in trade) and other property excluded by the Internal Revenue Code.

> *intangible asset.* An asset that is not a physical thing and only evidenced by a written document. For example, a debt that is owed to a taxpayer is an intangible asset.

> *tangible asset.* An asset that is a physical thing, such as land, buildings, and goods.

assign *v.* **1** To transfer one's duty, interest, or right to another, especially regarding property or under a contract, so that the transferee has the same duty, interest, or right as the transferor had. See also **assignment** and **delegate.** **2** To appoint. **3** To identify.

assignable *n.* Capable of being assigned. Certain rights and duties cannot be assigned while others are not assignable without the consent of the other parties involved. For example, a

world-renowned author cannot unilaterally assign her contract to write a book to another writer.

assigned counsel   See **counsel.**

assignee *n.* One to whom a duty, interest, or right is assigned.

assignment *n.* The transfer of a duty, interest, or right from one party to another. See also **subrogation.**

> *assignment for benefit of creditors.* An assignment of most of a debtor's property to another who, acting as a trustee, consolidates and liquidates the assets and pays the debtor's creditors with any surplus being returned to the debtor.

> *assignment of a lease.* An assignment of a lessee's entire interest in a lease. The assignor remains secondarily liable to the landlord and will have to pay the rent if the assignee does not. See also **sublease.**

assignment of error *n.* The list in an appellant's brief of the trial court's alleged errors, upon which the appellant seeks a modification, reversal, or vacation of the trial court's decision.

assignor *n.* One who transfers a duty, interest, or a right to another.

assigns *n.* The plural of assignee. See **heirs and assigns.**

assisted suicide   See **suicide, assisted.**

assize *n.* **1** Often spelled assizes: a session of a court or legislative body. **2** The time or place of, or a law enacted by, such a session. **3** A cause of action, especially one relating to the ownership or possession of land. **4** A trial, especially one presided over by an itinerant judge and held in the county that is the location of the land, dispute, or crime in question.   **5** The jury at such a trial.

> *general assize.* The action, or the trial or jury in an action, to determine the ownership of land.

assizes   See **assize.**

associate   *n.* **1** A colleague, companion, partner, or fellow employee.   **2** A junior member of an association, institution, organization, profession, or society.   **3** A junior member of a law firm who typically works on salary and does not share in the ownership, profits, or decision-making of the firm.

associate judge   See **judge.**

association   *n.* A group of individuals meeting or associated for fellowship or a common purpose. See also **freedom of association.**

> *unincorporated association.* An organized, but unincorporated group of individuals. Thus, the organization does not have a legal existence separate from its members. However, if it has certain characteristics, such as centralized management, that make it more like a corporation than a partnership, it may be treated and taxed as a corporation.

> *joint stock association.* Same as joint stock company. See also **company.**

> *professional association.* **1** A group of members of a profession organized to practice their profession together. The association may be a partnership, corporation, or some other entity.   **2** A group of members of a profession organized to promote, improve, regulate, or deal with the public on behalf of their profession, such as a bar association.   **3** In some states, the same as a **professional corporation.** See also **corporation.**

> *trade association.* An association of businesses or business organizations that share common concerns or engage in similar activities, such as a chamber of commerce or a trade council.

Association of American Law Schools *n.* A national organization of law schools that have each graduated at least three classes of students and have offered instruction for at least five years. Abbreviated AALS.

assumpsit   *n. Latin.* He undertook.   **1** An enforceable promise or undertaking that is not under seal.   **2** An action for expectation damages caused by the breach of a promise or a contract not under seal.

> *express assumpsit.* Such a promise that is made orally or in writing.

> *implied assumpsit.* Such a promise that is presumed due to individual's conduct or the circumstances of the situation.

> *general assumpsit.* An action based the breach of an implied promise or contract to pay a debt. Also called common assumpsit.

> *special assumpsit.* An action for expectation damages based on the breach of an express promise or contract to pay a debt.

> *non assumpsit.* A defendant's claim, in the form of a pleading, that he or she did not promise or undertake any obligation as alleged in a complaint.

assumption   *n.* **1** Something the truth of which is taken for granted; a supposition.   **2** The act of taking for or on oneself, especially accepting, or agreeing to take the responsibility for, the obligation of another.

assumption of risk *n.* **1** In contract law, the act or agreement to take on a risk of damage, injury, or loss, often stated as the risk "passes" to the purchaser upon the occurrence of a certain event, e.g., shipment of goods. **2** In contract law, an employee's express agreement to undertake the risks that normally accompany or arise from that occupation. **3** In tort law, that a plaintiff voluntarily accepted or exposed himself to a risk of damage, injury, or loss, after appreciating that the condition or situation was clearly dangerous, and nonetheless made the decision to act; in such cases, the defendant may raise the plaintiff's knowledge and appreciation of the danger as an **affirmative defense**. Successful invocation of assumption of risk as an affirmative defense will result in a reduction or elimination of damages assessed against the defendant. This defense has been strictly limited in many states, and is unavailable in certain types of actions, e.g., product liability cases. See also **negligence.**

assurance **1** *n.* a promise or guarantee, an act that inspires confidence. **2** *v.* the act of promising or assuring.

asylum *n.* A place of refuge, sanctuary, or shelter, especially an institution for the maintenance and care of people requiring special assistance.

> *political asylum.* **1** The decision by a country's government to allow within its border a person from another country and to protect that person from prosecution and persecution by that other country's government. **2** The protection and refuge granted by a country to citizens and residents of other countries who obtain entry unto the premises of its foreign embassies and consulates.

at bar See **bar.**

at equity See **equity.**

at issue See **issue.**

at large *adj.* **1** Free from confinement, control, or restraint. **2** Chosen by the electorate of, or representing the residents of, an entire political unit, such as a state, country, or city, as opposed to a subdivision of the unit, such as a district, riding, or ward. **3** Not ordered or organized by topics, especially when referring to a group of statutes or ordinances.

at law *adj.* Relating to law, as opposed to **equity.** See **equity** and **operation of law.**

at will *n.* A status or relationship that can be terminated for any reason, or for no reason, at any time without prior notice.

at-risk *adj.* Characterization of person or property subject to unique jeopardy or threat, as in the case of youth "at-risk" for increased likelihood of delinquency due to home and environmental factors, or finances "at-risk" due to vagaries of stock market, global instability, health issues of individual having such finances, etc.

atrocious *n.* An act that is outrageously cruel, vile, and wicked and that demonstrates a depravity and insensitive brutality, especially when using senseless, excessive, or extreme violence during the commission of a crime.

attach *v.* **1** To add, affix, annex, bind, fasten, or join as a part. **2** To seize or take by legal process; to carry out an attachment, for example, to attach the funds in a debtor's bank account to pay a judgment. **3** To adhere or become legally effective, especially in connection with something or upon some event. For example, certain rights and responsibilities attach to becoming a parent.

attachment *n.* **1** The seizure or freezing of property by court order while an action is pending so that its ownership can be determined, it can be secured to be sold to satisfy a judgment, or its sale or transfer can be prevented so that any future judgment arising from the action may later be secured or satisfied. See also **garnishment** and **replevin.** **2** The writ ordering such a seizure or freezing of property. **3** In commercial law, the creation of a security interest in property when the debtor agrees to the security, receives value from the secured party, and obtains rights in the property.

attainder *n.* In common law, the automatic elimination of one's civil rights and liberties when sentenced to death or declared an outlaw for committing a felony or treason. See also **civil death** and **bill of attainder.**

attempt *n.* The intentional and overt taking of a substantial step toward the commission of a crime that falls short of completing the crime. The mere planning of a crime, as well as soliciting another to commit the crime, does not constitute an attempt to commit the crime. Attempt is a crime distinct from the offense that the criminal was attempting to commit. Various legal tests are used to determine when, between planning a crime and committing it, a person's actions constitute an attempt. See also **conspiracy** and **solicitation.**

attendant *adj.* Accompanying; resulting in. For example, in criminal law, the definitions of several crimes require the presence or absence of attendant circumstances; for example, the absence of consent to be touched is required for an offensive touching to be considered a battery.

attest *v.* **1** To bear witness; testify. **2** To affirm as accurate, genuine, or true.

3 To certify by oath or signature. **4** To affirm a document's authenticity by signing it as a witness to its execution by another person.

attestation *n.* The act of authenticating a document by observing its execution at the request of the party signing the document, and then signing it as a witness.

attorn *v.* **1** To turn over or transfer something to another. **2** To acknowledge a new landlord and agree to become his or her tenant.

attorney *n.* Lawyer; one who dispenses legal advice to clients and advocates for them.

> *attorney in fact.* One who is the agent or representative of another and is authorized, pursuant to a **power of attorney**, to act on their behalf.

> *attorney at law.* **1** One who is specially trained and licensed by a state to practice law. **2** One whose profession is to provide advice or to act or represent others in legal matters. See also **district attorney, public defender,** and **counsel.**

> *attorney of record.* The attorney at law or the law firm designated in a court's records as representing a particular party in a particular action. As long as a party is represented by an attorney of record, all documents, correspondence, and other communications that are intended for that party, whether from the court or the other parties in the action, must go instead to the attorney of record.

attorney-client privilege See **privilege.**

Attorney General   *n.* The chief legal officer of the United States or of a state, who advises the federal or state government on legal matters, represents the federal or state government in litigation, and heads the United States Department of Justice or a state's legal department. Abbreviated A.G. See also **solicitor(s) general** and **United States Attorney.**

attorney, power of   See **power of attorney.**

attorney's fees   *n.* The sum charged to a client by an attorney at law for the professional services performed for the client. The sum reflects a contingent fee, flat fee, hourly fee, compensation for out-of-pocket expenses, or some combination thereof. See also **contingent fee** and **retainer.**

attorney's lien   *n.* An encumbrance asserted by a lawyer against a client's file, money or property as security for unpaid legal fees. Strictly limited right to assert such a lien in most jurisdictions, and prohibited by ethical rules in others. Also referred to as a charging lien or retaining lien.

attractive nuisance doctrine   *n.* In tort law, the doctrine that one who has a dangerous condition or thing on his property that is likely to attract a curious child is under a duty to take reasonable steps to protect the child from it. For example, one has a duty to fence or cover an unsupervised swimming pool. The fact that the child is a trespasser does not negate the duty, but is one of many factors to be taken into account in determining the exact extent of the property owner's duty and the level of care required of him.

auction   See **sale.**

audit   *n* A formal inspection of the accounting procedures and records and the financial situation of an individual, business, organization, or government entity to verify the accuracy and completeness of the records or their compliance with another set of standards.

authenticate   *v.* **1** To prove that something, such as a document, is what it purports to be, especially so that the item can be admitted into evidence at a trial or hearing. For example, a party wishing to admit a letter into evidence may ask the witness whether it is, indeed, the letter he received, does he recognize the handwriting, and similar questions.   **2** To place a mark, such as a signature or a stamp, on a document to signify that it is authentic, effective, or valid.   **3** To approve or adopt a writing as one's own.

self-authentication   *n.* The act of proving that something, usually a document, is genuine or true without the use of extrinsic evidence. For example, notarized documents and certified copies of public records are usually deemed to be self-authenticating.

authority   *n.* **1** The authorization, permission, power, or right to act on another's behalf and to bind them by such actions. See also **agency, agent,** and **principal.**   **2** The right or power to command, govern, or enforce obedience. **3** A legal writing, such as a judicial decision, law review article or legal treatise, or a statute's legislative history that provides information or insight on how to interpret and apply the law. See also **precedent.**

> *actual authority.* Authority, express or implied, intentionally given by a principal to an agent.

adverse authority. Authority that is detrimental to a party's argument or position regarding a question or an issue. Usually, when a lawyer finds such authority, he is under an ethical obligation to reveal it to the court, but it is done in such a way (for example, arguing that the decision in a previous case should be narrowly construed or was wrongly decided) as to minimize the authority's effect upon his client's case.

apparent authority. Authority that can be reasonably inferred by a third party to have been given to an agent based upon the third party's dealings with the principal or upon the principal's representations even if the principal did not intend to give the agent such authority.

binding authority. See **precedent.**

persuasive authority. Authority that is not binding on a court but still merits consideration. For example, a scholarly work or the decision of a higher court in another jurisdiction.

primary authority. Authority that is issued by law-making bodies, such as a court's decision or a statute's legislative history.

secondary authority. Authority that analyzes and explains the law, but is not issued by a court or legislature. For example, an annotation, law review article, or legal treatise.

automatic stay   See **stay.**

automobile guest statute   See **guest statute.**

autopsy   *n.* The post-mortem examination of a human body, including its dissection and the removal and inspection of the major organs, to determine the cause of death.

autoptic evidence   See **evidence.**

autre or auter   *n. French.* Other, another. See also **estate.**

autrefois acquit   *n. French.* Formerly acquitted. A plea by a person indicted for a crime for which he or she had previously been tried and acquitted. See also **double jeopardy** and **autrefois convict.**

autrefois convict   *n. French.* Formerly convicted. A plea by a person indicted for a crime for which he or she had previously been tried and convicted. See also **double jeopardy** and **autrefois acquit.**

autre (or auter) vie   *n. French.* Another's life. See **estate.**

aver   *v.* To formally assert as a fact, such as in a pleading; to allege.

averment   *n.* **1** The act of averring.   **2** A positive affirmation, allegation, or declaration of facts, especially in a pleading, as opposed to an argumentative statement or a statement based on induction or inference; generally this term is used in civil proceedings, as opposed to **allegation** in criminal proceedings.

averment of notice. See also **notice.**

immaterial averment. An averment that provides unnecessary information and detail.

negative averment. An averment that is stated in the negative, but is actually affirmative in substance. For example, the negative averment "he is not old enough to marry" really means that "he is too young to marry." Although one who makes a simple denial in a pleading does not carry the burden of proof, the party who asserts negative averment has the burden to prove the averment's affirmative substance.

a vinculo matrimonii   *adv. Latin.* From the bond of marriage. See **divorce.**

avoid   *v. Slang.* To annul, cancel, make void, or nullify for some legal reason a transaction to which one is a party or owes an obligation. For example, a child who is under the age of capacity may disavow a contract and avoid her obligations under it because she lacks the legal capacity to enter into a contract. See also **annul, voidable,** and **ratify.**

avoidance   *n.* **1** The act of keeping away from, escaping, evading, or preventing.   **2** Same as **confession and avoidance.**   **3** Same as **tax avoidance.** **4** Same as voidance.

avulsion   *n.* The sudden and perceptible removal or severing of land from the property or jurisdiction of which it was a part by natural forces such as a flood or an abrupt change in the course of a river. Despite the removal or severing of the land, the boundaries between jurisdictions or properties are not altered by avulsion. For example, if a river was the boundary between two states, the boundary remains the same although the course of the river has changed. See also **alluvion, accretion** and **reliction.**

award   **1** *n.* The final decision of an arbitrator.   **2** The final decision of a court, jury, or administrative tribunal granting damages or other relief to a party.   **3** *v.* To formally grant such relief. See also **confirmation, judgment,** and **order.**

AWOL   *abbr.* See **absent without leave.**

B

BAC *abbr.* Blood alcohol content.

bad character *n.* A person's predisposition to commit evil acts.

bad check See **check.**

bad debt *n.* An uncollectible debt arising due to the debtor's refusal to pay, insolvency, or bankruptcy.

bad faith *n.* Dishonesty of purpose; lack of fairness and honesty; the continuous and willful failure to fulfill one's duties or obligation. See also **good faith.**

badge of fraud *n.* The facts or circumstances surrounding a transaction that indicate that one party is trying to hinder or defraud another party, especially a court, an opposing party in an action, or a creditor. Such badges include, among other things, the transfer of property in anticipation of litigation or execution. See also **fraud.**

badge of slavery *n.* **1** A legal disability imposed on a slave, such as the inability to vote, own property, or enter into a contract. **2** Any visible trace of slavery, such as racial discrimination in public education. **3** Any public or private act of racial discrimination that Congress can prohibit under the Thirteenth Amendment to the United States Constitution.

bad title See **title.**

bail **1** *n.* Security, such as cash, a bond, or property, pledged or given to a court by or on behalf of one accused of committing a crime, to obtain release from incarceration and to ensure the person's future appearance in court when required during the criminal proceeding. See also **preventive detention** and **recognizance.** **2** *v.* To obtain for oneself or another the release from incarceration by providing security to ensure the person's future appearance at every stage in a criminal proceeding. **3** *v.* To temporarily give possession of personal property to someone. See also **bailment.**

> *excessive bail.* Bail set in an amount greater than what is reasonable, in light of the seriousness of the alleged crime and the risk that the defendant might flee, to ensure the person's appearance at every stage of a criminal proceeding. The Eighth Amendment to the United States Constitution prohibits the setting of bail in excessive amounts.

bail bond See **bond.**

bail bondsman See **bailsman.**

bailee *n.* One who temporarily possesses the personal property of another pursuant to and agreement between them. See also **bailment.**

bailer See **bailsman** and **bailor.**

bailiff *n.* **1** A court officer charged with maintaining order in the courtroom, with taking care of the judge's and jury's needs, and, in criminal proceedings, with the custody of the defendant. **2** A sheriff's deputy or other officer who executes writs and serves processes and warrants of arrest. **3** One who oversees the administration of land, goods, and other property, including the collection of rent, for the owner.

bail jumping *v.* To flee, hide, or otherwise avoid an appearance at any stage in a criminal proceeding while free on bail.

bailment   *n.* The delivery of personal property from one person (the **bailor**) to another (the **bailee**) in trust for some special purpose, as according to an express or implied contract. Only the lawful possession of the property, and not ownership, is transferred. The rights and duties of the parties as to the property depend on the purpose of the bailment and the terms of the contract. See also **lease.**

> *actual bailment.* A bailment created by the actual or constructive delivery of personal property to a bailee or his agents.

> *bailment for hire.* A bailment in which the bailor merely takes possession of personal property in exchange for compensation.

> *bailment for mutual benefit.* A bailment in which the bailee, in exchange for compensation, provides the bailor with some additional benefit as to the bailor's personal property, such as cleaning or repair work.

> *constructive bailment.* A bailment in which, due to the particular circumstances, the bailee has a legal obligation to return the personal property to its owner, even if the owner is not the bailor or if the bailee did not voluntarily take possession of the property.

> *gratuitous bailment.* A bailment in which the bailee accepts personal property without expecting compensation. For example, a gratuitous bailment is created when a bailee borrows the bailor's property. In gratuitous bailments, the bailee is liable to the bailor for the loss of or damage to the property only if it was caused by the bailee's gross negligence.

> *involuntary bailment.* A bailment in which the bailor, without any negligence, unavoidably or accidentally leaves personal property on the bailee's person or land. If the bailee refuses to return the property upon the bailor's demand or refuses to permit the bailor to remove the property, he can be liable for conversion. See also **property.**

bailment offense   See **offense.**

bailor   *n.* **1** Same as **bailsman.** **2** One who temporarily gives possession of personal property to another, pursuant to an agreement between them. The bailor does not have to be the owner of the property. See **bailment.**

bailsman   *n.* One who provides bail to secure the release of a criminal defendant.

bait and switch   *v.* The practice of advertising a product or service at a low price to bring customers into a store and, once they are there, urging them to buy a more expensive product or service by disparaging the original item or by saying that it is no longer available. This is illegal in most states, especially when the original product or service was not available at the time it was advertised.

balance   **1** *n.* To determine the difference between the sum of the credits and the sum of the debits of an account. **2** *v.* The act of estimating, measuring, or weighing two things in comparison to each other. For example, the balancing of the risks and benefits of filing a lawsuit. **3** *v.* To offset or counteract. **4** *v.* To place or keep in equilibrium or proportion, such as balancing competing interests. **5** *n.* The result of balancing.

balance sheet   *n.* A financial statement that indicates the value of an entity's current fiscal situation as of a specific date, consisting of a summary of the value of assets and a summary of the value of its liabilities and the owners' equity.

balancing of the equities *n.* A court's weighing of such factors as policy and the convenience or hardship to the parties in order to determine the fairness of granting or denying equitable relief (such as an injunction).

balancing test *n.* The weighing, especially by a court, of competing values and interests and deciding which one will prevail, in an attempt to achieve equality or fairness between those values and interests.

balloon mortgage See **mortgage.**

balloon note See **note.**

balloon payment See **payment.**

banc See **en banc.**

B and E (or **B & E**) *abbr.* Breaking and entering. See **burglary.**

bank *n.* A financial institution, whether incorporated or not, with a substantial portion of its business consisting of receiving deposits and maintaining savings accounts and checking accounts. Most also issue loans and credit, exchange currencies, transmit funds, and deal in negotiable bonds and securities issued by corporations and the government.

> *commercial bank.* A bank, often organized as a public corporation, that offers the broadest range of services allowed by law, but that is required to keep a larger percentage of its deposits on reserve than is required of savings and loan associations and savings banks.

> *savings and loan association.* A financial institution, often organized and operated like a bank, with a primary purpose to make loans so that individuals can purchase or construct homes, but that also provide various banking services. See also **building and loan association.**

> *savings bank.* A bank that receives deposits, maintains savings accounts (from which funds can usually be withdrawn only after a set period of time or advance notice), pays interest on them at usually higher rates than commercial banks, and makes certain loans. However, a savings bank cannot maintain checking accounts and is allowed to invest only in certain types of corporate and government bonds and securities.

bankrupt *n.* **1** A person or entity unable to pay debts due to insolvency. **2** A person (or entity) who has filed a voluntary petition for bankruptcy or against whom an involuntary petition for bankruptcy has been filed. See also **debtor.** **3** The state of having been declared bankrupt by a Bankruptcy Court.

bankruptcy *n.* A federal judicial procedure by which most debts owed by a person or entity are extinguished or reduced or the payment of which are delayed.

> *Chapter 7 bankruptcy.* A bankruptcy proceeding whereby most of the debtor's assets are collected and sold, the proceeds are distributed among the creditors, and the debtor's liabilities are discharged. Also called a straight bankruptcy.

> *Chapter 11 bankruptcy.* A bankruptcy proceeding whereby a debtor, usually a business, is allowed to reorganize itself and restructure its finances under court supervision and to arrange and carry out a court-approved repayment plan with its creditors while continuing to operate its business. Also called **reorganization.**

> *Chapter 12 bankruptcy.* A bankruptcy proceeding whereby a farmer with a regular income who is insolvent can keep and continue operat-

ing his farm while arranging and carrying out, under court supervision, a repayment plan with his creditors.

Chapter 13 bankruptcy. A bankruptcy proceeding whereby a person with a regular income is allowed to propose a plan to reduce her obligations or extend the period to pay those obligations and allow her future earnings to be collected by a trustee and paid to the debtor's unsecured creditors. Also called **rehabilitation.**

involuntary bankruptcy. A bankruptcy proceeding initiated by a creditor to legally declare a debtor to be bankrupt and to impound all of the debtor's non-exempt property, distribute it or its proceeds to the creditors, and extinguish the debtor's liability.

voluntary bankruptcy. A bankruptcy proceeding voluntarily initiated by a debtor who files a petition with the bankruptcy court to be legally declared a bankrupt and, during the proceeding, surrenders his property in order to discharge his debts.

Bankruptcy Act *n.* The federal statute, adopted in 1898, that governed all bankruptcy cases filed before October 1, 1979.

Bankruptcy Code *n.* The federal statute, adopted in 1978, that governs all bankruptcy cases filed after September 30, 1979. Superseded Bankruptcy Act.

Bankruptcy Court *n.* A United States District Court, or the bankruptcy judges assigned to a given United States District Court, that deals only with bankruptcy proceedings.

bankruptcy judge *n.* A United States District Court judge appointed by a United States Court of Appeals to pre-

side exclusively over bankruptcy proceedings filed within a designated United States District Court's jurisdiction.

bankruptcy trustee *n.* See **trustee.**

bar 1 *n.* A legal obstacle or barrier that prevents or destroys a legal action or claim, especially one that prevents the relitigation of an issue or the formation of a valid contract. See also **double jeopardy, estoppel, merger, plea,** and **res judicata.** 2 *v.* To prevent, prohibit, or act as a bar to. 3 *n.* In bar. As a bar to an action. For example, if a defendant in a criminal action was acquitted earlier of the same charges that he is now accused, he may plead double jeopardy in bar. 4 *adj.* At bar. Now before the court. For example, an action that is before the court may be referred to as the case at bar. 5 *n.* The legal profession in general. 6 *n.* A group of attorneys admitted to practice law in a particular jurisdiction or before a particular court or who practice in a common field or area of expertise in the law. 7 *n.* The railing in a courtroom that separates the area used by the judge, lawyers, and court personnel to conduct judicial business from the seating provided for observers. See also **bench.**

bar association *n.* A professional organization of attorneys who practice law within a specific geographic area (for example, a state bar association) or who practice in a common field or area of expertise in the law (for example, a defense attorneys' bar association).

integrated bar. A bar association in which membership is legally required of all attorneys who practice law in that state or jurisdiction. Also called a **compulsory bar, mandatory bar,** and **unified bar.**

voluntary bar. A bar association that attorneys do not need to join in order to practice law.

bare license See **license.**

bar examination *n.* A written examination administered by a state or an established licensing authority, such as a state bar association, usually lasting two or more days, that tests the legal knowledge of individuals seeking a license to practice law in a particular state. See **admission.**

bargain **1** *n.* A voluntary agreement between parties for the exchange or purchase of goods or services, regardless of whether the transaction is legal or the consideration is sufficient for the agreement to constitute a contract. Synonymous with **contract.** **2** *v.* To negotiate the terms of an agreement.

bargain and sale *n.* A written contract to convey the legal title of, and raise a use in, real property in exchange for valuable consideration recited in the agreement without requiring the parties to enter the land and perform a livery of **seisin.** Unless it includes a covenant of seisin and right to convey, the agreement contains no guarantees as to the seller's title to the property. See also **deed.**

bargainee *n.* The purchaser of land in a bargain and sale. See also **bargainor.**

bargaining unit *n.* A group of employees represented by a labor union or other group engaged in collective bargaining with a company or industry. Also called a collective bargaining unit.

bargainor *n.* The seller of land in a bargain and sale. See also **bargainee.**

barrato See **barrator.**

barrator *n.* One who commits barratry. Also called **barrato** or **common barrator.**

barratry *n.* The persistent incitement or initiation of groundless lawsuits and quarrels. Was a crime under the common law and is a statutory crime in most states. See also **abuse of process, champerty,** and **maintenance.**

barrister *n.* **1** In England, a lawyer who argues cases in court. See also **solicitor.** **2** In the United States, a lawyer.

barter **1** *n.* The exchange of goods or services without the use of money. **2** *v.* To negotiate, engage in, or conclude a barter.

basis *n.* The amount or value assigned to a taxpayer's cost of acquiring, or investment in, an asset. Primarily used when determining the taxpayer's gain or loss when the property is sold, bartered, or exchanged or the asset's depreciation.

adjusted basis. The value of a taxpayer's basis in an asset, after making additions or subtractions to his or her original basis, to reflect certain events, such as capital improvements and depreciation, that affect the value of the property subsequent to the taxpayer's acquisition of or investment in the asset.

carryover basis. The basis of an asset transferred from one owner to another by gift or in trust at the time of the transfer.

recovery of basis. See **recovery.**

stepped-down basis. The taxpayer's basis in an asset after the basis has been decreased to a certain value (usually its fair market value) upon a certain date or event. For example, the basis of inherited property is its fair market value as of the date of the decedent's death or an alternate valuation date and the decedent's stepped-down (or stepped-up) basis in the asset is the new owner's original basis.

stepped-up basis. The taxpayer's basis in an asset after the basis has been increased to a certain value (usually its fair market value) upon a certain date or event.

substituted basis. The basis of one asset that substitutes for that of another asset when the first asset has been exchanged or otherwise transferred in return for the second asset. The taxpayer does not incur any gain or loss, but substitutes the basis of the asset she transferred to the property she acquired.

bastard   *n.* **1** Same as illegitimate child. See **child.** **2** The child of a married woman whose father is not the woman's husband or whose paternity is not conclusively established.

bastardy proceeding   *n.* See **paternity suit.**

battered-person syndrome   *n.* The medical and psychological condition of a person who has suffered (usually persistent) emotional, physical, or sexual abuse from another person. Also called battered child syndrome or battered woman syndrome depending on the circumstances. In the case of a woman, her husband or partner inflicts the injuries. See also **abuse.**

battery   *n.* The harmful or offensive touching of any part of another person's body or of something, such as clothing or carried umbrella, that is so closely attached to the person that it is customarily regarded as part of the person. The touching may be in anger or a result of some other intentional wrong. Any amount of touching is considered a battery, even if harmless, if it is offensive to the person who is touched. See also **assault** and **mayhem.**

aggravated battery. See **aggravated.**

sexual battery. The forced penetration of or contact with another per-

son's or the perpetrator's sexual organs. See also **rape.**

simple battery. A battery with no accompanying aggravated circumstances and not resulting in serious bodily injury.

battle of the forms   *n.* The conflict between the incompatible terms in preprinted standardized forms exchanged by a buyer and seller while negotiating a contract.

bearer   *n.* A person in possession of a negotiable instrument, document of title, security, or other similar document that is marked "payable to bearer" or is indorsed in blank. Depending upon its nature, the document is called a bearer bond, bearer instrument, bearer paper, or the like and, if it is for the payment of money, it is said to be payable to bearer.

before the fact   See **accessory.**

below   *adv.* **1** Later in the same document. See also **infra.** **2** Of or in a court whose decision can be appealed. For example, when referring to a lower court's decision, an appellant court may rule that "the decision below" is affirmed or reversed.

bench   *n.* **1** Judges collectively or of a particular court. See also **bar.** **2** The area in the courtroom where the judge sits.

bench memo   See **bench memorandum.**

bench memorandum   *n.* A short memorandum summarizing the facts, issues, and arguments in a case, prepared either by a judge's law clerk or by the lawyers in the case, for the judge to use when preparing for trail, for hearing the lawyers' oral arguments, or in drafting a decision. Also called **bench memo.**

bench ruling *n.* An oral decision given, or a written decision read aloud, by a judge to the parties and their lawyers from the bench.

bench trial See **trial.**

bench warrant See **warrant.**

beneficial *n.* A right or interest that derives from something other than legal title. See **estate, interest, owner, use,** and **equitable.**

beneficiary *n.* A person entitled to an advantage, benefit, or profit (such as an inheritance under a will or the proceeds of an annuity, insurance policy, or property held in trust) arising from an appointment, assignment, disposition, instrument, or legal arrangement.

> *creditor beneficiary.* A third-party beneficiary who is to receive the benefit of a contract in satisfaction of a debt, duty, or liability owed to them by the party who purchased the benefit. Under certain circumstances, the execution of the contract itself may discharge the obligation. In any case, the contract must be primarily for the third person's benefit.

> *donee beneficiary.* A third-party beneficiary who is to receive the benefit of a contract as a gift from the party who purchased the benefit.

> *incidental beneficiary.* A person who is not a party to, but is the unintended beneficiary of, a contract or trust. Such a person has no legally enforceable right to the benefit they receive.

> *intended beneficiary.* A person who is not a party to a contract or trust, but is intended by the parties to benefit from the contract or trust. Such a person has the ability to legally enforce the contract or trust once their right to the benefit vests.

> *third-party beneficiary.* A person who is not a party to, but is the intended beneficiary of, a contract.

benefit *n.* That which is helpful; advantage; financial assistance; gain; privilege; profit.

benefit-of-the-bargain rule *n.* **1** In breach of contract cases, the principle that the aggrieved party is entitled from the party who breached the contract to everything that he would have received, including profits, if the breach had not occurred. **2** In cases involving fraud or misrepresentation of the value of property, the principle that the defrauded party is entitled to damages equal to the difference between the misrepresented value and the lower amount that represents the true value of the property. Also called loss of bargain. See also **out-of-pocket rule.**

bequeath *v.* **1** To give a gift of personal property by means of a will. See also **devise.** **2** In some states, to give a gift of any type of property by means of a will.

bequest *n.* **1** A gift of personal property (usually other than money) by means of a will. Also, any personal property given by means of a will. See also **devise** and **legacy.** **2** In a broader sense, any gift of property by means of a will. Also, any property given by means of a will, including a devise or a legacy.

> *conditional bequest.* A bequest that is effective or continues unless some particular event does or does not occur. For example, a bequest from a parent to a child that is to effective only if the child is still a minor at the time of the parent's death is a conditional bequest, because the parent may die after the child reaches adulthood.

> *executory bequest.* A bequest that does not take effect until after the occurrence of a particular event. For example, a bequest from a parent to a child that is effective only if the child is 18 years of age or older at the time of the parent's death is

an executory bequest, because the child must have first reached his 18th birthday to receive it.

general bequest. A bequest of a general type of property rather than of a specific item of personal property. For example, a bequest of "furniture" rather than "oak chair." A bequest to be paid out of the general assets of the testator's estate.

pecuniary bequest. See **legacy.**

residuary bequest. A bequest of what remains in the testator's estate after the payment of debts and the satisfaction of all other bequests.

specific bequest. A bequest of a specific item of personal property.

best efforts *n.* Diligence beyond a mere good faith effort to fulfill an obligation. See also **good faith** and **diligence.**

best evidence rule *n.* The rule that, to prove the contents of a writing, recording, or photograph, the original is required unless it is not available for some reason other than the serious fault of the party trying to prove the contents thereof. If the original is unavailable, the testimony of the person who created the original or the person who read it (if a writing), listened to it (if a recording), or saw it (if a photograph) may testify to its content. However, modern evidentiary rules usually permit the use of mechanical, electronic, or other similar copy instead of the original.

bestiality *n.* **1** Sexual intercourse between a person and an animal. **2** In a broader sense, any sexual activity or contact between a person and an animal. See also **crime** *(crime against nature),* **buggery,** and **sodomy.**

betterment *n.* An improvement that adds to the value of real property.

beyond a reasonable doubt *n.* The standard for conviction in a criminal trial; evidence sufficient to convince a reasonable person beyond doubt of the guilt of the defendant. The requirement of proof beyond a reasonable doubt is not so stringent as to preclude the possibility of error, as is, "beyond the shadow of a doubt," nor as loose as, "the preponderance of the evidence," as is the standard in a civil trial.

BFOQ *abbr.* See **bona fide occupational qualification.**

BFP *abbr.* Bona fide purchaser. See **purchaser.**

bias *n.* A mental tendency, inclination, preconception, prejudice, taint.

bias crime See **crime** *(hate crime).*

bid **1** *n.* An offer to pay a specific price for something. **2** *n.* An offer to perform work or supply services at a specific price. **3** *v.* The act of submitting an offer to buy.

firm bid. A bid that is publicly announced when made and that is binding and cannot be revised until it is accepted or rejected.

open bid. A bid that is publicly announced when made and that the bidder may repeatedly revise as competing bids are announced.

sealed bid. A written bid that is secret and not disclosed until all submitted bids (which are also written and secret) are simultaneously opened and considered.

bid-shopping *v.* The legitimate practice whereby a general contractor, after being awarded a contract, tries to reduce his own costs by disclosing to interested subcontractors the lowest bids he received for subcontracts, and then inviting even lower bids.

bigamy *n.* **1** The crime of marrying a person while legally married to another. The second marriage is void. **2** In some states, the crime of cohabiting with a person of the opposite sex while legally married to another. See also **monogamy** and **polygamy.**

bilateral contract See **contract.**

bill **1** *n.* A draft of a proposed statute submitted to a legislature by one of its members for consideration and possible enactment.

> *appropriation bill.* A bill that, if enacted, would authorize the expenditure of government funds.

> *engrossed bill.* The draft of a bill as it is adopted by one house of a legislature and before it is sent to the other house for consideration. See also **enrolled bill.**

> *enrolled bill.* The final draft of a bill after it is adopted by both houses of a legislature, printed, checked for errors, and signed by the presiding officers of both houses before it is sent to the president or a governor for approval or rejection. See also **engrossed bill.**

> *omnibus bill.* **1** A bill that contains proposals on a variety of subjects. Usually, such a bill will have one major provision dealing with one topic and several minor provisions regarding matters unrelated to the major subject. **2** A bill that contains all proposals on a single (usually broad) subject, such as an omnibus education bill that includes all proposals regarding, however tangentially, the subject of education.

> *private bill.* A bill concerning the interests, or affecting, only one or a small number of individuals, entities, or localities.

> *public bill.* A bill concerning the general interests of, or affecting, the whole community, state, or country.

> *no bill or no true bill.* The words used in a grand jury's notation on a bill of indictment indicating that insufficient evidence exists to support a criminal charge set forth in the proposed indictment. Such a decision by the grand jury prevents the prosecution from pursuing a criminal action against the defendant based on those charges until a new grand jury is selected.

> *revenue bill.* A piece of legislation for the purpose of levying taxes. By the United States Constitution, all federal revenue bills must originate in the House of Representatives. A similar provision constraining the origin of revenue bills to one particular house of the state legislature is part of many of the various state constitutions.

> *true bill.* The words used in a grand jury's notation on a bill of indictment indicating that sufficient evidence exists to support a criminal charge set forth in the proposed indictment that, if proved, would result in the defendant's conviction. Once the bill of indictment is indorsed as a true bill and filed with the court, the prosecution must pursue a criminal action against the defendant based on those charges unless the court approves a dismissal.

2 *n.* A statement by one person or entity to another regarding money owed for goods sold and services performed. Usually, the statement is in the form of an itemized list of the goods and services, along with the amount owed for each item. **3** *v.* To submit a request for payment for goods sold and services performed. **4** *n.* In equity law, the initial pleading wherein a party sets out their cause of action. See also **complaint** and **petition.**

bill of attainder *n.* **1** Any legislative act that imposed a sentence of death and attainder upon one or more specific individuals or groups without a trial or other judicial proceeding. **2** In United States constitutional law, any legislative act that prescribes a punishment on one or more specific individuals or groups or denies them of civil or political rights without a trial or other judicial proceeding. Such enactments are prohibited by the United States Constitution. See also **attainder, bill of pains and particulars,** and **civil death.**

bill of certiorari *n.* In equity law, a pleading that seeks the removal of an action to a higher court for appellate review. See also **certiorari.**

bill of costs *n.* An itemized and certified (or verified) list of the expenses incurred by the prevailing party in a lawsuit. The pleading is submitted to assist the court in determining how many, if any, of these costs should be paid by the losing party.

bill of discovery *n.* In equity law, a pleading that seeks the disclosure of facts known by the adverse party. See also **discovery.**

bill of exceptions. *n.* **1** A written statement from a trial judge to an appellate court listing a party's objections or exceptions made during the trial and the grounds on which they were based. **2** In some states, a detailed record made, after a trial judge has excluded evidence, of what that evidence was so that, in case of an appeal, the appellate court can better determine whether it was proper for the evidence to be excluded at trial. For example, if the trial judge excluded a letter from evidence, the letter might be read into the record so its contents may be part of the bill of exceptions. See also **exception.**

bill of exchange See **draft.**

bill of indictment *n.* **1** A proposed indictment submitted by the prosecution to a grand jury, listing the deeds of criminal misconduct allegedly committed by a defendant. **2** An indictment as approved by a grand jury. See **indictment** and **bill.**

bill of lading *n.* A document issued by a carrier or by a shipper's agent that identifies the goods received for shipment, where the goods are to be delivered, and who is entitled to receive the shipment. Abbreviated B/L.

clean bill or *clean bill of lading.* A bill of lading with no added notations that change or qualify its terms.

order bill or *order bill of lading.* A bill of lading that is negotiable and that states that the goods can be delivered only when the bill of lading is presented to the carrier. Title to the bill of lading and to the goods identified in it can be transferred by the shipper, indorsing and giving up possession of the document to another, who is then entitled to receive the goods from the carrier.

straight bill or *straight bill of lading.* A nonnegotiable bill of lading that merely specifies the specific place and person the carrier is to deliver the goods to.

through bill or *through bill of lading.* A bill of lading issued by the first of multiple connecting carriers who are going to ship the goods. By issuing the document, the first carrier assumes responsibility for the other carriers for the shipment's eventual arrival and delivery at the designated place and person.

bill of pains and particulars n. Any legislative act similar to a bill of attainder that imposes a punishment less severe than death. Such enactments are forbidden by the United States Constitution's prohibition of bills of attainder. See also **attainder, bill of attainder,** and **civil death.**

bill of particulars *n.* In criminal law, a written statement of the charges brought against the defendant specifying the details of the alleged acts of wrongdoing that will be brought up at trial. Such a document is usually filed in response to a defendant's request for more specific information when the criminal charges are vague or ambiguous. In some states, a bill of particulars can also be used in civil actions.

bill of review *n.* In equity law, a pleading requesting a trial court to explain, revise, or reverse a final decree issued by the court.

bill of rights *n.* **1** A section or addendum, usually in a constitution of a country, state, or other similar political entity, specifying the civil and political rights of the entity's citizens or residents and the limits on the entity's government to infringe on or interfere with those rights. **2** Any formal list of rights given to a group of individuals by statutes or by adoption by an organization or institution. For example, a law concerning the provision of services for the elderly may include a senior citizens' bill of rights.

Bill of Rights *n.* The first ten amendments to the United States Constitution.

bill of sale *n.* A document that conveys title to personal property from a seller to a buyer.

bind *v.* To subject to a legal obligation.

binder *n.* **1** A document giving a person temporary insurance coverage until her application for insurance is rejected or until the insurance policy is issued. **2** A document in which the parties to a sale of real property declare their intention to transfer ownership of the property. The document usually includes a

memorandum of the important points of the parties' contract and is usually accompanied by the buyer's first payment. **3** The buyer's first payment toward the purchase of real property. See also **earnest money.**

binding *adj.* Obligatory.

binding agreement See **agreement.**

binding arbitration See **arbitration.**

binding authority See **precedent.**

binding over See **bind over.**

binding precedent See **precedent.**

bind over *v.* **1** To require a person to do something (usually to appear in court). **2** To imprison or place a person into a law enforcement officer's physical custody for imprisonment to guarantee the person's attendance at a judicial proceeding (usually a criminal trial). Also called binding over and bound over.

biological child See **child.**

B/L *abbr.* See **bill of lading.**

Blackacre *n.* The name of a fictitious piece of land frequently used, especially in law school, when discussing concepts and issues of the law concerning real property and future interests. When the discussion involves two fictitious pieces of land, the second tract is frequently referred to as Whiteacre.

black letter law Same as hornbook law. See **hornbook.**

blackmail See **extortion.**

blackmail suit See **suit.**

blanket bond See **bond.**

blanket search warrant See **search warrant.**

blank check   Same as blank indorsement. See **indorsement.**

blasphemy   *n.* The act of reviling, ridiculing, or being disrespectful or irreverent of, by words or conduct, God, religion, a religious doctrine, a religious icon, or anything considered sacred. A crime under the common law if the blasphemy was directed towards Christianity or Christian doctrine and icons and is still a statutory crime (although rarely enforced) in many states.

blockbusting   *v.* The inducement of people by a real estate agent to sell real property quickly, and frequently for less than what the property is worth, by spreading rumors about ethnic minorities moving into the neighborhood and thereby generating business for the real estate agent. This practice is outlawed by many state laws as well as by the federal Fair Housing Act of 1968.

blood alcohol concentration (or **blood alcohol content**)   *n.* The amount of alcohol in an individual's bloodstream expressed as a percentage of the total composition of one's blood. The percentage is used to determine whether the person is legally drunk, especially in regard to laws prohibiting the driving of vehicles while under the influence of alcohol.

Bluebook, the   *n.* The most frequently used guide on how to cite court case, statutes, treatises, law review articles, legislative debates and hearings, and other authorities on the status and interpretation of the law. Formerly titled, and now subtitled, "A Uniform System of Citation."

blue laws   *n.* Laws regulating or prohibiting certain otherwise legal activities, especially commercial activities, either on Sunday or all the time for essentially a religious reason. For example, an ordinance prohibiting the operation on Sunday of a dance hall within city limits is a blue law if it was enacted for religious purposes.

blue sky law   *n.* The popular name for the statute, found in every state, that regulates within the state the sale of corporate securities to the public. These laws are the states' counterpart to the federal securities acts. See **securities acts.**

board of directors   *n.* The governing body of a corporation elected by the shareholders to establish and carry out corporate policy, select the corporation's officers, make certain major decisions concerning the corporation's business and finances, and to oversee the corporation's operations.

board of pardons   *n.* A state agency authorized to grant pardons to and commute the sentences of convicted criminals. Also called a pardon board.

bodily heir   See **heir.**

bodily injury   See **injury.**

body politic   *n.* The people who are subjected to or owe allegiance to a single organized political governmental authority, such as a state or country.

boilerplate   *n.* Any standardized language or working that is almost always found in certain legal documents such as contracts and deeds. The terms are often in fine print and typically deal with matters that are either noncontroversial or nonnegotiable. See also **contract, fine print,** and **unconscionable.**

bona fide   *adj. Latin.* In good faith. Acting, being, carried out, or made in good faith; authentic; genuine; sincere.

bona fide occupational qualification
n. Employment practices that would constitute discrimination as to certain

individuals of a particular religion, gender, national origin, or age range (but not race or color) when the otherwise illegal discrimination is a bona fide qualification that is reasonably necessary for the normal performance of the duties of that particular occupation. For example, a designer of women's clothes by necessity is permitted to hire only female models to show off new designs. Such practices are not illegal under federal law. In addition, religious organizations and schools are allowed to hire only members of that religion even if religion is not a bona fide occupational qualification for that position (such as the requirement that all teachers in a parochial school be Catholic, even though they teach subjects that do not require Catholic background). Abbr. BFOQ.

bona fide purchaser   See **purchaser.**

bona fides   *n.* **1** Same as good faith. **2** Credential, documents, or other evidence of authenticity, good faith, legitimacy, or trustworthiness.

bond   *n.* A written promise to pay or forfeit money or perform some act upon the occurrence or nonoccurrence of a specific act or the passage of a specified amount of time. See also **indenture.**

> *appeal bond.* A bond required of the appellant in a civil case to ensure that the appellee's costs will be paid if the appeal is dropped or unsuccessful.

> *bail bond.* A bond given to a court by a surety to secure the release of a criminal defendant from incarceration and to guarantee the defendant's future appearance in court, when required, during the criminal proceeding pending against him. See also **bailsman.**

> *bearer bond.* A bond payable to whomever has possession of it. Whenever possession is trans-

ferred, so is also the ownership of the bond and the entitlement to the repayment of the debt and accompanying interest payments.

> *blanket bond.* A bond, frequently in the form of a fidelity bond, to protect against the wrongful action of one or more of a group or class of individuals. For example, a summer camp for children might provide a blanket bond against acts of child abuse by any of its camp counselors.

> *completion bond.* A bond to guarantee that a contractor will complete a project according to the terms of a contract. In the event of the contractor's default, the surety may complete the project or pay damages to the aggrieved party up to the amount of the limits of the bond. Also called performance bond.

> *convertible bond.* A bond that, under specified circumstances, can be exchanged for shares of stock in the corporation that issued the bond.

> *fidelity bond.* A bond to protect against the loss caused by the wrongful conduct of an employee.

> *fiduciary bond.* A bond required of a trustee, administrator, executor, guardian, conservator, or other fiduciary to protect against the loss caused by misconduct during the performance of the person's duties.

> *general obligation bond.* A government bond for which repayment is to be made from general tax revenues rather than from any specific fund or from the proceeds of any specific civic improvements or project. Also called a bond for general purposes.

> *judicial bond.* A bond to protect the adverse party in a civil case against the loss caused by any delay or inability to utilize property as a result of the lawsuit.

junk bond. A corporate bond that pays high interest, because the company issuing it has a great risk of going out of business.

municipal (or state) bond. A bond issued or guaranteed by a local or state government or governmental body.

payment bond. A bond to ensure that the employees, subcontractors, and suppliers of materials for a general contractor on a construction project will be paid by the bonding company, which acts as an insurer, if the contractor fails to pay them.

peace bond. A bond required by a court of a person who has previously engaged in public disturbances or disorderly conduct or has threatened to do so again to ensure that, if she breaches the peace in the future, she will pay the court an amount up to the limits of the bond. See also **breach** and **conduct.**

penal bond. A bond to secure payment of a specified sum as a penalty if an obligation is not met. Often used to ensure that the terms of a contract are performed. Also called a penalty bond.

personal bond. A bond issued by the party whose own potential action or default will trigger the payment or forfeiture of money up to the limits of the bond. See also **surety bond.**

registered bond. A bond that is not payable to an individual only because he or she has possession of the certificate evidencing the bond's existence, but instead is payable only to whomever the issuer's records indicate is the owner of the bond.

revenue bond. A bond issued to raise funds for a specific project. The money used to repay the debt can derive only from the proceeds of that project.

serial bond. One of several bonds issued at the same time, each of which has a different maturity date.

series bonds. A group or groups of bonds issued as a result of the same bond indenture, but offered to the public at different times and with different maturity dates and interest rates.

supersedeas bond. A bond required of the losing party in a civil action for the amount of the judgment. The bond is frequently a requirement for delaying the execution of the judgment while the losing party is appealing the case. Also called supersedeas.

surety bond. **1** A bond provided, usually for a fee, by one party, such as an insurance company, to protect against the potential actions or default of another party, by guaranteeing to perform certain acts or to pay an amount up to the limits of the bond if the other party acts or fails to act as prescribed in the bond. Also called a suretyship bond. See also **surety** and **suretyship. 2** A long-term, interest-bearing instrument, in the form of a certificate, issued to the public by a corporate or governmental entity as a way to borrow money. The obligor promises to repay the money on or before a specific date and makes regular interest payments until then. The owner of the bond is not a stockholder and has no ownership interest in the entity, but is only a creditor, and the debt is often secured by a lien on the entity's property. See also **debenture.**

zero-coupon bond. A bond for which no interest is paid before its maturity. It is purchased at a discount price and redeemed at its maturity for its face value.

bonded *adj.* Acting under, placed under, protected by, or secured by a bond. For example, a bonded contractor.

bond for general purposes *n.* See **bond** *(general obligation bond).*

bondholder *n.* The owner of a bond.

bond indenture See **indenture.**

bondsman *n.* **1** One who, usually for a fee, guarantees a surety bond for another. **2** Same as **bailsman.**

bonus *n.* **1** Wages paid in addition to the compensation ordinarily given or required under an employment contract. A bonus is payment for services (such as for recognition of exceptional work performance) or on consideration, and is neither gift nor gratuity. **2** Anything given or provided for free in addition to what is usual, agreed to, or legally due.

bonus stock *n.* Extra shares of stock, usually common stock, given without payment or other consideration by a corporation along with a bond or other stock, usually preferred stock, as an incentive for the public to purchase the bond or other stock.

book **1** *n.* A ledger or register recording particular transactions or events such as financial transactions and police arrests. **2** *v.* To enter or record the details of a transaction or event into such a book. **3** *v.* The process at a police station of completing an arrest, including fingerprinting and photographing the defendant.

book value *n.* The value according to a corporation's books of an asset's worth minus its accompanying liabilities. See also **market value.**

boot *n.* **1** In tax law, the extra money, unrelated or non-like-kind property, or assumption of liabilities included in an otherwise like-kind nontaxable exchange of property. The boot is subject to income tax. **2** In commercial law, money or property given or received to balance or equalize an exchange property.

bootleg **1** *v.* To make or distribute something illegally, without required authorization or registration, or without payment of the appropriate taxes. **2** *n.* Something that is made or distributed in such a fashion.

borrowed servant doctrine (or **borrowed servant rule**) *n.* The common law principle that the employer of a borrowed employee, rather than the employee's regular employer, is liable for the employee's actions that occur while the employee is under the control of the temporary employer. Sometimes referred to as borrowed employee doctrine.

borrowing statute *n.* A state statute specifying the circumstances when the statute of limitations of another state will be applied to in-state lawsuits whose cause of action arose in the other state.

bounty *n.* **1** A benefit, premium, or reward offered or given, especially by a government, to cause a person to take some specific action. **2** A gift or favor generously bestowed. **3** Liberality in giving.

bounty hunter *n.* A person who, for an reward or fee, pursues and captures bail jumpers or individuals who have not yet been arrested but are charged with or suspected of committing a criminal offense.

boycott *v.* **1** A concerted action by two or more individuals or entities to avoid commercial dealings with a business or to induce others to take the same action. This may include the refusal to work for the business and to purchase or distribute the company's products. While peaceful boycotts are generally legal, boycotts that use coercion or intimidation to prevent others from dealing with the targeted business are not. **2** To engage in a boycott. See also **picketing** and **strike.**

consumer boycott. A concerted refusal of consumers to purchase the products or services of a business to indicate displeasure with the manufacturer, seller, or provider of the product.

group boycott. A concerted refusal of a group of competing businesses to conduct commercial transactions with a company with whom they would otherwise do business. Such boycotts are illegal under the Sherman Antitrust Act.

primary boycott. A union-organized boycott of an employer with which the union's membership have a labor dispute. For example, a union involved in a dispute over wages with a business may encourage customers not to buy that company's products.

secondary boycott. A boycott of a targeted company's customers or suppliers with whom the boycotters have no direct dispute to compel those customers and suppliers to refrain from doing business with the targeted company. Such boycotts are illegal under the Taft-Hartley Act if organized by a union.

Brady rule   *n.* Evidence or information favorable to the defendant in a criminal case that is known by the prosecution. Under the United States Supreme Court case of *Brady v. Maryland* (1963), the prosecution must disclose such material to the defendant if requested to do so. Under subsequent United States Supreme Court cases, the material must also be disclosed, even if not requested, if it is obviously helpful to the defendant's case. These requirements are collectively known as the Brady rule.

brain death   See **death.**

brand name   See **trademark.**

Brandeis brief   *n.* A brief, usually an appellate brief, that utilizes economic, sociological, or other scientific and statistical evidence in addition to legal principle when presenting arguments in a case. Named after Louis D. Brandeis, who filed such a brief with the United States Supreme Court in *Muller v. Oregon* (1908) during his successful defense of a state law limiting the maximum workday of female laundry workers.

breach   *n.* A violation of a law, obligation, or promise.

breach of the close. The common law trespass of entering another's land either unlawfully or without authorization.

breach of duty. **1** The failure to perform a legal or moral obligation owed to a person or to the public. **2** The failure to act as required by the law.   **3** The failure to exercise the care that a reasonable person would exercise in the same or similar situation.

breach of fiduciary duty. The failure of a fiduciary to fulfill his duties with a high standard of care.

breach of the peace. The criminal offense of provoking violence, creating a public disturbance, or engaging in public conduct that offends public morals or undermines public safety. See also **bond.**

breach of promise. A common law action for breaking off a marriage engagement. Abolished in many states.

breach of trust. The breach by a trustee of the terms of a trust or of her general fiduciary duties.

breach of warranty. A violation of an express or implied agreement or warranty relating to the title, quality, content, or condition of goods sold or of goods delivered to a bailee.

breach of contract *n.* A violation of a contract by either failing to perform one's own contractual obligations or by interfering with another party's performance of their obligations.

anticipatory breach. A party's positive and unequivocal action or statement, before the time his contractual obligation is due, indicating that he does not intend or will not be able to perform when the time to do so arrives. In most states, the nonbreaching party may choose to treat the repudiation as an immediate breach of the contract and sue for damages without waiting for the time the breaching party's performance is actually due. The nonbreaching party can also urge the repudiating party to perform when performance is due, without giving up the right to sue. If the repudiating party withdraws his repudiation before there has been a material change in the nonbreaching party's position, the breach will be nullified. Also called anticipatory repudiation or constructive breach. See also **repudiation** and **voluntary disablement.**

material breach. A breach of a contract that destroys the value of the contract for the nonbreaching party, excusing her from the further performance of her own obligations under the contract and giving her the right to sue for damages. Also called total breach.

partial breach. A breach of a contract that does not substantially affect the value of the contract for the nonbreaching party. Thus, while the nonbreaching party has the right to sue for damages, he is not excused from the further performance of his own obligations under the contract. For example, if a person purchases a car with a radio, but the vehicle does not have one when it is delivered, the nonbreaching party can sue for the cost of the radio and its installation, but he is also obligated to pay for the automobile. Also called immaterial breach.

breaking and entering *n.* Two of the elements constituting the crime of burglary. Under the common law, forcible entry into a building (however slight) without permission used to be required, but many state laws now only require one to enter (for example, through an unlocked door or open window) or remain on the premises (for example, hiding in a closet until no one else is left in the building) without authorization.

Breathalyzer *n.* A device that measures that blood alcohol content of a person by analyzing the content of the moisture in her breath. Usually used by police when a person is suspected of driving while intoxicated.

bribe **1** *n.* Money or other valuable consideration (including a gift or favor) given or promised with the intent to corruptly influence the judgment or actions of a person, especially one in a position of trust such as a public official or juror. **2** *v.* To give or promise a bribe. **3** *v.* To gain influence by a bribe.

bribery *n.* The criminal act or practice of voluntarily giving, offering, receiving, or soliciting a bribe to influence the official conduct of a person in a position or office of public trust. See also **kickback.**

commercial bribery. The voluntary giving, offering, receiving, or soliciting of a bribe to influence the discretionary conduct or decision of an agent, officer, or employee of a business.

bridge loan *n.* Short-term loan to cover excessive or concurrent obligations, as in the case of a loan to cover two separate mortgages until borrower is able to sell one home.

brief **1** *n.* A written statement prepared by a lawyer and submitted to the court that outlines the pertinent facts of the case, the questions of law to be decided, the position of the lawyer's client as to those questions, and the legal arguments and authorities (for example, statutes and appellate court decisions) that support that position. See also **memorandum.**

> *amicus brief.* The brief submitted by an amicus curiae. Also called brief amicus curiae.

> *appellate brief.* A brief submitted when the case is on appeal.

> *reply brief.* A brief that responds to the arguments previously raised in an opponent's brief.

> *trial brief.* A brief usually submitted just before a trial.

2 *v.* to counsel in an advisory capacity, as in "to brief" one's senior partner on the status of the case before going to court.

broker *n.* A person or entity who, for a commission or a fee, brings together buyers and sellers of property or services and, while acting as the agent of one or both of the parties, helps them negotiate contracts.

brokerage *n.* **1** The business or office of a broker. **2** A broker's commission or fee.

brother *n.* A traditional term of collegiality (for example, "I respectfully disagree with my brother Smith on the issue of . . . ."), by which lawyers or judges refer to one another. When referring to more than one, the plural, brethren, is used. However, as more women enter the legal profession, more gender-neutral phrases, such as "my colleague," are being used.

buggery *n.* Anal sex with another person or with an animal. See also **bestiality** and **sodomy.**

bugging *v.* Intercepting, listening to, or recording a conversation, usually done covertly, by the use of an electronic device. See also **pen register** and **wiretap.**

building and loan association *n.* A quasi-public corporation to which its members contribute money that is loaned back to the members so they can buy or build homes. See also **bank.**

bulk sale *n.* Any sale of a large quantity of materials, merchandise, supplies, or other inventory that is not in the seller's ordinary course of business. Also called bulk transfer. Regulated by the Uniform Commercial Code that is designed to prevent a seller from making such a sale, and then spending or disappearing with the proceeds without first paying his creditors.

bulk transfer See **bulk sale.**

burden *n.* **1** A duty, obligation, or responsibility. **2** Something that causes anxiety or is grievous or oppressive. **3** In property law, anything that encumbers or restrict the use or value of land, such as an easement, restrictive covenant, or zoning ordinance. The burden indefinitely binds the current and all future owners until it is extinguished, so it is the land, and the landowner, that is burdened by the encumbrance or restriction. See **estate.**

burden of allegation *n.* The burden on a party seeking to raise an issue at trial to make allegations about it in a pleading. Also called burden of pleading or pleading burden.

burden of evidence   *n.* The burden on a party seeking to support a claim or defense at trial to produce sufficient evidence at trial to have the issue merit consideration by the fact-finder. Also called **burden of going forward** (with evidence), **burden of introducing evidence, burden of proceeding, burden of producing evidence, burden of production,** duty of producing evidence, and production burden. See also **proof** *(burden of proof),* **verdict, dismissal, nonsuit,** and **prima facie case.**

burden of going forward (with evidence)   See **burden of evidence.**

burden of introducing evidence   See **burden of evidence.**

burden of persuasion   *n.* The burden on a party at trial to present sufficient evidence to persuade the fact-finder, by the applicable standard of proof, of the truth of a fact or assertion and to convince the fact-finder to interpret the facts in a way that favors the party. Also called persuasion burden or risk of nonpersuasion. See also **proof** *(burden of proof).*

burden of pleading   See **burden of allegation.**

burden of proceeding   See **burden of evidence.**

burden of producing evidence   See **burden of evidence.**

burden of production   See **burden of evidence.**

burden of proof   See **proof.**

burden shifting   *v.* The shifting of the burden of proof from one party to another at trial, after each party presents sufficient evidence to initially persuade the fact-finder of the truth or falsehood of a disputed fact or assertion, the burden shifts to the other party to disprove such fact or assertion.

Burford abstention   See **abstention.**

burglar   *n.* An individual who commits burglary.

burglary 1   *n.* The common-law offense of forcibly entering a dwelling at night to commit a felony therein. **2** *v.* Under many modern statutes, the act of breaking and entering into any building at any time with the intent to commit a felony (or, in some states, a felony or petit larceny and, in other states, any crime) therein. See also **larceny** and **robbery.**

business, course of   See **ordinary** *(ordinary course of business).*

business invitee   See **invitee.**

business judgment rule   *n.* The legal doctrine that a corporation's officers and directors cannot be liable for damages to stockholders for a business decision that proves unprofitable or harmful to the corporation so long as the decision was within the officers' or directors' discretionary power and was made on an informed basis, in good faith without any direct conflict of interest, and in the honest and reasonable belief that it was in the corporation's best interest.

but-for cause   See **cause.**

but-for test   *n.* In criminal and tort law, the principle that causation exists only if the harm suffered by a party would not have happened in the absence of ("but for") the defendant's conduct.

buyer   *n.* One who buys or agrees to make a purchase. See also **purchaser.**

    buyer in the ordinary course of business. A person who buys goods in the usual manner from a person in the business of selling such goods and who does so in good faith and without knowledge that the sale violates another person's ownership rights or security interest in the goods. Such a buyer will have good title to the item purchased. See also **holder in due course.**

ready, willing, and able buyer. A person who is legally and financially able and has the disposition to make a particular purchase.

straw buyer. See **straw person** (or man).

buy-sell agreement *n.* An agreement among the owners of a business or the stockholders of a closed corporation to purchase, or to have the business or corporation purchase, the interest or shares of any withdrawing or deceased owner or stockholder. See also **continuation agreement.**

by-law (also **bylaw**) *n.* A rule or administrative provision adopted by an association, corporation, or other body, subordinate to the body's articles of incorporation, charter, or constitution, that regulates the body's self-government and the rights and duties of its officers and members. See also **ordinance.**

C

C & F   *n. abbr.* Cost and freight. Both the initials and phrase are used in offers and contracts for the sale of goods to indicate that the quoted price includes the cost of the freight to a named destination as well as the cost of the goods. See also **C.I.F.**

calendar   *n.* A list of the civil and criminal cases scheduled on a particular day, week, or other time period for trial or some other hearing (such as an arraignment, sentencing, or the hearing of arguments concerning pretrial motions) to be conducted before a judge.

calendar call   *n.* A courtroom procedure in which the judge or a court officer calls out the names of the cases on the calendar, is advised by the parties or their lawyers whether they are ready to proceed, and, if they are, sets a date for trial. In doing so, the judge or court officer is said to "call the calendar."

call   *n.* **1** In property law, an identifiable natural landmark that serves to delineate the boundary of land. See also **metes and bounds.** **2** A demand for the payment of money or the delivery of a security, such as a bond, by someone entitled to make such a demand. See also **puts and calls**.

calumny   *n.* A false and malicious statement about someone that is intended to injure his or her reputation. See also **obloquy, defamation,** and **slander.**

cancel   *v.* **1** To blot out, deface, mark off, perforate, destroy, or otherwise physically alter a writing to render it void.   **2** To annul, terminate, or revoke a promise or obligation.

cancellation   *n.* **1** The act, or the marks or perforations made in the act, of canceling something.   **2** A remedy by which a court calls in, annuls, and retains possession of a void or rescinded written legal document because it may cause unnecessary litigation or make a person's title to property unclear. For example, a court may call in, annul, and retain possession of a void deed to real estate that a party used to falsely claim title to someone else's real property, in order to prevent any such claims in the future.

canon   *n.* **1** A rule or principle, especially one that is fundamental.   **2** A rule or standard of conduct, in the form of a general maxim, adopted by a professional organization to guide the conduct of its members. See also **Model Rules of Professional Conduct.**

capacity   *n.* **1** The function, office, position, or role in which one acts.   **2** A legal qualification, such as age, that determines one's ability to do something that has legal consequences (such as making a contract or getting married). Also called legal capacity.   **3** The mental ability to perceive, understand, and appreciate all relevant facts, to make a rational decision based thereon, and to understand the nature and effect of one's actions. See also **sane.**

> *criminal capacity.* The mental ability required to sufficiently distinguish right from wrong to hold a person liable for his criminal acts. See also **insanity** and **infancy.**

> *diminished capacity.* Reduced mental ability caused by such factors as alcohol or drug use, disease, mental retardation, or injury, that prevents a person from sufficiently distinguishing right from wrong to hold

them liable for his criminal acts. See also **insanity.**

testamentary capacity. The mental ability a person must have at the time he signs a testamentary document, such as a will, for the instrument to be valid. Although it varies from state to state, it usually requires the person to understand who are the natural objects of his bounty, the nature and extent of his property, and the consequences of executing the document. See also **mind.**

capital   **1** *n.* Money or other assets used or available for the production of wealth.   **2** *adj.* A crime punishable by or involving the death penalty.

capital crime. Same as capital offense. See **offense.**

capital offense. See **offense.**

capital punishment. See **punishment.**

capital asset. See **asset.**

capital expenditure. The expenditure of money to purchase, improve, or repair property that has, or whose improvement has, a useful life that is substantially longer than the length of the taxable year in which the purchase, improvement, or repair is made. Not deductible for income tax purposes, but may be subject to depletion or depreciation. Also called capital expense.

capital expense. See *capital expenditure.*

capital gain. See **gain.**

capital gains tax. See **tax.**

capital loss. See **loss.**

capital stock. See **stock.**

capitalism   *n.* An economic system in which the means of production and distri-

bution are owned and controlled mostly by private individuals and businesses for profit, thus what is produced and the quantities thereof are determined by consumer demand and competition.

capricious   *adj.* **1** Characterized by or resulting from caprice, inconsistency in feeling or purpose, a whim, or an unpredictable or impulsive behavior. See also **arbitrary.**   **2** Contrary to the evidence or law.

caption   *n.* **1** The heading of a pleading that contains the names of the parties and court, the case index or docket number, and the type of pleading the document is.   **2** The taking or carrying away of an object. See also **larceny, robbery,** and **trespass.**   **3** The arrest or seizure of a person pursuant to legal process.

care   *n.* **1** Serious attention, concern, interest, or regard.   **2** In negligence law, the level of caution and prudence demanded in the conduct of a person in a given situation. The appropriate level is determined by measuring the potential dangers in the particular situation, the risk that the person's actions might bring the risk to fruition, and the possible ways of minimizing or eliminating the risk. In some situations, the level of care owed is determined by statute. See also **reasonable man, malpractice,** and **negligence.**

degree of care. The level of care to be exercised in a particular situation.

due care. **1** A phrase used to describe the level of care that an ordinarily reasonable, intelligent, and prudent person would use under the same or similar circumstances. For example, "Smith's failure to exercise due care before the accident constitutes negligence." Depending upon the seriousness of the particular situation and the known risks, due care may be reasonable care or a higher or lower degree of care. **2** See *reasonable care.*

highest degree of care. The highest degree of care that a very attentive, watchful, and cautious individual would exercise when dealing with a particular situation. Among other things, this is the degree of care that trustees and other fiduciaries are required to exercise when carrying out their fiduciary duties. Also called extraordinary care and highest degree of care. See also **breach.**

ordinary care. See *reasonable care.*

reasonable care. The degree of care that an ordinarily reasonable, intelligent, and prudent person utilizing diligence and good judgment would exercise or reasonably be expected to utilize under similar circumstances. Also called *due care* and *ordinary care.*

carjacking See **hijack.**

carrier *n.* A person or commercial enterprise (such as an airline) in the business of transporting people or goods.

common carrier. A carrier who is legally required to accept all business from the public, so long as the approved fee for the transport of passengers or freight is paid.

private carrier. A carrier who is not legally required to accept business from the public, but who is hired in particular cases to deliver passengers or goods.

carryback *n.* The part of an income tax credit or deduction, such as a net operating loss, that cannot be entirely claimed in a given tax year, but that a person may apply against (and thereby reduce) his tax liability for a previous year. See also **carryover.**

carryforward See **carryover.**

carryover *n.* The part of an income tax credit or deduction that cannot be entirely claimed in a given tax year, but that a person may apply against (and thereby reduce) their tax liability for a subsequent year. See also **carryback.**

cartel *n.* A group of independent producers or sellers in a particular industry, or a group of businesses with a common interest, who have joined together to reduce competition between themselves by allocating markets, sharing knowledge, or controlling the price and production of a product or service. See also **monopoly** and **oligopoly.**

case *n.* **1** An action, cause of action, controversy, proceeding, or suit at law or in equity filed with a court. **2** Same as trespass on the case. See **trespass.** **3** The aggregate of the evidence presented at trial by a party in support of their argument or position.

agreed case. See case stated.

case at bar. A case that is proceeding towards resolution or trial or is under the particular or immediate attention of the court. Also called instant case and present case. See also **bar** and **sub judice.**

case in chief. **1** The primary case presented by a party that satisfies that party's initial burden of proof, as distinguished from the "rebuttal case".

case on point. A previously decided case with facts or legal issues that were similar or comparable to those in a case at bar. See also **precedent.**

case of first impression. A case that presents a legal issue that has never been considered or decided by any court in that jurisdiction. See also **stare decisis.**

test case. A case initiated or selected from a group of cases that involve the same or substantially similar facts and questions of law for the purpose of testing the constitutionality of a law or establishing an important legal principle.

prima facie case. The evidence presented at trial by a party that is sufficient to satisfy the party's burden of proof and to allow the fact-finder to decide the case in that party's favor. See also **verdict, dismissal,** and **nonsuit.**

rebuttal case. The evidence presented at trial by the plaintiff or prosecution to contradict the evidence presented during the defendant's case in chief.

surrebuttal case. The evidence presented at trial by the defendant to contradict the evidence presented in the plaintiff's or prosecution's rebuttal case.

case law   *n.* **1** The law based on judicial opinions, including decisions that interpret statutes, rather than law based on statutes and other sources. See also **administrative law, casus omissus,** and **common law.**   **2** The collection of reported judicial decisions within a particular jurisdiction dealing with a specific issue or topic. Also called decisional law.

cash-basis method   See also **cash method.**

cash method   *n.*   An accounting method that records income and expenses when they are received or paid rather than when they are earned or incurred. See also **accrual method** and **completed contract method.**

casual employee   *n.* An employee of less than full- or part-time status; an occasional or temporary employee.

casualty   *n.* **1** An individual or property that has been destroyed, injured, lost, or otherwise made ineffective.   **2** The harm to an individual or property as a result of a sudden, unexpected, or unusual event.   **3** An accident, especially one that is fatal or serious.

casus omissus   *n. Latin.* Case omitted. A legal issue or situation not governed by statutory or administrative law or by the terms of a contract. The resolution of any legal dispute arising from such an issue or situation is governed by the case law or, if it is a case of first impression, by whatever guidance the court finds in the common law.

caucus   **1** *n.* A meeting of the leaders, members, or representatives of a political party to select the party's nominees or convention delegates, plan a campaign, or develop party policy or strategy.   **2**   *n.* An organized group of members of a legislative body who share a common interest and work together to further those interests through legislation.   **3** *n.* Any group or meeting organized to advance a particular cause.   **4** *v.* To meet in or hold a caucus.

causa   *n. Latin.* Case, cause. See also **cause.**

> *causa mortis. Latin.* Because of death. Something done or made by a person in anticipation of his own imminent death. See also **gift.**

> *causa proxima. Latin.* The nearest cause. See also **cause.**

> *causa sine qua non. Latin.* A cause without which not. Same as but-for cause. See **cause.**

causality   *n.* The relationship between an action or event and the effect that it produces. Also called **causation.**

causation   *n.* The act of causing or producing an effect or a result. See also **chain of causation, causality,** and **cause.**

cause *n.* **1** An action, event, or force that produces or contributes to an effect or result. Also called **causation.** **2** The ground or reason for a choice made or action taken. **3** A matter to be decided by a court.

but-for cause. A cause without which the events or results that follow could not occur. Also called causa sine qua non. See also **but-for test, causa,** and *proximate cause.*

concurrent cause. **1** One of multiple causes that simultaneously produce an effect or result that no single cause could. **2** One of multiple causes that simultaneously produce an effect or result that any one of the causes could have produced alone.

for cause. In support of a request made or an action taken. See also **challenge** and **excuse.**

good cause. A substantial or legally sufficient reason for a choice made or action taken or for seeking a particular court order. What constitutes good cause usually rests upon the circumstances of a particular situation. See also *insufficient cause.*

immediate cause. The last of a series of causes, although not necessarily the proximate cause, of an effect or result.

insufficient cause. An insubstantial or legally insufficient reason for a choice made or action taken or for seeking a particular court order. See also *good cause.*

intervening cause. A contributing cause that arises or occurs after the initial action, event, or force and alters the sequence of later actions, events, or forces to produce a final effect or result. For example, if a person walks into a ditch, the digging of the ditch is the initial (that is, but-for) action, and the subsequent removal of the barricade and warning signs that kept people

away is the intervening cause. Also called *supervening cause.*

legal cause. See *proximate cause.*

proximate cause. A cause that directly, without the contribution of any subsequent action, event, or force, produces an effect or result, and without which the effect or result would not have occurred. Furthermore, the effect or result produced by the proximate cause would have occurred even if there were a subsequent action, event, or force that contributed to the eventual effect or result. For example, if a person is fatally injured in an accident, the cause of the accident is the proximate cause of his death and not the poor medical care they received after the accident. Also called *causa proxima, direct cause, efficient cause,* and *legal cause.* See also *remote cause.*

remote cause. A cause that contributes to, but is not necessary for, the production of an effect or result. See also *proximate cause.*

sole cause. The only cause responsible for the production of an effect or result.

superseding cause. A cause that arises or occurs after the initial action, event, or force, and so substantially alters the sequence of later actions, events, or forces that the persons responsible for all previous causes are not liable for the final effect or result, even if their own actions were a substantial factor in bringing about the final effect or result. For example, a parent may be negligent for letting her 14-year-old child drive a car, but the subsequent theft of the vehicle from the child would absolve the parent of liability for any damages or injuries caused by the thief's use of the vehicle.

supervening cause. See *intervening cause.*

cause of action   *n.* **1** A collection of facts that, if true, would entitle a party to be awarded a remedy from another party by a court; the facts that give a person the legal right to sue. See also **claim for relief** and **right of action.**   **2** A lawsuit.   **3** In many states, the same as a **claim for relief.**

cautionary instruction   *n.* An instruction given to a jury by the judge, usually during trial, to disregard certain testimony or evidence that was improperly introduced, in lieu of calling a **mistrial.**

caveat   *n. Latin.* Let him or her beware. **1** An admonition, caution, or warning. **2** A formal notice or warning given by a party to a judge or other court officer concerning his or her behavior and requesting a suspension of the proceeding until the merits of the notice or warning are determined.   **3** A formal notice to a court or public official that the notifier has an interest in a matter or property and requests the suspension of some procedure or proceeding concerning the matter or property until the notifier is given a hearing.

caveat emptor   *n. Latin.* Let the buyer beware. The legal principle that, unless the quality of a product is guaranteed in a warranty, the buyer purchases the product as it is and cannot hold another liable for any defects. Statutes and court decisions concerning products liability and implied warranties have substantially altered this rule.

C corporation   See **corporation.**

C.D.   *abbr.* See **certificate of deposit.**

cease and desist order   *n.* A court or administrative agency's order prohibiting a person or entity from continuing or undertaking a particular activity or course of conduct. See also **injunction** and **restraining order.**

cede   *v.* To assign; give up; relinquish; surrender; transfer; yield.

censor   **1** *v.* To officially inspect books, films, letters, newspapers, and other media or methods of communication in order to suppress them or to delete any portions thereof deemed offensive or objectionable for moral, political, religious, or other reasons.   **2** *n.* A person who censors the media or other methods of communication.

censure   *n.* An official condemnation, reprimand, or expression of adverse criticism, usually by a legislative or other formal body, of the conduct of one of its members or of someone whose behavior it monitors.

census   *n.* The official counting of people of a country, state, or other similar political entity.

cert.   *abbr.* See **certiorari.**

certificate   *n.* **1** An official or sworn document that formally attests something to be true. Also called **certification.**   **2** A formal document certifying some interest, permission, right, or status granted to its bearer.

certificate of deposit   *n.* **1** A certificate from a bank acknowledging the receipt of money and a promise to repay it at a specified time and with interest determined at a specified rate.   **2** A bank document evidencing a time deposit. Abbreviated C.D.

certificate of incorporation   *n.* **1** In most states, a certificate issued by the state indicating that a corporation's articles of incorporation have been filed, the corporation has come into existence, and that the corporation has the right to operate as a corporation.   **2** In some states, the same as **articles of incorporation.**

certificate of occupancy *n.* A certificate from a local government agency indicating that a building or dwelling adheres to the local building codes and is ready for occupancy, generally a prerequisite to taking possession.

certificate of service *n.* The section of a pleading or motion that certifies that the party filing the document has sent a copy of the document to the opposing party or his lawyer.

certificate of title *n.* **1** A certificate issued by the state or local government identifying the owner(s) of personal or real property, and often listing any encumbrances on the property. **2** A certificate issued by a title insurance company indicating that it has conducted a diligent examination of the title of a piece of real property and that, except for the encumbrances noted in the certificate, a person has good title to the land. This is not, however, a guarantee or insurance of good title.

certification *n.* **1** The act of certifying. **2** The state of being certified. **3** See **certificate.** **4** The same as **certiorari** in some states. **5** The procedure whereby a federal appellate court requests the United States Supreme Court or the highest court of a state to review an issue concerning the application or interpretation of a law that has arisen in a case pending before the appellate court, in order to give it guidance.

certified copy See **copy.**

certified mail *n.* A delivery service offered by the United States Postal Service that is often used to send legal notices to addresses within the United States. Upon the payment of a fee, the sender is given a receipt when an item is mailed and a record of the delivery is kept by the addressee's local post office. For an additional fee, the sender may have the addressee sign another receipt when the item is delivered, and that receipt is returned to the sender, in which case the service is known as "certified mail, return receipt requested." Some court rules provide that service by certified mail is acceptable.

certify *v.* **1** To attest, authenticate, or verify something in writing. **2** To issue a certificate. **3** To judicially determine that a person is mentally or otherwise not competent. **4** To judicially determine that a group of individuals or entities meets the requirements to proceed with a class action. See also **certification** and **decertify.**

certiorari *n. Latin.* To be more fully informed. A writ issued at the discretion of an appellate court directing a lower court to certify and deliver the record of a case that is not appealable **as of right** to the appellate court for possible review. See also **appeal** and **writ of error.**

cession **1** *v.* The act of surrendering or transferring title to real property. **2** *n.* Something that is surrendered or transferred, especially real property.

cf. *abbr.* Compare. In legal citation, a direction to the reader to review a cited authority in which an explanatory or an analogous (but supportive) proposition might be found.

> *but cf.* In legal citation, a direction to the reader to review a cited authority in which a analogous (but contradictory) proposition might be found.

C.F. *abbr.* See **C & F.**

C.F.I. *abbr.* See **C.I.F.**

C.F.R. *abbr.* Code of Federal Regulations.

chain of causation　A series of events, each of which was caused by the immediately previous event. See also **causation.**

chain of custody　*n.* The order of places where, and the persons with whom, physical evidence was located from the time it was collected to its submission at trial.

chain of title　*n.* The history of a parcel of real property or of a commercial paper from its original owner or issuer to its current owner or issuer, including all conveyances and owners in between. Any gap in the history casts doubt on the current owner's claim of title. See also **abstract of title** and **title insurance.**

challenge　**1** *n.* An objection, exception, or other formal questioning of the capability or legal qualifications of a person, the existence of a right, or the legality of an action or thing.　**2** *n.* An objection by a party or a lawyer to a potential juror or jury panel and his or her request that a judge disqualify the individual or the panel from hearing that party's cause or trial.　**3** *v.* To call into question.

　　as-applied challenge. An argument, claim, or lawsuit that a law or government policy, although otherwise constitutional, is unconstitutional when applied to a particular party or situation.

　　Batson challenge. A defendant's claim that the plaintiff or prosecution excluded potential jurors due to their race, color, ethnic background, or gender by use of peremptory challenges. Named for the United States Supreme Court case of *Batson v. Kentucky* (1986), which forbids such a use of peremptory challenges in criminal cases. The principle in *Batson* was extended to civil cases in *Edmonson v. Leesville Concrete Co.* (1991).

　　facial challenge. An argument, claim, or lawsuit that a law or government policy always operates in violation of the United States Constitution or a state constitution.

　　challenge for cause. A challenge to a prospective juror based on a specific cause or reason, such as bias, prejudice, or a financial or other interest in the outcome of the trial. Usually, there is no limit to the number of challenges for cause available to each party.

　　challenge to jury array. See *challenge to the array.*

　　challenge to the array. An objection to an entire jury panel based on the manner that the panel was selected. Also called challenge to jury array.

　　peremptory challenge. A challenge to a prospective juror that may be made without any specific cause or reason. The number of peremptory challenges allowed to each party is usually limited by statute or court rule.

chamber(s)　*n.* **1** The office of a judge. **2** Any location where a judge conducts official business when court is not in session. See also **in camera.**

champerty　**1** *n.* An agreement between a litigant and a person who is not a party to the action, including the litigant's lawyer, for that person to pursue or financially support the litigant's claim in exchange for a portion of any damages awarded. The practice was once prohibited by the common law and it is still forbidden in some states, thereby casting doubt on the legality of lawyers advancing costs for their clients, as in the payment of expert witness fees.　**2** *v.* To financially support or otherwise maintain or promote another person's claim.

chancellor *n.* **1** Traditionally, the title of the chief judge of a court of chancery. **2** Any judge who sits in a court of equity.

chancery (or **chancery court**) *n.* **1** The traditional name for a court of equity. **2** Equity or proceedings administered in courts of equity. Also called *court of chancery.*

change in circumstances *n.* A modification, usually substantial, unanticipated, and involuntary, in the emotional, financial, or physical condition of one or both parents, warranting a modification of a child custody or child support order.

change of venue *n.* The transfer of a case from a court in one location to a court in another, or from one court to another in the same judicial district, for reasons of fairness or for the convenience of the parties or the witnesses. See **venue.**

character evidence See **evidence.**

character witness See **witness.**

charge *n.* **1** The formal allegation, contained in an indictment, information, or presentment, that a person committed a specific crime. **2** An instruction to the **jury. 3** A claim, debt, encumbrance, or lien. **4** An individual or thing placed in another's care.

> *Allen charge.* An instruction given, generally in a criminal trial, encouraging a jury to continue its deliberations after reporting a **deadlock,** on the basis that considerable expense and time has gone into the trial of the matter and the jury should make every effort to come to a resolution. See also **jury instruction(s).**

charge conference *n.* A meeting between a judge and the parties' lawyers, after the parties have closed their cases and before the jury is charged, to determine the content of the

instructions to the jury and to note any objections the lawyers may have to the instructions proposed by the judge. See **charge** and **jury instruction(s).**

charitable contribution *n.* A voluntary contribution of money or property to an organization involved in charitable activities and without getting or expecting to receive anything of value in return. See also **charitable organization.**

charitable deduction See **deduction.**

charitable organization *n.* An organization that meets the requirements of section 501c(3) of the Internal Revenue Code, operated solely for a religious, charitable, scientific, literary, educational, or similar purpose.

charitable trust See **trust.**

charter *n.* **1** A formal document by which a sovereign or a government grants rights, powers, and privileges to a person, business, or the people. **2** The highest law of any organization. See also **articles of incorporation** and **by-law. 3** The lease or rental of an airplane, bus, ship, or similar mode of transportation.

> *corporate charter.* **1** A legislative act that establishes a corporation (including its purpose and basic governing structure) or defines a corporate franchise. **2** See **certificate of incorporation. 3** See **articles of incorporation.**

> *Great Charter.* See **Magna Carta.**

chattel *n.* Any tangible property that is moveable or transferable. See also **personal property** and **real property.**

> *chattel personal.* Any moveable property, tangible personal property, or an intangible right in such property (such as a patent). Also called personal chattel.

chattel real. Any interest in real property less than a freehold or a fee (such as an easement). Also called real chattel.

chattel mortgage. A lien on assets other than real estate that secures a loan.

chattel paper. A writing or writings that evidence a monetary obligation as well as a security interest in or a lease of specific goods. Generally used when a consumer buys goods on credit by signing a promissory note that promises payment in the future as well as grants the seller a security interest in the goods. See also **accommodation paper** and **commercial paper.**

check *n.* A draft signed by a person (the drawer or maker) that directs a bank (the drawee) to pay, on demand and without conditions, a specific sum of money to another person (the payee). Usually the funds are withdrawn from an account or a deposit that the drawer or maker has with the bank. Also called cheque.

bad check. A check that is not honored by a drawee bank because it is forged, the account it is drawn on has insufficient funds or does not exist, or the check is in some other way defective. See also **check kiting.**

canceled check. A check with a notation (for example, the word "paid") on it made by the drawee bank that indicates that the check has been paid.

cashiers check. A check drawn by a bank upon its own account rather than that of an individual depositor and made payable to another person, to the same bank, or to a different branch of the same bank.

certified check. A check with a certification or notation written upon it (for example, the word "certified"), indicating that the drawee bank has

set aside sufficient funds from the drawer's or maker's deposit to guarantee payment of the check on demand.

NSF check. abbr. Not sufficient funds check. A check that a drawee bank may not pay because the drawer has insufficient funds on deposit to cover it when it is presented for payment. See also **check kiting.**

raised check. A check whose face amount has been increased. Unless done with the agreement of the drawer or maker, the charge constitutes a material alteration and discharges the drawer or maker, as well as the drawee bank, from paying any amount on the check.

check kiting *v.* To write a check while knowing that there are insufficient funds in one's account to cover it. Depending on the circumstances, check kiting is often a crime, especially if the drawer or maker has previously deposited a check from another bank into his account and hopes that the funds from that check will reach his account before the outgoing check is paid. Also called kite and kiting. See also **check.**

checks and balances *n.* A system of distribution of power among the executive, legislative, and judicial branches of government, in relatively equal proportions, such that each branch has the ability to counter the actions of the other two and thus prevent the entire government from being controlled by any single branch. See also **separation of powers.**

Chief Justice of the United States *n.* The formal title of the presiding justice of the United States Supreme Court.

child *n.* **1** A person under the age of majority. See also **age.** **2** Under the common law, a person who is under 14 years of age. **3** The son or daughter of a person or an individual who is treated as such.

after-born child. A child born after a certain event, such as a child born after the execution of a will or the death of its testator parent.

biological child. **1** A child born to his parents. Also called **natural child.** **2** A child genetically related to a specified parent. Also called **genetic child** and **natural child.** See also **adoption.**

delinquent child. **1** A minor who intentionally and constantly engages in antisocial behavior. **2** A minor who does something that would be a crime if committed by an adult. Whether the child would be subject to the juvenile court's jurisdiction would depend on whether the child is over the statutorily established age. See also **juvenile delinquent.**

foster child. A child cared for and raised by an adult, usually selected by a government agency, who is not his or her natural or adoptive parents.

illegitimate child. A child who was not conceived or born in lawful wedlock and who is not later legitimated. Also called **bastard.** See also **paternity suit.**

legitimate child. **1** In common law, a child born or conceived in lawful wedlock. **2** Under most modern statutes, a child born or conceived in lawful wedlock or later legitimated by her parents' subsequent marriage, her father's acknowledgement of paternity, or a judicial determination of paternity.

neglected child. A child whose parents or legal custodians fail to safeguard the child's emotional and physical health and general well-being.

posthumous child. Traditionally, a child born after his father's death. However, because it is now medically possible in some situations to keep a deceased pregnant woman on life-support machine until the birth of her child, the term can include a child born after his mother's death.

child abuse See **abuse.**

child and dependant care credit See **tax credit.**

child custody See **custody.**

child labor law *n.* A state or federal statute that regulates employment of children.

child molestation *n.* Subjecting a child to any sexual advances, contact, or other activity.

child neglect *n.* The failure of a person responsible for a child's care and upbringing to safeguard the child's emotional and physical health and general well-being. See also **abuse.**

child pornography See **pornography.**

chilling effect *n.* In constitutional law, the inhibition or discouragement of the legitimate exercise of a a constitutional right, especially one protected by the First Amendment to the United States Constitution, by the potential or threatened prosecution under, or application of, a law or sanction.

Chinese Wall See **ethical wall.**

choate *adj.* Completed or perfected in and of itself. See also **inchoate.**

choice of forum clause *n.* **1** A provision in a contract in which the parties stipulate that any lawsuit between them arising from the contract shall be litigated before a particular court or in a particular jurisdiction. Because the parties cannot confer jurisdiction upon a court, they must select a court and place that would otherwise have jurisdiction; however, since more than one court may have jurisdiction, the parties opt to designate in advance which one they choose.　**2** A provision in a contract in which the parties stipulate that any arbitration or conciliation between them arising from the contract shall be held before a particular arbitrator or conciliator or group of arbitrators or conciliators or at a particular place. Also called forum selection clause. See also **choice of law clause.**

choice of law　*n.* The issue of which jurisdiction's law shall apply in an action that involves events that have occurred or have an impact in more than one jurisdiction. See also **conflict of law(s).**

choice of law clause　*n.* A provision in a contract in which the parties stipulate that any dispute between them arising from the contract shall be determined in accordance with the law of a particular jurisdiction. If the dispute is litigated, the choice is not binding, but is normally honored, by the court hearing the lawsuit. The choice is binding if the dispute is arbitrated. See also **choice of forum clause.**

churning　*v.* In securities law, the excessive and inappropriate trading of securities in a customer's stock investment account for the purpose of earning the stockbroker more commissions than what would have been earned if the stockbroker was concerned only with the furtherance of his customer's interests. This practice is illegal under the Securities Exchange Act of 1934; however, there is usually no right of action for churning.

C.I.F.　*abbr.* Cost, insurance, and freight. Phrase used in an offer or a contract for the sale of goods indicating that the quoted price includes the combined cost of the goods, insurance, and the freight to a named destination. See also **C&F.**

circuit　*n.* **1** Historically, a judicial district wherein a judge would travel from town to town to preside over hearings. **2** A judicial district established in some states wherein one or more courts have jurisdiction to hear cases.　**3** One of the twelve judicial districts (along with a special nationwide thirteenth circuit) in which the United States is divided for the appellate review of federal trials by a United States Court of Appeals.

circumstance　*n.* An act, condition, event, or fact connected with another act, condition, event, or fact either as an accessory or as a contributing or determining element.

> *aggravating circumstance.* A circumstance that increases the culpability or liability of a person or the measure of damages or punishment for a crime or tort.

> *exigent circumstance.*　**1** An urgent situation that demands extraordinary or immediate action. Such a circumstance often allows for the circumvention of procedures that would otherwise be required by law. For example, if a car hits a child, the fact that immediate medical attention is needed to save the child's life is an exigent circumstance that excuses the physician's treatment of the child before parental consent is obtained.　**2** An urgent situation in which a law enforcement officer who has probable cause must take immediate steps to make an arrest, search, or seizure without a warrant because someone's life or safety is at risk or because there is an imminent threat that a suspect will escape or evidence will be removed or destroyed.

mitigating circumstance. **1** A circumstance (such as having a mental defect at the time of the wrongdoing) that does not exonerate, but reduces the culpability of, a person for a tort or crime he has committed and that may result in a reduction of the damages or punishment to be imposed. See also **diminished capacity. 2** A circumstance (such as turning oneself in for arrest) that does not reduce a person's culpability for a crime he has committed, but that may result in a reduction of the punishment to be imposed. See also **negligence** and **defense.**

circumstantial evidence See **evidence.**

citation *n.* **1** A writ issued by a court ordering a person to appear at a specific time and place and, at that time and place, do a specific act or to show the court sufficient cause why he or she cannot do so or should not be required to do so. See **show cause order. 2** An order issued by a law enforcement officer to appear in court at a specific time to defend oneself against the criminal allegations contained in the order. See also **summons. 3** A reference to a legal authority, such as a statute, court decision, or treatise, that supports or contradicts a legal argument or position. See also the **Bluebook.**

parallel citation. An additional reference to a court decision that has been published in more than one reporter. For example, the citation for the United States Supreme Court's famous Miranda case is *Miranda v. Arizona* (1966), with the main citation to the *United States Reports* and with parallel citations to the *Supreme Court Reporter* and to the *Lawyer's Edition.*

pinpoint citation The reference to a specific page where a particular quote or passage is found in a judi-

cial decision. For example, in *Miranda v. Arizona,* 384 U.S. 436, 444–445 (1966), the numbers 444 and 445 are the pinpoint citation to the pages where the rule is enunciated.

cite **1** *v.* To bring forward, provide, or refer to as authority, illustration, precedent, proof, or support. **2** *n.* A citation to a statute, judicial decision, treatise, or other legal authority.

citizen *n.* **1** A person who, due to place of birth, naturalization, or other reasons (for example, citizenship of parents) is a member of a political community or of a civil state, such as a country or state, and is entitled to all the civil rights and protections thereof and owes allegiance to its government. See also **naturalization** and **resident. 2** For purpose of federal diversity of citizenship lawsuits, a corporation that is incorporated or has its principal place of business in a state, or an alien granted permanent residence in the United States and residing in a state, is a citizen of that state.

citizen's arrest See **arrest.**

citizenship clause *n.* The provision in the Fourteenth Amendment to the United States Constitution declaring that all persons born or naturalized in the United States and subject to its jurisdiction are citizens of the United States and of the state each resides in.

civil *n.* **1** Of or pertaining to all matters concerning the law except for matters arising under criminal law and military law. See also **civil law. 2** Secular. **3** Of or pertaining to the duties, rights, and status of citizens and other residents of a country or state. See also **civil disobedience** and **civil right.**

civil action See **action.**

civil contempt   See **contempt.**

civil court   See **court.**

civil death   *n.* **1** Historically, the loss of all civil rights by a person who had been sentenced to death or declared an outlaw for committing a felony or treason. This included the loss of right to contract, the right to sue, and the right to protection under the law. See also **attainder** and **bill of attainder.** **2** Today, the loss of certain civil rights, such as the right to vote by a person convicted of or sentenced to imprisonment for a felony. The rights lost, and for what crimes or sentences, varies state to state.

civil disobedience   *n.* The deliberate, public, and usually nonviolent breaking of a law in order to call attention to the unfairness or undesirability of a statute (usually the one that is broken) or some governmental policy, and to influence public opinion concerning the same.

civil disorder   *n.* A public disturbance by three or more people involving acts of violence that cause immediate danger, damage, or injury to others or their property.

civil forfeiture   See **forfeiture.**

civil law   *n.* **1** A legal system derived from Roman law and based on fixed rules and statutes rather than on a court's interpretation of broad principles. Prominent in continental Europe, Latin America, Scotland, Quebec, and Louisiana. See also **common law** and **natural law.** **2** The law pertaining to civil or private rights and duties rather than to matters arising under administrative, criminal, or military law.

civil liability   See **liability.**

civil liberty   *n.* The freedom to exercise a right of personal autonomy or political expression or participation, such as the freedom of speech or religion, without governmental influence or limitation. See also **civil right, liberty,** and **right.**

civil procedure   See **procedure.**

civil right   *n.* **1** Any governmentally recognized or constitutionally or legally protected economic, personal, or political liberty or right of an individual.   **2** In the United States, any of the liberties and rights guaranteed by the Bill of Rights, the Thirteenth, Fourteenth, Fifteenth, and Nineteenth Amendments to the United States Constitution, and legislation designed to protect or encourage the exercise of those rights. **3** Freedom from discrimination, especially that based on race. See also **civil liberty, liberty,** and **right.**

Civil Rights Act   *n.* One of the federal statutes adopted either after the Civil War (1861–1865) or in the 1950s and 1960s for the purpose of protecting and encouraging the exercise of the liberties and rights guaranteed by the Thirteenth, Fourteenth, Fifteenth, and Nineteenth Amendments to the United States Constitution, especially the exercise of voting rights and the prohibition of discrimination in employment, education, and public accommodations on the basis of age, color, race, religion, or sex.

civil union   *n.* A relationship between cohabiting members of the same sex, legally recognized in some states, that conveys to the couple some or all attributes, benefits, and rights of marriage for purposes of that state's law, but not for purposes of other states' laws or federal law. See also **cohabitation** and **marriage.**

C.J.   *abbr.* **1** Chief justice. **2** Chief judge. **3** Circuit judge. **4** Corpus juris.

C.J.S.   *abbr.* Corpus Juris Secundum.

claim **1** *v.* A demand for money or property. **2** *n.* An assertion that one is entitled to, or the perceived or actual right to receive, money or property. **3** *n.* The totality of facts that gives rise to a right to receive money or property that is enforceable in court. **4** *n.* In some states and in the federal courts, the same as **claim for relief.**

claimant *n.* An individual or entity who asserts a right or demand to money or property.

claim for relief *n.* An assertion of a collection of facts that, if true, would entitle a party to be awarded a remedy from another party by a court. See also **cause of action** and **claim.**

class *n.* **1** A category of activities, objects, people, or qualities that have, or are considered to have, certain attributes or characteristics in common. **2** An identifiable group of individuals that a regulation or statute deals with or acts upon differently than it does other people. If the group is identified by gender, race, national origin, or religion, such a group is called a protected class or a suspect class. See also **suspect classification.** **3** A group of individuals who have, with the plaintiff in a civil action, a common interest in the subject, facts, and legal issues that the action is based on and who seek to collectively participate in the action so all their claims can be adjudicated in a single proceeding. For example, the passengers of a cruise ship who became ill due to the cruise line's negligence may constitute a class.

> *testamentary class.* A group of individuals who will share a testamentary gift upon the death of a testator but whose exact number and identity is not known until the testator's death. For example, if a gift is "to my children who survive me," it will not be known until the testator's death who those children are. See also **gift.**

class action See **action.**

Clayton Act *n.* A federal statute, adopted in 1914, that amends the Sherman Antitrust Act and prohibits certain business practices, such as price discrimination as well as particular mergers and acquisitions, if the practice might substantially reduce competition or create a monopoly in a line of commerce. See also **antitrust law** and **Sherman Antitrust Act.**

CLE *abbr.* See **Continuing legal education.**

clean hands *n.* The quality of a person who acted in an equitable way (that is, fair, just, proper, reasonable, with good faith) in a dispute or transaction, for which he or she is now seeking relief or asserting a defense in an action in equity. See also **unclean hands.**

clear and convincing evidence See **evidence.**

clear and present danger *n.* In constitutional law, the principle that the government, notwithstanding the First Amendment to the United States Constitution, may restrict, prohibit, or punish speech or the printing and distribution of words if it is necessary to prevent a clear and present danger of an event that the government has a right to prevent. For example, the government may prohibit a person from falsely crying out "Fire!" in a crowded room in order to prevent panic and injury. This principle was first articulated in the United States Supreme Court case of *Schenck v. United States* (1919).

clearinghouse *n.* **1** A place where banks daily exchange the checks, drafts, and other forms of indebtedness that are held by one bank and owed to another, and settle their balances all at one time. **2** A place where brokers in stock or commodities exchanges daily settle their debits and credits with one another. **3** A place for the exchange of information concerning a specific topic.

clearly erroneous *n.* The standard that an appellate court normally uses to review a trial judge's findings of fact when a civil case that was tried without a jury is appealed. The appellate court may not reverse the decision merely because, based on the facts, it would have reached a different conclusion. However, it may reverse the decision if the appellate court determines that the trial court's decision was clearly erroneous, even if there is some evidence in the facts to support the decision. See also **abuse of discretion** and **error.**

clear title   See **title.**

clemency *n.* **1** An act of mercy or leniency. **2** The grant by the president or by the governor of a state of an amnesty, pardon, or reprieve or of a commutation of a criminal sentence.

clerk *n.* One who keeps records or accounts, attends to correspondence, or does other similar duties in an office.

> *court clerk.* The court official in charge of some or all of the administrative aspects of the court's operations, including the filing, processing, and maintenance of court records; preparing summons and other papers that commence a lawsuit, including endorsement or placement of raised seal to signify that the papers are official documents of the court; and entering judgments.

> *law clerk.* **1** A law student who is employed as an assistant to a lawyer or judge and does legal research; helps with the writing of briefs, opinions, and other legal documents; and performs similar tasks. **2** A lawyer, usually a recent graduate of a law school, who is employed as an assistant to a judge and does

legal research and helps with case management and the writing of opinions.

client *n.* One to whom a lawyer formally renders legal advice, pursuant to an oral or written agreement for such advice to be given; any individual to whom a lawyer provides advice about legal matters.

close   **1** *n.* An enclosed place or tract of land. **2** *n.* The visible boundary around an enclosed place or tract of land, consisting of a fence, hedge, wall, or similar structure, or the invisible boundary around an unenclosed place or tract of land. The boundary is "broken" if anyone crosses the boundary without permission or an invitation from the land's owner. See also **breach. 3** *n.* The legal interest of one who owns a particular piece of enclosed or unenclosed land. **4** *v.* To consummate, conclude, or bring to an end, especially a discussion or negotiation. See also **closing.**

close corporation   See **corporation.**

closed session   See **session.**

closed shop   See **shop.**

closely held corporation   See **corporation.**

closing *n.* **1** The final step in the purchase of real property or of an interest in real property when a deed or another instrument of title is conveyed to the buyer, the purchase price or a portion thereof is paid, and collateral matters, such as the exchange or transfer of any assignments, insurance policies, leases, and mortgages, are finalized. **2** The termination of the administration of a decedent's estate after the estate's assets are distributed, taxes and other liabilities are paid, and all the necessary documents have been filed with the court.

closing argument   See **argument.**

closing statement   *n.* **1** Same as closing argument. See **argument.** **2** A detailed written summary of the costs (bank fees, legal fees, purchase price, and so on) involved in conveyance of real property or an interest in real property.

cloud on title   *n.* A defect or potential defect in the record of the title to real property that evidences a possible outstanding claim or encumbrance (such as an easement or a lien) that could annul or impair title to the property.

COBRA   *abbr.* See **Consolidated Omnibus Budget Reconciliation Act of 1985.**

co-conspirator   See **conspirator.**

co-conspirator exception   *n.* An exception to the hearsay rule that allows the acts and statements of one conspirator, as long as they were done or said during or in furtherance of the conspiracy, to be admitted into evidence at the trial of another conspirator, even if done or said in the defendant's absence. In federal court and in some states, the act or statement is admissible even if done or said after the conspirators were arrested and in custody.

code   *n.* **1** A systematized collection of regulations, rules, or statutes of a particular jurisdiction. See also **Code of Federal Regulations** and **United States Code.** **2** A systematized collection of all statutes, or a single comprehensive statute, dealing with one area of the law. See also **Bankruptcy Code, Uniform Consumer Credit Code,** and **Uniform Commercial Code.**

co-defendant   *n.* One of multiple defendants sued in the same civil action or formally accused of committing together the same crime. See also **joinder.**

Code of Federal Regulations   *n.* The official annual compilation of all regulations and rules promulgated during the previous year by the agencies of the United States government, combined with all the previously issued regulations and rules of those agencies that are still in effect. Abbreviated CFR.

Code of Military Justice   Compilation of laws and procedures governing court martials and all court proceedings involving military personnel.

Code of Professional Responsibility   See **Model Rules of Professional Conduct.**

code pleading   See **pleading.**

codicil   *n.* A testamentary document that adds to, subtracts from, qualifies, modifies, revokes, or otherwise alters or explains an existing will. To be valid, it must be executed with the same formalities as a will.

codify   *v.* **1** To arrange, compile, organize, and systematize into a code the statutes, or the entire body of law (including case law) of a country or state or the statutes or the body of law concerning a particular area of the law. **2** To enact a statute that restates the body of a particular area of law including applicable common law principles and the judicial interpretation of previous or existing statutes. See also **statute.**

codification   *n.* The process of codifying existing statutes or an existing body of law into a code.

codifying statute   See **statute.**

coerced confession   See **confession.**

coercion   *n.* **1** Constrain or restrain by physical force or the threat of such force. See also **duress** and **undue influence.** **2** The improper use of economic power to alter, shape, or otherwise control the actions of another.

cogent *adj.* Convincing; strongly appealing; compelling action, assent, or belief.

cognation *n.* Relationship by blood, whether through a common female or male descendant, rather than by marriage.

cognizable *adj* 1 Within the jurisdiction of a court, a dispute that a court has the power to adjudicate. 2 Capable of being known or recognized.

cognovit *n. Latin.* He has conceded. An acknowledgment of a debt or liability in the form of the debtor's written consent to a judgment taken against the debtor by the creditor, if a particular event does or does not occur.

cognovit clause *n.* A contractual provision whereby a party agrees to the entry of a judgment against him in a particular court or courts without any notice or opportunity to present a defense if he should default on his obligations or otherwise breach the contract. The use of such clauses are outlawed or restricted in most states.

cohabitation *n.* The act of a man and a woman, unmarried to each other, publicly living together in an intimate relationship as if husband and wife. Although a crime in most states, it is seldom prosecuted. Where illegal, it is also called illicit cohabitation, lascivious cohabitation, and notorious cohabitation. See also **fornication, bigamy, civil union,** and **marriage.**

collateral 1 *adj.* Secondary; subordinate; supplemental. 2 *n.* Property, including accounts, contract rights, and chattel paper, that is subjected to a security interest in exchange for credit or as security for a debt. 3 *adj.* Indirect; on a parallel or diverging line.

collateral ascendant. A relative, such as an aunt, uncle, or cousin, who has a common ancestor with a person but is not that person's ancestor. Also called collateral. See also **ancestor** and **descendant.**

collateral attack. An attack in a judicial proceeding against another judicial proceeding or a judgment entered in another court. For example, a party in Florida may attack a judgment entered against him by an Alaska court on the grounds that Alaska did not have jurisdiction over him or the underlying cause of action. See also **habeas corpus** and **direct.**

collateral consanguinity. See **consanguinity.**

collateral estoppel. See **estoppel.**

collateral heir. See **heir.**

collateral source rule. In tort law, the doctrine that any compensation, such as insurance benefits, received by an injured party from a source that is independent of the tortfeasor does not reduce the damages that the tortfeasor is obligated to pay. See also **subrogation.**

collation *n.* The addition to the estate of an intestate of the value of the advancements made by the intestate to his or her children so that the estate can be divided in accordance with an intestacy statute. See also **advancement.**

collective bargaining *n.* In labor law, negotiations between an employer and a labor union or other group representing employees concerning the terms and conditions of the employees' work. See also **bargaining unit** and **lockout.**

collective mark *n.* A servicemark or trademark used by the members of an association, club, union, or other group to identify and distinguish themselves or their products or services. When referring to a collective mark that signifies membership in a group, also called collective membership mark.

colloquium *n.* In a case of libel or slander, the assertions or allegations in the plaintiff's pleading, or the evidence presented by the plaintiff at trial, showing that the alleged defamatory statement or writing by the defendant referred to the plaintiff. See also **inducement** and **innuendo.**

colloquy *n.* Any formal conference, conversation, or discussion between the lawyers and the judge during a judicial proceeding.

collusion *n.* **1** An agreement between two or more individuals to perpetrate a fraud or to commit an illegal act. **2** In divorce law, in states that do not have no-fault divorce, an agreement between husband and wife to suppress facts, manufacture false evidence, or to do some act that would create or appear to create a ground for divorce. If discovered, the agreement will cause the divorce to be denied.

color *n.* **1** A false appearance; disguise; pretext; especially the false appearance of a claim to legal right, authority, or office. See also **color of law** and **color of title.** **2** The skin complexion of people who do not belong to the Caucasian or Caucasoid ethnic group. The term is frequently added to "race" in constitutional provisions and statutes barring discrimination.

Colorado River abstention See **abstention.**

colorable *adj.* That which appears plausible or reflective of reality, but is deceptive, intended to conceal, does not correspond with reality, or is not authentic or valid.

color of law *n.* The conduct of a police officer, judge, or another person clothed with governmental authority that, although it superficially appears to be within the individual's lawful power, is actually in contravention of the law. For example, a police officer who makes a false arrest while on duty, or while off duty but when they are wearing a uniform or badge, is acting under color of law. In some circumstances, the phrase also applies to the conduct of private individuals that is specifically authorized or approved by a statute. Depriving a person of his or her federal civil rights under color of law is, in and of itself, a federal crime and a ground for a cause of action. Also called under color of law. If the conduct violates a federal civil right or criminal law, it is also called **state action.** See also **color of title.**

color of title *n.* A written instrument, such as a forged deed, that falsely appears to convey title. See also **color of law.**

comity *n.* The deference and recognition that the courts of one jurisdiction give to the law and the judicial decisions and proceedings of another jurisdiction as a matter of courtesy and respect rather than out of obligation. For example, comity normally prevents a federal court from interfering with a state criminal action. Likewise, American courts usually recognize the judicial decisions (for example, a judgment or a divorce decree) of another country if it is determined that the judicial procedures of that country are substantially fair. See also **abstention, full faith and credit,** and **relinquishment.**

comity clause See **privileges and immunities.**

comment *n.* **1** A scholarly article or essay, usually written by a law student and published in a law review, analyzing a judicial decision and its context in the law. See also **annotation** and **note.** **2** An explanation of a statute, code section, or administrative rule written by the drafters of the statute, section, or rule. See also **annotation.**

comment on evidence *n.* Statements made during a trial by a judge or lawyer regarding his or her own opinion about the evidence and the credibility of the witnesses. In many states, judges are not permitted to make such statements. Furthermore, a prosecutor may not comment on the defendant's refusal to testify in a criminal action. When made, such prohibited statements are sometimes called an impermissible comment on the evidence.

commerce *n.* The exchange of goods, materials, products, and services or the travel of people.

> *foreign commerce.* Commerce that involves the transport of goods, materials, products, services, or people across international boundaries.

> *interstate commerce.* Commerce that involves the transport of goods, materials, products, services, and people within the United States but across state boundaries.

> *intrastate commerce.* Commerce that completely takes place within the boundaries of a state.

commerce clause *n.* The provision in the United States Constitution that gives Congress the sole power to regulate the United States' foreign commerce, interstate commerce, and commerce with Native American tribes.

commerce power See **commerce clause.**

commercial frustration See **frustration.**

commercial name See **tradename.**

commercial law *n.* The substantive law concerning the purchase and sale of goods and related matters such as the financing of credit, secured transactions, and negotiable instruments. Most commercial law in the United States is set out in the Uniform Commercial Code.

commercial paper *n.* A negotiable instrument evidencing a debt to be unconditionally paid on demand or at a specified time and payable to order or to the instrument's bearer; includes such instruments as certificates of deposit, checks, drafts, and notes. The use of commercial paper is generally governed by the Uniform Commercial Code. Also called **paper.** See also **accommodation paper** and **chattel** *(chattel paper).*

commercially reasonable See **reasonable.**

commercial unit *n.* A unit of goods that is regarded by trade or commercial usage to be a single whole that cannot be divided without materially diminishing or harming its character, market value, or use; for example, a chair is a commercial unit.

commingling of funds *n.* The mixing by a fiduciary, trustee, or lawyer of the money or property of a customer or client with his own without a detailed and exact accounting of which part of the common funds and property belong to the customer or client.

commission *n.* **1** A formal written document from a government or court empowering the individual named therein to hold an appointive office or to perform official duties. In the case of an appointive office, the individual must receive the commission before she can act in their official capacity. **2** See **administrative agency. 3** A group of individuals appointed by a governmental authority to perform some public service on an ad hoc basis. **4** The act of committing or perpetrating a crime. **5** Compensation paid to an agent, employee, executor, or trustee based on a percentage of the money collected or to be collected in a transaction or a percentage of the value of the property involved. See also **kickback** and **royalty.**

commit *v.* **1** To do; perpetrate. **2** To order a person's placement in, or to send a person to, a hospital, mental health facility, prison, or similar institution, especially pursuant to court order.

commitment *n.* **1** A promise, vow, or agreement to do something. **2** An order, especially one from a court, directing that a person be taken to and placed in the care or custody of a hospital, mental health facility, prison, or similar institution.

civil commitment. The commitment of a person to a hospital, mental health facility, or similar institution upon a civil court's finding that the person is ill, incompetent, addicted to drugs, or in some similar circumstances and is a danger to himself or others.

diagnostic commitment. **1** The incarceration of a person while it is determined whether she is competent to participate in the preparation and presentation at trial of a defense in a criminal action. **2** The incarceration of a person after she has been convicted of a crime while an appropriate sentence is determined.

mandatory commitment. The automatic commitment of a person found not guilty of a crime by reason of insanity to a hospital, mental health facility, or similar institution. Required under federal law when dealing with a person charged with a federal crime, but not required by law in most states.

mortgage commitment. See **mortgage.**

voluntary commitment. The commitment of a person to a hospital, men-tal health facility, or similar institution at the request or with the consent of the individual.

committee *n.* **1** A person or group of people who are members of a larger body or organization and are appointed or elected by the body or organization to consider, investigate, or make recommendations concerning a particular subject or to carry out some other duty delegated to it by the body or organization on an ad hoc or permanent basis. **2** A person who has been civilly committed. **3** The guardian of a civilly committed person or the individual into whose care an incompetent person has been placed. See also **conservator.**

commodity *n.* Any tangible good or product that is the subject of sale or barter.

common area *n.* **1** In landlord-tenant law, a part of the premises that is used by all the tenants, of which the landlord retains control and is responsible to maintain in a reasonably safe condition; for example, an elevator, hallway, or stairway. **2** An area that is owned and used by the residents of a condominium or similar housing development.

common carrier See **carrier.**

common law *n.* **1** A legal system derived from the broad and comprehensive principles encompassed within the unwritten laws of England and applied in most English-speaking countries, including the United States (except the state of Louisiana). The principles are created and modified by judicial decisions; passed on through custom, traditional usage, and precedent; are adaptable when applied to new facts and circumstances; and are changeable when required. Although much of what was once part of the common law, such as commercial law and criminal law, has been codified, other areas of the law, such as contract law, property law, and tort law, are still primarily governed by the principles of the common law. See also **case law, casus omissus, civil law,** and **natural law.** **2** The legal procedures and decisions of courts of law as distinguished from courts of equity. Also called **law.**

> *federal common law.* The case law derived from federal court decisions interpreting federal statutes or addressing other matters of federal concern.

common law marriage   See **marriage.**

common law property state   See **common law state.**

common law state   *n.* A state whose rules governing the ownership, division and inheritance of income and property acquired by a husband or wife during the course of their marriage holds that, subject to various qualifications, each spouse owns and has complete control over his or her own income and property. Also called common law property state and separate property state. See also **elective share, equitable distribution, property,** and **community property state.**

commonwealth   *n.* **1** The people of a state or country. **2** A state or country where sovereignty is vested in the people.

communication   *n.* **1** The exchange, imparting, or transmission of ideas, information, opinions, or thoughts, transmitted electronically or by gestures, speech, or writing. **2** A message so exchanged, imparted, or transmitted.

> *confidential communication.* A communication made during the course of a confidential relationship that is legally protected from involuntary disclosure and may be withheld from evidence. See also **privilege.**

> *privileged communication.* A communication made, whether or not during course of a confidential relationship, that is legally protected from involuntary disclosure and may be withheld from evidence. See also **privilege.**

community   *n.* **1** A group of people living together or in the same locality or who share interests or a sense of identity.   **2** The area, district, locality, neighborhood, or vicinity where a group of people lives.

> *marital community.* A married couple in a community property state.

community notification law   See **Megan's Law.**

community of interest   *n.* A common grievance, interest, or other similarity among a group of people that justifies treating them as a class for legal purposes. See also **action.**

community property   *n.* In a community property state, the income and property acquired by a couple during the course of their marriage, except for the income or property obtained solely by one of them by gift or inheritance. See also **property, equitable distribution,** and **tenancy.**

community property state   *n.* A state in which income or property acquired by a husband or wife during the course of their marriage, except for the income or property obtained solely by one of them by gift or inheritance, is community property.

commutation   *n.* In criminal law, the president's or governor's substitution of a less severe punishment for a greater one that was imposed by a court in a criminal action. See also **amnesty, pardon,** and **reprieve.**

commutative justice   See **justice.**

compact *n.* An agreement between two or more parties, especially between states or a treaty between countries.

> *interstate compact.* An agreement between two or more states that has been approved by Congress.

compact clause *n.* A provision in the United States Constitution that prohibits a state from entering into an agreement with another state or a foreign country without Congressional approval.

company *n.* A group of individuals, such as an association, corporation, partnership, or union, associated for the purpose of carrying out, maintaining, or performing a commercial or industrial enterprise.

> *holding company.* A company, usually a corporation, organized to influence or control other companies by such means as owning large amounts of stock in other corporations. See also **company.**

> *joint stock company.* An unincorporated company whose owners pool capital into a common fund in exchange for a number of shares proportionate to their respective investments. However, unlike a partnership, the shares can be transferred without the express consent of the other owners and, unlike a corporation, the owners are personally liable to the company's creditors if the company cannot pay its bills. See also **company.**

> *limited company.* A company, usually a corporation, in which the investor or shareholder's liability is limited to the amount invested or the value of the person's share.

> *limited liability company (LLC).* An entity that blends features of a corporation and a partnership, but is neither; owners are called "members" and may consist of one or more individuals, corporations, or even other LLCs. Members have some of the same protection as stockholders in a corporation, especially, no personal liability.

> *parent company.* A corporation that owns more than half of the voting stock of another corporation. Also called parent corporation. See also **affiliate, company, corporation,** and **subsidiary.**

> *personal holding company.* A holding company, usually with a limited number of shareholders and with over half of its income coming from such passive sources as capital gains, dividends, interest, rent, and royalties. The income is subject to a special tax in order to prevent individuals from avoiding income taxes by placing their assets in such corporations.

> *trust company.* A company, usually incorporated, that provides trust services, such as administering trusts and managing funds and property held in trust. Trust companies sometimes operate as commercial banks as well.

comparative negligence See **negligence.**

compelling governmental interest test See **compelling interest test.**

compelling interest test *n.* In constitutional law, a method for determining the constitutionality of a statute that restricts the practice of a fundamental right or distinguishes between people due to a suspect classification. In order for the statute to be valid, there must be a compelling governmental interest that can be furthered only by the law in question. Also called compelling governmental interest test and, in the case of a state statute, the compelling state interest test.

compelling state interest test See **compelling interest test.**

compensating use tax Same as use tax. See **tax.**

compensation *n.* **1** Payment for work done. **2** Payment for injury, loss, or otherwise depriving a person of something he or she is entitled to. See also **damages.**

> *deferred compensation.* **1** Payment at some agreed time in the future for work already done. **2** Payment for work done paid in a tax year subsequent to when the payment is earned or paid in a manner, such as contributing to a qualified pension or profit-sharing plan, that postpones the employee's tax liability for the payment.

> *just compensation.* The compensation to a property owner required by the Fifth Amendment to the United States Constitution whenever a state government or the federal government takes possession of private property by means of eminent domain for public use. Generally, the amount of compensation is the market value of the property at the time of the taking. See also **eminent domain.**

compensatory damages See **damages.**

competent **1** Possessing sufficient mental ability to understand an issue, problem, or situation; to make a reasonable decision concerning it; and to understand and appreciate the potential consequences of the decision. See also **capacity, compos mentis,** and **insanity. 2** Possessing the legal authority, jurisdiction, qualification, or legally required mental ability to perform a task.

> *competent evidence.* See **evidence.**

> *competent witness.* See **witness.**

competition *n.* Rivalry, as between two individuals or entities, a quest to secure an advantage over another; in business, rivalry for customers or a share of the marketplace. See **unfair competition.**

compilation *n.* **1** In copyright law, an assemblage of data or preexisting literacy works that is selected and arranged in such a way that it results in an original work of authorship. **2** A collection of updated statutes that have been rearranged to make their use more convenient.

complainant *n.* **1** One who enters a complaint against another in a civil action. **2** One who signs and swears to a criminal complaint.

complaint *n.* The initial pleading of a plaintiff in a civil action that identifies the court's jurisdiction, the alleged facts that entitle the plaintiff to relief, and the relief sought. See also **ad damnum clause, bill, petition,** and **prayer.**

> *amended complaint.* A complaint that substitutes for the original complaint and adds to, corrects, revises, or subtracts from the alleged facts contained in the original complaint.

> *criminal complaint.* A document, signed and sworn to by a victim or witness to a crime or by a police officer, alleging facts that give rise to a reasonable belief that a crime has been committed and that a person named in the instrument committed that crime. Also called a complaint.

> *third-party complaint.* A complaint by the defendant in a civil action against a person or entity who is not a party to the proceeding, to whom the defendant alleges a right of contribution or indemnity from that person, should the defendant

be found liable to the plaintiff. See also **action.**

well-pleaded complaint. A complaint in a civil action that identifies the court's jurisdiction, the alleged facts that entitle the plaintiff to relief, and the relief sought in a manner sufficient for the defendant to respond to the issues contained therein.

completed contract method An accounting method that does not record the income and expenses of a long-term project until the project is completed. See also **accrual method** and **cash method.**

completion bond See **bond.**

compos mentis *adj. Latin.* Master of one's mind. In sound mind; mentally competent. Sometimes shortened to compos. See also **non compos mentis.**

compound *v.* **1** To determine the interest on the principal and on whatever interest has already accrued. **2** To settle a claim or debt for an amount less than what is alleged to be due. **3** To agree, in exchange for consideration, not to prosecute a crime or seek punishment for the convicted criminal. See also **compounding a crime.**

compounding a crime *n.* The offense committed by a victim of a crime when he or she fails to report or prosecute the offender or agrees to hamper prosecution in exchange for a bribe, act of atonement, or making of amends by the criminal. In some states, it is not a crime if the victim agrees not to prosecute when the criminal returns what was taken or pays remuneration to the victim for the injury or loss. See also **misprision of felony.**

compound interest See **interest.**

compromise **1** *n.* An agreement between two or more parties to settle differences between them by mutual concessions. **2** *n.* The result of such concessions. **3** *v.* To end a dispute by compromise. **4** *v.* To adjust by concessions. **5** *n.* Something midway between two or more conflicting, different, or opposing things. **6** *n.* A partial payment made by a debtor in exchange for the creditor's promise not to seek payment of the remainder owed or claimed.

compromise verdict See **verdict.**

compulsory *adj.* Compelled, mandated, obligatory, or required, especially if by legal process or a statute.

compulsory appearance See **appearance.**

compulsory arbitration See **arbitration.**

compulsory counterclaim See **counterclaim.**

compulsory joinder See **joinder.**

compulsory nonsuit See **nonsuit.**

compulsory process *n.* The right of a defendant to utilize the subpoena power to compel the appearance of favorable witnesses at trial. In civil actions, the right is established by statute and, in some states, by the state constitution. In criminal cases, it is established by the due process clause of the Sixth Amendment of the United States Constitution. In some cases, the right is also available during hearings or investigations conducted by an administrative agency or a legislative committee.

computer crime See **crime.**

computer fraud See **fraud.**

concealed carry law *n.* A state statute that allows private individuals to conceal loaded handguns upon or about their bodies.

concealed weapon See **weapon.**

concealment *n.* **1** The act of hindering or preventing the discovery, knowledge, or sight of something. **2** The hiding or placement of an object out of notice or sight.

> *active concealment.* The concealment by deeds or speech of something that one has a duty to reveal.

> *fraudulent concealment.* The failure to inform another of a material fact that one has a duty to reveal, with the intention that the other party rely upon the omission to his or her detriment.

> *passive concealment.* The concealment of something by maintaining silence when one has a duty to speak.

concealment rule *n.* The legal doctrine that when a plaintiff is hindered or kept from discovering the existence of a claim by the actions of a defendant, the statute of limitations is tolled until the plaintiff discovers or should have discovered the claim.

concerted action *n.* Activity that is planned, agreed upon, arranged, and carried out by parties acting together with the shared intent to pursue some scheme or cause. Typically, each party involved is civilly and criminally liable for the actions of all the other parties committed in furtherance of the scheme or cause. Also called concert of action. See also **conspiracy, tortfeasor,** and **concert of action rule.**

concert of action See **concerted action.**

concert of action rule *n.* In criminal law, the doctrine that two or more parties who agree to commit a particular crime cannot be prosecuted for conspiracy or concerted action if the agreed-upon crime can be committed only by the exact number of parties involved. However, if any additional parties also participate in the underlying crime, all participants may be liable for conspiracy or concerted action. Also called Wharton Rule. See also **concerted action, conspiracy,** and **tortfeasor.**

conciliation *n.* **1** The amicable resolution of a dispute. **2** A method of alternative dispute resolution whereby a third party, who is usually but not necessarily neutral, meets with the parties and assists them to find a way to settle their dispute. See also **arbitration, mediation,** and **summary proceeding. 3** In family law, an attempt by a third party to assist a couple to settle their differences and stay together. See also **mediation.**

conciliator *n.* A person who helps parties to find a way to resolve their disputes. See also **conciliation, arbiter, arbitrator,** and **mediation.**

conclusion of fact *n.* A deduction reached without applying any substantive law, but entirely from facts that are observed or shown to be true or genuine. For example, the determination that Jones' bicycle had a flat tire when he purchased it is a conclusion of fact. See also **conclusion of law** and **findings of fact.**

conclusion of law *n.* An inference reached by applying substantive law to the facts. For example, unless there is an express or implied warranty or products liability law that applies to Jones' bicycle, the substantive legal principle known as **caveat emptor** will prevent

Jones from holding the seller of the bicycle liable for the bike's flat tire. See also **conclusion of fact** and **findings of fact.**

conclusive presumption See **presumption.**

concur *v.* **1** To agree, approve, or consent to, especially regarding an action or opinion. **2** Regarding a decision of a court or court panel that has more than one judge, to agree with the opinion of another judge, but not necessarily for all the same reasons or for a different reason altogether. See also **dissent.**

concurrent *adj.* **1** Existing or occurring at the same time. **2** Cooperating; coordinated; united in purpose, action, or application. **3** Simultaneously having authority or jurisdiction over the same legal action, dispute, or matter.

condemn *v.* **1** To expropriate private property, usually land, for public use. See also **appropriation** and **eminent domain.** **2** To adjudge someone guilty of a crime or to impose sentence, especially a severe penalty such as death or life imprisonment. **3** To adjudge something, often a building, to be illegal, unfit for public use, or a hazard to the public and order it to be destroyed.

condemnee *n.* **1** A person or entity whose property has been condemned or is about to be expropriated. **2** A person or entity who claims an interest in property that is being expropriated.

condemnor *n.* A governmental or semi-public entity that has condemned, or has the power to condemn, private property.

condition *n.* **1** A prerequisite or stipulation in an instrument. **2** A future and uncertain event, fact, or circumstance whose existence or occurrence is necessary for the existence or determining the extent of an obligation or liability. See also **estate** and **fee simple.**

concurrent condition. A condition precedent that must exist, occur, or be performed at the same time as another, but separate, condition before a duty or obligation arises.

condition precedent. A condition (other than lapse of time) that must exist, occur, or be performed before a liability or obligation arises.

condition subsequent. A condition that, if it occurs or comes into existence, will extinguish a duty or obligation.

condominium *n.* An individual residential or commercial unit in a multi-unit building wherein each unit's owner also owns the common areas, such as the hallways and elevators, as a tenant in common with the other units' owners. See also **cooperative.**

condonation *n.* **1** The forgiveness, purposeful disregard, or tacit approval by a victim of another's illegal or objectionable act, especially by treating the other person as if nothing happened. **2** In family law, an act (especially participation in sexual relations) indicating forgiveness by one spouse of the other spouse's improper conduct (such as adultery) when that wrongful conduct is a potential ground for divorce. In some states, condonation is an affirmative defense in a divorce action if the act asserted as grounds for the divorce is the act that was condoned, the act was not repeated after the condonation, and the spouse who acted wrongfully does not deny conjugal rights to the other spouse. See also **connivance.**

confession *n.* An admission that one has committed a crime or any other incriminating statement made by a person.

coerced confession. A confession induced by the police or other law enforcement officers' use of threats or force.

involuntary confession. **1** A confession induced by the police or other law enforcement officers' use of coercion, deceit, promises, or psychological pressure. **2** A confession obtained in violation of the Miranda Rule.

oral confession. See *voluntary confession.*

voluntary confession. A confession that is not involuntary. Also called an oral confession.

confession and avoidance *n.* A pleading in which a defendant admits the allegations against him, but alleges additional facts that negates the adverse legal effect of what he has admitted. For example, in a state where adultery is a ground for divorce, a plea of **condonation** would be a confession and avoidance.

confession of judgment *n.* **1** A person or entity's voluntary agreement to the entry against them of a judgment in favor of another person or entity upon the occurrence or nonoccurrence of an event without the cost, formality, or time of a legal action or the presentation of a defense in court. Also called **cognovit** judgment. **2** A judgment taken against a defendant by a plaintiff pursuant to such an agreement, especially if the defendant owes money to the plaintiff at the time the agreement was made, and the event that allows the plaintiff to enter the judgment is the defendant's failure to pay the amount owed or a portion thereof on time. Also called **cognovit** judgment. **3** The document wherein a defendant made such an agreement before the judgment was entered.

confidence game *n.* An intentional misrepresentation of past or present facts in order to gain a person's trust so that she will transfer money or property to the individual making the misrepresentation. Also called a con game.

confidential communication See **communication.**

confidential relation *n.* Any relationship that carries with it a special trust or dependency based on history, pattern of dealing, familial relationship, or special circumstances.

confirmation *n.* **1** An action, declaration, document, or statement that corroborates, ratifies, verifies, gives formal approval, or assures the validity of something. See also **advice and consent.** **2** A court order enforcing an arbitrator's decision. See also **award, order,** and **judgment.** **3** In commercial law, an agreement, usually by a bank, to honor a letter of credit issued by someone else, usually another bank, and to seek reimbursement from the instrument's issuer. **4** In property law, a conveyance of an interest in real property to one who has or claims an existing interest in the property, thereby curing a previous conveyance that was defective, increasing or making permanent a previously conveyed interest, or making avoidable estate certain and no longer voidable. See also **deed.**

confiscation *n.* The appropriation of private property without just compensation for the public use or treasury, often as a penalty resulting from a criminal prosecution or when possession of the property is itself a crime. See also **condemn.**

conflict of authority *n.* **1** A difference of interpretation regarding a point of law between two or more courts, often courts of equal importance or rank (such as the highest appellate court in two states). **2** A difference of opinion regarding a point of law between two or more legal scholars, especially on a point or in an area of law where there is little or no case law.

conflict of interest *n.* **1** The real or apparent conflict between one's personal interest in a matter and one's duty to another or to the public in general regarding the same matter. **2** The real, apparent, or potential conflict between the duty owed to one in a matter and the duty owed to another regarding the same matter, especially if the person who owes the duty is a lawyer (such as one who represents two defendants in the same case).

conflict of law(s) *n.* **1** A conflict between the laws of two or more states or countries that would apply to a legal action in which the underlying dispute, transaction, or event affects or has a connection to those jurisdictions. **2** The area of law that deals with the problems arising from such a conflict. See also **choice of law, comity, federalism, forum nonconveniens, full faith and credit, lex loci contractus, lex loci delicti,** and **uniform laws.**

conformed copy See **copy.**

conforming use See **use.**

confrontation clause *n.* The provision in the Sixth Amendment to the United States Constitution guaranteeing a criminal defendant the right to hear and cross-examine at trial all the witnesses against them.

confusion of goods *n.* The mixing of items of personal property of like kind or nature belonging to different owners to such an extent that it is impossible to identify which specific items belong to which owner.

con game See **confidence game.**

conglomerate *n.* A corporate entity that owns or otherwise controls a group of other corporations that engage in unrelated businesses or industries.

congress **1** *n.* A formal assembly, conference, or meeting of delegates or representatives. **2** *v.* To meet at a congress. **3** *n.* The legislature of various countries.

> *Congress.* The national legislature of the United States consisting of two branches, the House of Representatives and the Senate, and created by the United States Constitution.

congressional immunity See **immunity.**

congressional intent See **legislative intent.**

conjecture **1** *n.* A conclusion or inference based upon incomplete or uncertain evidence. **2** *v.* To make a conclusion or inference based upon such evidence.

conjugal **1** *adj.* Pertaining to marriage, the state of being married, or the relationship between a husband and wife. **2** *n.* The sexual relationship or relations between a husband and wife.

conjugal rights *n.* The mutual rights and privileges between two individuals that arise from the state of being married. These include, among other things, affection, companionship, co-habitation, joint property rights, and sexual gratification. See also **alienation of affections** and **consortium.**

conjugal visit *n.* A visit by a person to his or her institutionalized spouse (for example, a prison inmate) during which privacy is provided to the couple, usually to permit them to engage in sexual relations.

conjunctive denial See **denial.**

connect up See **connecting-up doctrine.**

connecting-up doctrine *n.* The rule that allows evidence to be admitted at trial, provided the party submitting it will later present other evidence to show its admissibility or relevance. Typically, the introduction of subsequent evidence will "connect up" the earlier evidence, but if the original evidence is never connected to the case, it will be disregarded by the factfinder.

connivance **1** *n.* The assent to, encouragement of, or promotion of another's wrongdoing by silence or feigned ignorance. See also **conspiracy.** **2** *v.* To be in collusion with another person. See also **conspiracy.** **3** *n.* In family law, the consent by one spouse of the other spouse's improper conduct (such as adultery), either in advance of the conduct or while it is occurring, when that wrongful conduct is a potential ground for divorce.

consanguinity *n.* The relationship between people who share a common ancestor. See also **degree, heir,** and **affinity.**

> *collateral consanguinity.* The relationship between people who share a common ancestor but are not ascended or descended from one another.

> *lineal consanguinity.* The relationship between people who are ascended or descended from one another.

conscience of the court *n.* A trial court's equitable power to resolve a dispute by applying the community's (but not the judge's personal) notions of decency, fairness, and justice.

> *shocks the conscience of the court.* Phrase used when a trial judge determines that a jury or the parties to an action acted beyond certain limits of decency and fairness. Such a determination will be grounds for invalidating an award or verdict of the jury or a contract or other act of the parties.

conscientious objector *n.* A person who, due to religious belief, refuses to participate as a combatant in any war. By law, such an individual is exempt from serving as a combatant, but may be required to perform an alternative form of service to the country in a civilian or non-combatant military role.

> *selective conscientious objector.* A person who does not object to all wars, but only to those he considers unjust. Such an individual is not exempt from service as a combatant.

conscious parallelism *n.* A decision by a business, made independently and without any agreement with a competitor, to follow a particular course of conduct that a competitor has already taken. See also **conspiracy.**

consecutive sentences See **sentence.**

consecutive tortfeasors See **tortfeasor.**

consent *v.* To acquiesce, agree, approve, assent, to voluntarily comply or yield, to give permission to some act or purpose. See also **acquiescence.**

> *age of consent.* See **age.**

> *express consent.* Consent that is clear, definite, exact, and unmistaken.

> *implied consent.* Consent that is not specifically expressed, but that is inferred from one's conduct.

> *informed consent.* Consent given after being completely advised of the nature, benefits, costs, and risks of a suggested course of action.

consequential contempt Same as constructive contempt. See **contempt.**

consequential damages See **damages.**

conservator *n.* **1** The court-appointed custodian of the property or financial affairs of a person who is under the age of capacity or who has been declared legally incompetent. See also **committee** and **guardian.** **2** In some states, the same as **guardian.**

consideration *n.* Something of value to either the promisee or the promisor of a contract (usually cash, but also property, a promise to do something or not to do something, and so on) that is given or will be given by the promisee to the promisor in exchange for a performance or a promise of a performance by the promisor. For the contract to be enforceable, the consideration must be something that the promisee, to his or her detriment or loss, is giving up, or something that benefits the promisor.

gratuitous consideration. Consideration that is neither a detriment or loss to a promisee nor a benefit to the promisor. For example, the promise to pay for an item with something that is worthless to both the promisee and the promisor is gratuitous consideration. A contract based on such consideration is unenforceable.

illegal consideration. Consideration that contravenes the law, public policy, or the public interest. For example, the promise to physically harm someone in exchange for an item is illegal consideration. A contract based on such consideration is unenforceable.

nominal consideration. Consideration that is so small that it has no meaningful value in light of the performance or promise that it is being exchanged for. For example, when buying a $10 million business for only one dollar, the dollar is nominal consideration. Traditionally, courts did not consider the value of the consideration when determining the enforceability of a contract, but today a nominal consideration might be viewed as evidence that the contract is unconscionable or is, in reality, a gift rather than a contract.

past consideration. Consideration consisting of an act performed or promise given in the past. For example, the promise to pay a debt that one is already obligated to pay is past consideration. A contract based on such consideration is usually unenforceable because, typically, the original performance was done or the original promise was made for some reason other than to exchange it for the current performance or promise of the promisor.

sufficient consideration. Consideration that is of a great enough value to be meaningful in light of the performance or promise that it is being exchanged for.

valuable consideration. Consideration that is of a great enough value to be meaningful in light of the performance or promise that it is being exchanged for and that has a measurable financial value to either the promisee or the promisor.

consideration, failure of See **failure of consideration.**

consideration, want of See **want of consideration.**

consignee *n.* One who receives custody, but not ownership, of goods that are consigned. See also **consignment.**

consignment *n.* The bailment of goods by their owner (the consignor) to another person (the consignee) to have the consignee sell the goods on behalf of the consignor in exchange for a portion of the proceeds or to deliver them to a designated recipient. See also **consignee.**

consolidated appeal　See **appeal.**

Consolidated Omnibus Budget Reconciliation Act of 1985　*n.* A federal statute requiring employers who provide a group health insurance plan for their employees to continue providing coverage to an employee for 18 months following termination or firing, or to a spouse of an employee in the event of divorce, for a period of 36 months following the entry of the divorce decree, provided that the spouse was covered by the employee's health insurance during the marriage. Obligation for payment of the health insurance premium is borne by the terminated employee or, in the event of divorce, by the party designated in the divorce papers, but in no event by the employer.　Abbreviated **COBRA**.

consolidation　*n.* **1** The act of combining two or more things into one.　**2** In corporate law, the union of two or more corporations into a new corporation along with the dissolution of the original corporations. See also **merger. 3** In civil procedure, the court-ordered combination of two or more actions that involve the same parties or issues. In the end, there may be a single judgment for all the actions or a separate judgment for each original action. See also **joinder.**

consortium　*n.* **1** The affection, companionship, and sexual gratification that one receives from another, especially from a spouse or, in some states, a fellow participant in a civil union. See also **alienation of affections** and **conjugal rights. 2** In some states, the affection and companionship between a parent and a child. See also **alienation of affections.**

loss of consortium. The loss of such affection, companionship, and sexual gratification as a result of the negligent or intentional injury or death of a spouse. May be the basis

for a tort action for alienation of affections or an element in determining the damages awarded in a wrongful injury or death lawsuit.

conspiracy　*n.* **1** An agreement or combination by two or more individuals to commit a crime or to commit a lawful act by unlawful means. Making the agreement is a crime, even if the unlawful act that is planned is never performed, but most states require overt action by one of the conspirators to further the conspiracy before the making of the agreement becomes criminal. A conspiracy to harm someone is also a tort. Also called partnership in crime. See also **tortfeasor, concert of action rule, accessory, accomplice, aid and abet, attempt, connivance, conscious parallelism,** and **solicitation. 2** Two or more individuals acting together to commit a crime or to commit a lawful act by unlawful means even if they are not aware of each other's participation or role in the conspiracy. For example, Smith and Jones prepare to commit a crime. Jones enlists Adam's help. Even though Adams and Smith are unaware of each other's participation, there is a conspiracy between the two to commit the crime and they will be held liable for each other's actions.

seditious conspiracy. See **sedition.**

conspirator　*n.* One who participates in a conspiracy. Also called **co-conspirator.**

unindicted co-conspirator. One who is alleged to have participated in a conspiracy, but is not indicted for the crime even though one or more fellow conspirators are. Also called unindicted conspirator.

constant search　*n.* A search that is conducted after a person who is authorized to do so waives his Fourth Amendment rights. The burden of proof is thereafter on the prosecution to show that the consent was freely given, with no threats having been brought to bear.

constitution *n.* **1** The fundamental and organic laws and principles of a country or state that create a system of government and provides a basis against which the validity of all other laws is determined. **2** The fundamental rules governing an association.

> *Constitution.* The Constitution of the United States, written in 1787 and put into effect in 1789.

> *unwritten constitution.* The body of fundamental and organic laws and principles contained in a series of statutes, court decisions, governmental proclamations, and tradition that has been accepted as such by the government and people (often over generations or centuries). For example, the United Kingdom has an unwritten constitution that includes the Magna Carta (written in 1215), the Bill of Rights of 1689, and other documents and tradition.

> *written constitution.* A single written document that embodies all the fundamental and organic laws and principals of a country or state. For example, the United States has a written constitution.

constitutional *adj.* Consistent with, pertaining to, or mandated by the constitution of a country or state. See also **unconstitutional.**

constitutional issue See **constitutional question.**

constitutional law *n.* The body or branch of law concerned with the study, interpretation, and application of a country or state's constitution, including the issues of governance, the powers of the branches and levels of government, civil liberties, and civil rights.

constitutional question *n.* An issue whose resolution requires the interpretation of a constitution rather than that of a statute.

constitutional right *n.* A liberty or right whose protection from governmental interference is guaranteed by a constitution. See also **bill of attainder, contracts clause, due process, equal protection, ex post facto law, freedom of contract, overbreadth, search,** and **self-incrimination (privilege against).**

construction *n.* The process of interpreting, or the interpretation of, a constitution, statute, or instrument. See also **legislative history** and **intent.**

> *canon of construction.* Any of the general principles that courts apply to construe a statute or instrument whose meaning is in dispute.

> *liberal construction.* The interpretation of a constitutional or statutory provision that applies the original intent, purpose, and spirit of the writing to circumstances that are not specifically addressed by the constitution or statute. Also called broad interpretation.

> *strict construction.* The interpretation of a constitutional or statutory provision that applies only the literal words of the writing to circumstances that are not specifically addressed by the constitution or statute. Also call narrow construction.

constructive Something that, while not actually true, is imputed by the law to exist or to have occurred and treated as if it were actually so. For example, to say "I'm giving you my car" and to turn over the car keys would probably be considered a constructive delivery of the vehicle itself. See also **legal fiction, actual, apparent,** and **impute.**

constructive bailment. See **bailment.**

constructive contempt. See **contempt.**

constructive delivery. See **delivery.**

constructive eviction. See **eviction.**

constructive fraud. See **fraud.**

constructive notice. See **notice.**

constructive service. See **service.**

constructive trust. See **trust.**

constructive-receipt doctrine Same as constructive receipt of income. See **income.**

constructive receipt of income See **income.**

construe *v.* To analyze, explain, interpret. See also **construction.**

consultative privilege Same as deliberative process privilege. See **privilege.**

consumer *n.* One who purchases or leases goods or services for his or her own personal, family, household, or other nonbusiness use.

consumer goods See **goods.**

consumer loan See **loan.**

consumer protection law *n.* A state or federal law designed to protect consumers against improperly described, damaged, faulty, and dangerous goods and services as well as from unfair trade and credit practices.

contemner (or contemnor) *n.* A person or entity who is guilty of contempt before a judicial or legislative body.

contemplation of death *n.* The anticipation of one's own death, whether imminent or not, as the major cause for transferring property to another. See also **gift** and **causa.**

contempt *n.* The willful defiance, disregard, or disrespect of judicial or legislative authority or dignity, especially any disobedience of an order or any conduct that disrupts, obstructs, or interferes with the administration or procedures of a court or legislature. See also **contemner.**

civil contempt. Contempt that consists of the failure to comply with a court order that is issued for another's benefit. The usual penalty is the daily imposition of a fine or imprisonment until the person in contempt agrees to obey the order.

consequential contempt. See *constructive contempt.*

constructive contempt. Contempt that occurs outside of a judge's presence or the immediate vicinity of a courtroom.

criminal contempt. An act or omission that is in disrespect of the court and obstructs its administration or procedures. For example, a party who shouts insults at a judge during a trial would be committing an act of criminal contempt. The usual penalty is a fixed fine or term of imprisonment.

direct contempt. Contempt that occurs openly in the presence of a judge or immediate vicinity of a courtroom.

indirect contempt. See *constructive contempt.*

purge[ing] contempt. To comply with court order so as to have sentence of contempt lifted.

content-based restriction *n.* In constitutional law, a restriction on the exercise of free speech based upon the subject matter or type of speech. Such a restraint is permissible only if it is based on a compelling state interest and is so narrowly worded that it achieves only that purpose. For example, a statute cannot ban all public demonstrations, peaceful or otherwise, on the subject of gun control while allowing demonstrations concerning other topics of controversy. However, a statute can ban all inflammatory speeches, regardless of the topic, that might incite imminent violence. Also called content discrimination. See also **discrimination.**

content discrimination See **content-based restriction.**

contiguous *adj.* **1** Touching at the edge, at a point, or along a boundary. **2** Close, nearby, or in close proximity, but not touching. See **adjacent** and **adjoining.**

contingency *n.* A future event or circumstance whose occurrence is not certain.

> *contingency fee.* A fee charged for a lawyer's services in an action that is paid only if the client wins his or her lawsuit or receives a payment from an out-of-court settlement. Usually, the fee is a percentage of the amount recovered. Furthermore, whatever the result of the action, the client will pay the court costs and the other out-of-pocket expenses (postage, subpoena fees, and so on) incurred by the lawyer during the course of the action. Although contingency fees are frequently charged for a lawyer's services in a civil action, it is unethical to charge this way for services in a criminal action. Also called contingent fee. See also **attorney's fees** and **champerty.**

contingent *adj.* **1** Possible, but not certain to happen. **2** Dependent upon a future event or circumstance that is not certain to happen. See also **vested.**

contingent beneficiary See **beneficiary.**

contingent estate See **estate.**

contingent fee Same as contingency fee. See **contingency.**

contingent interest See **interest.**

contingent legacy See **legacy.**

contingent liability See **liability.**

contingent remainder See **remainder.**

continuance *n.* The adjournment or postponement to another date of a trial or other proceeding. See also **adjourn.**

continuation agreement *n.* An accord between business partners that, should the partnership dissolve, the business will continue without the liquidation that would otherwise occur. See also **buy-sell agreement.**

continuing injury See **injury.**

continuing jurisdiction See **jurisdiction.**

continuing legal education *n.* **1** The training available to lawyers, usually through seminars, to continue their legal education, hone their skills, and keep up with the latest developments within a particular area of the law. Abbreviated **CLE.** **2** The industry of the providers of seminars, books, and other materials designed to provide such training to lawyers. Abbreviated **CLE.**

> *mandatory continuing legal education.* Such training to the extent it is required by a state or a state bar association. In most states, lawyers are required to devote a particular number of hours every year, usually by attending seminars, in furtherance of their legal education and in improving their skills. Abbreviated MCLE.

continuing objection See **objection.**

continuing trespass See **trespass.**

contra *adj. Latin.* **1** Against; in contradiction or opposition to; in answer or reply to. See also **precedent.** **2** In legal citation, an indication to the reader that the cited authority supports a contrary position.

contraband *n.* **1** Any goods that are unlawful to possess, sell or otherwise distribute or transport, or whose very existence is illegal. **2** Smuggled goods.

contract **1** *n.* Any legally binding agreement voluntarily entered into by two or more parties that places an obligation on each party to do or not do something for one or more of the other parties and that gives each party the right to demand the performance of whatever is promised to them by the other parties. To be valid, all parties must be legally competent to enter a contract, neither the objective nor any of the obligations or promised performances may be illegal, mutuality of the agreement and of its obligations must exist, and there must be consideration. See also **acceptance, offer, privity, tender, breach of contract,** and **bargain. 2** *v.* To enter into or settle by a contract or to make a legally binding promise. **3** *n.* The document containing the terms of a contract.

> *adhesion contract.* A contract that is so highly restrictive of one party's rights and liabilities, but not of the other, that it is doubtful that it is a truly voluntary and uncoerced agreement. The concept typically arises in the context of standard-form contracts that are prepared by one party, not subject to negotiation, and offered on a "take it or leave it" basis. If the terms of the contract are extremely burdensome or oppressive, the court may not enforce it on the grounds that it is unconscionable. Also called contract of adhesion. See also **boiler plate, fine print,** and **unconscionable.**

aleatory contract. A contract in which the performance promised by at least one party depends upon the occurrence of an uncertain future event. For example, a contract with an insurance company for the payment of proceeds in the event that an injury is suffered in the future in an automobile accident.

bilateral contract. A contract wherein each party is obligated to fulfill a promise made to the other party and is entitled to the completion of a promise made by the other party.

breach of contract. See **breach of contract.**

completely integrated contract. One or more documents adopted by the parties as expressing the complete and exclusive statement of all the terms of their contract. Also called entire agreement of the parties, entire contract, or entire contract of the parties. See also *partially integrated contract* and *severable contract.*

contract implied in fact. See *implied-in-fact contract.*

contract implied in law. See *implied-in-law contract.*

contract of adhesion. See *adhesion contract.*

contract under seal. A promise to do or not do something that is physically delivered to the promisee in a sealed instrument. Under common law, such a promise bound the promisor even if there was no consideration, but the use of such contracts has been modified or eliminated in most states. Also called **covenant** and **sealed instrument.**

cost-plus contract. A contract in which the payment for work done or supplies provided equal the total costs that the contractor incurs, plus a fixed fee or a percentage of the profits. Frequently used in transactions with the government.

divisible contract. See *severable contract.*

executed contract. **1** A contract in which all the promises owed by the parties have been performed and all the obligations have been discharged. See also *executory contract.* **2** A signed contract.

executory contract. A contract in which all or a portion of the promised contained therein have not yet been performed. See also *executed contract.*

express contract. A contract whose terms have been clearly expressed in words, whether spoken or in writing, between the parties. See also *oral contract, written contract,* and *implied contract.*

freedom of contract. See **freedom of contract.**

illusory contract. A contract in which the only consideration given by one party is an illusory promise. For example, "For $500, I will provide housekeeping services whenever I am available for the next year." Traditionally, such a contract was unenforceable, but in modern court decisions, a duty to act in good faith is often read into the promise and the contract is enforced accordingly.

implied contract. **1** See *implied-in-fact contract.* **2** See *implied-in-law contract.* See also *express contract.*

implied-in-fact contract. A contract based on the tacit understanding or an assumption of the parties and evidenced by the parties' conduct. For example, if a person drives her vehicle to a service station and opens the gasoline tank so that the service attendant can fill it, there is an implied promise on the part of the driver to pay for the gasoline, even if nothing is said between the driver and the attendant. Also called contract implied in fact. See also *implied-in-law contract.*

implied-in-law contract. A contractual obligation imposed by the law because of the parties' conduct or a special relationship between them or to prevent unjust enrichment. For example, when someone receives and uses goods that were intended for another, the law will impose an obligation on the recipient of the goods to pay for them. The obligation is imposed even if there is opposition or no assent from the party whom the obligation is being imposed upon. Also called contract implied in law and *quasi contract.* See also *implied-in-fact contract.*

installment contract. **1** A contract in which the obligations of one or more parties (for example, the delivery of goods, performance of services, or payment of money) is authorized or required to be completed in a series of increments over a period of time. **2** Under the Uniform Commercial Code, a contract that authorizes or requires the delivery of goods in separate lots that will each be separately accepted. A severable contract; each delivery is, in reality, an independent contract.

integrated contract. One or more documents expressing one or more terms of a contract in its final form. See also *completely integrated contract, partially integrated contract,* and **integration.**

oral contract. An express contract that is not in writing or has not yet been signed by the parties who will be obligated to do or not do something under its terms. See also *written contract.*

output contract. A contract in which a buyer agrees to purchase at a set price all quantities of a particular good or service that the seller can provide over the duration of the contract. See also *requirements contract.*

partially integrated contract. An integrated contract of which one or more of its terms is not yet in its final written form. See also *completely integrated contract.*

privity of contract. See **privity.**

quasi contract. **1** See *implied-in-law contract.* **2** A name for a claim for relief for restitution, especially one for quantum meruit.

requirements contract. A contract in which a seller agrees to provide at a set price all quantities of a particular good or service that the buyer needs over the duration of the contract and the buyer agrees, during that time, to obtain those goods and services only from the seller. See also *output contract.*

sealed contract. See *contract under seal.*

severable contract. A contract with two or more distinct components any one of which, if breached or invalidated, may be considered as an independent contract and not affect the other components of the contract and the parties' rights and obligations thereunder or put the promisor in breach of the entire contract. For example, a contract to purchase an automobile and to have a radio installed in it before delivery may be regarded as severable if the radio is not installed when the vehicle is delivered. Also called divisible contract. See also *installment contract, completely integrated contract,* and **severability clause.**

standard-form contract. A contract containing set terms that is repeatedly used and usually mass produced or preprinted by a party or an industry with only a few blank spaces to be filled in and with a few predetermined alternate and optional clauses to choose from to accommodate slight additions and modifications.

subcontract. A contract whereby a party procures the performance of a part or all of his obligations under another contract by hiring another party to perform those obligations for him.

unilateral contract. A one-sided contract in which one party promises to do or not do something in exchange for the performance of an act that is not promised to be done. For example, if a reward is offered for the return of a lost watch, nobody is promising to return the watch, but if it is returned, the promisor will be required to pay the promised reward.

void contract. **1** A contract that is not legally enforceable. See also *voidable contract.* **2** A contract whose terms have been completely fulfilled.

voidable contract. **1** A contract that can be voided at the will of one or more parties. The power to void the contract is not necessarily available to all the parties of the contract. For example, a person who is under the age of capacity can reject her rights and obligations under a contract and make it void without any repercussions, but until she does so, the contract is valid. However, an adult who entered that same contract cannot void it, and any attempt to do so will be a breach of contract and make her liable for damages. **2** A contract that is void to a wrongdoer, but not to the party who is wronged unless the injured party decides to treat the contract as void. See also *void contract.*

written contract. An express contract that is written and has been signed by the parties who will be obligated to do something or not do something under its terms. See also *oral contract.*

yellow dog contract. An employment contract whereby an employee agrees, as a condition of employment, not to remain in or to join a union during the course of his employment and to quit his job if he does. Such contracts are unenforceable in federal courts and are illegal in most states.

contract, freedom of See **freedom of contract.**

contractor *n.* A party to a contract, especially one who agrees to provide goods or services to the other parties.

general contractor. A contractor who agrees to undertake a large project, such as the construction of a building, and who hires and coordinates subcontractors to complete parts of the project. Also called a prime contractor.

independent contractor. A contractor who agrees to provide services to another party, but who retains significant or complete control over how the work is done. See also **employee.**

subcontractor. A person retained by a contractor (usually a general contractor or another subcontractor) to complete a part or all of the obligations owed by the contractor under a particular contract or series of contracts. For example, general contractors who build houses frequently hire subcontractors to install the plumbing.

contracts clause *n.* A provision in the United States Constitution that prohibits states from impairing private contractual obligations. This clause has been interpreted so that the states can impose regulations governing such obligations, provided the regulations are reasonable and necessary.

contributing to the delinquency of a minor *n.* The offense of an adult causing or encouraging a minor to become involved in delinquent or illegal activity, to engage in conduct in the presence of a minor that is likely to lead to delinquent or illegal activity by the child, or to otherwise encourage a minor's disregard for the law. See also **juvenile delinquent** and **corruption of a minor.**

contribution *n.* **1** The right of a debtor who has paid the entirety of a debt owed by her and others to recover the others' proportionate share of the debt. **2** The right of a joint tortfeasor who has paid more than her proportionate share of a judgment to recover the amount in excess of her share from the other tortfeasors. **3** The right of a joint tortfeasor to demand that the other tortfeasors supply their proportionate share of what is required to compensate the injured party. **4** A payment made by a co-debtor or joint tortfeasor of her proportionate share of what is due. See also **indemnity.**

contributory negligence See **negligence.**

controlled substance *n.* Any drug whose production, possession, importation, and distribution is strictly regulated or outlawed. These include depressants (such as barbiturates), hallucinogens (LSD, mescaline, and peyote), marijuana, opiates (heroin, morphine, and opium), and stimulants (amphetamines and cocaine). The substances are listed in five categories, or schedules, according to their characteristics and the type and degree of regulation is determined by the category the particular substance is in.

controlling authority See **precedent.**

controversy *n.* **1** A difference in views, especially in public, between individuals taking opposite sides on a particular issue. **2** In constitutional law, an actual, definite, and concrete dispute over legal rights between parties with adverse interests wherein one party is seeking an adjudication of the dispute and specific relief of a conclusive nature. Also called case or controversy requirement. See also **adversary proceeding.**

 separable controversy. A cause of action or claim that is part of a lawsuit, but is independent and separate from the other causes of action and claims in the action and can be severed and litigated separately from them.

contumacy *n.* The willful disobedience of a court's direction, order, or summons or any other disrespectful or disruptive conduct that would justify a finding of contempt.

conversion *n.* In criminal and tort law, the intentional deprivation of another of the benefit and use of his property, without his authorization or lawful justification, by possessing or disposing of the property as if it were one's own or by an act (such as damaging or destroying it) that interferes with or is inconsistent with the owner's right to sue and possess the property.

convertible bond See **bond.**

convertible security See **security.**

convey *v.* To transfer or deliver property or the title thereto or a property right by a deed or another written instrument other than a will.

conveyance *n.* The voluntary transfer of an interest in property or a property right, usually by means of a written instrument other than a will. See also **alienation** and **grant.**

convict **1** *n.* One whom a court has determined is guilty of an offense, either by accepting a valid guilty plea from the individual or upon a verdict of guilty by a judge or jury. **2** *v.* To prove or officially find a person to be guilty of an offense. **3** *n.* One serving a prison sentence.

conviction *n.* **1** The act or process by which a judge or jury finds someone guilty of an offense. See also **judgment.** **2** A firm belief or opinion.

cooperative *n.* **1** An organization or business enterprise, organized as either an association (cooperative association) or corporation (cooperative corporation), owned by those who use its services. All profits are shared amongst the cooperative's members in proportion to the money or labor each member contributed. **2** A dwelling owned by a cooperative whose members lease their apartments or living quarters from the cooperative. See also **condominium.**

copy *n.* **1** A duplicate, imitation, reproduction, or transcript of an original. **2** One of multiple originals.

 certified copy. A copy of a document to which a statement, usually by the person who issued or is keeping the original, affirming or swearing that the copy and the original have been compared and that the copy is an exact reproduction of the original. Also called attested copy or verified copy.

 conformed copy. A copy of a document to which changes or insertions are made to reflect identical changes and insertions made in the original. For example, if a judge makes changes to a proposed order before signing it, a party would "conform" a copy by adding to it those same changes as well as writing in the judge's name where he or she signed on the original order.

copyright *n.* The exclusive statutory right of literary (authors, playwrights, poets), musical (composers, musicians), visual (painters, photographers, sculptors), and other artists to control the reproduction, use, and disposition of their work, usually for their lifetime plus seventy years. The Copyright Act of 1976 governs most copyrights in the United States. See also **copy** and **fair use.**

coroner *n.* A public official whose primary duty is to investigate the cause and circumstances of any deaths within his or her jurisdiction that were clearly not due to natural causes.

corp. *abbr.* See **corporation.**

corporal punishment See **punishment.**

corporate *adj.* Of or relating to a particular corporation or to corporations in general.

> *corporate law.* The substantive law concerning business organizations and transactions.

> *corporate opportunity doctrine.* The common law principle that the directors, officers, employees, and agents of a corporation may not use any information obtained in their corporate capacity to exploit for their own personal benefit a business opportunity that belongs, or should in fairness belong, to the corporation.

> *corporate veil.* The legal principle that a corporation is distinct from its owners and that the corporation's shareholders are not personally liable for the corporation's acts and debts. See also **alter ego, piercing the corporate veil, charter,** and **seal.**

corporation *n.* An entity, usually a business, created by a legislative act or by individuals who have agreed upon and filed articles of incorporation with the state government. Ownership in the corporation is typically represented by shares of stock. Furthermore, a corporation is legally recognized as an artificial person whose existence is separate and distinct from that of its shareholders who are not personally responsible for the corporation's acts and debts. As an artificial person, a corporation has the power to acquire, own, and convey property, to sue and be sued, and such other powers of a natural person that the law may confer upon it. Abbreviated **corp.** See **charter, corporate,** and **seal.**

> *brother-sister corporation.* See *sister corporations.*

> *C corporation.* A corporation that pays corporate income taxes on its income rather than having its profits taxed as the personal income of its shareholders. Any corporation that is not a S corporation is, by default, a C corporation. Also called subchapter C corporation. See also *S corporation.*

> *close corporation.* A corporation owned by a single individual or a small group of individuals, often all personally involved in the corporation's business or related to another, who frequently conduct the corporation's business without such formalities as annual shareholder meetings, and whose share of stocks cannot be sold to anyone outside the group without the prior permission of the other shareholders. The rights and privileges of such corporations vary state to state. Also called closed corporation, closely held corporation, or privately held corporation. See also *publicly held corporation.*

domestic corporation. **1** A corporation whose articles of incorporation have been filed in a particular state. (The corporation is a domestic corporation of that state.) See also *foreign corporation.* **2** For federal income tax purposes, a corporation whose articles of incorporation have been filed in the United States.

dummy corporation. A corporation whose sole purpose is to conceal the owners' identities and to protect them from personal liability.

foreign corporation. A corporation whose articles of incorporation have been filed in another state or country. (A corporation whose articles of incorporation have been filed in one state or country is a foreign corporation in every other state or country.) See also *domestic corporation.*

municipal corporation. A political entity, such as a county, city, town, village, or school district, that is created by and derives its limited powers of self-government (including the ability to enter contracts and to sue and be sued) from the state legislature. See also **immunity.**

nonprofit corporation. A corporation organized for a chartable, cultural, educational, religious, or some other purpose other than making a profit or distributing its income to its shareholders, officers, or others similarly affiliated with it. Usually, such corporations are given special treatment under state and federal tax laws. Also called not-for-profit corporation.

nonstock corporation. A corporation in which ownership is conferred by a membership charter or agreement that governs the owners' rights and liabilities rather than by the ownership of shares of stock. For example, mutual savings banks and fraternal organizations are usually nonstock corporations.

parent corporation. Same as parent company. See **company.**

private corporation. A corporation created and owned by private individuals for a nongovernmental, usually business or nonprofit, purpose. See also *public corporation.*

professional corporation. A corporation owned by a small group of individuals who practice a common occupation that requires a professional license (such are accounting, architecture, law, or medicine). Such a corporation has the same, but not all, of the characteristics of a private corporation. Abbreviated P.C. Also called P.A. or professional association.

public corporation. **1** A corporation created by a state or the federal government and, while often financially independent of the government, engages as a government agency in activities that benefit the general public. A publicly appointed board of directors manages such a corporation. See also *private corporation.* **2** See *publicly held corporation.*

publicly held corporation. A corporation whose shares of stock are sold to, freely traded amongst, and owned by a diverse group of shareholders who are members of the general public. See also *close corporation.*

S corporation. A corporation with a small number of shareholders that has elected, pursuant to Subchapter S of the Internal Revenue Code, to have its income treated as personal income to its shareholders for income tax purposes rather than have the corporation pay the normal corporate income taxes on the income. Also called subchapter S corporation. See also *C corporation.*

shell corporation. A corporation that has no business or ongoing activity (and sometimes no substantial assets) of its own and is typically used to conceal another corporation's business activities.

sister corporations. Two or more corporations that are subsidiaries of the same parent company. Also called brother-sister corporations. See also **affiliate** and **company.**

subsidiary corporation. A corporation in which a parent company owns enough shares to control its activities and the selection of its officers and directors. Also called a **subsidiary.**

corpus *n. Latin.* **1** The main body, mass, or part of something. **2** A collection of things that, when together, can be considered or regarded as a single thing (such as a collection of writing by an author). **3** The capital or principal sum (as opposed to income or interest). **4** The property or subject matter of a trust.

corpus delicti *n. Latin.* The body of the crime. The objective evidence that there has been an injury (physical or otherwise) or loss and that it was caused by the criminal act of some person or thing.

corpus delicti rule *n.* The legal principle that the prosecution cannot prove that a crime has been committed from the defendant's confession alone, but that the prosecution must prove that corroborating evidence exists that the crime that the defendant has confessed to did actually occur.

corpus juris *n. Latin.* Body of law. The law in general, especially when compiled, codified, and published in a single text or in a series consisting of a collection of individual laws. Abbreviated **C.J.**

Corpus Juris Secundum *n.* An authoritative legal encyclopedia that provides general background knowledge of the law with footnoted citation to relevant case law. Abbreviated **C.J.S.**

corroborate *v.* To confirm, ratify, strengthen, or support, especially by additional authority or evidence.

corroborating evidence See **evidence.**

corruption of a minor **1** *n.* The offense of engaging in sexual intercourse or other sexual activity with a person who is not one's spouse and who is under the age of consent or another age set by statute, especially if there is a considerable age difference (usually four years or more) between the offender and the victim. See also **rape.** **2** *v.* In some states, to assist or encourage a minor to commit an offense. See also **contributing to the delinquency of a minor.** **3** *n.* The arousal or encouragement of a child's destructive antisocial behavior by a parent, guardian, or other caregiver. See also **contributing to the delinquency of a minor.**

cosigner *n.* One who jointly signs a negotiable instrument with another person to assist the other signer to obtain a loan and, by doing so, assumes full liability for the loan should the other signer ever default on the loan contract. Also called a comaker. See also **accommodation party** and **surety.**

cost and freight See **C & F.**

cost basis See **basis.**

cost, insurance, and freight See **C.I.F.**

cost of completion *n.* A measure of damages in a breach of contract action representing the expense incurred by the nonbreaching party to complete the breaching party's promised performance or to have the performance finished by a third party. See also **damages** and **specific performance.**

cost-plus contract See **contract.**

costs *n.* The filing fees, jury fees, court reporter fees, and other expenses, excluding attorneys' fees, incurred in the prosecution of or defense against a civil suit. When allowed by statute, a court may order the losing party in a civil action to reimburse the successful party for his or her costs. Also called court costs. See also **bill of costs.**

counsel *n.* One or more lawyers who provide advice to or represent a particular client. In the singular, also called a **counselor.** See also **attorney.**

assigned counsel. A lawyer appointed by a court to represent at the government's expense a criminal defendant who cannot afford to retain his or her own lawyer.

counsel of record. Same as attorney of record. See **attorney.**

general counsel. A lawyer or law firm that provides most or all of the legal advice and representation utilized by a client, especially by one that is a corporation or engages in business activities.

independent counsel. **1** A lawyer or law firm retained to provide advice or representation on a particular matter when it would be a conflict of interest for the client's regular lawyers to do so. **2** A lawyer retained to conduct an unbiased investigation, especially one retained by a governmental body to investigate employees or officers of that body for alleged misconduct. See also **prosecutor.**

in-house counsel. One or more lawyers who are employees of a business and provide legal advice and representation only for that business.

lead counsel. When more than one lawyer or law firm is hired to represent a party or parties in an action, especially in an action involving more than one jurisdiction, or to represent various plaintiffs in a

class action, the lawyer or law firm that controls, coordinates, or manages the litigation and represents the interests of the parties or class as a whole.

local counsel. A lawyer licensed to practice law in a particular jurisdiction or before a particular court who assists a lawyer who is not licensed, but who has been given permission to provide advice and represent a client in an action in that jurisdiction or before that court, with matters regarding the application and interpretation of the local laws as well as with the local court customs, practices, and rules.

of counsel. **1** A lawyer who assists the attorney of record in a trial or appeal with the preparation, management, or presentation of a case. **2** A lawyer who is connected to a law firm, such as a retired partner who regularly provides advice, but who is not an associate, member, or partner of the firm.

special counsel. A lawyer brought in to assist another lawyer or a law firm in a matter requiring their special experience, knowledge, or skills or to serve as independent counsel.

counselor See **counsel.**

count *n.* **1** In a civil action, the statement of a distinct cause of action in a complaint or similar pleading. **2** In a criminal action, the distinct allegation in an indictment or information that the defendant committed a crime.

multiple counts. Two or more distinct causes of action or allegations that the defendant committed an offense contained in a complaint, indictment, information, or similar pleading.

separate count. Any of the individual causes of action or allegations that the defendant committed an offense in a complaint, indictment, information, or similar pleading.

counterclaim *n.* A cause of action or claim for relief asserted in opposition to or as a setoff against the plaintiff's own cause of action or claim for relief and contained in the defendant's answer to the plaintiff's complaint. See also **cross-claim.**

compulsory counterclaim. A cause of action or claim for relief that arises from the same occurrence, transaction, or subject matter as the plaintiff's cause of action or claim for relief. Generally, the failure to raise such cause of action or claim for relief in the defendant's answer will prevent the defendant from bringing it up in a subsequent action.

permissible counterclaim. A cause of action or claim for relief that does not arise from the same occurrence, transaction, or subject matter as the plaintiff's cause or action or claim for relief. The failure to raise such a cause of action or claim for relief in the defendant's answer will not prevent the defendant from bringing them up in a subsequent action.

counterfeit *v.* To copy or imitate something without the right to do so and with the intent to deceive or defraud by representing the copy or imitation to be the original or to be genuine if no original ever existed (such as passing off a painting as a particular work by Claude Monet when, in fact, Monet never painted such a piece of art).

counteroffer *n.* An offeree's counterproposal to a contract offer. Such a proposal constitutes a rejection of the original offer as well as an offer for the original offeree to consider.

countersign *v.* To sign one's own name next to one's own or someone

else's to authenticate, reinforce, or verify the first signature.

course of business See **ordinary** (*ordinary course of business*).

course of dealing *n.* The pattern of conduct during previous transactions between the parties of a more recent transaction from which a dispute has arisen. To resolve the dispute, the courts will look to that pattern to determine how the transaction in dispute was intended to be carried out. See also **course of performance** and **usage of trade.**

course of employment *n.* **1** The activities engaged in, the circumstances that exist, and the events that occur that are normally part of an employee's job, especially those directly related to the work that the employee was hired to do. **2** The time that the employee takes to complete his or her assigned tasks.

course of performance *n.* The pattern of completing a recurring obligation under a contract when all parties are aware of the nature of the obligation and have had the opportunity in the past to object to how it is done. If a dispute later arises regarding the performance of that obligation and there was no previous objection, the courts will look to the course of performance to determine how the parties intended the obligation to be completed. See also **course of dealing** and **usage of trade.**

court *n.* **1** A governmental body that adjudicates legal disputes by interpreting and applying the law to specific cases. See also **trial.** **2** The regular session of a court. **3** The judge or judges who sit on a court. **4** The building or other locale where a judge or judges adjudicate legal disputes.

appellate court. A court with jurisdiction to hear appeals from trial courts, administrative agencies, and, when there is an intermediate appellate court, lower appellate courts. See also *trial court*.

Article I court. A quasi-administrative, quasi-judicial federal court created by Congress under Article I of the United States Constitution to settle disputes arising from the implementation of a statutory scheme that Congress has established in the exercise of its legislative power. For example, pursuant to its power to impose and collect taxes under the United States Constitution, Congress has established the United States Tax Court to hear appeals from taxpayers who are unsatisfied with the decisions of the Internal Revenue Service. See also *legislative court* and *Article III court*.

Article III court. A federal court that is part of the judicial branch of the United States government and derives its jurisdiction from Article III of the United States Constitution. See also *constitutional court* and *Article I court*.

circuit court. **1** In a state with a judicial system that is divided into geographical units known as circuits for the purpose of holding trials, a trial court that sits in the circuit over which its geographical jurisdiction extends. Often, the jurisdiction of such courts is limited to more serious matters (for example, felonies as opposed to misdemeanors). If the circuit encompasses more than one county, the court may hold sessions in each county. **2** In a state with a judicial system that is divided into geographical units known as circuits for the consideration of appeals on the intermediate level, an intermediate appellate court that hears appeals from the circuit over which its geographical jurisdiction extends. **3** A court of the United States Court of Appeals that considers appeals of the trials conducted in those United States District Courts located within the states contained in the court's circuit. (The United States, for the purposes of the Court of Appeals, is divided into twelve circuits. There is also the special nationwide Federal Circuit, which hears appeals from federal courts and administrative agencies other than the District Court.)

civil court. A court that hears the trials of noncriminal cases.

constitutional court. A court named or described in a state constitution or the United States Constitution that exercises the judicial power of a state or the federal government. See also *Article III court* and *legislative court*.

county court. A state court with jurisdiction that encompasses a single county and with powers that are determined by a state statute or constitution. In some states, a county court is an administrative, rather than a judicial, governmental body or is a mixture of both.

court above. An appellate court to which a case may be appealed.

court below. A trial or intermediate appellate court from which a case is appealed.

court en banc. See *full court*.

court of appeals. **1** Usually a state intermediate appellate court. **2** In Maryland and New York, the highest appellate court in those states.

court of assize and nisi prius. See *nisi prius court*.

court of chancery. See **chancery** (or **chancery court**).

court of civil appeals. In some states, an intermediate court of appeal.

court of claims. See *United States Court of Federal Claims*.

court of common pleas. **1** In some states, a trial court of general jurisdiction. **2** In some states, an intermediate appellate court.

court of criminal appeals. In some states, the court of last resort for criminal actions.

court of equity. A trial court that adjudicates legal disputes primarily by applying the rules and principles of equity. Courts of equity have been merged with courts of law in most states. See also *court of law.*

court of first instance. See *court of original jurisdiction.*

court of general jurisdiction. A trial court with unlimited or nearly unlimited jurisdiction to hear any kind of action. See also *court of limited jurisdiction.*

court of last resort. The court from which a particular case can be appealed no further. Usually a state's highest appellate court or the United States Supreme Court. See also *intermediate appellate court.*

court of law. **1** A trial court that adjudicates legal disputes primarily by applying statutes and the rules and principles of the common law. **2** In states where courts of equity and courts of law have been merged, any trial court that adjudicates legal disputes. See also *court of equity.*

court of limited jurisdiction. A court with jurisdiction to adjudicate only specific kinds of legal disputes (based on either the subject matter of the action or the amount of damages sought). See also *court of general jurisdiction.*

Court of Military Appeal. An appellate court that may review decision of the *Court of Military Review.* For those appeals that this court declines to consider, this is the court of last resort. However, cases that are considered may be appealed to the United States Supreme Court. This court's decisions are also subject to review by the president of the United States.

Court of Military Review. An intermediate appellate court that reviews court-martial decisions.

court of original jurisdiction. A court in which, by statute or constitutional provision, a particular type of action must be initiated and where the evidence is heard, the facts determined, and the law applied to those facts for the first time. Also called *court of first instance* and *trial court.*

court of record. A court that is required to keep a permanent record of all conversations and statements made and non-verbal evidence produced during its proceedings by use of a stenographer or other means.

district court. In a state whose judicial system is divided into geographical units known as districts for the purpose of holding trials, a trial court that sits in the district over which its geographical jurisdiction extends. Often, the court's jurisdiction is limited to one county and to less serious matters (for example, misdemeanors as opposed to felonies). See also *circuit court.*

drug court. A state court with jurisdiction to adjudicate lesser offenses arising from drug use, usually with an emphasis on medical treatment and supervision rather than punishment for the drug user.

ecclesiastical court. A nongovernmental court that is part of the structure of an organized religion and adjudicates internal church issues according to church law. For centuries, such courts also had jurisdiction over matters like divorce and wills that are now within the jurisdiction of the civil courts.

en banc court. See *full court.*

family court. A state court with jurisdiction to adjudicate family law issues, such as divorce, child custody and visitation, child and spousal support, paternity, and domestic violence.

federal court. An Article III court. Most actions involving federal law are tried before one of the United States District Courts. An appeal of a District Court's decision would normally be heard first by one of the United States Court of Appeals, and then by the United States Supreme Court (the court of last resort in the federal judiciary). The Supreme Court also considers appeals of state court decisions involving questions of federal law. There are also a few specialized federal courts; see also *United States Court of Federal Claims.*

full court. In appellate litigation, a session of an appellate court where all the judges participate, typically resulting from a motion to reconsider the decision of a three judge panel. Also known as an **en banc** hearing.

inferior court. A court whose decision may be appealed to another court within the same judicial system, especially a court of limited, special, or statutory jurisdiction, such as a family or probate court.

intermediate appellate court. In those jurisdictions whose appellate court system is divided into two levels, the lowest appellate court, the decisions of which are subject to review by the jurisdiction's highest appellate court. See also *court of last resort.*

International Court of Justice. The principal judicial body of the United Nations whose fifteen judges usually meet at The Hague,

Netherlands, to provide advisory legal opinions to the United Nations and to adjudicate legal disputes between countries who voluntarily submit cases for the court's consideration. Abbreviated ICJ.

International Criminal Court. A permanent international court, tentatively established by the United Nations in 1998, to investigate and adjudicate the most serious violations of international law, such as genocide and war crimes, by applying, until the adoption of an international criminal code, the general principles of international criminal law. Abbreviated ICC.

justice court. A state court, presided over by a justice of the peace, that has jurisdiction over certain minor civil and criminal actions that arise outside the city limits of any municipality. See also *municipal court.*

juvenile court. A state court with jurisdiction over cases involving children under eighteen years of age or another age set by the state legislature, especially one concerning cases where the child is alleged to have committed what would be an offense if done by an adult.

kangaroo court. **1** A court that has no legal authority, is often self-appointed or established by criminals or vigilantes, and where few or none of the authorized and regular judicial procedures are usually followed. **2** A lawful court whose procedures are so unauthorized or irregular that its proceedings are extremely improper or unfair. **3** A lawful court that followed authorized and regular procedures, but is so biased against a party as to render its judgment or verdict unfair.

legislative court. A court created by a state legislature or the Congress to settle disputes arising from the implementation of a statutory scheme that the legislature or Congress has established in the exercise of their legislative powers, as opposed to a court authorized by a state constitution or the United States Constitution as part of the government's judicial branch. See also *Article I court* and *constitutional court.*

magistrate's court. A state court presided over by a magistrate with jurisdiction over minor offenses and civil actions.

military court. A court-martial, military commission, the Court of Military Review, and the Court of Military Justice. These are not Article III courts, but courts established by Congress as a part of its power to raise and maintain a military force under the militia clause found in Article I of the United States Constitution.

moot court. A fictitious court consisting of law professors or lawyers, before which law students and other lawyers argue moot or hypothetical cases or cases pending before a court to learn or practice oral advocacy skills and trial techniques.

municipal court. A city court with exclusive jurisdiction over violations of city ordinances and sometimes jurisdiction over certain minor civil and criminal cases that arise within the city limits. See also *justice court.*

nisi prius court. Same as court of assize and nisi prius. See *nisi prius court.*

open court. **1** A court that, when in session, the public is allowed to attend so long as they are orderly and peaceful. **2** A court that, when in session, is attended by all the parties and their lawyers. See also **ex parte** and **in camera.**

out of court. Accomplished or conducted without litigation, without the involvement of a court, or outside a courtroom.

probate court. A state court with jurisdiction over proceedings regarding the validity of wills, the administration and disposition of estates, and, in some states, the adoption of minors and the care, custody, guardianship, and protection of minors, incompetent individuals, and their assets. Also called surrogate court.

small claims court. A state or municipal court that has the jurisdiction to adjudicate civil actions involving very small sums of money while using informal courtroom procedures without, usually, the presence or participation of lawyers.

superior court. **1** In some states, a trial court of general jurisdiction. **2** In some states, an intermediate appellate court.

supreme court. **1** In most states, the court of last resort. **2** In New York, a court of general jurisdiction with trial and appellate divisions.

Supreme Court of the United States. The court of last resort in the federal judiciary pursuant to Article III of the United States Constitution, with original jurisdiction in all cases involving ambassadors and other public ministers and consuls as well as in all cases in which a state is a party. The court also has appellate jurisdiction over all cases in federal court as well as those cases in state court involving questions of federal law. Unless it is otherwise clear, the phrase "Supreme Court" always means this court.

surrogate court. See *probate court.*

tax court. A state court that adjudicates disputes between the taxpayer and the state's tax collection agency over the individual's tax liabilities.

Tax Court. An Article I court that adjudicates disputes between the taxpayer and the Internal Revenue Service over the individual's tax deficiencies. (Disputes over the taxpayer's claim for a refund are considered by the United States Court of Federal Claims.)

term of court. A session of court, defined by the court's schedule; may refer to a single session or a schedule of sessions over a period of time.

trial court. See *court of original jurisdiction.*

United States Court of Appeals. The intermediate appellate court in the federal judiciary that hears appeals from trials conducted by the United States District Courts and other lower federal courts and appeals of administrative decisions from some federal agencies. See also *circuit court.*

United States Court of Federal Claims. An Article I court with jurisdiction to hear all claims against the United States government that are based on the United States Constitution, a federal statute or regulation, a contract with the federal government, or other cause of action not involving a tort. Formerly called the United States Claims Court.

United States District Court. A federal trial court having original jurisdiction for most criminal offenses against the United States and for most of the civil matters described in the United States Constitution.

United States Supreme Court. See *Supreme Court of the United States.*

court costs   See **costs.**

court en banc   Same as full court. See **court.**

court-martial   *n.* An ad hoc military court whose judges are commissioned officers of higher rank than, and of the same branch of the armed services as, the accused. This court is convened to try a member of the armed services who is accused of violating the Uniform Code of Military Justice.

> *general court-martial.* The highest military court, comprised of five officers (unless the defendant decides to be tried by only one judge) with jurisdiction to try all offenses under the Uniform Code of Military Justice and to impose any sanction permitted by the code (including death).

> *special court-martial.* An intermediate military court, comprised of three officers (unless the defendant decides to be tried by only one judge) with jurisdiction to try all noncapital offenses under the Uniform Code of Military Justice. However, the sanctions this court can prescribe may be no greater than a dismissal from the armed services or six months imprisonment.

> *summary court-martial.* The lowest military court, comprised of one officer. The type of offenses this court can try and the sanctions it is allowed to impose are very limited. Furthermore, the accused may refuse trial by a summary court-martial, in which case he or she will be tried by a general or special court-martial.

court recorder   *n.* A court reporter who uses electronic recording equipment in his job.

court reporter   *n.* A person (often certified) who makes, by stenography, electronic recording devices, or other means, a verbatim record of all that is said in a trial, deposition, or similar proceeding and from which, if requested (and usually for a fee), a transcript can be prepared.

court reports See **advance sheets, reports,** and **slip opinion.**

court rules *n.* A regulation, often having the force of law, governing the procedures of a court and how various matters pending before court are handled and processed. Also called local rules and rules of the court.

covenant *n.* **1** A written and legally enforceable agreement or promise that is often a part of a contract or deed, especially one to maintain the status quo of something or to do or not do something during the term of the covenant. **2** An implied promise that is incidental to a contract or deed. **3** A warranty, especially one made in connection with the sale or transfer of land. **4** Same as contract under seal; see **contract. 5** An action under the common law to recover damages for the breach of a contract under seal. See also **assumpsit.**

concurrent covenant. A covenant that requires one party to fulfill her promise to do or not do something at the same time the other party to the covenant has to fulfill his promise.

covenant against encumbrances. A covenant of title, whereby the grantor promises that there are no undisclosed encumbrances (such as easements, liens, or mortgages) on the property.

covenant appurtenant. See *covenant running with the land.*

covenant not to compete. A provision, often found in employment, partnership, and sale-of-business contracts, in which one party agrees not to conduct any business or professional activity similar to that of the other party. Such covenants are enforceable for the duration of the business relationship between the parties, but not afterward except for the period of time, scope, and territorial limits that are deemed reasonable by a court in light of the adequacy of consideration given in exchange for the covenant, the hardship that the enforcement of the covenant or lack thereof would impose upon the parties, and the need of the party seeking to enforce the covenant to protect trade secrets and the like. Sometimes also called *restrictive covenant.*

covenant not to sue. In a settlement of a claim, dispute, or lawsuit, a promise not to assert or pursue in court a right of action arising from the subject of the claim, dispute, or lawsuit.

covenant of further assurance. A covenant of title whereby the grantor promises to do whatever is reasonably necessary to give the grantee full title if the title conveyed in the deed later proves to be imperfect.

covenant of (or for) quiet enjoyment. **1** A covenant of title, whereby the grantor promises that the grantee's unimpaired use and enjoyment of the land will not be disturbed by anyone with a lien or superior right to the land. **2** A covenant of title, whereby the grantor promises to indemnify the grantee against any defects in the title to the land conveyed or any disturbances of the unimpaired use and enjoyment of the land. Often considered synonymous with *covenant of warranty.*

covenant of right to convey. See *covenant of seisin.*

covenant of seisin. A covenant of title, whereby the grantor promises that he or she has at the time of the grant the full ownership, or the right to convey, an estate of the quality and size that they are purporting to convey to the grantee. Also called covenant of right to convey.

covenant of (or for) title. A type of covenant usually given by a grantor in a warranty deed conveying real property to ensure that title is complete and secure. Also called warranty of title. In the plural, also called usual covenants.

covenant of warranty. A covenant of title, whereby the grantor promises to defend the title against all reasonable claims of a superior right to the land by a third party and to indemnify the grantee against any losses arising from the claim. Often considered synonymous with *covenant of quiet enjoyment.*

covenant running with the land. A covenant that relates to a particular parcel of land without which the land cannot be conveyed and that is binding for an indefinite time on all successor grantees. Also called covenant appurtenant and running covenant.

covenant under seal. See *contract under seal.*

racially restrictive covenant. A covenant that purports to limit all future transfers of a piece of real property to successor grantees of, or to successor grantees who are not of, a particular race, color, or ethnic group. Once very common, these covenants are now unenforceable.

restrictive covenant. **1** A covenant that restrict the use, occupancy, or disposition of real property (such as specifying the size of lots that the property can be divided into or the types of buildings that may be constructed on the land). **2** See *covenant not to compete.*

covenantee   *n.* One to whom a promise is made in a covenant or has a right to enforce it.

covenant marriage   See **marriage.**

covenanter   *n.* One who makes a promise in a covenant or is bound by it.

cover   *v.* **1** In commercial law, to buy, or the purchase of, goods on the open market that are similar to those that a seller of such goods had promised, but failed, to deliver. Under the Uniform Commercial Code, the buyer is entitled from the seller the difference between the cost of the substituted goods and the original contract price if the buyer acted in good faith and without unreasonable delay when obtaining the substituted goods.   **2** In insurance law, to currently protect a particular person against loss or to currently protect someone or something against a particular risk.

coverture   *n.* Under the common law, the legal condition of a woman, whereby her legal existence was largely submerged into that of her husband so that he had almost unlimited control over her personal and real property and she could not enter into a legally binding contract or exercise any power or right over her own property without her husband's consent. In every state except community property states, statutes have been enacted that have effectively abolished coverture by giving wives almost unlimited control over their personal and real property free of their husbands' authority, claims, or interests.

credibility   *n.* The quality of something capable of being believed or relied upon or that is worthy of confidence. See also **veracity.**

credit   **1** *n.* Approval; deference; respect. See also **full faith and credit.** **2** *n.* Belief; faith; trust.   **3** *n.* The ability to borrow money, the amount made available as a loan, or the ability to purchase goods and services without immediate payment, based on the creditor's faith in one's ability and intention to repay the loan or to pay for the goods and services in the future. **4** *n.* A reduction in an amount owed or an addition to one's net worth or revenue. **5** *v.* A form of security offered to a seller that provides for payment by a bank or financial institution upon certain conditions being met, including delivery of goods within specified time and whatever other conditions are applicable to the transaction. See also **letter of credit.**

creditor *n.* One to whom money is owed or who gives credit to another. See also **debtor.**

> *account creditor.* One to whom the balance of an account is owed. See also **debtor.**

> *judgment creditor.* One who has the legal right to collect a specific sum because of a judgment entered in his or her favor in a civil action. See also **levy, writ,** and **debtor.**

> *secured creditor.* A creditor who has been given or pledged collateral to protect against loss if the debtor fails to fully pay the debt owed.

> *unsecured creditor.* A creditor who is not a secured creditor.

creditor beneficiary See **beneficiary.**

creditor's bill (or **suit**) *n.* A proceeding in equity in which a judgment creditor seeks to discover and have delivered to him property that cannot be reached by the process available at law to enforce a judgment.

crime *n.* An act or omission that violates the law and is punishable by a sentence of incarceration. See also **felony, misdemeanor, offense,** and **violation.**

> *anticipatory crime.* See *inchoate crime.*

> *bias crime.* See *hate crime.*

> *common-law crime.* An offense that was a crime under the common law. Nearly all crimes, including offenses that were common-law crimes, are now defined by statute and are, thus, *statutory crimes.* Also, most states no longer recognize common-law crimes.

> *computer crime.* A crime, such as committing fraud over the Internet, that requires the knowledge or utilization of computer technology. Also called cybercrime.

> *crime against nature.* One of the three sexual acts (oral sex and anal sex, whether with a person of the opposite or same sex, and sex with animals) that were considered crimes under the common law and that, in some cases, are currently a statutory crime. Also called unnatural act. See also **bestiality** and **sodomy.**

> *crime of passion.* A crime committed in a moment of sudden or extreme anger or other emotional disturbance sufficient enough for a reasonable person to lose control and not reflect on what he or she is doing.

> *crime of violence.* See *violent crime.*

> *cybercrime.* See *computer crime.*

> *hate crime.* A crime motivated mostly by bias, ill will, or hatred toward the victim's actual or perceived race, color, ethnicity, country of national origin, religion, or sexual orientation. Many states impose extra penalties if a crime is committed due to such motivation. Also called bias crime. See also **freedom of speech.**

> *high crime.* A crime whose commission offends the public's morality.

> *inchoate crime.* One of the three crimes (attempt, conspiracy, solicitation) that are steps toward the

commission of another crime. Also called anticipatory crime, anticipatory offense, and **inchoate** offense.

infamous crime. **1** Under common law, any one of the crimes that were considered particularly dishonorable and the punishment for which included ineligibility to hold public office, to serve on a jury, or to testify at a civil or criminal trial. These crimes included treason, any felony, forgery, and perjury, among other offenses. **2** Any crime punishable by death or by imprisonment of more than one year. See also **punishment.**

status crime. A crime that is defined by a person's condition or character rather than by any wrongful act that they have done. For example, the "crime" of being an alcoholic as opposed to being intoxicated in public or drinking alcohol while driving a vehicle. The United States Supreme Court has held that to impose a sanction for such crimes violates the ban found in the Eighth Amendment to the United States Constitution against cruel and unusual punishment. See also **vagrancy.**

statutory crime. **1** An offense that was not a crime under the common law, but has been made a crime by a statute. **2** Broadly, any crime that is defined by a statute. See also *common-law crime.*

victimless crime. A crime, such as drug use, gambling, and a crime against nature, that directly harms no person or property except that of the consenting participants.

violent crime. Any crime that has as an element the use, attempted use, or threatened use of physical force against the person or property of another or any felony that entails a substantial risk that physical force will be used against the person or property of another. Also called a crime of violence.

white-collar crime. Any business or financial non-violent crime, such as bribery, consumer fraud, corruption, embezzlement, and stock manipulation, committed by business executives, professionals, and public officials.

criminal *n.* **1** One who has committed a crime. **2** One who has been convicted of a crime. **3** Constituting, implying, or involving a crime or an element of a crime. **4** Pertaining to some aspect of the penal code or its administration.

career criminal. One who repeatedly commits crimes, especially of the same type. See also *habitual criminal.*

habitual criminal. One who has been convicted of one or more crimes in the past and, as a result, is subject to a more severe sentence under the habitual offender statute of a state for any subsequent crime that they commit. Also called habitual offender. See also *career criminal* and **three-strikes law.**

criminal conversation *n.* In tort law, having sexual relations with another person's spouse, especially the act of a man having sexual intercourse with another man's wife. This tort has been abolished in most states. See also **alienation of affections, adultery, fornication,** and **rape.**

criminal disenfranchisement *n.* The loss of the right to vote by a person convicted of or sentenced to imprisonment for a felony. See also **civil death.**

criminal intent See **intent.**

criminalist *n.* One who collects and scientifically analyzes the physical evidence of crimes, through such techniques as ballistic testing and tissue analysis, to try to determine what happened when the crime was committed. See also **criminologist.**

criminality *n.* 1 The state, practice, or quality of being a criminal. 2 The act or series of acts that constitute a crime.

criminalize *v.* 1 To make a particular conduct or omission a crime and to establish penal sanctions for it. 2 To make a person, or to be the cause of making that person, a criminal. See also **decriminalization.**

criminal law *n.* The area of law pertaining to the violation of offenses as well as the investigation, charging, prosecution, and punishment of offenders. See also **civil law.**

criminal negligence See **negligence.**

criminal procedure See **procedure.**

criminal record See **record.**

criminologist *n.* One who studies the biological and sociological causes and consequences of crime and criminal behavior (such as the effects of mental defects and social environment). See also **criminalist.**

cross appeal See **appeal.**

cross-claim *n.* A cause of action or claim asserted between co-defendants or co-plaintiffs against one another and not against the plaintiff or defendant on the opposite side of a civil action. For example, a defendant's assertion of a right of contribution from a fellow defendant is a cross-claim. See also **counterclaim.**

cross-complaint *n.* 1 A cause of action or claim asserted by a defendant in a civil action against another party in the same action. 2 A cause of action or claim asserted by a defendant in a civil action against one who is not a party to the action that concerns a matter related to the underlying dispute in the action. 3 The pleading in which one asserts a cross-claim.

cross-examination See **examination.**

cruel and unusual *adj.* Characterization of punishment that is unduly harsh and goes beyond the recognized purposes of punishment in a civilized society. "Cruel and unusual punishment" has frequently been asserted in connection with attempts to overturn death penalty statutes or forms of execution, e.g., electric chair.

cruelty *n.* As a ground for divorce, the intentional and malicious infliction of physical or psychological abuse by a married person upon his or her spouse that endangers or severely impairs the spouse's life or physical or mental well-being or creates a reasonable apprehension in the spouse's mind of physical or mental harm. The extent of abuse that a spouse is expected to tolerate varies state to state, but a single act of cruelty is normally not enough to constitute grounds for divorce. See also **abuse.**

culpable *adj.* Deserving of blame.

culpable mental state See **mens rea.**

cumulative voting See **voting.**

curable defect See **defect.**

curtesy *n.* Under the common law, a husband's entitlement to a life estate in all the land that his wife possessed at her death in either fee simple or fee tail, provided the couple had a living child who was capable of inheriting his or her mother's estate. This right has been abolished in most states. See also **dower.**

curtesy consummate. The name of a husband's right of curtesy after his wife's death.

curtesy initiate. The name of a husband's right of curtesy before his wife's death, once the right is created upon the birth of the couple's first child.

curtilage   *n.* The land immediately surrounding a dwelling, such as a yard and outbuildings, where some of the regular activity of the occupant's home life takes place, where the occupant has a reasonable expectation of privacy, and that is usually demarcated, fenced off, or otherwise clearly protected from public scrutiny. Such land is regarded as a part of the dwelling itself and is protected from warrantless searches under the Fourth Amendment to the United States Constitution. Also called open fields doctrine or messuage.

custodial interrogation   See **interrogation.**

custody   *n.* **1** The immediate control, guarding, or keeping of a thing for its care, inspection, preservation, or security.   **2** Any significant restraint or control over a person's freedom to ensure his or her presence at a hearing or trial in a criminal action.   **3** The restraint and control over a person who is incarcerated following that person's conviction of an offense.

child custody. The physical control over a minor awarded by a court to a parent in a divorce or separation proceeding or in a similar action between the unmarried parents of the child. Such control usually includes the right to have the child live with the parent who is awarded custody, the right to determine the upbringing of the child (including the care, discipline, education, religion, and residence of the child), the right to make all legal decisions concerning the child, and the duty to care for and maintain the child. See also **visitation rights.**

joint custody. An arrangement ordered by a court or agreed upon by the divorced or separated parents of a minor by which the parents share all authority, decisions, and responsibilities concerning the care and upbringing of their child,

although the minor still primarily resides (usually) with only one of the parents.

sole custody. An arrangement ordered by a court or agreed upon by the divorced or separated parents of a minor by which only one parent makes all the decisions and has all the authority and responsibilities concerning the care and upbringing of his or her child, to the exclusion of the other parent.

custom   *n.* A practice, particularly in business, that is so old and universal that it has obtained the force of law.

custom and usage. See **usage of trade.**

customs   *n.* **1** Taxes imposed on imports and exports; the United States Constitution prohibits Congress from imposing taxes on goods exported from a state. Also called duties.   **2** The agency or procedure for collecting such taxes, or the place where they are collected.

cybercrime   Same as computer crime. See **crime.**

cyberfraud   Same as computer fraud. See **fraud.**

cyberlaw   *n.* The area of law dealing with the use of computers and the Internet and the exchange of communications and information thereon, including related issues concerning such communications and information as the protection of intellectual property rights, **freedom of speech,** and public access to information.

cyberpiracy   See **cybersquatting.**

cybersquatting   *n.* The registering of a domain name on the Internet in the hope of selling or licensing it at a profit to a person or entity who wishes to use it. If the domain name is identical or confusingly similar to a trademark used by that person or entity, the owner of the trademark has a cause of action against whoever registered and is holding on to the name. Also called cyberpiracy, domain name grabbing, and domain name piracy.

cyberstalking   *v.* **1** Using the Internet, through chat rooms and e-mail, to find, identify, and arrange to meet a person whom one intends to criminally victimize. **2** Sending multiple e-mails, often on a systematic basis, to annoy, embarrass, intimidate, or threaten a person or to make the person fearful that she or a member of her family or household will be harmed. Also called e-mail harassment.

cy pres   *n. French.* As near as. The equitable doctrine that a deed or will whose terms cannot be carried out may be modified by a court so that the intent of the instrument's maker can be fulfilled as closely as possible.

D

speculative damages. Damages claimed for possible future harm. These are considered uncertain or impossible to prove and generally are not awarded.

treble damages. A tripling of the actual damages, generally awarded pursuant to a law or statute; intended to deter bad conduct.

damnify *v.* To harm by causing loss or damage.

dangerous weapon See **weapon.**

date rape *n.* The rape of an individual with whom the perpetrator is acquainted, typically during a social engagement. See also **rape.**

d/b/a *abbr.* Doing business as, identifying an individual's trade name; for example, John James d/b/a James Productions.

dead man's statute *n.* An evidentiary rule at trial that excludes statements made by a deceased person if offered in support of a claim against the deceased's estate.

death *n.* The end of life, when physical functions and vital signs stop.

brain death. An irreversible end to the functioning of the brain. Often used as the legal definition of death.

death certificate *n.* An official document setting forth particulars relating to a dead person, including name, date of birth and death, and cause of death, usually certified to by a doctor as to the cause of death.

death penalty *n.* The court- ordered imposition of a sentence of execution as punishment for a crime. See also **punishment** (*capital punishment*).

death warrant *n.* A warrant signed by an appropriate official, such as the governor of a state, directing that a sentence of execution be carried out.

damages *n. pl.* Financial compensation demanded by, or directed by a court to be paid to, a claimant as compensation for a financial loss or injury to person or property.

actual or *compensatory damages.* Damages intended to compensate for a quantifiable loss.

consequential damages. Damages resulting indirectly from the act complained of.

incidental damages. Under the Uniform Commercial Code, expenses reasonably incurred by either party to a transaction in caring for goods after the other party's breach of the contract.

liquidated damages. A contractually agreed upon amount to be paid in the event of a breach of the contract, in lieu of performance or quantification of actual damages sustained.

nominal damages. A small or insignificant amount of money awarded by a court or jury to demonstrate that a defendant is at fault, but that the injury sustained was minor or non-existent.

punitive damages. Damages awarded by a court or jury, typically in addition to *actual damages,* when the party against whom the award is made is deemed to have behaved egregiously; for example, with particular recklessness or malice.

debenture *n.* A corporate debt secured by the revenues, reputation, and credit standing of the debtor, and that lacks a security interest in other property; an instrument that embodies this type of debt.

debt *n.* A specific sum of money due as a result of a written or verbal agreement or by operation of law.

debtor *n.* One who owes a fixed sum of money to another; a person or entity filing, or becoming the subject of, a bankruptcy action.

> *debtor-in-possession.* A debtor allowed by the bankruptcy court to continue operation of the business during the proceedings.

> *joint debtors.* Two or more persons both liable for the same debt.

> *judgment debtor.* One who owes a sum of money to another by virtue of a judgment that has previously been rendered.

decedent *n.* A person who has died; the term is usually used in trusts and estates and personal injury matters.

deceit *n.* **1** The intentional imparting of a false impression. **2** A misrepresentation of fact, which, when made with the intention that the other party will rely on it to his detriment, constitutes the torts of fraud or misrepresentation. See also **fraud** and **misrepresentation.**

decertify *v.* To cancel or annul a certification, as of a labor union or of a class in a class action.

decision *n.* The written determination of a court or administrative tribunal disposing of motions or claims in a case or matter before it.

declarant *n.* A person who makes a verbal statement or signs a written one.

declaration *n.* **1** A statement made in connection with a case or legal matter, or intended to have a formal status or effect. **2** A written document, synonymous in some jurisdictions with **affidavit** and in others (although antiquated) with **complaint.** **3** A written document governing rights and obligations among property owners, as in declaration of condominium or declaration of covenants and restrictions.

> *declaration against interest.* A statement that is assumed to be truthful because it is contrary to the **declarant**'s self-interest when made, and is therefore admissible in court as an exception to the **hearsay** rule.

> *dying declaration.* A statement that is assumed to be truthful because it is made by an individual aware of impending death (and thus thought to have no incentive to lie), and that is therefore admissible in court as an exception to the **hearsay** rule.

declaratory judgment *n.* Order rendered by a court which establishes rights between parties where there is uncertainty, usually as to a written contract or document. Does not generally result in award of damages, only determination by Court as to meaning or obligations.

decree *n.* A court judgment, especially in a court of equity, bankruptcy, admiralty, divorce, or probate.

> *consent decree.* A written settlement by the parties to a litigation, in the form of a decree signed by the judge.

> *decree absolute.* A final decree entered by the court, after the waiting period set in a *decree nisi* has expired, without the adverse party persuading the court to set it aside.

> *decree nisi.* A proposed final decree by a court, which will not become final until the expiration of a time

period, during which the adversely affected party is given the opportunity to show the court why it should be set aside.

decriminalization　*n.* The legislature's act of amending laws to permit a previously illegal act.

dedication　*n.* A grant of land, a copyright, or of some other property, or the right of use in land or other property (an easement), for a public purpose.

deductible　*n.* In an insurance policy, the monetary amount of the loss that must be paid by the insured before the insurer becomes responsible for any reimbursement.

deduction　*n.* A monetary amount that a taxpayer is permitted by law or regulation to subtract from income when determining income tax.

> *itemized deduction.* An expense, such as state and local taxes paid, or annual interest on a mortgage, that is listed on a tax return as a **deduction.** Includes charitable deductions.

> *standard deduction.* A dollar amount that a taxpayer is permitted by law to subtract from taxable income in lieu of listing itemized deductions.

deed　**1** *n.* A written conveyance of an interest in real property. **2** *v.* The act of granting a deed in property to another.

> *quitclaim deed.* A deed conveying the grantor's interest in real property, as is, including any defects in title, and with no warranty that title is valid.

> *warranty deed.* A deed that contains one or more warranties, such as the validity of the grantor's title, the recipient's right of "quiet enjoyment" of the property, and the right to resell it free of any encumbrances; contrast *quitclaim deed.*

deem　*v.* To consider or assume that a thing has the attributes or qualities of something else; for example, for certain legal purposes, a corporation is deemed to be a person.

deep pocket　*n.* A person or entity that has significant financial resources and is therefore an attractive target for litigation.

de facto　*adj.* In fact. Description of a person or action that exists for all intentions and purposes, but which lacks official legitimacy.

defalcation　*n.* The theft or misuse of funds, generally refers to improper use of money by government official or private trustee.

defamation　*n.* The utterance of a false statement that harms the reputation of another. Although most state laws require that a defamatory statement be made with knowledge of its falsehood, in some jurisdictions a cause of action exists for negligent defamation. **Libel** (involving a written false statement, including statements transmitted on the Internet) and **slander** (spoken, as opposed to written, false statements), are both forms of defamation.

defamatory　*adj.* Used in reference to an utterance, to indicate that it is false and harmful to the reputation of another.

default　**1** *n.* The failure to perform a legal or contractual requirement, such as the payment of a debt by the due date. **2** *v.* To fail to perform such a requirement.

default judgment　*n.* A judgment entered against a party to a litigation as a result of that party's failure to appear or contest the claim.

defeasance　*n.* The abrogation of an interest in real property.

defeasible *adj.* Description of a right or interest that is capable of being terminated, or which will terminate upon occurrence of a condition subsequent.

defect *n.* An error or flaw in a process or product, affecting performance and potentially causing harm; a shortcoming in a legal document that may lead to its invalidity, or in a pleading that may lead to its dismissal.

> *apparent defect.* A flaw or error that should have been noticed by a reasonably observant individual. Also known as a *patent defect.*

> *design defect.* An error or flaw introduced, or not detected, during the design of the process or product.

> *fatal defect.* Pertaining to a contract or a pleading, an error or flaw of such gravity that it may invalidate the document in question.

> *manufacturing defect.* An error or flaw in a product, introduced during the manufacturing rather than the design phase.

> *marketing defect.* The failure either to inform users of the appropriate way to use a product so as to avoid harm, or to disclose an error or flaw in a product that may cause harm to a user.

defective *adj.* Of a product or process, that it contains an error or flaw affecting performance; of a pleading or document, that it contains a shortcoming potentially causing its invalidity or leading to its dismissal.

defend *v.* In litigation, to oppose a claimant's case; to advance or protect one's own adverse interests. Also, as an attorney, to represent the defendant in a criminal case or civil proceeding.

defendant *n.* In a criminal trial, the accused; in a civil proceeding, the person or entity against whom a claim is made.

defense *n.* Collectively, the attorneys representing a defendant and any laypeople assisting them in their efforts, particularly in a criminal trial. In litigation, generally a factual denial or an assertion of facts or law that counters or negates a claim made by the other party. See also **self defense.**

> *affirmative defense.* A statement of fact in a responsive pleading that, if true, has the effect of canceling or rendering ineffective a claim of the other party. For example, the truth of an allegedly **defamatory** statement is an affirmative defense.

> *equitable defense.* A defense derived from those historically used in courts of equity, such as mutual **mistake.**

deferred compensation *n.* Compensation that is paid to an employee at a time later than the one at which it was earned, with the tax on that compensation deferred as well. Often in the form of stock options in the employer corporation.

deficiency judgment *n.* A judgment for the balance of a debt already partly paid, typically through a forced sale of personal or real property.

degree *n.* **1** A step or level in the accomplishment of an act or a duty, or in the determination of a relationship. The level of an offense, such as murder and determining the appropriate punishment for it.

> *degree of care.* The standard to which a party is responsible for exercising a duty or responsibility in order to avoid an implication of negligence.

2. In trusts and estates or family law matters, degree pertains to genetic proximity (the *degree of consanguinity*).

dehors *adj. French.* Outside or beyond the bounds of, as in matters that are dehors the trial record or the pages of a written agreement.

del credere *adj. Italian.* Of belief or trust. Used in connection with agents who guarantee the good faith or financial capability of the persons or entities on whose behalf they act. See also **agent.**

delegable duty *n.* A responsibility that can be delegated to another to perform. See also **duty.**

delegate **1** *n.* One who acts on behalf of one or more others in an official capacity. **2** *v.* The act of granting another the power to act on one's behalf.

delegation *n.* The act of granting another the power to act on one's behalf in an official capacity; a group of delegates.

deliberate **1** *adj.* Intentional and premeditated, of an act performed with prior planning; with full consideration and thoroughly, as in "with all deliberate speed." **2** *v.* The process by which jurors determine the outcome of a case.

delict *n.* From the Latin *delictum,* an offense. A breach of criminal or civil law.

delinquency *n.* **1** A failure, by act or omission, to perform a legal or contractual obligation. **2** an unpaid amount due.

delinquent **1** *n.* A person who fails to perform a legal or contractual obligation, or who is guilty of illegal or disorderly behavior. **2** *adj.* Of a person failing to perform a legal or contractual obligation, or who is engaging in illegal or disorderly behavior.

delivery *n.* The act of granting legal possession, custody, or control of something, to another; the thing so transferred.

Constructive delivery. Absent actual delivery of goods or item, an action or communication which conveys property to another, even if actual possession is not taken, as opposed to actual delivery, which is complete upon transfer of property, or conditional delivery, in which property is delivered but ownership is subject to further action, e.g., payment.

demand **1** *n.* A claim for money or other relief or the assertion of a legal right. **2** *v.* To claim money or other relief, or assert a legal right.

demise *n.* The conveyance of an interest in real property for a specified time period by will or lease; the death of a person or cessation of a corporate entity.

demonstrative evidence *n.* See **evidence.**

demur *v.* To deny the legal sufficiency of an adversary's claim, without admitting or denying the truth of the underlying facts, usually on a technical legal basis rather than the merits of the claim; to file a **demurrer.**

demurrer *n.* In a litigation, a pleading or motion denying the legal sufficiency of an adversary's claim. The term is archaic but is still used in a few jurisdictions, where such a denial would either be included in the **answer** or advanced in a **motion to dismiss** or preliminary objections.

denial *n.* In litigation, a rejection of a claim or request; an assertion in a pleading rejecting facts asserted by the other party in its own pleading.

general denial. A response that questions all of the material accusations in a petition or complaint.

specific denial. A separate response to several of the plaintiff's charges individually denying them, while not denying all of them.

deny *v.* Of a court, to reject a party's claim for money or other relief; of a litigant, to reject in a pleading assertions made by the other party in its own pleading.

dependent *n.* A person relying on another for financial support; a relative for whom a taxpayer may claim an exemption on his income tax return.

deplete *v.* To draw out in its entirety, or use up, money or a nonrenewable resource such as oil.

depletion *n.* The act of drawing out in its entirety, or using up, money or of a nonrenewable resource such as oil.

deponent *n.* A person who, in connection with a litigation, makes a sworn statement, usually orally, in **deposition;** occasionally in a writing such as an affidavit. See also **affiant.**

deport *v.* To expel an illegal alien, or someone whose immigration status has expired or been revoked, to a foreign country.

deportation *n.* The act of expelling an illegal alien, or someone whose immigration status has expired or been revoked, to a foreign country.

depose *v.* To take a person's **deposition;** to make a written, sworn statement, such as an affidavit.

deposit *n.* The act of placing money or property with another who will hold it in trust, or who has a fiduciary duty with regard to it, or otherwise will hold and manage it for the benefit of the owner; the money or property so placed.

deposition *n.* In litigation, a proceeding outside the courtroom in which a party or witness gives sworn testimony under oath before a court reporter, who then creates a written document; the written document created as a result of such a proceeding.

> *deposition de bene esse.* The deposition of a witness who is unlikely to be available to appear at the trial.

deposition of corporate designee. The deposition of a person representing a corporation or entity, in which that person is held out to have the most knowledge of the subject at hand. Testimony taken in this manner is binding upon the corporation or entity.

depraved-heart murder *n.* A murder resulting from an act of reckless disregard for the safety of others. See also **murder.**

depreciation *n.* A decline in the value of an asset over time, due to its increasing obsolescence or the wear and tear due to its use; a **deduction** on an income tax return of part of the asset's cost, transforming its declining value into a benefit for the taxpayer.

derelict **1** *n. Archaic.* An object that has been abandoned by its owner; an individual who is homeless, drunk or disorderly. **2** *adj.* Of property, that it is abandoned; of a person, that he is remiss in his duties.

dereliction *n.* **1** The committing of a breach, typically of a **duty.** **2** An increase in land caused by the recession of sea, river, or other body of water formerly covering it. Ownership is a function of how rapidly the water receded. See also **reliction.**

derivative action *n.* Litigation brought by a shareholder on behalf of a corporation against an officer, on the theory that the corporation is powerless to act on its own behalf.

derivative work *n.* In copyright, a work that is based on another, in whole or part, in the same or another medium, such as a sequel to a novel or a live musical based on a movie. A derivative work cannot be published without the permission of the creator of the original, or the permission of any successor to the creator's rights.

derogation   *n.* In legislation, partially repealing or limiting the scope of common law or prior statutes.

descendant   *n.* A person's child, grandchild, great-grandchild, or other offspring in the direct line of descent.

descent   *n.* The transfer of real estate by inheritance, whether by will or intestacy. See also **distribution** and **succession.**

desecrate   *v.* To harm or insult a sacred thing.

desegregate   *v.* The act of removing laws and policies that provide for a mandatory separation of the races.

desegregation   *n.* The removal of laws and policies enforcing a separation of the races.

desertion   *n.* The intentional and indefensible abandonment of a responsibility, such as to military service or to a spouse.

design defect   See **defect**.

destructibility   *n.* The capacity of being destroyed by an event, a person's action, or by law.

detainer   *n.* The act of keeping a person or thing in one's custody or possession; an order authorizing a prison to continue holding a prisoner beyond his or her release date, typically while proceedings are commenced in another jurisdiction.

> *unlawful detainer.* The illegal holding of real property by a formerly lawful tenant beyond the date of legal possession, as in the holdover of a lease.

detention   *n.* The act of keeping an individual imprisoned or in custody.

> *preventive detention.* The holding in custody of an accused criminal or mentally ill individual who is deemed to be a threat to him- or herself or to others, or to represent a flight risk.

determinate sentence   See **sentence**.

determination   *n.* A final ruling by a court or agency; the cessation of an interest in property or of a power granted by law.

determination letter   *n.* A ruling by the Internal Revenue Service issued at the request of a taxpayer, seeking assurance as to the tax implications of a particular transaction.

detinue   *n.* At common law, an action to recover personal property wrongly held by another.

detrimental reliance   See **reliance**.

device   *n.* An invention, typically a mechanical object; a tactic or contrivance for the purpose of committing a deception or fraud.

devise   *n.* The act of transferring real property by will; a clause of a will describing such a transfer; the property disposed of in such a transfer.

devisee   *n.* The individual or entity receiving real property as the result of a **devise.**

devisor   *n.* The person making a transfer of real property by **devise.**

devolve   *v.* The grant or transfer of authority and/or responsibility to another.

dictum   *n.* In a court's decision, a statement of opinion or of a general rule that is explanatory or suggestive only, and not binding on courts in future cases, because it does not form part of the court's central argument. For example, a judge's suggestion as to how she might decide a related controversy not presently before her would be considered dictum.

digest   1 *n.* A book or series in which cases are summarized and indexed by topics, such as legal issues involved in the case or statutes on which the court ruled.   2 *v.* To create a summary of a case.

diligence   *n.* The effort required to carry out a responsibility or to meet a standard of care.

> *due diligence.* A thorough review of documents, financial statements, and other relevant information pertaining to a proposed corporate transaction such as an acquisition or merger; *lack of due diligence* by one undertaking an examination of books and records may give rise to liability of that individual if the entity being acquired has lower value than expected.

dilution   *n.* **1** Diminution or weakening of a shareholder's interest in a company by the issuance of more shares to other shareholders.   **2** Of a trademark, by its use as a term of general description or in other derogatory or unauthorized ways.   **3** Of the voting rights of a particular party or group by reapportionment of one or more legislative districts (see **gerrymandering**).

diminished capacity   *n.* An alteration to a defendant's mental state, a reduced ability to understand, usually the result of mental retardation, alcohol or drug intoxication, or some other factor, which exists at the time of the commission of a crime, not sufficient to support an **insanity defense,** but that raises the issue of whether the defendant was able to form the intent to commit the crime.

Typically offered as a defense in partial mitigation to obtain conviction on a lesser included charge or to receive a lesser sentence.

diplomatic immunity   *n.* An **immunity** granted by law or treaty to ambassadors and others with diplomatic status.

direct   *v.* To order or cause a person or entity to carry out a course of action; more generally, to govern an enterprise or activity. Of a judge, the giving of a verbal instruction to a witness or jury to behave in a certain way, as in, "the witness is directed to answer yes or no to the questions" or "the jury is directed to disregard the defendant's outburst."

direct examination   *n.* At trial, the initial questioning of a witness by the lawyer who called that witness. Followed by *cross examination* by the opposing attorney and, in some cases, *redirect examination* by the attorney who conducted the direct examination.

director   *n.* Of a corporation, an individual selected to serve on its **board of directors** and thereby oversee the management of its affairs.

disability   *n.* An injury or medical condition that interferes with an individual's ability to perform one or more of the functions of daily life or of work; a legal status that prevents an individual from exercising one or more of a citizen's rights.

> *civil disability.* The status of an individual who has had one or more legal rights (such as the right to vote or to drive) revoked as a result of the conviction of a crime.

disbarment   *n.* The act of revoking an attorney's license to practice law, usually because he or she has committed a crime or violated a legal rule of ethics.

discharge *n.* A debtor's release from a debt upon payment in full or upon adjudication of bankruptcy; the release of an inmate from prison; the termination of an employee; the act of releasing jurors from any further obligation, upon the giving of a verdict or the settlement or dismissal of the trial in which they serve.

discharge in bankruptcy *n.* The release of a debtor from his obligation to pay all or part of his debts, upon the adjudication of a bankruptcy court.

disciplinary proceeding *n.* An administrative proceeding considering the suspension or expulsion from a profession of a licensed individual, as the result of a crime for which he or she was convicted, or of a disciplinary infraction such as a breach of a code of ethics.

disclaimer *n.* A clause in a contract or other writing, stating that the producer or seller of product, device, or process makes no promises about its quality or performance and will not be responsible for harm resulting therefrom.

disclosure *n.* The release of information about a person or entity. Of a corporation, the filing of documents and statements required by law; in litigation, the release of documents and other information subpoenaed or otherwise sought by the other side. See also **discovery.**

discontinuance *n.* The voluntary termination of litigation by a plaintiff who has elected not to pursue it or by both parties pursuant to a settlement.

discovery *n.* In litigation, the compulsory release by a party of documents and other evidence sought by the other party, under rules set by the court. Means of discovery include depositions, written interrogatories, requests for admissions, and requests to produce documents or to inspect property. See also **disclosure.**

discretion *n.* The freedom of choice and of action of a judge, prosecutor, or other public official, within the defined scope of his or her responsibilities. For example, in a criminal matter a judge may have wide discretion to release the defendant on recognizance or to demand bail in any amount, based on the judge's view of the defendant as a flight risk.

discrimination *n.* The act of denying rights, benefits, justice, equitable treatment, or access to facilities available to all others, to an individual or group of people because of their race, age, gender, handicap or other defining characteristic. See also **reverse discrimination.**

disenfranchise *v.* To take away from an individual or group the ability to exercise a right, such as the right to vote.

disenfranchisement *n.* The act of taking a right away from an individual or group.

dishonor *v.* To refuse to pay a claim embodied in a written document, such as a check or other negotiable instrument, when presented; to treat disrespectfully an object considered to have a public or sacred nature, such as a flag.

disinheritance *n.* The act of creating or modifying a will to deprive a potential heir of property or assets that would otherwise pass to the heir under a will.

disinterested *adj.* Neutral, impartial; lacking a financial interest in, or other predisposition toward, a particular resolution of a controversy or issue.

dismissal *n.* **1** The termination of a legal proceeding by the judge, before a trial or hearing, typically on the grant of a motion to dismiss by the adverse party, or because the claimant failed to proceed with the action or comply with an order of the court, or because the claimant has agreed to end the proceeding. **2** Of employment, the firing of an employee.

dismissal without prejudice. A dismissal that allows the claimant to bring the same claim again at some time in the future, within any applicable period of limitations.

dismissal with prejudice. A dismissal that bars the claimant from bringing the claim again at any time in the future.

involuntary dismissal. A dismissal of a claim that the claimant desired to pursue.

voluntary dismissal. A dismissal by the claimant or with the claimant's consent to withdraw the claim.

disorderly conduct *n.* An individual or group's pattern of acts that has the effect of creating a public nuisance or threatening safety.

disparage *v.* To make an untrue statement that harms the reputation of another's business or product.

disparagement *n.* An untrue statement that harms the reputation of someone else's business or product.

dispossess **1** *v.* To evict someone from a tenancy in, or the possession of, real property. **2** *n.* A document, such as a legally required notice, advising someone that an eviction proceeding will be commenced if he or she does not vacate the premises within a specified time period.

dispossession *n.* The act of removing someone from a tenancy in, or the possession of, real property.

dissent *n.* Of a judicial decision, a non binding opinion by one or more judges who disagree with the majority's holding; a withholding of consent to a decision or outcome; the exercise of free speech to express disagreement with a government action or policy.

dissolution *n.* The termination, cessation, or **winding up** of a legal entity such as a corporation or partnership; the consensual or judicially ordered undoing of a contract by placing the parties back into the positions they held before entering into it; the termination of a marriage.

distinguish *v.* In a judicial decision, or an argument such as a brief in support of a particular legal outcome, to note or argue that a prior decision of the same or another court is inapplicable as precedent, because of significant differences in the facts or in the legal posture of the two cases.

distrain *v.* To seize personal property of an individual, typically a tenant, to compel the performance of an obligation, such as the payment of rent. See also **distress.**

distress *n.* The act of distraining another's property. See also **distrain**.

distributee *n.* An heir or beneficiary entitled to receive payment or personal property from an estate.

distribution *n.* At common law, the transfer of personal property to the heirs of an individual who died **intestate.**

district *n.* A geographical subdivision of a county, municipality, or similar entity, for political, judicial, or administrative ends; for example, a *court district* (in which a particular court has jurisdiction over certain matters arising within the borders or pertaining to people who live there) or a *voting district* (where all the franchised inhabitants are required to vote at a particular polling station).

district attorney *n.* A **prosecutor** in the state or municipal court system, often an elected official.

district court   *n.* A court in the state or federal system, typically the lowest level trial court serving a particular geographical area. See also **district**.

diversity jurisdiction   *n.* A form of federal court **jurisdiction** over state law disputes, based on the parties' residence in different states (or one party being a noncitizen of the United States).

diversity of citizenship   *n.* The state of affairs giving rise to **diversity jurisdiction,** when a legal dispute is between citizens of two or more states or when one party to the dispute is a noncitizen of the United States.

dividend   *n.* A distribution of shares or money made by a corporation to its shareholders, representing a pro rata percentage of the company's earnings.

divorce   **1** *n.* The termination of a marriage by court order; the state of having terminated a marriage.   **2** *v.* To terminate a marriage to someone by obtaining a court order, usually referred to as a divorce decree.

divisible divorce. A proceeding in which the marriage is terminated but other issues pertaining to alimony, distribution of assets, or custody of children are reserved for another proceeding in another jurisdiction or under the laws of another state. Also known as a limited divorce.

divorce a mensa et thoro. (Archaic. Latin.) Divorce from bed and board. A proceeding, current in Britain until the nineteenth century, that resulted in the parties remaining married but living separately. The term is still used in a few jurisdictions.

divorce a vinculo matrimonii. (Latin.) Common law, meaning, from the bonds of marriage; a form of divorce based on grounds that preexisted the marriage, which resulted in a legal fiction that the marriage never existed (with the result that any children of the marriage are then considered illegitimate).

mail-order divorce. A divorce received through the mail or otherwise without the presence of the parties in the court granting it. Not recognized in the United States because of the lack of personal jurisdiction.

migratory divorce. A divorce obtained by a spouse who moves or travels to another jurisdiction to obtain it.

no-fault divorce. A divorce granted at the parties' request without any adjudication of wrongdoing (such as abandonment, infidelity, or mental cruelty).

DNA identification   *n.* A method for identifying a particular individual as the source of the deoxyribonucleic acid (human genetic material) in a sample such as semen, blood, or hair. Commonly used to prove the individual's commission of a crime such as murder or rape.

docket   **1** *n.* A court's official record, in summary form, of the hearings held, parties' appearances, and papers filed in a proceeding; a court's calendar of the dates on which hearings are to be held or papers filed.   **2** *v.* To enter a case, hearing, or filed paper in such a record or calendar.

Doctor of Juridical Science   *n.* A graduate degree in law, equivalent to a Ph.D., sought by those who already have the basic **Juris Doctor** degree and an **L.L.M.**

doctor-patient privilege   *n.* A legal **privilege,** arising from a doctor's obligation of confidentiality, that forbids the doctor from disclosing any information or testifying about confidential health matters or communications from a patient, unless the patient waives the privilege.

doctrine *n.* A widely accepted legal tenet.

document **1** *n.* Information captured on paper or in electronic format. Under the rules of evidence, the term receives the broadest possible interpretation and may include such items as photographs, audiotapes, etc. **2** *v.* To record something, typically in writing, or to produce documents to substantiate an assertion.

document of title *n.* Under the Uniform Commercial Code, a **document** (such as a **bill of lading**) giving a specified individual the right to take custody of and dispose of goods.

domain *n.* Real estate; the ownership of such real estate. In Internet parlance, an Internet address (such as www.aol.com) to be registered with the appropriate authorities.

domestic *adj.* Pertaining to the internal affairs or products of a country; relating to matters of the family.

domicile *n.* An individual or corporation's permanent legal residence, of which there may only be one; for an individual or corporation with multiple residences, the primary one, determining the proper jurisdiction for matters such as taxation, voting, and so on. In the case of multiple residences, an individual's domicile is that to which he always intends to return.

dominant estate See **estate.**

donee *n.* The recipient of a gift.

donee beneficiary *n.* A third party who receives the benefit of a gift made to a donee.

donor *n.* The maker of a gift. **2** One who creates a trust. See also **settlor.**

double indemnity *n.* A clause in an insurance policy providing that the policy's benefit will be doubled if a loss occurs as the result of a particular instrumentality or under particular circumstances, typically in the event of an accidental injury or death.

double jeopardy *n.* The fact or risk of being prosecuted more than once for the same (or substantially the same) offense. Double jeopardy is prohibited by the United States Constitution; however, separate proceedings under state and federal law for offenses arising out of the same incident do not constitute double jeopardy (for example, a state trial for murder and a federal trial for deprivation of civil liberties involving the same killing).

dower *n.* Common law; the right of a wife to one third of the real property owned by her husband at his death, for the duration of her life.

draft *n.* A written order for the payment of a specified sum of money to a certain individual or to the bearer (for example, a check). A draft may involve three parties: the **drawer,** who writes or creates it, the **drawee,** who has custody of the funds to be paid (for example, a bank), and the **payee,** who will receive the funds.

> *sight draft.* A draft payable upon receipt.

> *time draft.* A draft payable as of a certain date.

draw *v.* To prepare and execute a financial instrument such as a draft or check; to prepare a legal document such as a will or contract; to withdraw funds from a bank account.

drawee   *n.* A person or entity to whom a **draft** is sent, instructing him or it to release funds to the **payee.**

drawer   *n.* The maker of a **draft** or **check.**

driving while intoxicated   *v.* The criminal law offense of operating a vehicle after having drunk an amount of alcohol sufficient to raise one's blood alcohol content above a legal limit, commonly referred to by the acronym DWI. Also known as driving under the influence (DUI), which, in some jurisdictions means that the driver had a lower level of intoxication than DWI, but was still impaired.   In some jurisdictions, the term driving while impaired is used.

drug   **1** *n.* A chemical or organic substance used to treat a medical or psychological condition; such a substance used illegally to alter consciousness or mood.   **2** *v.* The act of giving someone such a substance, with the implication that it is against the recipient's will and has an adverse effect. See also **controlled substance.**

drug-free zone   *v.* A geographical area (typically surrounding a school or other place where children are found) in which, under an applicable criminal law, the distribution of illegal drugs is penalized with a sentence or fine greater than is applicable elsewhere.

drug paraphernalia   *n.* Items such as pipes or syringes used for the preparation or ingestion of illegal drugs.

duces tecum   *n. Latin.* To bring along. A type of **subpoena** that requires a witness to bring specified documents when he or she appears in court or for a **deposition.**

due   **1** *adj.* A proper or appropriate standard or level, as in due care. **2** *adv.* Of a **debt**, **draft,** or other financial instrument, that it is payable immediately.

due process   *n.* A Constitutionally determined doctrine requiring that any legal proceeding or legislation protect or respect certain rights of the persons or groups involved in the proceedings or affected by the legislation. See also **fundamental fairness.**

procedural due process. The requirement that a legal proceeding affords an affected person, such as the defendant in a criminal case, certain rights such as that of notice of the charges or claims, and an opportunity to contest them before a neutral tribunal. These rights are defined by the Fifth and Fourteenth Amendments to the United States Constitution and by court cases thereunder.

substantive due process. The Constitutional requirement that federal, state, and local legislation should not interfere with the rights defined by the Fifth and Fourteenth Amendments, unless such legislation serves a compelling governmental interest in the subject matter, and utilizes the least restrictive means to accomplish that interest.

DUI   *n. abbr.* Abbreviation for driving under the influence. See **driving while intoxicated.**

dummy corporation   See **corporation.**

dumping   **1** *n.* The act of selling goods at less than fair market value, typically for the purpose of injuring a competitor and gaining market share.   **2** The illegal disposal of pollutants.

durable power of attorney   *n.* A **power of attorney** that remains in effect after the grantor becomes mentally incompetent.

duress *n.* The application of force, or the threat of force, to compel another to act against his or her will. Used as a defense in criminal and contractual matters, for example, that a defendant participated in a crime because held at gunpoint, or signed a contract only under the threat of physical harm. See also **economic duress.**

duty *n.* A legally-defined responsibility to perform certain acts or meet certain standards of performance; an essential element of proof in a tort action is that the defendant had a **duty** to act in a certain manner, such as the duty to use due care in the operation of a motor vehicle. Duties may be mandated by law, such as the duty to pay taxes, or may be voluntary, such as those assumed under a contract.

delegable duty. A duty that may be transferred to another.

nondelegable duty. A duty that one must perform personally, and that may not be delegated to another.

DWI See **driving while intoxicated.**

dying declaration See **declaration.**

E

earned income   *n.* **Income** received as payment for labor or services performed.

earnest money   *n.* A down payment, typically for real estate, that demonstrates the prospective purchaser's intent to proceed with the transaction.

easement   *n.* A right of use of another's land for a particular purpose; for example, an easement permitting a person to cross another's land to fish in a pond located there, or use of a common driveway.

> *affirmative easement.* An easement that grants another the right to perform certain related actions on the property.

> *easement appurtenant.* An easement that benefits another property; for example, a right to pass across land to reach a neighboring tract.

> *easement by necessity.* A statutory or natural encumbrance that occurs in situations such as its being necessary to cross another's land in order to gain access to water or to a road.

> *easement in gross.* An easement that benefits an individual who does not necessarily own any adjoining land; for example, an easement permitting someone to hunt or fish on the property.

> *implied easement*   *n* An easement imposed by law where it is clear that the parties to a transaction intended an easement to exist, even if not specifically stated.

> *negative easement.* An easement that prohibits the property owner from performing some action.

> *prescriptive easement.* An easement gained by the uninterrupted occupation of a another person's land for a statutory period, often equal to that required for adverse possession.

economic duress   *n.* An act of **duress** involving a threat of financial harm.

effective assistance of counsel   *n.* Diligent, competent legal representation in a criminal case that meets the minimum standards of due care expected of an attorney.   Failure to receive effective assistance of counsel is a common basis for appeal in serious criminal matters, particularly death penalty cases.

effective date   *n.* The date as of which a contract or other instrument, or a law, enters into force.

e.g.   *abbr.* From the Latin term *exempli gratia,* meaning for example.

eggshell skull   *n.* A principle of **tort** law for which a **tortfeasor** is responsible, even for the unforeseeable results of his or her wrongful act; the term derives from a case in which a light blow to the head killed an individual, thereby subjecting the hitter to liability, even though one would not have expected serious injury or death from the force of the blow.

eject   *v.* To remove from premises; to push out or cast off.

ejectment   *n.* The removal of a tenant or owner from property he or she occupies; a legal action by which a person removed from property seeks to recover it.

ejusdem generis   *n. Latin.* Of the same category. A legal principle stating that a general phrase following a list of specific items refers to an item of the same type as those in the list.

elder law *n.* A relatively recent body of law dealing with rights and privileges of the elderly, including estate matters, pensions, health issues, and Social Security.

election *n.* The process by which an individual is chosen to occupy a public office, or, in some cases, a private one (such as a director serving on a corporate board); in litigation, the making of a choice among remedies, whereby the selection of one may preclude the use of others; in estate law, a choice between inheriting under a will, and pursuing a legal remedy other than as provided in the will. See also **elective share.**

elective share *n.* In trusts and estates, a share, mandated by law, that a spouse or child may elect to take of the estate, in lieu of inheriting under the will.

elector *n.* A member of the **electoral college;** the maker of an **election;** a voter eligible to vote in an **election.**

electoral college *n.* A group of electors, chosen according to the popular vote in each state, who elect the president and the vice president of the United States.

elements of crime *n.* The required facts of a crime, such as intent, to be proven in the course of a prosecution.

emancipation *n.* The liberation of an individual or a group from a constraint, such as the emancipation of slaves; in family law, the process by which a minor child becomes legally and financially independent of his or her parents and receives the legal rights, at least in some respects, of an adult.

Emancipation Proclamation *n.* Executive order issued by President Abraham Lincoln on January 1, 1863, freeing all slaves held in geographical areas in rebellion against the United States.

embezzle *v.* To illegally misappropriate property under one's care, particularly property to which one has a public **trust** or **fiduciary** duty.

embezzlement *n.* The illegal taking of property under one's care, particularly property to which one has a public **trust** or **fiduciary** duty.

embracery *n.* The act of illegally influencing or corrupting a juror or an entire jury to reach a particular result.

emendation *n.* The act of revising a document.

eminent domain *n.* The government's right, upon the payment of fair compensation, to seize privately held land for a public purpose, such as the widening of a highway, or the construction of a public building; the act of exercising such a right.

emolument *n.* A payment or other benefit received as a result of employment or of the holding of a public office.

emotional distress *n.* A negative emotional reaction—which may include fear, anger, anxiety, and suffering—endured/experienced by the victim of a **tort,** for which monetary damages may be awarded.

empanel *v.* The formality of seating a jury following **voir dire** at the commencement of a trial.

employee *n.* A person who works in the service of another (the employer) subject to a contract for hire, where the employer controls the conditions of work performance. See also **agent.**

employee benefit plan *n.* A benefit other than salary (such as health insurance or pension) granted by an employer to its employees, subject to a written plan document, the taxable status of which is governed by the federal

Employee Retirement Income Security Act of 1974.

Employee Retirement Income Security Act of 1974.   *n.* Federal legislation enacted in 1974 that sets forth rules for employee benefit plans. Abbreviated **ERISA.**

employment   *n.* The state of working for another under a contract of hire that provides that one's services are subject to the other's direction and control.

en banc   *n. French.* On the bench. Of appeals courts, before a full court, with all judges present. Federal appeals are typically heard by a panel of three judges, but may be reheard by the full circuit court of appeals sitting en banc.

encroach   *v.* To unlawfully gain access to or take the property or possessions of another, particularly by stealth.

encumbrance   *n.* A financial obligation, such as a mortgage, that is attached to or burdens a property right and is transferred with that right.

encumbrancer   *n.* The holder of an encumbrance, such as a mortgagor.

endorsement   *n.* A change to an insurance policy.

enfranchise   *v.* To grant rights to an individual or group, such as a right to vote or to have personal freedom (for example, the **Emancipation Proclamation** enfranchised the slaves).

engross   *v. Archaic.* To prepare a document, such as a **deed** or a legislative bill, for **execution** or passage.

enjoin   *v.* To order or compel to stop or prohibit commencement of an activity; of a judge: to grant a court order directing a party to cease a particular activity.

enjoy   *v.* To have the undisturbed use or possession of something, particularly real property.

enlarge   *v.* To make greater in size, extend; to free from detention.

enrolled bill   *n.* A final copy of legislation passed by the United States House of Representatives and the Senate, which is then sent to the president for signature.

entail   *n. Archaic.* At common law, an interest in real estate that passed only to direct issue of the owner and not to collateral heirs.

enter   *v.* In real property, to pass upon or into; of litigation, to file or present to the court—for example, to enter an appearance into the record; of a contract, to enter into it means to sign or execute it.

entice   *v.* To invite someone to commit a wrongful or illegal act.

entire contract   *n.* A contract that must be performed in its entirety; its parts are not severable from one another; a description of a contract that is complete.

entirety   *n.* The whole of a thing; something incapable of being divided.

entitlement   *n.* A benefit that must be granted to anyone who meets the criteria for receiving it.

entrapment   *n.* Of law enforcement, the act of leading or guiding a suspect into committing a criminal act the suspect otherwise would not have committed.

entry   *n.* The act of entering upon real property; the making of a notation in a court or business record; in criminal law, the act of intruding into a residence with the intention of committing a crime. See also **enter.**

  illegal entry. In immigration law, the act of an alien coming into the country without proper documentation or credentials.

enumerated power *n.* A governmental power that is described in a foundation document such as a constitution.

environmental impact statement *n.* A report required to be filed by entities seeking federal or state monies, analyzing the environmental implications of proposed projects and legislation.

environmental law *n.* A body of law intended to protect the environment, by regulating activities that cause pollution, such as fossil fuel emissions and the dumping of wastes; by prohibiting certain inconsistent uses of land designated as federal parkland; and by providing regimes of protection for endangered species.

equality before the law *n.* The doctrine that all persons, regardless of wealth, social status, or the political power wielded by them, are to be treated the same before the law.

eo instante *n. Latin.* At that moment.

eo nomine *n. Latin.* In the name of.

equal protection *n.* The constitutional guarantee that all persons shall receive the same protection of the laws as are afforded all other persons under the same circumstances.

Equal Protection Clause *n.* The provision of the Fourteenth Amendment to the United States Constitution that prohibits states from denying equal protection of laws to its citizens.

equalization *n.* The act of revising assessed values of real property to make tax rates consistent or of amending the tax rates themselves to achieve consistency among similar taxes.

equitable *adj.* Fair, under widely held moral principles, often embodied in court precedents; or referring to a remedy available in a court of **equity.**

equitable distribution *n.* In **divorce** law, a remedy under which the court makes a fair (not necessarily equal) distribution of the marital assets. This is the alternative to the community property (equal) approach followed in some jurisdictions.

equity *n.* Fair dealing under widely held moral principles, often embodied in court precedents; a body of common law founded on such principles, providing special remedies, such as injunctions, in cases where monetary damages are not available or will not suffice.

ergo *conj., adv. Latin.* Therefore.

Erie doctrine *n.* The legal doctrine requiring a federal court exercising **diversity jurisdiction** over a state law issue to apply the substantive (as opposed to procedural) law of the state where the court is located.

ERISA See **Employee Retirement Income Security Act of 1974.**

error *n.* A mistake as to facts or law.

harmless error. A mistake by the judge that does not interfere with a party's rights or remedies, and that therefore does not warrant reversal of the decision.

plain error. An error that is so obvious and causes such an adverse effect, that an appeals court reverses a decision despite the affected party's failure to object to it during trial.

reversible error. A mistake by the judge that adversely affects a party's rights or remedies, and is, therefore, grounds for reversal on appeal.

escheat *n.* The transfer of property to government ownership when its owner dies without a will or any heirs; property that is so transferred.

escrow *n.* An arrangement under which something (money, a document, or property) is held in trust by a third party until the occurrence of a condition allowing its release to a party to an underlying transaction. For example, a down payment may be held in escrow, typically by the realtor or a lawyer, until the closing of a real estate transaction.

estate *n.* The totality of an individual's ownership of money, real and personal property.

> *decedent's estate.* Such assets after the death of the owner, as involved in the **probate** of a will or an **intestacy** proceeding.

> *residuary estate.* The remainder of a decedent's estate after all applicable payments and transfers have been made, including gifts and taxes.

> *contingent estate.* From the common law. An asset, typically real property, that vests only upon the occurrence of a condition.

> *dominant estate.* Real property that benefits from an **easement** on adjoining property.

> *equitable estate.* An estate recognized under the rules of **equity.**

> *possessory estate.* A right of possession in an estate, which may not include actual ownership.

> *servient estate.* Real property upon which an **easement** has been granted.

> *vested estate.* An estate that an individual has a present right to **enjoy,** or a noncontingent right to do so in the future.

estop *v.* To stop or prevent from occurring.

estoppel *n.* A doctrine that holds, under certain circumstances, that a claim or assertion cannot be made if it contravenes a prior claim or assertion of the same party, or if it contradicts the factual holding of a court whose decision is not directly binding on the parties.

> *collateral estoppel.* Estoppel created by the findings of another court upon the same facts, even though the other proceeding did not involve all of the same parties or was otherwise not directly binding on the current court.

> *equitable estoppel.* At **equity,** the doctrine that a party who has caused another harm in reliance on the party's promise or statement, may be barred from taking certain actions to escape liability for such harm.

> *estoppel by silence.* An estoppel created by the failure to speak of a party who had an obligation to do so.

> *promissory estoppel.* A doctrine that prevents a party from pleading lack of **consideration** as an affirmative defense, if that party made a statement upon which the other party foreseeably relied to his or her detriment.

et al. *abbr. Latin.* And others; typically used in the caption of court documents following the first named party, to signify that more than one individual is aligned on one side of the case.

ethical *adj.* In accordance with widely held norms of behavior, or of written standards of conduct adopted by the members of a profession.

ethical wall *n.* A process for avoiding conflicts of interest by limiting disclosure of information to certain attorneys or individuals within a firm or corporation, thereby building a metaphorical wall between the holders of information and colleagues who represent interests or hold opinions which conflict. Also known as a Chinese wall.

euthanasia *n.* The process of terminating the life of another by merciful or painless means, to prevent further suffering.

evict *v.* To remove a tenant or other occupant from real property.

eviction *n.* The action of removing a tenant or other occupant from real property.

> *actual eviction.* The physical removal of an individual from real property.

> *constructive eviction.* Wrongful acts of a landlord that make premises uninhabitable, with the intent or result of forcing the tenant to leave.

> *retalitory eviction.* Eviction in retaliation for a tenant's complaints to or about the landlord with regard to living conditions. If eviction occurs within a narrow timeframe following such complaints, it is presumed to be retaliatory. Retaliatory eviction is illegal under the statutes of most states.

evidence *n.* A thing, a document, or the testimony of a person that bears on the truth or falsity of an assertion made in litigation; the totality of such items introduced in a trial; the legal doctrines pertaining to the admission, use, and evaluation of such items.

> *character evidence.* Evidence attesting to one's character and moral standing in the community; character witnessed to attest to same. See also **reputation witness.**

> *competent evidence.* Evidence that pertains to the matters being decided by the court and that may be considered by the court under the applicable rules of evidence.

> *cumulative evidence.* Additional evidence that tends to prove the same assertions as evidence already admitted.

> *demonstrative evidence.* Visual evidence, such as a chart, image, or model, prepared by attorneys or consultants, that demonstrates or clarifies information relevant to the trial.

> *direct evidence.* Evidence based on the witness' personal observation of events.

> *documentary evidence.* Documents introduced as evidence.

> *evidence in chief.* Evidence supporting the basic premises of a party's case.

> *extrinsic evidence.* Evidence pertaining to a contract and contradicting or supplementing its terms. Extrinsic evidence is not permitted where the contract is unambiguous.

> *opinion evidence.* A witness' personal opinion about the facts of the dispute.

> *real evidence.* Tangible evidence directly involved in the underlying events of the case.

> *rebuttal evidence.* Evidence offered to contradict the other party's assertions.

evidentiary fact *n.* A fact that is an indispensable step in determining the truth or falsehood of an assertion.

ex. *adj. Latin.* Previous, from.

examination *n.* In litigation, the questioning of a witness under oath, either at trial or in a **deposition;** the Patent and Trademark Office investigation into the validity of a patent application.

> *cross examination.* The questioning of a witness by a lawyer or other party other than the one who called that person, with respect to matters about which the witness has testified during direct examination.

direct examination. A witness's initial questioning by the lawyer who called that person, in order to introduce matters of fact in a case. **Leading questions** should be avoided by the attorney conducting direct examination.

redirect examination. Questioning of a witness by the party who called that witness, following cross examination, to attempt to clarify or rebut any damaging testimony that might have come out during cross examination. Normally, **redirect,** as it is also known, is limited to the scope of the subject matter examined in cross examination, although the judge may make an exception.

exception   *n.* In litigation, a formal statement made by a party indicating to the court that he or she wishes to preserve an issue for appeal.

excess insurance   *n.* A secondary insurance policy covering a loss in excess of that covered under a primary policy; may be referred to as excess policy.

excessive force   *n.* In criminal law, the unjustified use of force, determined by the circumstances.

excessive verdict   *n.* Term applied to a jury verdict that "shocks the conscience of the court" as being unduly high; generally thought to result from extraneous factors such as bias against the defendant or unusually dramatic facts.

excise   *n.* A tax on income-producing activities or on actions involving goods, such as their manufacture or sale.

excited utterance   *n.* An exclamation made at the moment of an accident or other unexpected and disturbing event, considered under the rules of evidence to be likely to be truthful because of the urgency of the surrounding circum-

stances and, therefore, an exception to the hearsay rule. See also **hearsay.**

exclusion   *n.* Of taxes, an item that is not required to be included in gross income; of insurance, the occurrences that will not receive coverage under the policy.

exclusionary rule   *n.* Of litigation, a body of rules that provide that evidence may not be introduced if it was obtained in violation of a party's constitutional rights.

exclusive jurisdiction   *n.* The provision, made in the United States Constitution, in legislation, or in a contract, that a particular court is the sole forum in which a certain type of case may be brought.

exculpate   *v.* To clear of suspicion; to determine the innocence of another.

excusable neglect   *n.* An act of neglect that occurs not as a result of a party's fault but due to circumstances beyond his or her control.

excuse   *n.* A defense or justification of an individual's act or failure to act; a defense in criminal law that an individual's actions cannot constitute a crime because of **coercion,** or some other cause that places the actions beyond the individual's volition or control.

execute   *v.* To sign a contract, will, or other legal document; to carry out a duty; to recover funds under a judgment; to put a criminal defendant to death.

executed   *adj.* Of a legal document, that it has been signed; of an action, that it has been carried out.

executive   *n.* The branch of government including the president and those responsible to him or her for implementing the laws of the United States.

executive clemency *n.* The power granted to the governor by most state constitutions and vested in the president by the United States Constitution as chief executive officer to pardon or to commute any sentence imposed by a court within that officer's jurisdiction. See also **clemency, commutation, pardon,** and **reprieve.**

executive privilege *n.* A legal **privilege,** exempting the president of the United States and other members of the **executive** branch from being compelled to disclose information to the public about matters of foreign policy or of national security.

executor *n.* An individual named in a will who will be responsible for seeing that its bequests and other provisions are performed.

executory *adj.* Something that has not yet been fully performed.

exemplar *n.* A representative example of a type of object or thing. In criminal law, a physical sample, such as a fingerprint or hair, taken from the defendant for evidentiary purposes.

exemplary damages *n.* See **damages** *(punitive damages).*

exempt *adj.* Not subject to a responsibility held by others.

exemption *n.* The state of not being subject to a responsibility held by others; in taxes, an amount subtracted from gross income to determine taxable income.

exhaustion of remedies *n.* A legal principle stating that, before a particular remedy is sought, all lesser remedies (typically available at a lower or parallel level of jurisdiction, or from an administrative body) must have been attempted, without satisfactory results. For example, all state remedies must have been tried before a state prisoner files a writ of **habeas corpus** in a federal court.

exhibit *n.* A document or thing introduced as evidence in court, or attached to a contract or to a motion.

exigent circumstances *n.* Events that justify a departure from usual legal procedures such as the obtaining of a warrant, typically in order to save a life, preserve evidence, or prevent a suspect from fleeing.

exonerate *v.* To clear of guilt or responsibility, particularly to establish the innocence of a prisoner on death row. See also **exculpate.**

ex parte *adj.* A judge's action in conducting a hearing or conference with one party only, without notice to the other party; typically improper, except under the limited circumstances in which a party is seeking a temporary restraining order and alleging that notice to the adverse party will result in the destruction of evidence or other illegal action. Also used as an adverb, such as, "the judge conducted the hearing ex parte." It also refers to a party's attempts to make such contact with the judge.

expectancy *n.* The expectation that an heir or legatee will acquire property at another's death; of real estate, a **remainder** or **reversion.**

expert *n.* An individual of recognized knowledge in a particular topic, typically confirmed by academic standing and publications, who is called upon by one of the parties to testify in court as to his or her opinion of the underlying facts. Also referred to as expert witness.

ex post facto *n. Latin.* After the fact.

ex post facto law   *n.* A law intended to apply to crimes or events that took place before its passage. The United States Constitution forbids the passage of ex post facto criminal laws, on the principle that it is wrong to punish an act which was not illegal when committed.

express   *adj.* Direct, immediate, clear.

expropriate   *v.* Of government: forcibly to divest another of a property interest, as by **eminent domain.**

expropriation   *n.* Of government: the action of forcibly divesting another of a property interest, as by **eminent domain.**

expungement of record **1** *n.* The eradication of a criminal conviction from official records after a specified period of time or upon the happening of a specific event. **2** *v.* the process of removing criminal records from official rolls.

extort   *v.* To wrongfully take something of value from another by the threat of force or other coercive measure.

extortion   *n.* The wrongful taking of something of value from another by the threat of force or other coercive measure.

extradite   *v.* To transfer through legal process a captured fugitive to the jurisdiction where he or she is sought.

extradition   *n.* The act of transferring a captured fugitive to the jurisdiction where he or she is sought; the legal process for such a transfer.

extrajudicial   *adj.* Of an action, that it is of the nature of something that should be accomplished by legal process but has been done outside of the court system; for example, a statement made out of court is an extrajudicial statement. See also **hearsay.**

extralegal   *adj.* Outside of the domain of the law.

extraordinary remedy   See **remedy.**

extraordinary writ   *n.* A **writ** for an **extraordinary remedy.**

extraterritorial   *adj.* Beyond the boundaries or reach of a particular jurisdiction. See also **jurisdiction.**

extrinsic evidence   *n.* Evidence that pertains to a contract, but is not contained with the "four corners" of the contract document; generally offered to contradict or explain the terms of the written document. Extrinsic evidence is generally not permitted unless the contract is ambiguous on its face.

eyewitness   *n.* An individual who saw the occurrence of an event and may be called upon to testify about it in court.

face *n.* The front part of a document or thing, or the part with writing on it; the appearance or tendency of a thing, for example, the face of the evidence.

facilitation *v.* Criminal law, the act of assisting another to commit a crime by making it easier.

fact *n.* Something that exists or has happened; an irreducible element of real existence or occurrence.

   collateral fact. A fact that is not central to the main issue or controversy.

   evidentiary fact. A fact that tends to prove, or is a necessary prerequisite for the proof of, another fact.

   jurisdictional fact. Such a fact as must exist before a court will exercise jurisdiction over a matter; for example, in a diversity case in federal court, that the parties are citizens of different states and that the amount in controversy is above a threshold level.

   probative fact. See evidentiary fact.

   ultimate fact. An essential fact, arrived at by inference from the evidence and testimony, that causes the final determination or conclusion of law.

fact-finder *n.* The person or persons in a particular trial or proceeding with responsibility for determining the facts. The jury typically acts as the fact-finder in any case where there is one; otherwise, the judge will perform that func-

tion along with that of making determinations of law.

fact-finding *n.* The process of acting as the **fact-finder.**

factor *n.* One who buys accounts receivable for an amount less than their face value and collects the full amount, pocketing the difference as his or her commission; one who sells goods received on consignment.

factum *n.* From Latin, meaning a fact or an action.

fail *v.* To break; not to succeed in reaching a standard or goal; to perform ineptly or faultily; to become bankrupt.

failure of consideration *n.* The doctrine that a contract is unenforceable where there is no reciprocity of benefits, because one party has given nothing in return for what he or she has received; the circumstances under which a contract becomes unenforceable for such a lack of reciprocity.

failure of issue *n.* In trusts and estate law, that a decedent had no children to inherit his or her estate.

faint pleader *n.* A dishonest manner of filing a legal pleading, typically involving fraud or conspiracy among the parties.

fair *adj.* Neutral; balanced; just; reasonable.

fair comment *n.* A defense to a charge of defamation, that the statements were based on sincere opinion about a matter of public interest.

fair hearing *n.* A court or administrative hearing conducted so as to accord each party the **due process** rights required by applicable law.

fair market value *n.* Market value, the price that can be had for property in a reasonable commercial marketplace; in corporate law, the intrinsic value of shares of stock, for purposes of determining a buy-out price.

fair trial   *n.* A trial by a neutral and **fair** court, conducted so as to accord each party the **due process** rights required by applicable law; of a criminal trial, that the defendant's constitutional rights have been respected.

fair use   *n.* Copyright law: the doctrine that one may use a small portion of a copyrighted work without the author's permission, in scholarly works, reviews, or other contexts where the use is considered reasonable and limited.

fair warning   *n.* Adequate notice in a law that certain acts constitute criminal behavior.

false advertising   *n.* The act of knowingly advertising a product or service that does not exist or does not function as represented.

false arrest   *n.* An arrest made by a person who falsely claims to be a law enforcement officer or by a law enforcement officer who has no legal grounds for making an arrest; restraint of an individual's free movement. See also **false imprisonment.**

false imprisonment   *n.* The act of detaining or restraining another without proper legal authority; a **false arrest.**

false pretenses   *n.* The act of obtaining a benefit or property by fraud or misrepresentation.

false statement   *n.* An intentionally untrue **statement** made to mislead.

family   *n.* A group of individuals who share ties of blood, marriage, or adoption; a group residing together and consisting of parents, children, and other relatives by blood or marriage; a group of individuals residing together who have consented to an arrangement similar to ties of blood or marriage.

family law   *n.* Collectively, those laws dealing with matters of significant impact on **family** relationships, particularly adoption, divorce, custody, and abuse.

fast-track   **1** *n.* An expedited litigation or **discovery** schedule ordered by the court, generally in relation to civil cases. See also **speedy trial.**   **2** *v.* to expedite a case schedule.

fatal   *adj.* Deadly, causing actual or metaphorical death; causing the undoing of a claim, assertion, or legal document ("a fatal flaw in the pleading"). See also **fatal defect.**

fatal defect   *n.* Pertaining to a contract or a pleading, an error or flaw of such gravity that it invalidates the document in question.

fatal variance   *n.* In criminal procedure, a distinction between two assertions or documents that ought to be the same, leading to a **due process** violation; frequently, a difference between the language of the indictment and the theory pursued or proof presented at trial, thereby denying the defendant fair notice of the charges.

fault   *n.* A negligent or intentional failure to act reasonably or according to law or duty; an act or omission giving rise to a criminal indictment or a civil **tort** lawsuit.

federal   *adj.* Pertaining to a system of government such as that adopted in the United States, in which a national government oversees a federation of local governments, with distinctly defined but overlapping responsibilities.

federal common law   See **common law.**

Federal Insurance Contributions Act   *n.* A federal law authorizing a Social Security tax partly withheld from employee paychecks and partly paid directly by employers.

federalism *n.* Generally, the allocation of authority and responsibility to the different levels of government in a federal system.

federal law *n.* A body of law at the highest or national level of a federal government, consisting of a constitution, enacted laws and the court decisions pertaining to them. The federal law of the United States consists of the United States Constitution, laws enacted by Congress, and decisions of the Supreme Court and other federal courts.

federal question *n.* An issue or case arising under federal law, particularly the Constitution of the United States or an Act of Congress; a basis for invoking the jurisdiction of federal courts.

federal question jurisdiction See **jurisdiction.**

fee *n.* A payment invoiced or made for the performance of services; an interest in or ownership of real estate See **fee simple.**

fee simple *n.* At common law, the broadest possible ownership interest in real estate, inheritable by any heir of the owner.

fee simple absolute. A fee simple with no conditions placed upon it and that will endure as long as there are descendants of the original owner to inherit it.

fee simple defeasible. A fee simple that is terminable despite the existence of heirs, because of the occurrence of a particular event or condition.

fee simple determinable. A fee simple that terminates and reverts to the grantor upon the occurrence of a particular event or condition; commonly a grant of property to be used for charitable purposes and that reverts if no longer used in this way.

fee tail *n. Archaic.* A fee estate granted to a particular individual and his or her specified heirs (typically direct issue, not collateral heirs) and that reverts if the individual dies without such heirs.

felon *n.* An individual previously convicted of a **felony.**

felonious *adj.* Pertaining to, involving, or of the nature of a **felony.**

felony *n.* A grave or serious form of crime, typically punishable by imprisonment for more than a year, as opposed to a **misdemeanor.**

felony murder *n.* A murder occurring during the commission of a felony.

felony murder rule *n.* Doctrine that a death which occurs during the commission of another felony crime, even where the perpetrator did not intend to cause death; for example, during a bank robbery, shall be punishable as murder.

fence **1** *n.* An individual who buys and resells stolen goods or receives them on consignment. **2** *v.* To buy stolen goods for resale, or receive them on consignment.

fertile octogenarian rule *n.* A legal-fiction, to alleviate the **rule against perpetuities,** that a woman could become pregnant for so long as she is alive.

fiduciary **1** *n.* An individual owing another a legal duty of care and good faith in the management of a business, money, or property; for example, a corporate officer or the executor of a will. **2** *adj.* Descriptive of a relationship that confers special higher responsibilities. See **fiduciary relationship.**

fiduciary relationship *n.* A legally defined relationship in which one individual acts as a **fiduciary** protecting the interest of the other (for example, an attorney and client, or a trustee and beneficiary).

fighting words *n.* Speech not protected by the First Amendment because it is intended to bring about a violent response.

file **1** *n.* A court's or a lawyer's record of a case.   **2** *v.* The act of submitting a document, generally to a court.

final judgment See **judgment.**

finder *n.* One who brings together two or more parties for a business transaction, such as a merger or a loan, but who is not usually involved in the negotiation or preparation of the details of the transaction.

finder's fee *n.* The **fee** paid to a **finder** for his services in bringing about the transaction.

findings of fact *n.* The conclusions of a judge, jury, or administrative tribunal regarding the underlying facts of the case under consideration.

fine *n.* An amount of money paid as a penalty for a criminal or civil infraction.

fine print *n. Colloquial.* Of a contract, referring to matter within it that is obscurely phrased and generally adversarial to the less powerful party's interests, such as disclaimers of liability or penalties for late payment or performance. Derived from the custom of printing the parts of standard form contracts that contain such matter, in tiny, hard-to-read print.

first-degree murder See **murder.**

first offender *n.* An individual never previously convicted of a crime.

fixture *n.* Personal property that is attached to a structure or to land in such a way as to be considered a part of it.

> *Trade fixture.* Items attached to premises by a tenant for purposes of conducting a business; for example, ovens in a restaurant.

FOIA See **Freedom of Information Act.**

forbearance *n.* the act of delaying enforcement of a legal right, as with a creditor who grants the debtor extension of time to pay.

for cause *n.* Of an action, such as the termination of a contract or a relationship of employment, that it is based on a breach, misfeasance, or other inappropriate action of the other party.

force *n.* Power or strength.

> *deadly force.* Force used which is known or expected, or should be expected to cause death.

> *in force.* Legal validity, as with a law or regulation that is "in force."

force majeure *n. French.* Greater force; a natural or human-induced disaster that causes a contract to fail of performance.

forcible detainer See **eviction**.

forcible entry. *n.* The taking of or entry onto property using unlawful or illegal force, or any entry done without consent of occupier or owner.

foreclosure *n.* An action brought by the holder of a security interest in property to terminate the owner's interest in order to take possession of, or to sell the property, in satisfaction of the secured debt.

foreign *adj.* Relating to another country or jurisdiction.

forensic *adj.* Relating to the gathering, preparation, or presentation of evidence in court. *n.* the application of scientific or medical principles to the law.

foreseeability *n.* Tort law: that which should be anticipated as the natural consequence of an action or inaction; predictable.

foreseeable *adj.* Tort law: Of an action or event, that it was predictable or should be anticipated.

forfeiture *n.* The loss or compulsory transfer to another, without compensation, of a right or property interest, usually as a penalty.

forgery *n.* A false banknote, document, work of art, or other imitation of a thing of value, created to be passed off as real; the act of creating such an object.

form *n.* A standard legal document sold or published to be used as a model, or to be prepared by filling in blanks; the outward appearance of something, as opposed to its substance.

fornicate *v.* To have sex with someone to whom one is not married.

fornication *n.* Consensual sex between two individuals not married to one another.

forum *n.* A public place, typically devoted to communication or expression; in litigation, a particular court or jurisdiction.

forum conveniens *n. Latin.* In litigation: the most appropriate court for the resolution of a particular dispute.

forum nonconveniens *n. Latin.* In litigation: the doctrine that a court may decline jurisdiction of a case, based on factors such as residence of the parties, thus allowing or causing another more convenient court to take the case.

forum-selection clause *n.* A clause in a contract stating that all disputes will be resolved in a particular court and waiving the right to file suit in any other.

forum shopping *n. Colloquial.* A party's action of looking for a court or judge that is deemed likely to render a favorable result.

foundation *n.* Of evidence, that it indicates or leads to the admissibility of other evidence; a nonprofit organization created to fund or promote charitable causes.

four corners *n. Colloquial.* The entirety of a written contract or document, referring to matters that are, or are not, found within the document.

franchise *n.* A right granted by or pursuant to legislation, particularly the right to vote; the exclusive right under a licensing agreement to utilize a trademark and distribute the trademarked products or services in a particular area.

fraud *n.* An intentional misrepresentation uttered to cause another to rely on it to his detriment.

> *constructive fraud.* A misrepresentation deemed by the law to be fraud even though unintentional.

> *fraud in the factum.* The nature of a legal document is misrepresented to a party who is induced to sign it based on an incorrect understanding of its nature.

> *fraud in the inducement.* A party is induced to sign a contract by misrepresentation, not of the terms of the contract itself, but of the level of risk or the surrounding circumstances.

mail fraud. A fraudulent act involving misrepresentations made through the United States Postal Service for financial benefit.

wire fraud. A fraudulent act involving misrepresentations made via telephone or other form of electronic communications.

fraudulent concealment See concealment.

fraudulent conveyance *n.* A transfer of real property to another, typically lacking any or significant consideration, made for the purposes of protecting the property from a creditor who would otherwise seek its sale or forfeiture.

freedom of association *n.* The right, protected by the First Amendment to the United States Constitution, to gather or associate with others for any purpose that would be lawful if pursued individually.

freedom of contract *n.* The right of individuals to consent to binding contracts without government intervention.

freedom of expression *n.* Collectively, the rights, guaranteed by the First Amendment to the United States Constitution, to engage in freedom of speech, freedom of association, freedom of the press, and freedom of religion.

Freedom of Information Act *n.* A federal law that allows individuals and organizations to compel the federal government to release copies of documents it might not otherwise choose to disclose. Abbreviated **FOIA.**

freedom of religion *n.* The right, guaranteed by the First Amendment to the United States Constitution, to choose religious practices or to abstain from any without government intervention.

freedom of speech *n.* The right, guaranteed by the First Amendment to the

United States Constitution, to communicate ideas and opinions without government intervention.

freedom of the press *n.* The right, guaranteed by the First Amendment to the United States Constitution to publish and distribute information in books, magazines, and newspapers without government intervention.

freehold *n.* An ownership estate or possessory interest in land, particularly a **fee simple** or **life estate.**

fresh pursuit *n.* Law enforcement: the pursuit of a suspect in flight. A police officer may leave his or her jurisdiction while in active pursuit, or may search a building the suspect has entered without first obtaining a warrant.

friend of the court *n.* Litigation: An individual or organization filing an **amicus curiae** brief in an action to which he or it is not a party. A friend of the court must show a strong interest in the matters under consideration by the court. See also **amicus curiae.**

frisk **1** *v.* To search another for a weapon or contraband. **2** *n.* The search of another for a weapon or contraband. See also **search.**

frivolous *adj.* Of a claim or assertion in litigation, that it lacks merit or substance; often a pejorative term, implying bad faith or negligence by the pleading party.

frolic *n.* In tort law: of an employee, that he or she, during business hours, deviated from the scope of employment to the extent that the employer will not be held responsible for harm resulting from the employee's actions. The term typically refers to circumstances in which the employee pursued a personal interest during the hours of employment.

fruit of the poisonous tree *n.* Constitutional law: otherwise competent evidence obtained from an illegal search, which will not be admitted at trial because of the illegality of the manner in which it was obtained.

frustration *n.* Contract law: an inability to carry out a contract or perform a term of the contract due to supervening circumstances beyond the parties' control, such as an event of **force majeure.**

full age *n.* The age of majority, when an individual can marry, sign contracts, and so on.

full court See **court.**

full faith and credit *n.* The requirement under the United States Constitution, Article IV, that a state respect the laws and court decisions of other states.

full warranty *n.* Contract law: as opposed to a limited warranty, a warranty that completely covers the repair or replacement of any defect in a consumer product.

fundamental fairness *n.* A synonym for due process; the conditions under which due process is obtained.

fundamental right *n.* A basic or foundational right, derived from natural law; a right deemed by the Supreme Court to receive the highest level of Constitutional protection against government interference.

fungible *adj.* Of goods or products, that they are all of a kind, not unique, and replaceable by other goods of the same kind; for example, crops are fungible while a painting by Rembrandt is not.

further assurance *n.* A clause in a deed in which the transferor of real property promises to execute any other documents that may be needed to complete the transfer or protect the interest granted to the transferee.

future interest *n.* With real property, an ownership or possessory interest that does not presently exist, but will come into being upon the occurrence of an event or condition.

G

GAAP See **generally accepted accounting principles.**

GAAS See **generally accepted auditing standards.**

gag order *n.* In litigation, a court's order to the parties and witnesses not to speak to the press or public about the case.

gain *n.* The profit on a sale (the selling price minus costs).

>   *capital gain.* In tax law, the taxable profit realized from the sale or exchange of real property, stock, or other capital property.

garnish *v.* To seize a debtor's property, held by a third party, in order to recover a debt; commonly against debtor's earnings from an employer.

garnishee *n.* An individual or entity in possession of a debtor's property or monies that a creditor seeks to **garnish.**

garnishment *n.* In litigation, a judicial process in which a creditor seeks the seizure of a debtor's property, held in possession by a third party.

garnishor *n.* A creditor who brings an action of **garnishment.**

GATT See **General Agreement on Tariffs and Trade.**

General Agreement on Tariffs and Trade *n.* An international agreement governing imports and exports; predecessor to the World Trade Organization.

generally accepted accounting principles *n.* Standards adopted by the accounting profession for the form and content of financial statements. Abbreviated as GAAP.

generally accepted auditing standards *n.* Standards adopted by the accounting profession governing the audit of corporations and organizations. Abbreviated as GAAS.

generation-skipping transfer *n.* A grant of assets to a grandchild or other grantee who is more than one generation removed from the grantor.

generation-skipping transfer tax *n.* A tax assessed upon a **generation-skipping transfer.**

generation-skipping trust *n.* A trust created for the purpose of carrying out a **generation-skipping transfer.**

generic *adj.* In trademark law, a term or phrase that is merely descriptive and cannot be trademarked; with pharmaceuticals or other products, a non-trademarked equivalent offered in competition against a brand-name product.

generic-drug law *n.* A law allowing pharmacists to offer customers less expensive generic drugs when filling prescriptions for a brand-name drug.

generic name *n.* A word or phrase that cannot be trademarked because it is only descriptive of a product or service.

genetic mother *n.* The mother who provided the egg from which an embryo developed and, therefore, contributed to the genetic makeup of the ensuing child.

gentlemen's agreement *n. Colloquial.* An unwritten agreement, not enforceable by law but backed by the parties' good faith.

germane *adj.* Pertaining to the subject matter at hand.

gerrymandering *v.* Apportioning legislative districts in a way calculated to give an undue advantage to a political party, by concentrating its members or separating those of another party from one another; implies lines drawn in an otherwise illogical way.

gift 1 *n.* Property given as a present. 2 *v.* The action of making a present of property.

> *class gift.* A gift made to a group of persons, the number of whom is determined at the time of the gift.

> *gift causa mortis. (Latin.)* A gift made by a donor in the expectation that he or she will die soon after.

> *gift over.* A gift that becomes effective only upon the expiration of a prior transfer (such as a life estate).

> *inter vivos gift.* An irrevocable gift made during the owner's lifetime.

> *testamentary gift.* A gift made by will.

gift tax *n.* A tax levied on the value of property given as a **gift,** imposed upon the donor of the gift.

give *v.* To make a gift; to transfer property to another without payment; to grant something to another.

going concern *n.* A business that is being actively conducted.

good behavior *n.* In criminal sentencing law, the conduct by a prisoner that may justify a reduction in his or her sentence.

good cause *n.* A necessary showing by a litigant to convince a court to issue an order favorable to that litigant.

good faith *n.* A party's state of mind in acting or carrying out an action or transaction, evincing honesty, fairness, full communication of any hidden issues or information, and an absence of intent to harm other individuals or parties to the transaction.

good faith exception *n.* A doctrine that evidence may be introduced at trial, despite the invalidity of a warrant for its seizure, if the police acted in the **good faith** belief that the warrant was valid.

goods *n.* Items of personal property offered or sold in commerce.

Good Samaritan doctrine *n.* The doctrine that an individual reasonably acting to rescue or aid another shall not be held liable for contributory negligence in causing injury to the person aided.

Good Samaritan law *n.* A state law protecting from lawsuits individuals who reasonably attempt to rescue or aid another; designed to encourage public acts of assistance.

goods and chattels *n.* Personal property.

government *n.* 1 The political organization by which a state or nation is ruled. 2 In criminal cases, the prosecution is occasionally referred to as the **government**.

grade *n.* A level of seriousness of a crime, which assists in determining the sentence to be given.

grand *adj.* An offense that involves an aggravating factor, such as the theft of a larger sum or the use or threat of force, and, therefore, warrants a higher sentence; for example, **grand larceny.**

grand larceny *v.* The taking, with intent to keep, of property valued above a certain dollar amount which varies from one jurisdiction to another.

grandfather *v.* To include a person or entity in the benefits conferred by a **grandfather clause.**

grandfather clause *n.* A legislative provision stating that anyone who has previously enjoyed a particular status may continue to do so, despite a change in the applicable law or rules denying that status to anyone newly applying for it.

grant **1** *n.* A transaction in which a **grantor** transfers a subset of his or her own rights in property; the rights so transferred. **2** *v.* To transfer rights in real or personal property; in litigation, accession by the court to a party's request made by motion or pleading.

grantee *n.* The recipient of a **grant.**

granting clause *n.* The section of a contract that sets forth the terms of a **grant.**

grantor *n.* The individual or entity making a **grant.**

grantor trust *n.* A trust whose maker retains control over the management of the trust assets and the distribution of its income.

gravamen *n.* The substance or core argument of a legal document or position taken.

green card *n.* An identification card granted by the United States Immigration and Naturalization Service to legal, permanent residents.

greenmail *n.* The act of purchasing shares in a publicly traded company that could be used to support a hostile takeover, and then selling them back to the company at a profit.

grievance *n.* In labor law, a complaint filed with or by a union to challenge an employer's treatment of one or more union members.

ground lease *n.* A lengthy lease of real property (often for 99 years).

guarantee **1** *n.* A commitment by a third party to make good in the event of a default by a party to a contract, by paying the money or providing the perform-

ance due from the defaulting party. **2** *v.* To promise to make good in the event of a default by a party to a contract by paying the money or providing the performance due from the defaulting party.

guarantor *n.* One who makes a **guarantee.**

guaranty See **guarantee.**

guardian *n.* An individual designated by law to care for another's person and property because of the former's incompetence to make his or her own decisions.

guardian ad litem *n.* Representative appointed by a court to protect and represent the interests of one incapable of acting on own behalf, such as child or incompetent person.

guest statute *n.* A law that bars, or strictly limits, a nonpaying guest in a private vehicle from suing the driver for damages resulting from an accident; such laws vary from state to state and are now rare.

guilt phase *n.* In a criminal trial, the portion of the trial in which the defendant's guilt is adjudicated, as opposed to the portion in which a sentence is determined for a defendant who was found guilty in the prior phase (the sentencing phase).

guilty *n.* The state of being deemed responsible for the commission of a crime, either as a result of a plea or the adjudication of a judge or jury.

gun-control law *n.* A statute regulating the private ownership of firearms.

H

habeas corpus *n.* In criminal procedure, a process to challenge the detention of a prisoner; frequently used as a way to attack a conviction in federal court when state appeals have been exhausted.

habendum clause *n.* In real estate, the language in a deed setting forth the interest being granted and any limitations upon it.

habitability *n.* In real estate, the condition of being amenable for occupancy; the absence of conditions that would interfere significantly with a tenant's ability to occupy the premises.

halfway house *n.* A transitional facility to which convicted criminals are paroled for some period of time, in advance of full release into the community.

hand down *v.* For a judge or court to release a decision upon a motion or at the resolution of a trial or appeal.

hand up *v.* For a grand jury to process an indictment of an accused.

hanging judge *n. Pejorative.* A judge who has the reputation of applying overly harsh sentences in criminal cases.

harassment *n.* Unjustifiable conduct, typically persistent and repetitive, aimed at an individual, that causes distress or discomfort.

hard labor *n.* Physical work imposed on prisoners as an aspect of punishment.

hardship *n.* The difficulty or distress resulting to an individual or entity from a court decision, zoning decision, or passage of a law; taken into account as one factor in an **equity** proceeding.

harmless error *n.* A mistake by the judge that does not interfere with a party's rights or remedies and that, therefore, does not warrant reversal of the decision.

hate crime See **crime**.

hate speech *n.* Speech not protected by the First Amendment, because it is intended to foster hatred against individuals or groups based on race, religion, gender, sexual preference, place of national origin, or other improper classification.

headnote *n.* A note prepared by an editor and placed in front of the published version of a court decision, analyzing or summarizing the facts, precedents, and legal impact of the decision.

head of household *n.* The individual providing the primary support for a family.

hearing *n.* **1** In litigation or administrative procedure, any proceeding in which the parties have the opportunity to present evidence or testimony to the court or **fact-finder.** **2** In legislation, a session at which legislators hear witnesses on the advisability or efficacy of proposed legislation.

hearsay *n.* An out of court statement offered for the truth of the matter asserted. Testimony of a witness as to statements made by another individual who is not present in the courtroom to testify; generally not admissible because of unreliability (the hearsay rule), but there have been many significant exceptions to the rule, where there are certain indicia of reliability. See also **excited utterance.**

heat of passion   *adj.* characterization of acts done while actor is in state of extreme stress or explosive anger. See also **voluntary manslaughter.**

heir   *n.* Colloquially used to refer to anyone who inherits under a will or otherwise.

> *collateral heir.* A descendant through an indirect line, such as the issue of a sibling or cousin. See also **issue.**

> *heirs and assigns. Archaic.* A phrase formerly necessary for the creation of a **fee simple.**

> *lineal heir.* An heir who is above or below the decedent in the direct line of descent, such as a parent or child.

hereditary succession   *n.* Inheritance pursuant to the common-law doctrines of succession.

hidden defect   *n.* A **defect** not discoverable by a reasonable inspection by the purchaser.

hidden tax   *n.* A tax on goods that is passed to the consumer in the form of higher prices.

hijack   *v.* To take over control of a vehicle or airplane by use of the threat of force.

hit-and-run statute   *n.* A state law requiring a car involved in an accident not to leave the scene, pending the arrival of the authorities.

HLA test   *n. abbr.* A paternity test utilizing genetic material.

holder   *n.* An individual or entity that has ownership or legal possession of a negotiable instrument, security, or other document of title.

holder in due course   *n.* Under the Uniform Commercial Code, one who has given value in exchange for the possession of a negotiable instrument and is unaware of any defects in title.

hold harmless   *v.* To **indemnify** another against financial liability arising from a transaction.

holding   *n.* The decision of a court or judge; the reasoning underlying such a decision.

holding company   See **company.**

holding period   *n.* The period for which an asset must be held to be entitled to the more favorable capital-gains tax rate.

holdover   *n.* The act of staying beyond the end of a lease.

holograph   *n.* A handwritten document.

holographic will   *n.* A will set forth completely in handwriting; many states do not recognize such documents as valid, while others recognize the validity only if the entire instrument is written in the handwriting of the deceased.

home rule   *n.* The allocation of power to local governments over matters that might otherwise be regulated at the state level.

homestead   *n.* Houses, other buildings, and land comprising a residence.

homicide   *n.* The killing of a human being, committed by another.

> *justifiable homicide.* The killing of a human excused by the law as appropriate or necessary; for example, in self-defense.

> *negligent homicide.* The killing of another by an act of irresponsibility or lack of attention to duty, rather than by intentional act.

vehicular homicide. The killing of another by operation of a motor vehicle; generally the driver's acts must be more than just negligent; for example, in a motor vehicle accident arising from the intoxication of the driver, where another is killed.

horizontal privity See **privity.**

hornbook *n. Colloquial.* A law textbook, often one relied upon as authoritative in the field.

hornbook law. *adj.* A term used to characterize a proposition of law that is so basic and well-known that it is accepted without further proof or citation.

hostile possession *n.* Possession in derogation of the owner or others who have conflicting rights in property.

hostile witness *n.* A witness who is expected to make assertions that are adverse to those being set forth by the party calling the witness. Because of the adverse nature, the questioning lawyer is given wide latitude to question the hostile witness by way of leading questions, not ordinarily permitted on direct examination. Typically called to establish the truth of matters that cannot be proved through a friendly witness.

hung jury *v.* For a jury to be deadlocked and unable to reach a verdict.

husband-wife immunity See **spousal immunity.**

hypothecate *v.* To grant a security interest in something as collateral for a debt.

hypothetical question *n.* A question, based on assumptions rather than facts, directed to an expert witness intended to elicit an opinion.

I

ibid. *abbr. Latin.* When citing a work, indicates that the citation is to the same volume and page as the previous citation.

ICC *abbr.* See **Interstate Commerce Commission.**

id. *abbr. Latin.* Like **ibid.,** indicates that a citation is identical to the immediate past one.

identity *n.* A sameness between two items or designs such that one violates patent rights held by the other.

ignorantia juris non excusat *Latin.* Ignorance of the law is no excuse; typically refers to criminal charges, in which such ignorance is not a cognizable defense.

illegally obtained evidence *n.* Evidence obtained in violation of a law or a constitutional requirement.

illegitimacy *n.* The status of being born to parents who are not married to one another.

illegitimate *adj.* **1** Of a child, that he or she was born to parents not married to one another. **2** Wrongful or unlawful.

illusory *adj.* Deceptive or insubstantial.

> *illusory promise.* A promise to do something that is unenforceable or meaningless because the promisor has means of avoiding the commitment.

immediate cause See **cause.**

immigration *n.* The act of entering a country with the intention of remaining there permanently.

immunity *n.* **1** An exemption from a duty or penalty. **2** A permanent status, as for a diplomat, exempting one from being sued or prosecuted for certain actions. **3** A special status, granted by a prosecutor, exempting a witness from being prosecuted for the acts to which he or she testifies.

> *sovereign immunity.* The doctrine (subject to certain exceptions) that a government may not be sued in its own courts or in courts of another nation or level of government; many limitations on this doctrine apply and vary from state to state. Sometimes referred to as governmental immunity.

> *transactional immunity.* A grant of immunity to a witness by a prosecutor that exempts the witness from being prosecuted for the acts about which the witness will testify.

> *use immunity.* A grant of immunity to a witness by a prosecutor, under which the prosecutor promises not to use the witness' testimony against him or her, but reserves the right to prosecute the witness for the underlying action.

impact rule *n.* The rule that a plaintiff cannot claim damages for **negligent infliction of emotional distress** unless there has been some physical impact, such as an assault. Example: a parent of a child injured in an auto accident cannot recover for his/her own distress in seeing child physically injured, unless parent also sustained own physical injury.

impair *v.* Of property or a contractual right, to interfere in such a way as to diminish its value.

impeachment *n.* **1** An attack on the credibility of a witness for reasons relating to prior inconsistent testimony or evidence of lying. **2** An administrative procedure, defined in the United States Constitution, under which the president or another government official is brought up on charges and tried by the Congress, and, if convicted, is removed from office.

impertinent matter *n.* Irrelevant material in a pleading.

impleader *n.* A procedure under which one of the parties brings in a third party, typically in an attempt to hold the third party liable on a claim or counterclaim made against the party who is bringing in the third party.

implication *n.* An inference.

implied *adj.* Of something that is inferred, rather than plainly expressed.

implied authority *n.* Authority of an agent inferred from surrounding circumstances, such as the principal's previous acquiescence to the exercise of similar authority.

implied consent See **consent.**

implied contract *n.* A contract inferred from the actions of the parties.

implied easement See **easement.**

implied notice See **notice.**

implied power *n.* A political power not expressly named in a constitution but that is inferred because it is necessary to the performance of an enumerated power.

implied warranty See **warranty.**

import **1** *n.* A product brought in the course of commerce into a country other than the one in which it originated **2** *v.* The process of bringing in such products.

impossibility *n.* The condition of being unable to happen or to be achieved.

> *factual impossibility.* Of an act that cannot physically be done.

> *legal impossibility.* In criminal law, a defense to charges on the basis that the acts committed were not illegal. In civil law, an act which is impossible by operation of law or rule, such as an attempt by a minor to enter into a binding contract.

impound *v.* To take personal property (such as an automobile) into police or judicial custody, pending further proceedings.

impoundment *n.* The condition of being taken into police or judicial custody, pending further proceedings.

improvement *n.* A modification to real estate that increases its value.

impute *v.* To infer or attribute responsibility or causation.

imputed income See **income.**

in absentia *n. Latin.* In the absence of.

inalienable *adj.* Of property, that it cannot be sold or assigned; of rights, that they cannot be abrogated.

in camera *n. Latin.* In the judge's chambers; implying a private, closed, or informal hearing or conference before the judge.

incapacity *n.* **1** A lack of physical or mental ability or standing. **2** Inability to take actions that are legally effective, such as signing a contract, due to age, mental status, or other factors.

incendiary *n.* **1** An arsonist. **2** A bomb or combination of chemicals used to start a fire.

inchoate *adj.* Commenced but not completed, partially done, generally used in contract law to describe an undertaking which has been agreed upon, but as to which all necessary formalities (for example, signatures on the document) have not been completed.

income *n.* Money received for services performed, products sold, as interest on investments, as royalties on inventions or creative works, or generally in exchange for some performance or consideration.

adjusted gross income. Gross income minus deductions permitted by the Internal Revenue Code.

gross income. Income prior to any exemptions, exclusions, or deductions.

imputed income. The doctrine that, under certain circumstances, a taxpayer realizes taxable income as a result of the use or consumption of his or her own property.

income in respect of a decedent. Income due to a person before death but not collected until afterward.

net income. Income after all exemptions, exclusions, and deductions.

ordinary income. Income from routine or everyday activities, such as the operations of a business or the labor of an individual.

taxable income. Same as net income.

income statement *n.* An accounting document setting forth the income and expense of a business organization over some period of time.

income tax *n.* A tax on the net income of an individual or business entity.

incompetency *n.* **1** Absence of legal capacity to perform certain acts, such as testifying at a trial. **2** Absence of the legal capacity to understand the charges against one and to participate in one's own trial.

incompetent *adj.* **1** Of evidence, that it is not admissible. **2** Of a witness, that he or she is not permitted to testify, on the grounds that his or her testimony is not relevant or is subject to some other disqualification.

incompetent evidence *n.* Evidence that is not admissible.

inconsistent *adj.* Of an assertion, that is contradictory or not supported.

incorporate *v.* **1** To form a business corporation. **2** To include or merge something into something else.

incorporation *n.* **1** The process of forming a business corporation. **2** The doctrine that the Bill of Rights is applied to the states by inclusion in the Fourteenth Amendment right of due process.

incorporeal *adj.* Having no tangible existence.

incorrigible child *n.* A child who cannot be managed by his parents or guardians.

increment *n.* A measurable or metaphorical increase in quantity or quality.

incriminate *v.* To reveal someone's involvement in criminal acts.

inculpatory evidence *n.* Evidence establishing the guilt of the accused.

indebtedness *n.* **1** The condition of owing money to another. **2** The money owed.

indecency *n.* Of speech, the state of being crude and offensive, typically in a sexual manner.

indecent *adj.* Of speech, that it is crude and offensive, typically in a sexual manner.

indecent exposure *n.* Publicly displaying portions of one's body, especially the genitals, that are usually covered by clothing.

indefeasible *adj.* Of a right, that it cannot be cancelled or defeated.

indefinite failure of issue *n.* Language used in wills to denote a descendant's death without children at any time in the future, with no time limitation applied.

in delicto *Latin.* In the wrong.

indemnify *v.* To promise to make good another's financial loss or liability resulting from a particular event or contingency.

indemnity *n.* **1** A duty, typically arising from contract, in which one promises to make good another's financial loss or liability, resulting from a particular event or contingency. **2** The act of making good another's financial loss or liability, resulting from the occurrence of a particular event or contingency. **3** The injured party's right to claim payment from the party with the duty.

indenture *n.* A document such as a mortgage or deed of trust, which provides for security for a financial obligation, and which sets forth essential terms such as interest rate and due date or maturity date.

independent contractor *n.* See **contractor.**

indictable offense *n.* A level of crime for which a defendant must be indicted by a grand jury in order to be prosecuted (typically a **felony**).

indictment *n.* **1** A charge made by a grand jury against a defendant. **2** The process of making such a charge.

indigency *n.* **1** A state of poverty. **2** In criminal/constitutional law, the state of not being able to afford an attorney.

indispensable evidence *n.* Evidence that is necessary for the proof of a particular assertion.

indispensable party *n.* A party who must be included in the case, due to the inevitablity of his or her interests being affected by the court's judgment in same.

individual retirement account *n.* A tax-deferred retirement account established by federal law. The portion of annual income contributed to the account is not taxed until it is drawn out after retirement age. Abbreviated IRA.

indorsee *n.* The person to whom a negotiable instrument is assigned by **indorsement.**

indorsement *n.* **1** The act of placing a signature on the back of a negotiable instrument in order to assign it to an **indorsee.** **2** The signature itself.

accommodation indorsement. A signature by a third party who is neither the **payor** or the **payee,** but is acting to **guarantee** payment by the former.

blank indorsement. A signature that names no payee, thereby making the instrument payable to the bearer.

restrictive indorsement. An indorsement placing special conditions upon the assignment of the instrument.

special indorsement. An indorsement naming the payee (or, for a transfer of goods, the person to whom they must be delivered).

indorser   *n.* A person who assigns a negotiable instrument to another by **indorsement.**

inducement   *n.* In contract law, the material reason for undertaking certain obligations. In criminal law, motive or that which leads to the commission of a crime.

ineffective assistance of counsel   *n.* Basis for appeal of criminal conviction, on grounds that lawyer did not properly represent the defendant.

in extremis   *Latin.* Upon the point of dying.

infamous crime   See **crime.**

infancy   *n.* **1** The earliest stage of childhood. **2** More generally used to describe a person prior to the age of majority.

inference   *n.* A logical conclusion drawn from available facts; the process of arriving at such a conclusion.

infirmity   *n.* Debility caused by ill health or advanced age.

informal proceeding   *n.* Any adversarial proceeding designed to be conducted rapidly and with a minimum set of procedural requirements; for example, a trial in small-claims court.

in forma pauperis   *Latin.* In litigation, to proceed as an indigent. Abbreviated i.f.p.

information   *n.* A criminal charge, typically for a lesser offense, that is filed by a prosecutor without resorting to a grand jury.

information and belief   *n.* In litigation, language traditionally used in an affidavit to denote that the deponent has received from others, and believes, the information that he or she is communicating.

information return   *n.* A tax return intended to communicate information about the taxpayer's activities or status to the Internal Revenue Service, but upon which no tax is due.

informed consent   See **consent.**

informer   *n.* One who, privy to the commission of a crime, confidentially communicates with the police or other governmental entity about it.

infra   *adj./adv. Latin.* See below; referring to the placement of a particular citation or assertion in a text.

infringement   *n.* Violation of a copyright, patent, or trademark.

in futuro   *adv. Latin.* In the future.

ingress   *n.* **1** The action of entering land or premises.   **2** Access to land or premises.

inherent power   *n.* A power that must be deemed to exist in order for a particular responsibility to be carried out.

inherit   *v.* To receive a transfer of property under intestacy laws, or as a bequest, upon the death of a relative.

inheritance   *n.* **1** Property received via bequest or intestate succession.   **2** The act of receiving such property.

initiative   *n.* An electoral process available in some states in which citizens vote on proposed legislation.

injunction   *n.* A judge's order to a party compelling or prohibiting certain described conduct.

mandatory injunction. An injunction compelling a party to perform an action.

permanent injunction. An injunction granted after a trial on the merits, which forms part of the final judgment in the case.

preliminary injunction. An injunction granted before trial, to preserve the status quo pending the court's final determination. Also known as an *interlocutory injunction.*

injury *n.* A violation of rights, or harm inflicted on an individual, for which damages or relief may be sought in court.

in kind *adv.* Payment made in goods or services, rather than in cash.

in limine *adv.* A motion presented at the outset of a case to determine the admissibility of certain evidence.

in loco parentis *adj./adv. Latin.* Acting in place of a parent.

inmate *n.* An individual confined in a correctional or psychiatric institution.

innuendo *n. Latin.* **1** An indirect or suggestive remark, usually a disparagement of someone. **2** A section in a **libel** pleading explaining the plaintiff's construction of the defendant's allegedly libelous utterances.

in pais *adv. Archaic.* Outside of court.

in pari delicto *adv. Latin.* At equal fault.

in pari materia *adj. Latin.* On the same topic or pertaining to the same subject matter.

in perpetuity *adv.* For eternity; without limit of time.

in personam *adj. Latin.* Pertaining to a person or personal rights or interests, as opposed to **in rem.**

in posse *adv. Latin.* Latent; not currently in existence.

in praesenti *adv. Latin.* Currently; at present.

inquest *n.* **1** An inquiry into a suspicious death conducted by a coroner or medical examiner. **2** An inquiry into a particular subject matter by a special jury. **3** A judge's determination of damages after a defendant's default.

inquest jury *n.* A jury empanelled to investigate the circumstances of a death.

in re *Latin.* In regard to. Used in the title of cases involving an interest in property.

in rem *adj. Latin.* Pertaining to a thing or to property. Litigation in rem (as opposed to **in personam**) determines the respective rights to property that has been brought before the court.

quasi in rem. A type of case initiated by the seizure of property that is within the court's jurisdiction, as a step toward obtaining monetary damages against an individual who is outside the jurisdiction of the court.

insanity *n.* A mental disorder that deprives a criminal defendant of capacity to be tried.

insanity defense *n.* A defendant's assertion that a mental disorder excuses the defendant from legal responsibility for a crime.

insolvency *n.* The status of being unable to pay one's debts when due.

inspection *n.* A detailed examination of objects, such as goods or discovery materials, to determine qualities such as fitness, relevance, or consistency with a prior description.

installment *n.* A partial payment of a debt scheduled to be made at regular intervals.

installment contract See **contract.**

installment sale *n.* A contract for the sale of goods such as furniture, in which the purchaser makes periodic payments and the seller retains a security interest in the goods until paid in full.

instrument *n.* A written legal document defining the parties' rights and liabilities to one another.

> *negotiable instrument.* Under the Uniform Commercial Code, a writing that reflects an unconditional promise to pay, such as a check or note, but does not also include security for the payment.

insufficient evidence *n.* Evidence so inadequate to prove an assertion that it will not even support a presumption.

insurable interest See **interest.**

insurance *n.* An agreement by an insurer to provide compensation or another benefit upon the occurrence of a specified risk causing harm to property or the person of an **insured.**

> *casualty insurance.* Insurance for loss or injury to person or property.

> *indemnity insurance.* Insurance which protects against loss, as opposed to insurance against one's liability to others.

> *liability insurance.* Insurance which protects against one's liability to others, as with automobile insurance that provides coverage for accidents in which the policyholder is at fault, or homeowners' insurance, which provides coverage for injury to those who are injured while on the homeowner's property.

> *life insurance.* Insurance for loss of life.

insured *n.* A person who pays for and receives the prospective benefit of an insurance policy.

intangible *n.* Impalpable; not capable of being touched or otherwise detected by the senses.

integration *n.* **1** The merger of all agreements and understandings between parties pertaining to a particular subject matter into a single written agreement. **2** The removal of racial barriers in society, providing equal access to all public facilities.

intendment *n.* The legislature's intention in passing a particular law.

intent *n.* **1** The perpetrator's frame of mind in committing an criminal act. **2** The wishes and desires of the framers of the United States Constitution or of legislation.

> *original intent.* The view that the United States Constitution should be strictly construed in light of the framer's intentions, rather than with modern values and interpretations.

intentional infliction of emotional distress *v.* Intentionally causing another person extreme psychological suffering through one's actions.

inter alia *adv. Latin.* Among others.

interest *n.* **1** Ownership of, or other right in, property. **2** Legitimate concern with the outcome of a case or controversy, because of a likelihood that the outcome will affect one's property rights or other rights or privileges. **3** Compensation for making a loan, placing money on deposit, or other use of funds, expressed as a percentage of the principal, calculated and payable on a regular schedule.

> *compound interest.* Interest calculated both on the principal and on previously accrued interest.

Insurable interest. A legal interest in the safety of property or the health and wellbeing of another person sufficient to permit the purchase of an insurance policy.

interim relief *n.* Preliminary relief, such as an injunction, granted by the court to preserve the status quo pending trial.

interlocutory *adj.* Of an order, that it is temporary, pending a trial on the merits.

interlocutory order *n.* A preliminary order granted by a court pending a trial on the merits.

Internal Revenue Service *n.* A federal government agency charged with the collection of income taxes. Abbreviated IRS.

international agreement *n.* A contract or treaty signed by two or more sovereign nations.

International Court of Justice *n.* A tribunal established by the United Nations to hear cases submitted by the consent of United Nations members.

international law *n.* The entire body of rights and responsibilities existing between nations, including treaties and customs.

interpleader *n.* **1** An action by the neutral custodian of property to determine its proper owner. **2** One who brings such a suit.

interrogation *n.* The detailed questioning of a suspect by the police or other law-enforcement authorities.

interrogatory *n.* A form of **discovery** involving the submission of written questions to the other party.

in terrorem *adj./adv. Latin.* A characteristic marked by threat or warning.

in terrorem clause *n.* A provision in a contract or will that warns a beneficiary or party not to engage in certain behavior, by providing a prospective penalty for such behavior.

inter se *Latin.* Among themselves.

interstate commerce *n.* Business, including the sale of goods, conducted across state borders.

Interstate Commerce Commission *n.* A federal agency, no longer in existence today, that regulated interstate carriers.

intervening cause *n.* An event that interrupts the chain of causation by providing an independent cause of the final result, possibly relieving the original actors of liability.

intervention *n.* A procedure under which a nonparty who has a significant interest in the outcome of a case enters into and becomes a party in the case.

inter vivos *adj. Latin.* A conveyance of property between living parties and not by bequest.

intestate *adj.* The condition of having died without a will.

intestate succession *n.* The process used to distribute the property of one who died without a will.

in toto *adv. Latin.* In entirety.

intoxication *n.* The condition of being mentally or physically impaired due to the ingestion of alcohol or drugs.

intrinsic evidence *n.* Evidence appearing within a written document.

intrinsic fraud *n.* Fraud in a party's conduct of a prior litigation.

inure *v.* **1** To be given or to be attributable to. **2** To become used to.

invalid *adj.* Legally ineffective; unfounded.

invasion of privacy *n.* **1** An unjustifiable intrusion into one's personal affairs and information.

invest *v.* **1** To grant authority. **2** To place money in an income-producing opportunity.

investment tax credit *n.* A provision of law, now largely repealed, that permitted a portion of the purchase price of capital goods to be utilized as a credit against income taxes.

invitee *n.* One who enters upon premises with the permission of the owner.

involuntary *adj.* Performed against one's will.

involuntary bailment See **bailment.**

involuntary confession See **confession.**

involuntary manslaughter See **manslaughter.**

ipse dixit *Latin.* Asserted but unproven.

ipso facto *Latin.* As a matter of fact.

IRA See **individual retirement account.**

IRC *abbr.* Internal Revenue Code. Contains the current federal tax laws and is located in Title 26, United States Code.

irrelevant *adj.* With evidence or testimony, not pertinent to the claims or defenses in the case.

irreparable injury *n.* An injury not capable of being redressed by money damages, and that therefore supports a request for injunctive relief.

irresistible impulse test *n.* A form of insanity defense in which the defendant must establish that he or she was incapable of resisting the urge to commit the crime.

IRS See **Internal Revenue Service.**

issue *n.* **1** A question of law or fact disputed by the parties. **2** In estate law, the descendants of a common ancestor; offspring.

> *collateral issue.* Incidental to the central issue in a matter.

> *material issue.* An issue which directly bears on the outcome of a matter; significant to the determination of a fact in dispute.

itemized deduction *n.* A deduction listed separately as a line item on an income tax return.

J

J. *n. abbr.* Judge or justice.

jail *n.* A confinement facility whose inmates are individuals awaiting trial or convicted of lesser offenses.

J.D. *n. abbr.* **Juris Doctor** (a law degree).

Jencks material *n.* Written or recorded statements by a prosecution witnesses that must be disclosed to the defense.

jeopardy *n.* A defendant's risk of punishment.

JJ. *n. abbr.* Judges or justices.

joinder *n.* The combination of separate parties or claims into a single lawsuit.

> *compulsory joinder.* The required joinder of a party without whom a dispute cannot be fully resolved.

> *misjoinder.* The joining of a party who is not properly a part of the case.

> *nonjoinder.* The failure to join a party who should be part of the case.

> *permissive joinder.* The optional joinder of parties or claims because of an overlap in the issues or interests involved.

joint *adj.* An ownership interest or expectation shared by two or more individuals, as in a bank account or an estate.

joint account *n.* A bank account in the name of two or more individuals, each of whom has an undivided right to the entire balance.

joint and several liability *n.* Responsibility for a loss that is borne both individually and collectively by a group of defendants.

joint custody See **custody.**

joint enterprise *n.* **1** In criminal law, a conspiracy or cooperation of two or more individuals to commit a crime. **2** In tort law, a business enterprise conducted by several individuals, who each share in the liability arising from their activities.

joint liability See **liability.**

joint ownership *n.* Undivided ownership of the whole of an asset by two or more individuals. Upon the death of any one, his or her rights pass to the surviving owners rather than to the heirs of the decedent.

joint return *n.* A tax return filed by a husband and wife, each of whom is individually liable for the entire tax due.

joint-stock company See **company.**

joint tenancy See **tenancy.**

joint tortfeasors *n.* Two or more individuals or entities who contributed jointly to the harm suffered by the plaintiff and who may be held individually or collectively responsible.

jointure *n. Archaic.* A **life estate** that reverts to a wife after her husband's death.

joint venture *n.* An unincorporated business venture with two or more participants who share the financial risk and gain.

journalists' privilege *n.* A law or doctrine, arising out of the First Amendment, that shields reporters from being compelled to name confidential sources in court proceedings.

joyriding   *n.* The temporary appropriation of another's vehicle for use, typically without the intention of selling or destroying it.

J.P.   See **justice of the peace.**

judge   *n.* An appointed or elected official responsible for conducting a court in which he or she resolves legal controversies.

judge-made law   *n.* Legal doctrine established by court decisions rather than by statute.

judgment   *n.* A court's final resolution of the issues before it at trial or upon a dispositive motion.

> *default judgment.* A judgment entered due to the failure of the defendant to answer or otherwise respond to the claim.

> *deficiency judgment.* A judgment in favor of a creditor following a forced sale of property, for the difference between the amount owed and the amount collected as a result of the sale, so as to fully compensate the creditor.

> *final judgment.* A judgment which fully ends a case, on its merits (as opposed to on procedural grounds). A final judgment is generally necessary before a party can file an appeal.

> *foreign judgment.* A judgment of a different state or country than the one in which the judgment is being challenged or as to which enforcement is sought.

> *judgment creditor.* A creditor who has obtained, through judicial process, a judgment against a debtor; commonly used in bankruptcy proceedings to distinguish such a creditor from others to whom the debtor owes money but do not have judgments. Judgment creditors may be entitled to preferential distribution of a debtor's money if there are insufficient assets to pay all creditors.

> *judgment debtor.* A debtor who owes money to a creditor who has obtained a judgment against the debtor in that amount. See *judgment creditor.*

> *judgment docket.* A roll or listing of judgments maintained by a clerk or administrative office of a court.

> *judgment in rem.* A judgment that disposes of property, or resolves competing interests in a piece of property, as opposed to a judgment that is against a person ordering payment of money.

> *judgment lien.* A lien against property that results from a judicial proceeding in which a monetary award has been made and has been reduced to judgment; until payment of the judgment, a lien will be placed against all real property (and some personal property) of the individual or entity that owes payment of the judgment.

> *judgment non obstante veridicto. Latin.* Judgment notwithstanding the verdict. In rare cases, a judge may enter a judgment in favor of one party despite a jury's award against that party; generally in cases where the evidence was such that no reasonable jury could have come to the determination that it did. Abbreviated j.n.o.v.

> *judgment of conviction.* The final decision in a criminal case, which includes the plea taken by the defendant, the verdict, any court findings, and the ultimate sentence.

> *judgment of dismissal.* A judgment invalidating or otherwise disposing of the plaintiff's or the prosecutor's claims prior to a trial.

judgment on the merits. A judgment issued after the parties have had a full chance to present evidence and witnesses at trial.

judgment on the pleadings. A judgment that is issued on the pleadings alone, either on the basis that the plaintiff's pleadings are inadequate or that the defendant has failed to plead any fact that negates the plaintiff's claims or raises an affirmative defense.

personal judgment. A judgment imposing personal liability on a defendant.

judgment proof *adj.* Of a defendant, that he or she has no assets against which a **judgment** may be executed.

judicature *n.* **1** The administration of justice via a court system. **2** The judges serving in such a court system. **3** The office and duties of a **judge.**

judicial activism *n.* A usually pejorative phrase implying that a judge is applying his or her own political views, rather than basing decisions on law or prior precedent.

judicial admission *n.* An admission made by a party in court as to an opposing party's assertion, or a failure to formally dispute an assertion, resulting in that assertion being treated as an incontrovertible fact in the remaining court proceedings.

judicial discretion *n.* Of matters left within the personal choice of a judge, not to be reviewed or overruled by a higher court.

judicial economy *n.* Efficiency in the management of a particular litigation or of the courts in general; refers to measures taken to avoid unnecessary effort or expense on the part of the court or the court system.

judicial immunity *n.* The **immunity** of a judge from civil action for official activities.

judicial notice *n.* Regarding evidence, the court's acceptance of the truth of certain universally admitted facts without the necessity of proof.

judicial restraint *n.* The doctrine that cases should be decided on the narrowest possible grounds, without resolving unnecessary issues, especially political or social controversies.

judicial review *n.* A court's power of review of the decisions of lower courts or of the actions of other branches of government.

judiciary *n.* **1** The court system. **2** The branch of government in which judges serve. **3** Collectively, the judges in a particular court system or in all court systems.

jump bail *v.* See **bail jumping.**

jural *adj.* Pertaining to law or legal matters.

jurat *n. Latin.* A certification at the bottom of an affidavit or deposition by a notary public that states the paper was signed, and thereby sworn to, in his or her presence by the individual who signed it.

jurisdiction *n.* **1** The power wielded by a government over its subjects, their property, and the land and natural resources within its boundaries. **2** A court's authority over persons or property brought before or appearing before it. **3** The geographical area within which a government's or a court's power may be applied.

ancillary jurisdiction. The authority of a court to decide secondary or subsidiary claims raised by a case properly before it.

appellate jurisdiction. An appeals court's power of review of the decisions of lower courts.

concurrent jurisdiction. The overlapping jurisdiction of two or more courts over the same cause of action.

exclusive jurisdiction. The sole court or forum in which an action may be heard or tried, as no other courts or tribunals have authority over the person or the subject matter.

federal question jurisdiction. The authority of the federal district courts to try cases that raise an issue of federal or constitutional law.

in personam jurisdiction. The court's authority over an individual who resides or is found within the court's geographical area.

in rem jurisdiction. The court's authority to adjudicate rights in real or personal property located within the court's geographical area.

jurisdictional amount. The minimum or maximum amount to invoke a particular court's jurisdiction over the matter; in some lower courts, e.g., small claims court, there may be a limitation above which relief must be sought in a higher court; in federal court, a minimum amount in controversy is required in certain cases, e.g., diversity cases.

limited jurisdiction. Jurisdiction over only certain types of cases, or claims under certain financial limits or subject to other restrictions.

original jurisdiction. A court's status as the first court that has authority to hear a particular claim.

pendent jurisdiction. A court's authority over claims that would not ordinarily be brought before it, but that are secondary or subsidiary to claims properly before it.

subject matter jurisdiction. A court's authority over particular types of cases or of relief.

Juris Doctor   *n.* The law degree conferred by most American law schools. Abbreviated **J.D.**

jurisprudence   *n.* **1** The study of the fundamental structure of a particular legal system or of legal systems in general. **2** A body of case law serving as precedent.

jurist   *n.* **1.** A **judge.** **2** A legal scholar.

juror   *n.* An individual selected and sworn in to serve on a **jury,** deciding factual issues in a civil or criminal case.

jury   *n.* A group of individuals selected and sworn in to serve as the finders of fact in a civil or criminal trial, or in the case of a **grand jury,** to decide whether the facts warrant an **indictment** of the defendant.

> *blue-ribbon jury.* A jury for which only highly educated individuals have been selected, because they will be dealing with technical subject matter.

> *grand jury.* A jury selected and sworn in by a prosecutor to determine whether to issue indictments.

> *petit jury.* A jury selected to decide the facts in a trial (effectively, any jury other than a **grand jury**).

jury instruction   *n.* An instruction given by the court to a jury at the conclusion of presentation of all evidence in a trial, and after the lawyers' closing arguments, to advise the jury of the law that applies to the facts of the case, and the manner in which they should conduct their deliberations.

jury trial   *n.* A trial in which a **jury** will serve as the finder of fact.

just compensation   See **compensation.**

jus tertii   *n. Latin.* The rights of third parties affected by a controversy or claim.

justice   *n.* The balanced and equitable administration of law.

justice of the peace   *n.* A local official, not necessarily an attorney or judge, with jurisdiction over limited matters such as performing weddings or resolving minor civil or criminal complaints.

justiciability   *n.* Of a claim or controversy, the condition of being suitable for adjudication by a particular court.

justifiable homicide   See **homicide.**

justification   *n.* A showing of an appropriate reason for one's actions.

juvenile court   See **court.**

juvenile delinquent   *n.* A minor who has committed criminal acts.

K

kangaroo court *n. Pejorative.* Of an unfair court, in which justice cannot be obtained.

Keogh plan *n.* A tax-deferred retirement plan available only to the self-employed and their employees.

key-number system *n.* A scheme of numerical classification of cases utilized by West Publishing Company in its legal treatises and case reporters.

kickback *n.* A form of bribery in which a percentage of the revenues from a contract or other financial award is illicitly returned to the person awarding the contract or benefit.

kidnapping *n.* The felony of abducting an individual by force.

kin *n.* A relation, typically by blood; sometimes used to refer to relations by marriage or adoption.

knowing *adj.* Conscious, deliberate, with cognizance of pertinent information.

knowledge *n.* An awareness of factual information. Includes actual knowledge (positive or definite), personal knowledge (based on one's own observation), and constructive knowledge (based on other circumstances).

L

Labor Management Relations Act *n.* A 1947 federal law designed to protect employers, employees, and the public. It governs union activities and provides an arbitration mechanism for strikes that cause national emergencies. Abbreviated **LMRA.**

laches *n.* Equitable doctrine that precludes or limits relief to one who delays in acting or bringing a claim.

lame duck *adj. Colloquial; often pejorative.* An elected official whose successor has already been elected, and who is serving out the remainder of a term.

land *n.* **1** Real property. **2** An area of ground with defined boundaries, including minerals or resources below the surface and anything growing on or attached to the surface.

landlord *n.* The lessor of real property.

landmark decision *n.* A decision that is notable and often cited because it significantly changes, consolidates, updates, or effectively summarizes the law on a particular topic.

Landrum-Griffin Act *n.* A 1959 federal law regulating labor unions, for the purpose of reducing corruption in unions.

Lanham Act *n.* 1947 federal law that defines and regulates trademarks.

land use planning *n.* Collectively: zoning, real estate permitting, planning and use, and those aspects of environmental law as apply to such real estate matters.

lapse *n.* The termination or expiration of a right because it has not been exercised or because of the occurrence or nonoccurrence of some contingency.

larceny *n.* The wrongful appropriation of personal property with the intention of permanently depriving the owner of its possession and use.

last clear chance doctrine *n.* The doctrine that a plaintiff who committed contributory acts of negligence may nonetheless recover damages against a defendant who had the last opportunity in time to avoid the damage. Very limited applicability in most states.

last will and testament See **will.**

latent ambiguity *n.* An ambiguity that is not apparent from the wording of a document but is caused by external circumstances.

latent defect *n.* A hidden flaw that cannot be readily ascertained from mere observation.

lateral support *n.* A person (in property law) has the right to have his land supported at the sides by his neighbor's land; the principle that an adjoining landowner cannot alter the perimeter of his property in such a manner that his neighbor's land is adversely affected or weakened.

law *n.* **1** The complete body of statutes, rules, enforced customs and norms, and court decisions governing the relations of individuals and corporate entities to one another and to the state. **2** The subset of such statutes and other rules and materials dealing with a particular subject matter. **3** The system by which such statutes and rules are administered. **4** The profession of interpreting such statutes and rules. **5**

A bill that becomes effective after enactment by the legislature and signature (or failure to veto) by the executive.

lawful *adj.* Permissible; not contravening a law.

law of the case *n.* In appellate litigation, the doctrine that the decision in an earlier appeal is binding on the appeals court considering a later one in the same case.

law of the land *n. Colloquial.* The laws effective in a particular nation.

lawsuit *n.* A litigation or action brought in a court. See also **suit.**

lay witness See **witness.**

leading case *n.* Synonym for a **landmark decision.**

leading question *n.* A question posed to a witness that is phrased so as to suggest or elicit a particular answer desired by the attorney conducting the examination.

learned treatise *n.* Book or treatise regarded as authoritative, generally of long-accepted value within a profession or field of study.

lease *n.* An agreement in which the right of occupancy or use of real property, or the right to use personal property, is conveyed to another for a set period of time in return for consideration, typically in the form of periodic payments.

> *gross lease.* Lease in which a tenant pays a flat sum inclusive of all utilities and other expenses.

> *month-to-month lease.* Rental of property without a long term contractual obligation; in actuality, not a lease. May require one month's

notice in order to terminate, depending on local or state law.

> *net lease.* Lease in which tenant pays a rental amount for property, plus additional obligations for utilities, taxes, etc.

> *parol lease.* Oral agreement for tenancy; see **parol.**

> *percentage lease.* Business lease agreement whereby the amount to be paid is based on a specified percentage of tenant's gross or net profits; usually a minimum rental amount is stated.

> *sublease.* An agreement under which the **lessee** of real property conveys his rights, or some subset of them, to a third party.

leasehold *n.* Generally, a tenant's interest in the real property used or possessed pursuant to a **lease.**

leave no issue *adj.* To die without children or descendant heirs (spouse is not considered issue).

leave of court *n.* The court's permission to perform, or to forego, an act for which the court's consent is required.

legacy *n.* A grant by will of personal property or of money.

> *alternate legacy.* A legacy in which the recipient is given a choice among various items.

> *contingent legacy.* A legacy that depends on an event that has not yet occurred.

> *demonstrative legacy.* A legacy paid from a particular source if there are sufficient funds.

> *general legacy.* A legacy from the assets or proceeds of an estate, paid in cash or in fungible personal property, such as stock.

residuary legacy. A bequest of all property not specifically mentioned in will.

specific legacy. A legacy that consists of a piece of property that is clearly distinguishable and separable from the remainder of the property that forms the estate of the testator.

legal aid *n.* The free or inexpensive services of an attorney, provided to individuals, typically criminal defendants, who are not otherwise able to afford an attorney.

legal assistant *n.* A **paralegal.**

legal capacity to sue *adj.* Right or ability to bring suit, determined by age and mental status in general. See also **capacity.**

legal duty *n.* A duty created by the operation of law or arising from the terms of a contract. See also **duty.**

legal entity *n.* Anything other than a person that, by virtue of certain characteristics, is conferred with a status that it has certain rights or obligations, can sue or be sued.

legal fiction *n.* The assumption by the law that a particular assertion is true (even though it may not be) in order to support the functioning of a legal rule.

legal heir See **heir.**

legal impossibility See **impossibility.**

legal injury *n.* A harm caused by the infringement of a legal right.

legal secretary *n.* A secretary employed by a lawyer or a law firm, whose expertise includes the typing and filing of contracts, pleadings, or other legal documents.

legal separation See **separation.**

legal tender *n.* A nation's official monetary bills and coinage.

legal title See **title.**

legatee *n.* One who receives property via a will.

legislation *n.* **1** A bill being considered by a legislature that will become law if enacted. **2** The entire body of such bills under consideration or already enacted as law by a legislature. **3** The process of enacting bills into law.

legislative history *n.* The legislature's intentions in enacting a bill into law, as embodied in an explanatory document attached to the bill or in the record of debates pertaining to the bill's enactment.

legislative intent *n.* The legislature's intentions in enacting a bill into law, frequently derived from the **legislative history.**

lend *v.* To provide something temporarily to another, often in exchange for compensation.

lessee *n.* The **tenant** of real property, or holder of personal property, under a **lease.**

lesser included offense *n.* A more minor category of criminal act (or one with a lesser penalty), all of the elements of which are included in the more serious crime being charged.

lessor *n.* The owner of real or personal property, an interest in which is granted by **lease.**

let *v.* **1** To consent to or allow. **2** To rent or lease (something).

letter of credit *n.* A financial instrument, typically issued by a bank, in which the issuing institution commits to pay a **draft** presented by a third party in a specified format or meeting certain criteria.

letter of intent *n.* A non-binding summary of the proposed terms of a contract contemplated by the parties.

letter ruling *n.* An advisory statement issued by the Internal Revenue Service to a taxpayer asking about the tax consequences of a proposed transaction.

letters of administration *n.* A document issued by a probate court appointing an administrator for an estate.

letters of guardianship *n.* An entrustment of care of an incompetent or child unto another, generally a lawyer or officer of the court.

letters rogatory *n.* Court order or subpoena issued in one jurisdiction, seeking to compel citizen of another jurisdiction to testify in the first jurisdiction; requires court approval in second jurisdiction.

letters testamentary *n.* A document issued by a probate court approving the executor of a will.

leverage *n.* **1** Generally, the use of borrowed money to engage in transactions with a high rate of return that will allow repayment of the loan. **2** The ratio between a company's debt and equity.

levy *n.* **1** A tax or penalty. **2** The state's acting of seizing and selling property to satisfy a tax or other liability.

lewdness *n.* Indecent behavior offensive to observers.

lex fori *n.* Law of the jurisdiction where an action is pending.

Lexis *n.* A computerized legal research service.

lex loci contractus *n. Latin.* The law of the place where a contract was signed or is to be performed.

lex loci delicti *n. Latin.* The law of the place where a wrong was committed.

liability *n.* **1** A legally enforceable obligation. **2** More generally, a debt or other legal obligation to pay an assessed amount (for example, taxes).

joint and several liability. Liability that is jointly payable by multiple parties, but that may (or must, depending on jurisdiction) be paid in full by one or more of them if the others are not to be found or are incapable of paying their share.

joint liability. Liability that is jointly payable by multiple parties, of which none may be required to pay more than his or her share.

primary liability. Liability for which one is directly responsible, without the claimant being obligated to resort to any other source for payment.

secondary liability. Liability that one is not obligated to pay unless the party with primary liability fails to make payment.

strict liability. In tort law, a financial responsibility to compensate a harm in the absence of any negligence; an absolute responsibility to ensure the safe functioning of a dangerous instrumentality.

vicarious liability. The liability of an employer or supervisor for the acts of an employee, based on the employer-employee or supervisory relationship. See **respondeat superior.**

libel *n.* **1** A false and defamatory statement expressed in writing or in an electronic medium. **2** The first document or pleading filed in an admiralty action, which is now called a **complaint.**

liberal construction *n.* A loose or expansive interpretation of a statute or writing, as opposed to a strict or literal construction.

liberty *n.* **1** Freedom from government or private interference or constraints. **2** The ability to exercise the rights enumerated by a constitution or available or under natural law.

license *n.* **1** The grant by the owner of intangible or intellectual property, such as a trademark or software program, of the rights to make certain uses of the property. **2** A permission granted by government to perform an act or service regulated by law (for example, a license to fish or to practice law). **3** A right to enter onto land or property and use it, without any ownership rights being conferred.

> *bare license.* A license under which no property is exchanged, and the licensee receives the right to not be treated as a trespasser. Same as *social guest,* or a hotel guest.

> *exclusive license.* A right to carry on an activity to the exclusion of all others.

licensee *n.* The recipient or grantee of a **license**; one who uses property subject to a license, as opposed to one who has been actually or constructively invited onto the property, for the benefit of the owner of the property (**invitee**).

licensor *n.* One who grants a license.

lie *v.* Available, to exist. Example: No cause of action will **lie** for trespass if the landowner gave his permission to enter onto the land.

lien *n.* A security interest, held by a creditor in a debtor's property, to secure a loan.

> *attorney's lien.* See **attorney's lien.**

> *mechanic's lien.* A lien against real property to secure payment of amounts owing to contractors, service people, etc., who performed work on the property.

lien theory *n.* The concept that a **mortgage** is a form of **lien** on the property that does not grant the **mortgagee** any ownership rights until a foreclosure occurs.

life estate *n.* An estate held for the duration of life of a person (usually, the occupant).

life interest *n.* A property interest granted for the duration of a person's life. See **life estate.**

life tenant *n.* The occupant of property under a **life estate.**

like-kind exchange *n.* An exchange of property for other property of the same nature.

limine out *v.* To exclude evidence from trial by the grant of a motion in limine.

limitation *n.* **1** A restriction. **2** The act of placing a limit or restriction. **3** A condition or restriction placed upon real estate.

> *limitation of actions.* Period of time during which an action must be filed. See *statute of limitations.*

> *statute of limitations.* See **statute of limitations.**

limited jurisdiction See **jurisdiction.**

limited liability *n.* Liability upon which limits are set by contract or by statute.

limited partnership See **partnership.**

lineage *n.* The overview or totality of the marriage and blood relationships within a family, including the ancestors and descendants of a particular individual.

lineal *adj.* Regarding trusts and estates, of a direct, as opposed to a collateral, descendant.

lineal heir   See **heir.**

lineup   *n.* A procedure in which the police show a witness a suspect and several other individuals to see whether the witness can distinguish the suspect from other individuals not involved in the crime.

liquidate   *v.* **1** In bankruptcy or insolvency, to terminate a business by the sale of its assets to pay its liabilities. **2** To pay a debt. **3** To convert hard assets into cash. **4** To set, by contract or stipulation, a fixed amount for damages resulting from a particular harm.

liquidated amount   *n.* To set by agreement a specific amount or a formula for calculating such an amount, in compensation for the losses resulting from a breach.

liquidated damages   See **damages.**

lis pendens   *n.* **1** A court's authority over property resulting from a pending lawsuit. **2** A notice filed in a government office with the title documents pertaining to real property, giving notice to the public that the property is the subject of a litigation.

listing   *n.* **1** In securities, the action of having a corporation's securities registered and traded on a particular exchange. **2** In real estate, the action of registering a house, building, or land with a broker for sale.

litigant   *n.* A party to a legal action.

litigation   *n.* A legal action; the process of bringing and carrying on a legal action.

living will   *n.* A document signed by an individual directing manner in which he wishes to be medically treated if in a vegetative or terminal state, designed to give guidance to loved ones and health care providers as to the desires of an individual if he is no longer able to properly communicate such desires.

L.J.   *n. abbr.* Law journal.

L.L.B.   *n. abbr.* The law degree formerly granted by American law schools, most of which now confer the **J.D.** degree.

L.L.M.   *n. abbr.* Master of Laws degree.

LMRA   See **Labor Management Relations Act.**

loan   *n.* The giving or granting of something, particularly a sum of money, to another, with the expectation that it will be repaid (typically with interest) or returned.

loan-sharking   *n. Colloquial.* The illegal business of lending money at usurious rates, typically with the threat or use of violence to ensure repayment.

lockdown   *n.* The confinement of prisoners to their cells for the duration of a security alert caused by events or conditions at the prison.

lockout   *n.* An employer's refusal to allow employees to work, in retaliation for union activity or a labor dispute.

locus   *n. Latin.* The place or location of a thing or event.

locus delicti   *n. Latin.* The place where a crime was committed.

locus in quo   *n. Latin.* The place where an event allegedly occurred.

loitering   *n.* The crime of being in a public place without a valid reason.

long arm   *adj.* Of or pertaining to long arm jurisdiction or statutes.

long arm statute   *n.* A law providing for civil jurisdiction over a nonresident defendant based on his or her contacts with the jurisdiction.

loss   *n.* **1** The death of an insured person or damage to insured property.   **2** The amount that the value of personal or real property exceeds the proceeds from its sale.   **3** Generally, the complete or partial diminishment of the value of an asset or of a human life.

loss-of-bargain rule   *n.* The concept that damages for breach of contract should put the plaintiff in the position he or she would have enjoyed if the contract had been fully performed.

lost property   *n.* Property no longer in the owner's possession, due to accident or negligence, which cannot be located.

lower of cost or market method   *n.* In accounting, an approach under which the value of goods held for sale is set at the lower of acquisition cost or market price.

lump-sum payment   *n.* A payment made once in a single amount, as opposed to smaller payments over time.

lying in wait   *v.* The act of waiting in concealment with the intention of killing or committing serious physical harm upon a prospective victim.

MACRS See **Modified Accelerated Cost Recovery System.**

magistrate *n.* A judicial officer of limited jurisdiction or responsibility; colloquially used as a synonym for judge.

Magnuson-Moss Warranty Act *n.* A federal law that requires warranties of consumer products to set forth their terms, including limitations, in plain English.

mailbox rule *n.* **1** The rule that the acceptance of a contract is effective upon being mailed, unless the contract provides otherwise. **2** In litigation, the rule that a pleading is served as of the date it is mailed.

maintenance *n.* **1** Financial support paid by one ex-spouse to another pursuant to a legal separation or divorce. **2** The effort and expense of the upkeep of property. **3** To assist a party to a lawsuit with which one has no connection by providing financial or other support to enable the party to pursue the matter.

majority *n.* **1** The status of having attained the age of adulthood as set by law. **2** More than fifty percent of a total (usually referring to people in a group voting in an election or on a matter placed before them).

majority opinion *n.* The holding of a court consisting of multiple members, typically an appellate court, issued together by the majority of the members, and establishing the formal legal result of the case, as opposed to a dissenting opinion.

maker *n.* A person who issues a promissory note.

malfeasance *n.* An unlawful act, particularly one committed by a public official.

malice *n.* The state of mind of one intentionally performing a wrongful act.

> *constructive malice.* Malice which can be imputed to the actor because of the nature of the acts committed and the result thereby.

malice aforethought *n.* The requisite state of mind for murder to be charged under the common law, involving an intent to kill or to cause serious physical harm, depraved indifference to human life, or an intent to commit another serious felony that results in a death.

malicious arrest *n.* An arrest made for a dishonest purpose and lacking probable cause.

malicious mischief *n.* The intentional destruction or damaging of another's property.

malicious prosecution *n.* **1** The pursuit of a criminal proceeding for a dishonest purpose and without probable cause. **2** The pursuit of a civil proceeding for a dishonest motive.

malpractice *n.* The negligent actions of a professional, such as a doctor or lawyer, as evinced by a failure to perform services consistent with the standards of such profession.

malum in se *n. Latin.* An act, such as murder, that is inherently evil or immoral.

malum prohibitum *n. Latin.* An act that is wrong solely because prohibited by law, as opposed to **malum in se.**

mandamus   *n.* A writ issued by a court to compel a public official (including the judge of a lesser court) to perform a task or duty.

mandate   *n.* **1** The voters' show of support, typically greater than a simple majority, for a particular political candidate or party.   **2** A court's order directing a lower court or judicial officer to perform a particular action.

mandatory injunction   *n.* See **injunction**.

mandatory sentence   *n.* See **sentence**.

manifest weight of the evidence   *n.* A doctrine under which a verdict will be overturned only if it is substantially unsupported by the evidence in the case.

Mann Act   *n.* A federal criminal law penalizing the transporting of anyone in interstate commerce for purposes of prostitution.

manslaughter   *n.* The act of killing another person without **malice aforethought.**

> *involuntary manslaughter.* The accidental killing of another during the commission of a crime or as a result of criminal negligence.

> *voluntary manslaughter.* Killing in the heat of passion.

margin   *n.* **1** The difference between the amount of a loan and the market value of the collateral securing it.   **2** Cash or other collateral given or paid to a stockbroker to secure him or her against losses incurred extending credit to an investor.   **3** The investor's equity in stocks purchased by a broker extending credit to the investor.

marital agreement   *n.* An agreement between spouses resolving issues pertaining to their joint and individual property during the marriage and/or after divorce.

marital communications privilege   *n.* A right not to give testimony concerning discussions with one's spouse that may be asserted at the option of the witness spouse. See **spousal privilege**.

marital deduction   *n.* An estate or gift tax **deduction** for the value of property that was assigned or has passed to the taxpayer's spouse.

marital property   *n.* All property acquired during marriage, regardless of how titled, that will be divided between the spouses in the event of a divorce.

market price   *n.* Actual price, that which is available in ordinary course of free trade.

market value   See **fair market value.**

marketable title   *n.* A real estate title that lacks any defect discoverable by a reasonable purchaser.

marriage   *n.* The legal relation of a man and woman as husband and wife.

> *common-law marriage.* Marital relationship arising not from formal ceremony but from intention to hold out as a married couple, combined with living together for a requisite period of years that may be specified by statute; abolished in many states.

marshal   *n.* **1** A federal court employee with police-like powers who provides security, guards prisoners, and seizes property in execution of judgments, among other functions.   **2** A state or local official with responsibilities like those of a sheriff. **3** Arranging in order of priority or in a logical pattern.

martial law   *n.* Civil law exerted over citizens by military, generally in times of war or emergency.

Mary Carter agreement   *n.* A device for settling cases that involves multiple defendants, with one or more defendants paying money to plaintiff in exchange for a release from further liability, but with an ongoing role to participate in the trial of the case, a portion of any monies received by the plaintiff from other defendant(s) is paid to the settling defendant(s).

master *n.* **1** A special official appointed by a court to assist it, typically by making findings or rulings pertaining to matters specified by the court, typically, a "master" in divorce or custody, or a "master" to render an accounting; sometimes referred to as a "special master". **2** *Archaic.* One who has authority over another's person and services.

master and servant *n.* The relationship between an employer or other person having authority to direct and control the performance of services; the person performing those services.

master plan *n.* In land-use planning, a government entity's plan for the overall utilization of a particular area, including its allocation for residential or manufacturing uses and the corresponding environmental impacts.

material *adj.* **1** Of evidence, that it is important or essential to an adjudication or determination. **2** Having a logical connection to the matters under consideration.

material alteration *n.* A substantial change in a contract or other document that changes its interpretation or effect.

material breach See **breach.**

material witness See **witness.**

maternal *adj.* Pertaining to one's mother.

matricide *n.* **1** The act of killing one's mother. **2** A person who has killed his or her mother.

matter *n.* An issue under consideration in a lawsuit.

> *matter in issue.* The crux of a case, the matter in controversy.

> *matter of fact.* An issue of the truth or falsity of a pertinent fact.

> *matter of law.* An issue pertaining to the applicability or interpretation of a particular law.

> *matter of record.* Any matter that has been made a part of the official court record.

mature *v.* A debt that has become payable.

maxim *n.* A key principle of law that has been repeated so often it has become a commonplace expression.

mayhem *n.* Violent, disorderly behavior.

measure of damages *n.* A formula for determining monetary damages, which varies among types of actions; for example, measure of damages in a contract case is generally the contract price less reduction for any incomplete performance by the selling party, while measure of damages in a tort action is that which fairly compensates a plaintiff for her expenses sustained as a result of the tortious act, plus compensation for any pain and suffering.

mechanic's lien See **lien.**

mediation *n.* A form of conflict resolution in which a neutral individual attempts to assist the parties to find a compromise acceptable to both. Distinguished from **arbitration** because it concentrates more on the search for terms acceptable to both parties and less on the legal resolution of their disputes.

meeting *n.* A gathering of persons for a specific purpose.

annual meeting. Corporate law, yearly gathering of board of directors to which stockholders are invited.

special meeting. Corporate law, gathering for a special or limited purpose.

meeting of the minds *n.* Actual understanding of and agreement to the terms of a contract.

Megan's Law *n.* A statute that requires sex offenders to register with local authorities and requires publication of information about them (including their residence in the community) to the public.

member *n.* One part of an organization or family, one person belonging to a partnership.

memorandum *n.* **1** A form of written internal communication utilized in businesses and other office environments. **2** A summary of the terms of an agreement (typically one to be drafted later). **3** A legal brief, typically on a motion or other issue arising at the trial level.

menacing *n.* An attempt to commit an assault.

mensa et thoro *n. Latin.* Bed and board.

mens rea *n. Latin.* The defendant's guilty state of mind, as an element in proving the crime with which he or she is charged.

mental cruelty *n.* Behavior by a spouse that threatens the life, bodily health, or psychological health of the other spouse.

merchant *n.* An individual or entity that buys goods and resells them for a profit, and that is assumed to be expert in the particular type of goods.

merchantable *adj.* Of goods, that they are fit for sale.

mere licensee *n.* One who enters property at the will of another.

merger *n.* **1** In contract law, the action of superceding all prior written or oral agreements on the same subject matter. **2** In criminal law, the inclusion of a lesser offense within a more serious one, rather than charging it separately, which might cause **double jeopardy.** **3** In litigation, the doctrine that all of the plaintiff's prior claims are superceded by the judgment in the case, which becomes the plaintiff's sole means of recovering from the defendant. **4** The combination under modern codes of civil procedure of law and equity into a single court. **5** In corporate law, the acquisition of one company by another, and their combination into a single legal entity.

merit *n.* **1** The substantive elements of a claim or defense. **2** The validity of a claim or defense (as in "the defense of impossibility is without merit").

on the merits. Description of adjudication of a matter on its substantive elements, not on procedural or technical grounds.

mesne *adj.* Occupying a middle or intermediate position.

metes and bounds *n.* The objective measurement of real property from recognized landmarks so as to situate it precisely in a description to be used in legal documents, such as deeds.

mineral lease *n.* The right given to use land for purpose of exploration, specifically for minerals, with concommitent right to remove minerals, if found, for a finite period of time, or indefinitely, upon payment of royalties to the landowner.

mineral rights *n.* A right to take minerals from land or to receive payment from the excavation of such minerals.

minimum contacts *n.* A defendant's activities within or affecting the state in which a lawsuit is brought, that are considered legally sufficient to support jurisdiction in that state's courts.

ministerial *adj.* Of the nature of a routine or mechanical function performed with a minimum of discretion.

minority *n.* **1** An ethnic, religious, or other defined group of people who may face discrimination from the majority as a result of their differences. **2** The condition of not yet being of legal age. **3** A group of less than half of eligible voters.

Miranda rule *n.* The rule, formed from constitutional law, that suspects must be advised of certain rights (such as the right to remain silent and the right to an attorney) before being questioned by the police.

misadventure *n.* **1** An accident or unlucky event. **2** An accidental homicide.

misapplication *n.* The illegal misuse of money or property in lawful keeping.

misappropriation *n.* The act of taking improperly, including the use of another's property or work.

miscarriage of justice *n.* The unjust and inappropriate outcome of a court proceeding.

misconduct in office *n.* The unlawful exercise of public authority.

misdelivery *n.* The delivery of goods at a time or place or in a manner not meeting contractual requirements.

misdemeanor *n.* A crime considered to be less serious than a felony, and that receives a lesser punishment (typically a sentence of one year or less).

misfeasance *n.* **1** Generally, an act of wrong-doing. **2** An otherwise legal act that is performed in an illegal fashion.

misjoinder *n.* The improper addition or inclusion of parties or claims in a civil case, or of charges in a criminal case.

mislaid property *n.* Property that has been left unattended by the owner with an intent to return to it later, but that can no longer be located.

misnomer *n.* An error in referring to or naming a person, location, or object, particularly in a contract or other legal document.

misprision of felony *n.* The offense of covering up of a felony committed by another.

misrepresentation *n.* A false statement typically made with the intention to mislead. See **fraud.**

mistake *n.* In contract law, a factual misunderstanding that may lead to a failure of a meeting of the minds.

> *mistake of fact.* Improper understanding of a fact that is material to a contract.

> *mistake of law.* Improper understanding of the law as applied to facts as to which a party has a correct and full understanding.

> *mutual mistake.* A mistake in which each party has an incorrect understanding of the other's position, or in which both parties share the same mistaken belief, generally a basis for canceling the contract.

> *unilateral mistake.* A mistake by only one party to a contract as to the underlying facts of the agreement, not generally a basis for avoiding the contract.

mistrial *n.* A trial that the judge orders ended without a verdict, either because the jury has deadlocked or because of an incident or mistake prejudicing the outcome.

mitigating circumstance *n.* A factual matter argued in defense that may lessen a defendant's liability or culpability, resulting in lesser damages or a shorter sentence.

mitigation-of-damages doctrine *n.* The doctrine that requires a plaintiff to use reasonable efforts to alleviate the injury caused by the defendant. For example, a merchant who fails to receive goods due to the manufacturer's breach is expected to replace those goods with similar ones from another source, and will then be able to sue only for the difference in price between the contracted-for goods and the ones actually purchased.

mixed nuisance *n.* See **nuisance**.

mixed question of law and fact *n.* An issue that can be resolved only by adjudicating facts and deciding relevant legal issues at the same time.

M'Naghten rules *n.* The insanity defense as codified in federal law and the law of many states, in terms of whether a mental disease or defect interfered either with the defendant's understanding of the nature of the criminal act or the difference between right and wrong.

m.o. *abbr.* See **modus operandi.**

model act *n.* Proposed legislation drafted by a national lawyer's conference for the purpose of providing a model for state laws.

Model Rules of Professional Conduct *n.* Ethical guidelines for lawyers drafted by the American Bar Association.

Modified Accelerated Cost Recovery System *n.* An accounting approach for the rapid depreciation of assets. Abbreviated **MACRS.**

modus operandi *n. Latin.* A method of operating.

moiety *n.* A portion of something, typically half.

money *n.* An official, government-created token of value, made of paper or metal, that may be exchanged for goods or services.

money demand *n.* A claim for a specified amount of **money.**

money judgment *n.* A judgment for a specified amount of **money,** awarded as damages.

monogamy *n.* A law or custom permitting a person to be married to only one spouse.

monopoly *n.* The domination of a commercial market by only one supplier, worldwide or in a particular region.

month-to-month lease *n.* A lease without a fixed term, because either it never included one or such term is expired, in which the landlord's acceptance of each monthly rent payment gives the tenant a right to stay for one more month.

moot *adj.* Of an issue, that it is not currently a controversy able to be decided, typically because it was resolved or otherwise removed from the court's purview by an intervening act or occurrence.

moot court *n.* A law-school competition in which students argue imaginary cases before professors sitting as judges.

moral certainty   *n.* High level of conviction that causes one to act in accordance therewith; beyond a reasonable doubt.

moral turpitude   *n.* Of conduct, that it is significantly wrong or immoral; used as a term of special condemnation.

mortgage   *n.* **1** A grant of a security interest in real property to secure a loan, often for the purchase of the property.   **2** A loan secured by an interest in real property.   **3** The paperwork reflecting such a loan and security interest.

> *purchase money mortgage.* A mortgage that secures debt incurred in connection with the property as to which the mortgage is given, for example, a mortgage on one's home given to secure a loan given in order to purchase that home.

mortgagee   *n.* The lender or creditor extending the loan involved in a **mortgage.**

mortgagor   *n.* The owner of the real property involved in a **mortgage.**

mortmain   *n. Archaic.* The permanent holding of lands by an ecclesiastical organization, without the right to dispose of them.

most favored nation clause   *n.* A provision in treaties according all citizens of the nations that are parties to the treaty a special status as to other nations that are parties to the treaties, such citizens are afforded all privileges available to most favored nations; general effect of such status is a lowering of duty on trade between such nations.

motion   *n.* **1** In litigation, a formal request, usually in writing, to a court for specified relief, under applicable procedural rules.   **2** In a legislature or other deliberative body, a request for procedural relief made by a member to the chairman or the body at large, under Robert's Rules of Order or other applicable procedural rules.

motion for arrest of judgment   *n.* A **motion** asking the court to overrule the judgment in a civil or criminal case, on the grounds that it was granted in error.

motion for judgment as a matter of law   *n.* A request for relief available to a party when there is no disputed fact issue.

motion for summary judgment   *n.* In civil litigation, a written submission made to the court following the discovery phase, asking for judgment before trial on the basis that the undisputed facts as adduced through discovery entitle the moving party to judgment as a matter of law; if granted, the case is over with no need for trial.

motion in limine   *n.* A **motion** to limit the evidence that will be submitted to the jury, by excluding matters that are not relevant, are prejudicial, or are otherwise inadmissible under applicable rules.

motion to dismiss   *n.* In civil litigation, a written submission to the court at a preliminary stage of the case, generally before the defendant answers, seeking dismissal of the case on one of several grounds, including lack of jurisdiction over the person or subject matter, and failure of the plaintiff to allege requisite elements of the cause of action asserted in the complaint, etc.; may be granted with or without leave given to plaintiff to amend his complaint to correct deficiencies.

motion to set aside   See **set aside**.

movant   *n.* The party making a motion to the court.

move *v.* To make a **motion;** to request relief from a court or a deliberative body.

moving expense *n.* In tax law, an expense incurred in connection with the transportation of one's household effects when changing one's residence.

mulct *n.* **1** To levy a fine. **2** To defraud someone.

multifarious *adj.* Referring or relating to the improper **joinder** of unrelated causes or parties in a lawsuit.

multipartite *adj.* Divided into several parts.

multiplicity of actions *n.* Multiple lawsuits filed by one party involving the same subject matter, usually against same defendant, generally of a frivolous nature or attempt to relitigate matter that has been unfavorably decided against the plaintiff.

municipal bond *n.* A **bond** issued by a city or other municipal entity.

municipal court *n.* A city court.

muniments (of title) *n.* Chain of documents that indicate title to property, from the beginning to the present.

murder *n.* The intentional and malicious killing of a human being.

first degree murder. Murder that is premeditated, or done during the commission of certain other felonies.

murder-suicide. Act of killing another followed by suicide, sometimes carried out in a pact, other times without the assent of the murdered person.

second degree murder. An unpremeditated murder not committed while carrying out another felony.

mute *n.* The act or condition of remaining silent when required to enter a plea.

mutuality of obligation *n.* The consent by both parties to a contract to pay, yield, or give up something in return for the benefits received.

mutuality of remedy *n.* The doctrine that **specific performance** must be available to both parties to a transaction in order for either to obtain it.

mutual mistake *n.* A **mistake** in which each party has an incorrect understanding of the other's position, or in which both parties share the same mistaken belief.

N

naked power *n.* Power over a person or thing unrelated to an interest in the well-being or continuation of that person or thing.

named insured *n.* The covered individual named in an insurance policy.

narcotic *n.* A drug that, by law, is illegal or designated a controlled substance.

National Association of Security Dealers Automated Quotation system *n.* An automated national stock exchange. Abbreviated **NASDAQ.**

National Labor Relations Act *n.* A federal law governing certain labor issues and creating the **National Labor Relations Board.** Abbreviated **NLRA.**

National Labor Relations Board *n.* A federal labor agency that oversees union elections and other labor issues. Abbreviated **NLRB.**

National Lawyers Guild *n.* A lawyer's association founded in 1937, which states as its mission a dedication to the need for basic and progressive change in the structure of the political and economic system, generally aligned with liberal and socially progressive causes.

natural child *n.* A biological, as opposed to an adopted, child.

naturalization *n.* The formal grant of U.S. citizenship to a foreigner.

natural law *n.* A philosophical explanation of the origins of law, grounding it in purported external facts (such as biology, religious conceptions of right and wrong, and so on) rather than in human custom or practice.

natural person *n.* An actual person, as opposed to one created by a legal fiction (such as a corporation).

n.b. *abbr. Latin.* Nota bene; used to emphasize or call notice to something.

Necessary and Proper Clause *n.* A section of the United States Constitution that enables Congress to make the laws required for the exercise of its other powers established by the Constitution.

necessary implication *n.* An implication that is very likely to be true.

necessary inference *n.* A conclusion that flows of necessity from a particular premise.

necessary party *n.* A party who, because of his or her relationship to or involvement in the underlying facts and issues, should be joined to a case if it all possible.

necessity *n.* A defense to a criminal charge or civil claim, that the party's actions were in response to a supervening state of emergency.

negative averment See **averment.**

negative easement See **easement.**

negative pregnant *n.* A limited and conditional denial of a part of an assertion that implies that the assertion may otherwise be true.

neglect *n.* The action or status of failing to care for or to maintain something.

negligence *n.* The failure to use reasonable care, resulting in harm to another.

comparative negligence. The plaintiff's own negligent acts that bring about a pro rata reduction of the damages owed by the defendant, depending on the degree of the plaintiff's own negligence; compare *contributory negligence.*

concurrent negligence. The negligence of two or more parties contributing to the ultimate harm.

contributory negligence. Any degree of negligence on the part of a plaintiff, which results in a total bar to recovery by the plaintiff, even if the defendant was negligent as well. States are either "comparative" or "contributory" negligence jurisdictions.

criminal negligence. Negligence so substantial it is grounds for a criminal prosecution.

culpable negligence. Negligent actions committed with a disregard of the consequences.

gross negligence. Extreme negligence, acts committed with utter disregard for the consequences, punishable by punitive damages.

negligence per se. Negligence as to which there is no disputed fact issue and that may therefore be determined by the court without recourse to a jury.

negligent infliction of emotional distress *n.* The act of inflicting emotional distress on another by one's negligent act.

negotiable instrument *n.* In commercial law, a writing that meets certain criteria, such as that it contains an unconditional promise to pay a specified amount on demand or at a particular date to the bearer or a particular person, and it is signed by the person making it.

negotiation *n.* Discussions between adverse parties, with the goal of resolving their differences.

net income *n.* Income after all exemptions, exclusions, and deductions.

net operating loss *n.* The amount by which operating expenses exceed revenues.

new and useful *adj.* Term used in patent law to define whether an item is patentable.

newly discovered evidence *n.* Material evidence bearing on innocence and discovered after the conclusion of a trial.

new matter *n.* A matter not previously raised by a party in a litigation.

new trial *n.* A second or later trial on all or part of the merits, ordered by the original trial judge or a court of appeals.

New York Stock Exchange *n.* A national exchange operated by an association of securities firms based in New York City. Abbreviated **NYSE.**

next friend *n.* An attorney or other competent person appointed to appear in a litigation to represent the interests of a minor or incompetent.

next of kin *n.* The individual(s) of closest consanguinity to a decedent.

nisi *adj. Latin.* Of an ex parte decision or ruling, that it is valid unless opposed by the adverse party.

nisi prius *n. Latin.* Refers to a court in which a jury is the ultimate finder of fact.

NLRA *abbr.* See **National Labor Relations Act.**

NLRB *abbr.* See **National Labor Relations Board.**

no bill   *n.* A grand jury's determination that there is not adequate evidence to indict someone.

no-fault   *adj.* Of claims or controversies, such as divorces or automobile accidents, in which adjudications or awards are made without reference to the parties' guilt or blame.

nolens volens   *adj./adv. Latin.* Willing or not.

nolo contendere   *n. Latin.* A plea available in certain jurisdictions in which a party declines to contest a charge without formally admitting guilt.

nominal damages   See **damages.**

nominal party   See **party.**

non compos mentis   *adj. Latin.* Mentally incompetent.

noncustodial sentence   *n.* A criminal sentence served elsewhere than in a prison (for example, on probation).

nondelegable   *adj.* Of a power, that it cannot be assigned or transferred to another to be performed.

nonfeasance   *n.* A failure to act in derogation of a duty to do so.

nonnegotiable   *adj.* **1** Of commercial paper, that it cannot be transferred.   **2** Of a contract term or demand, that the party proposing or making it refuses to discuss or make any modification.

non obstante veredicto   *n. Latin.* A judgment notwithstanding the verdict, in which a jury verdict is set aside by the judge as being factually or legally invalid.

nonprofit corporation   *n.* A corporation organized for other than commercial purposes; for example, for charity or to advance a viewpoint on policy.

non prosequitur   *n. Latin.* A judgment against a plaintiff who has abandoned the case.

nonrecognition provision   *n.* A rule that allows certain items not to be included in taxable income.

nonrecourse   *adj.* Pertaining to an obligation that cannot be enforced against the personal assets of the debtor.

non sequitur   *n. Latin.* A conclusion or a statement that does not logically follow from what preceded it.

nonsuit   *n.* **1** The dismissal of a case by the judge for procedural infirmity or lack of any evidence, without reaching a decision on the merits.   **2** A plaintiff's voluntary dismissal of a case.

nonsupport   *n.* A breadwinner's failure to provide support to a child, spouse, or other dependent.

noscitur a sociis   *Latin.* A rule of interpretation that states that the meaning of unclear language in a contract or other legal document should be construed in light of the language surrounding it.

notary public   *n.* An individual who performs the public functions of witnessing signatures, administering oaths, and comparing documents in order to attest to the validity of copies.

note   *n.* **1** In commercial law, a writing representing a promise by a maker to pay a specified amount of money to a payee or to the bearer, on demand or by a specified date.   **2** A short article in a law review, typically written by a law student.

not guilty   *n.* **1** A determination by a jury that the evidence is insufficient to convict the defendant beyond a reasonable doubt.   **2** A defendant's plea in court denying the prosecution's charges.

not guilty by reason of insanity. A jury verdict or plea that acknowledges that the defendant committed the crime but states that he or she was not responsible for his or her actions by reason of a mental disease or defect, and so could not have formed the requisite **mens rea,** and therefore, is not guilty.

notice *n.* **1** A state of awareness of a fact or thing, as required by law or contract. **2** A communication seeking to make its recipient aware of a fact or thing, as required by law or contract.

actual notice. Notice personally received by the person for whom it was intended.

constructive notice. Notice deemed to have been received by a party, due to publicly known facts or events of which that party had a duty to be aware.

implied notice. Notice deemed to have been received by a party, due to his or her knowledge of other information that should have led that party to become aware of the matter in question.

inquiry notice. Notice deemed to have been received by a party, due to the party's knowledge of other information that would have caused a reasonable person to inquire further.

judicial notice. Notice taken by a court that a fact is so obvious, well-known or commonly accepted that no proof is required to establish that fact; for example, judicial notice may be taken of the fact that many people died during the events of September 11, 2001, without proof being necessary as to the actual death of such persons.

personal notice. Actual notice received directly by the person for whom it was intended.

notice of appeal *n.* A formal written notice, filed with the court and served on the other parties, as required by procedural rules, that a party intends to appeal a judgment or order.

notice of appearance *n.* **1** A written document filed with the court (or in some cases, a verbal representation made in court) to notify it and the other parties that a party wishes to appear in or receive notice of the proceedings. **2** An attorney's written or verbal notice to the court that he or she represents one of the parties.

notice of dishonor *n.* Notice that payment of a note or other commercial paper is being refused.

notice of motion *n.* A party's written notice, under applicable procedural rules, that it is requesting the court's determination on an issue pertaining to a pending litigation. Motions are typically used to resolve procedural issues such as **discovery** disputes or issues of the excludability of evidence, but may also seek dismissal of the case on the grounds that the pleadings do not state a cause of action, or summary judgment on the grounds that there is no disputed fact issue on which the other party could prevail.

notice to quit *n.* A landlord's written notice to a tenant to vacate the premises for nonpayment or other material breach of a lease.

notorious possession *n.* Use or inhabitance of real property that is open and obvious to neighbors, leading to a presumption that the owner has notice of it. See also **adverse possession.**

novation *n.* In contract law, the replacement of an old obligation with a new one.

novelty *n.* an element required to obtain a patent. See **new and useful.**

NSF *abbr.* A banking term meaning "not sufficient funds."

nudum pactum *n. Latin.* A bare or scant agreement that is not enforceable because **consideration** is lacking.

nugatory *adj.* Of a law or a contract, that it is unenforceable.

nuisance *n.* An ongoing act or a condition that interferes with another's use or inhabitation of real property.

> *abatable nuisance.* A nuisance that may easily be repaired or avoided.

> *attractive nuisance.* A potentially dangerous element or entity on real property that may attract people, especially children, to use it to their own harm; for example, a swimming pool.

> *attractive nuisance doctrine.* See **attractive nuisance doctrine.**

> *mixed nuisance.* A nuisance that affects both public and private interests.

> *nuisance per se.* A nuisance that is very dangerous, or in some other way beyond conventional bounds of acceptability and risk, one that has certainty.

> *private nuisance.* A nuisance that affects private ownership interests.

> *public nuisance.* A nuisance that interferes with public interests, including those in health, safety, and transportation.

nullification *n.* The act or condition of negating the existence of a law, performed by individuals acting in a public capacity (for example, a jury) or by one level of government opposing the laws of another.

> *jury nullification.* A jury's verdict of "not guilty" despite overwhelming evidence of guilt, often in the face of the jury's collective belief of this guilt, because of its perception that the law is being immorally or improperly applied to the defendant; in other words, the jury nullifies the law because it believes the defendant has been unfairly treated.

nullity *adj.* Legally nonexistent; without force or effect.

nunc pro tunc *adj. Latin.* Of an order or decision, that it has a retroactive effect.

nuncupative will *n.* A verbal will made in contemplation of oncoming death from a wound or injury. Not valid in most states.

NYSE *abbr.* See **New York Stock Exchange.**

O

oath *n.* A solemn swearing to the truth of statements delivered orally and/or in written form. Making of false statements while under oath may result in prosecution for perjury. An **affidavit** is a written oath. See also **affirmation.**

> *oath of office.* A sworn promise to carry out the duties and responsibilities of a position, diligently and as required by law.

obiter dicta *adv. Latin.* "By the way . . . ." A passing statement reached in a court opinion that is irrelevant to the outcome of the case. See also **dictum.**

objection *n.* A statement opposing something that is about to occur in a courtroom, or has already occurred, as being improper, out of order, or against procedural rules. It is up to the judge to rule on the objection's validity, or to **overrule** it. A timely objection that is entered into the trial record, along with appropriate argument on its validity, may form the basis for an appeal to a higher court. See also **challenge** and **motion in limine.**

obligation *n.* **1** A moral or legal duty to perform or to not perform some action. **2** A binding, formal arrangement or an agreement to a liability to pay a specified amount or to do a certain thing for a person or group of persons. See also **duty** and **liability.**

obligation, mutuality of See **mutuality of obligation.**

oblige *v.* **1** To legally or morally bind; to obligate. **2** To bind someone by performing a service for that person.

obligee *n.* The person who is owed an obligation, generally a sum of money or a service.

obligor *n.* The person owing the money, service, or goods. See also **obligee.**

obloquy *n.* Abusive language; blame; disgrace or cause to be in ill repute; **calumny.** Obloquy may go to the extent where it constitutes **defamation.** See also **defamation** and **slander.**

obscene *adj.* Exceptionally repugnant to the contemporary standards of decency and morality within the community; grossly obnoxious to the notions of acceptable behavior.

obscene material *n.* According to a Supreme Court decision, material is obscene, and hence not protected by the free-speech provision of the First Amendment if it has three elements: It must have prurient appeal, as decided by the average person applying the standards of the community; it must portray sexual conduct in an offensive way; and it must be lacking in serious artistic, literary, scientific, or political value.

obscenity See **obscene material.**

obsolescence *n.* **1** A process or condition of becoming useless or obsolete. **2** A diminishing of a property's value or usefulness, especially because of innovations in technology, as distinguished from physical decay. See also **depreciation.**

obstruction of justice *n.* Delaying or impeding the timely and orderly administration of the legal system in some way, such as by giving false or misleading information, withholding information from legal authorities, or attempting to influence a witness or a juror. A criminal act in most jurisdictions.

obviate   *v.* **1** To anticipate and prevent something from happening; to dispose of something. **2** To make something no longer necessary.

occupancy   *n.* **1** The condition or act of possessing or living in a dwelling or on some property. **2** The period of time during which one rents, owns, or in some way possesses property. **3** Having actual possession of a place that has no owner so as to acquire legal rights to ownership. See also **adverse possession.**

occupant   *n.* One who inhabits or exercises direct control over a certain piece of property or premises, as distinguished from the one who has ownership of the property, although the same person(s) may do both.

occupational disease (or injury)   *n.* A disease or injury contracted as a result of prolonged exposure to unsafe substances or conditions in the natural course of one's employment, where the risk of such condition or injury is greater than that prevalent in the general population.

occupational hazard   *n.* A risk peculiar to the specific occupation or place of employment and that arises in normal work at such a job or workplace. Occupational hazards include the likelihood of accidental injuries and diseases.

Occupational Safety and Health Act *n.* A federal law enacted in 1970, setting forth workplace rules and regulations to promote safety of workers; administered by the **Occupational Safety and Health Administration.**

Occupational Safety and Health Administration   *n.* An agency of the federal government established by Act of Congress in 1970 that creates and enforces rules governing the safety of workers in the workplace. The agency routinely inspects workplaces and issues citations for businesses that are in violation of its standards. The agency is a part of the Department of Labor. Abbreviated **OSHA.**

occurrence   *n.* An event of happening.

odious   *adj.* Disgusting, disgraceful, hateful, vile, loathsome, scandalous. See also **odium.**

odium   *n.* **1** Hatred or distaste for, accompanied by contempt or disgust. **2** A condition of disgrace, usually as the result of some form of vile conduct.

offense   *n.* Any violation of the law for which the judicial code demands there be a penalty, including misdemeanors and felonies. See also **crime.**

offer   *n.* **1** The act of presenting something, such as a bargain, with the understanding that should the other party agree, that bargain will be complete. **2** A promise by one party to do something in exchange for something else being done by the second party. **3** An act demonstrating a willingness to enter into a contract in such a way that a reasonable person would recognize that acceptance of the terms will conclude in a binding agreement. See also **acceptance.**

offer of proof   *n.* **1** A presenting of evidence for the record, but outside of the presence of the jury (usually following a judge's ruling that such evidence is inadmissible) for purposes of preserving the evidence on the record for use in an appeal. **2** Such a presentation is an attempt to persuade the judge to allow the item's or testimony's introduction before the jury.

officer   *n.* A person who holds a position (office) of trust, command, or authority. In public affairs, the term usually applies to a person who holds a government position and is authorized to perform certain functions. In corporate law, it is a person appointed or elected by the company's board of directors. The term usually implies some form of tenure, duration, and emolument.

> *officer of the court.* Generally, a lawyer, in connection with his dealings with and in a court, is said to be an officer of the court as a result of his special relationship to the court and the trust placed in a lawyer by the court.

officious intermeddler *n.* A person who acts to benefit a person without having been asked to do so and without having had a contractual or legally recognized interest in doing so, and then seeks compensation or restitution for the act from the beneficiary, even though he has no legal grounds to do so.

offset **1** *v.* To pay for or compensate for; to calculate against: "The debtor is entitled to an offset against the amount due to the contractor for the amounts that are alleged to be properly deducted for poor workmanship." **2** *n.* Something that balances something else; for example, "The offset for the amount she spent was the house's improved appearance."

of record *adj.* **1** Matter that appears in official written documents, such as testimony taken by the court stenographer and filed deeds and mortgages. **2** Documented, as in the attorney of record or the court of record.

of the essence, time is See **time is of the essence.**

oligopoly *n.* An industry that is dominated by a small number of companies that manufacture substantially identical products. The American automobile industry and the tobacco industry are two examples. An oligopoly is far less competitive than one with many manufacturers, but slightly more competitive than a **monopoly.**

omission *n.* **1** Something left out or left undone. **2** The act of neglecting to do something required by law; especially one's duty. **3** The state of having been left out or undone. **4** The act of leaving something out or not done. An omission may be deliberate or unintentional.

omnibus *adj.* Having many purposes or treating with numerous things at the same time; including many things.

omnibus clause *n.* **1** A portion of a writing that confers rights or duties upon one not specifically named, or property not specifically mentioned, as in: an automobile insurance policy provision that extends the policy's coverage to any persons operating the motor vehicle, provided that the operator had the named insured's permission, or a clause in a will that bequeaths all unspecified property, or property not known at the time of testation.

on account *n.* Partial payment.

on all fours *adj. Colloquial.* Legal precedent or case law that is precisely on point with respect to the case at hand.

on demand *n.* When presented or asked for. Bills or notes that are payable when requested are known as demand notes. When the bank receives a demand note, it pays it, regardless of who the bearer may be.

one person (man), one vote *n.* A 1964 decision in *Reynolds v. Sims* affirmed the principle (based on the Equal Protection Clause) that each legislative district should have, as closely as possible, the same number of voters. See also **apportionment.**

on or about *n.* An expression popular in legal documents to indicate an approximate time or location.

on the brief   *n.* The identification of all attorneys and other persons who participated in preparing an appellate brief, usually listed on the brief's front cover.

on the merits   *adj.* Said of a judgment delivered after all the evidence in the case and the arguments of the parties have been heard. The judgment is rendered based upon the essential facts of the case, rather than on any technical or procedural rule, such as the failure of proper service.

on the pleadings   *adj.* Said of a judgment found after reading or hearing the complaint and the answer, and without waiting to hear or evaluate the evidence or the attorneys' arguments. See also **summary judgment.**

open   *adj.* **1** Free from concealment; readily viewable by the public; unobstructed.   **2** Apparent; notorious.   **3** Not closed, or final; still under consideration.

open account   *n.* **1** An as yet unsettled account.   **2** A series of transactions that result in a single liability. See also **account.**

open and notorious   Known by the public, and at odds with the community's accepted moral values. See also **notorious possession.**

open court   *n.* A functioning court attended by all interested parties and admitting the public, presided over by a judge. The term usually implies that all of the business of the court is done in a public judicial proceeding, rather than in a judge's office or **chamber(s).**

open end   *adj.* **1** Having room for future modifications or additions.   **2** Issuing or redeeming stocks or other shares on demand on a continuous, ongoing basis, at whatever their current net values happen to be.

opening statement   *n.* Introductory remarks made by an attorney at the commencement of a trial, in which he outlines the evidence that is expected to be proven. Although sometimes referred to as an "opening argument," this term is a misnomer, as the lawyers are not permitted to argue any points that have not yet been introduced into evidence.

open shop   *n.* A business that employs workers regardless of whether or not they are members of a labor union.

operation of law   *adj.* Description of an event that comes about automatically by virtue of application of law to a set of facts.

operative   *adj.* Description of words in a document that bring about the result of transaction.

opinion   *n.* The court's statement of its decision, usually written by a single judge, citing the facts, points of law, rationale, and decision or verdict. See also **decision, judgment** and **verdict.**

> *concurring opinion.* In appellate cases, a joining in by one or more judges to the principal opinion in the case, but for differing reasons or basis.

> *dissenting opinion.* An opinion written by one or more judges that disagrees with the one reached by the majority of the court.

> *majority opinion.* The opinion reached by the majority of the court; usually known simply as the opinion.

> *per curiam opinion. (Latin.)* By the court; an opinion reached by an appeals court and handed down without identifying its writer by name.

option   **1** *n.* The power or right to make a choice.   **2** *n.* A contract to keep an offer open for a specified period of time so that the person making the offer cannot suddenly withdraw it during that period.   **3** *n.* The right carried by that contract.   **4** *n.* The right to sell or buy a certain number of stocks or bond at a set price within a specified time period.   **5** *v.* To give or take an option on something.

oral   *adj.* Spoken or uttered, as distinct from written or hand-signaled.

oral argument   *n.* The spoken legal presentation by the attorneys before a court, in an effort to persuade same to decide in favor of his or her side.

oral deposition   *n.* See **deposition.**

order   *n.* A command, instruction, or direction by the court or by a judge intended to adjudicate some point or to direct some step in a legal proceeding.

> *final order.* An order that disposes of the entire case, but may be appealed to a higher court. See also **judgment.**

> *interlocutory order.* An order relating to only a portion of the case, but not a final disposition.

> *restraining order.* See **restraining order.**

> *show-cause order.* An order requiring a person to appear in court and explain why certain relief should not be granted.

order to show cause   See **order** (*show-cause order*).

ordinance   *n.* A local law, usually on the municipality level, that, when fully enacted, has the same effect and force as a statute within that municipality.

ordinary   *adj.* **1** Occurring in the usual course of events; usual and normal.   **2** When applied to a judge, having jurisdiction by virtue of office rather than by being assigned same.   **3** When applied to a jurisdiction, immediate and original; not delegated or devolved to.

> *ordinary care.* See **care** (*reasonable care*).

> *ordinary course of business.* Conduct of business under usual circumstances, going about business in everyday manner.

ordinary income   See **income.**

organic law   *n.* The body of laws that are fundamental to defining and creating a government and its legal system, whether written (such as a constitution) or unwritten.

organization expense   *n.* A deduction allowed to a newly formed corporation or partnership incurred establishing that company, which may be spread over a period of not more than five years.

organized crime   *n.* **1** A widespread group of professional criminals who rely on illegal activities as a way of life and whose activities are coordinated and controlled through some form of centralized syndicate.

original jurisdiction   *n.* The ability and authority to decide cases based on hearing testimony and viewing evidence, rather than on appeal. The distinction separates trial courts from appellate courts. When an appellate court tries a case de novo on appeal, it is said to be exercising its original jurisdiction rather than its appellate jurisdiction. State-and-county level trial courts have original jurisdiction. The federal courts have original jurisdiction in certain matters, as Congress expressly provides.   See **federal question** and **diversity jurisdiction.**

OSHA See **Occupational Safety and Health Administration.**

ostensible authority (or agency) *n.* A relationship between two parties that reasonably leads a third party to believe that one is the agent of the other; for example, an emergency room physician who may be employed by an outside contractor, not the hospital, may nonetheless be deemed the "ostensible agent" of the hospital.

ouster *n.* **1** The wrongful exclusion of a person from property or dispossession of same. **2** The removing from office of a public or corporate official.

out-of-court *adj.* Done outside a judicial proceeding, such as an out-of-court settlement.

out-of-pocket expenses *n.* Costs for necessary items, usually made in cash, and reimbursable at a later time.

out-of-pocket rule *n.* The principle that the damages in a breach of contract or warranty case should constitute the difference between what was paid for the goods or services and what their actual value is. See also **benefit-of-the-bargain rule.**

output contract See **contract.**

outstanding issue *n.* The total number of shares actually sold to shareholders less treasury stock; must be less than the authorized issue (the amount permitted by the company's charter).

overbreadth *adj.* A term used to describe a statute that prohibits certain behavior, but in so doing also restricts or inhibits behavior that is constitutionally guaranteed. See also **chilling effect.**

overreaching *n.* In commercial law, abusing one's superior bargaining power to take unfair advantage of another through fraudulent practices. Synonymous with **fraud.**

overrule *v.* **1** To void the findings of another court; overturn; set aside. **2** As a judge, to reject or rule against a courtroom objection.

overt *adj.* Unconcealed; open and observable; not secret.

overt act *n.* An open act; an act indicating an intent to commit a crime.

owner *n.* A proprietor; the one who has legal right to possess, use, and/or convey property to another.

ownership *n.* The total body of rights to use and enjoy a property, to pass it on to someone else as an inheritance, or to convey it by sale. Ownership implies the right to possess property, regardless of whether or not the owner personally makes constructive use of it.

oyez *v. French.* Literally, hear! An exclamation used to bring a court to order, or to gain attention for an official proclamation to be publicly made. A customary greeting uttered by a court bailiff to signify that court is in session.

P

P.A. *abbr.* Professional association. See also **corporation.**

pain and suffering *n.* Compensable results, whether physical or mental, from a wrong either suffered or committed. The loss of the ability to work due to emotional suffering, mental suffering, or physical pain are all appropriate elements of damage.

palimony *n.* A court-mandated payment by one of a former unmarried couple, who cohabited, to the other. The term originated in the reportage of *Marvin v. Marvin*, a 1976 California case. A portmanteau word, constructed from pal and alimony.

palm(ing) off *v.* Acting in a fraudulent manner, to pass something off as something other than what it is.

pander *v.* To pimp; to cater to others' lust. See **panderer.**

panderer **1** *n.* A manager, in the sex-for-money sense, of prostitutes; a person who causes a female to become a prostitute. **2** *v.* The act of selling obscene literature, movies, and/or other materials that appeal to one's prurient interest. See also **pander.**

panel *n.* **1** A list of persons summoned to be potential jurors. **2** The actual group of potential jurors, see also **venire.** **3** A group of judges selected from a larger group to hear a case. **4** Those sitting on an appellate bench.

paper *n.* Any written or printed document; any negotiable document or instrument evidencing the existence of a debt; stocks and bonds; securities. See **negotiable instrument, bearer, commercial paper.**

par/par value *n.* Equality between face value and actual selling price.

paralegal **1** *n.* A person not licensed to practice law, who assists a lawyer in a variety of tasks associated with a law office. **2** *adj.* As in "The assistant performed paralegal activities."

paramount title *n.* Real estate, title that is senior or superior to the title to which it is compared.

pardon See **clemency** and **reprieve.**

parens patriae *n. Latin.* Parent of his or her country. The state, in its role of provider of protection to people unable to care for themselves; a doctrine giving the government standing to sue on behalf of a citizen who is unable to pursue an action due to a legal disability.

parental liability *n.* The doctrine that parents are responsible for willful damage done to another's person or property by their minor children. All states have statutes to that effect, but most limit the amount to a few thousand dollars per tort.

parent corporation See **company** and **corporation.**

pari delicto See **in pari delicto.**

pari materia See **in pari materia.**

parimutuel *adj.* Of equal betting or wagering.

parole **1** *n.* A conditional release from a criminal sentence that permits the convict to serve the remainder of his or her term outside the confines of the prison as long as he abides scrupulously by certain preset conditions. **2** *v.* To effect what is described in the meaning of the noun.

parole board *n.* A group of individuals charged with assessing, as a group, the risks of granting early release to prisoners.

parole evidence rule *n.* The principle that a preexisting commitment cannot be used as evidence to contradict or in any way modify the terms of a written agreement. See also **integration** and **merger.**

partial breach   See **breach of contract.**

partially disclosed principal   See **principal.**

particulars, bill of   See **bill of particulars.**

partition **1** *n.* A separator of one space from another; a separation by a court of real estate owned jointly into two or more separately owned parcels, so that each of the former joint owners may enjoy having his or her own estate. **2** *v.* to separate a single parcel into two.

partnership *n.* A voluntary joining of two or more persons to jointly carry on and profit from a single business. A partnership is presumed to exist if the persons have agreed to proportionally share the losses and profits from that enterprise.

> *limited partnership.* A partnership comprised of one or more people in charge of the business who are personally responsible for the debts of the partnership (known as general partners) and one or more people who provide capital and share in the profits but who do not manage the business and are responsible only for the amount of their contribution (known as limited partners).

part-performance   See **statute of frauds.**

party *n.* A person taking part in a transaction or contract; a person or entity directly involved in a lawsuit.

> *aggrieved party.* A party whose pecuniary, personal, or property rights have been negatively affected by the actions of another or by a court's ruling. See also **aggrieved.**

> *indispensible party.* See **indispensible party.**

> *necessary party.* A party whose interests will be affected by his or her close connection to the case and who should be included if feasible, but whose absence would not require the proceedings' dismissal.

> *nominal party.* A party who appears on the record because of the technical rules of pleading, but who does not necessarily have any real interest in the outcome of the case.

> *party to be charged.* Contract law, the party against whom enforcement of the agreement is sought.

> *party wall.* Real property, a common support structure between two separately owned pieces of property.

> *prevailing party.* The party in whose favor a judgment is rendered, regardless of its magnitude or extent.

> *proper party.* A party not essential to the proceeding, but who may be joined in the case because of judicial economy or an interest in the subject matter of the litigation.

> *real party in interest.* A person who generally but not necessarily benefits from the suit's final outcome, and who is entitled under law to enforce the right the suit is based upon.

> *third party.*   A designation of any person not directly involved in a transaction or lawsuit.

passion   See **heat of passion.**

passive *n.* Not involving active participation, especially an enterprise in which an investor has no control whatsoever in its income-producing activity.

passive concealment   See **concealment.**

patent   *adj.* Obvious; manifest; apparent; clear; evident, as in "the contract had a patent ambiguity." See also **latent ambiguity.** Pronounced PAY-tint.

patent defect   See **defect.**

Patent and Trademark Office   *n.* A federal agency under the auspices of the Department of Commerce, which grants and regulates patents and trademarks.

patent (of invention)   *n.* The granting of a right or authority by the federal government; the document granting that right or authority; an exclusive right to make, use, or sell an invention granted to the inventor of a unique device or process for a specified period of time (usually 20 years). See **new and useful.**

> *design patent.* Patent granted for a new appearance to an existing item.

> *plant patent.* Patent granted for a new variety of plant, granted to person who discovers and reproduces same.

patent pending   *n.* A designation attached to a product while the Patent Office is considering the patent application. Such a designation imparts no protection against infringement unless the actual patent is eventually granted. Abbreviated **pat. pending.**

paternity   *n.* Fatherhood, the relationship of father to a child.

paternity suit   *n.* A proceeding initiated to determine the father of a child born out of wedlock, in order to provide for support for that child.

pat. pending   *abbr.* See **patent pending.**

patricide   *n.* The act of killing one's own father; a person who has killed his or her father.

patronage   *n.* The giving of protection or support; sponsorship; all of the clients or customers of a business; clientele; political favors, such as appointing to governmental positions in exchange for political support.

pauper   *n.* Someone who is unable to provide for his own support; a monetarily very poor person; an indigent person. Paupers are excused from paying court fees under the United States Constitution's Equal Protection Clause, so that they may avail themselves of equal access to the courts. See also **in forma pauperis.**

pawn   **1** *n.* An item of personal property given to secure a monetary loan; something held as security against a monetary loan.   **2** *v.* To borrow money against a piece of personal property that is held by the lender as security.

payables   See **account.**

payable to bearer   See **bearer.**

payable to order   *n.* To be paid only to a specific payee.

payee   *n.* Any person to whom a debt is to be paid; one to whose order a check or other negotiable instrument is made out.

payer (or **payor**)   *n.* A person who pays a debt or who is obliged to pay a debt by some written instrument.

payment   *n.* Delivery of funds in settlement of a claim or debt; fulfillment of a monetary obligation.

payment in due course   *n.* The payment of a negotiable instrument to the holder on or after its due date in good faith by the payer and with no notice of any defect in title. See also **holder in due course.**

payment into court *n.* The payment of money or other property by a party to a proceeding into the care of the court for later distribution in accordance with the suit's settlement or the court's judgment. See also **interpleader.**

payor See **payer.**

P.C. *abbr.* Personal computer; politically correct. See also **probable cause, professional corporation,** and **protective custody.**

PCR *abbr.* Stands for polymerase chain reaction, the newest (at this writing) method of **DNA** analysis. Using PCR technique, it is possible to analyze a biological specimen that is one-tenth the size of that required for the older **RFLP** method. It also gives quicker results, but the analysis is not as discriminating as RFLP.

PCR actions See **post-conviction relief proceedings.**

P.D. *abbr.* Police department; also **public defender.**

peaceable possession *n.* A continuous possession of property that is uninterrupted by legal suits or other action intended to oust the possessor from the property. Peaceable possession does not preclude there being adverse claims against the possessor, so long as no actual attempt has been made to dispossess him or her.

peculation *n.* **1** The fraudulent misuse of funds by one to whom they have been entrusted for purposes for which those funds were not intended, especially the misuser's own benefit. **2** Embezzlement, especially when done by a public official.

pecuniary *adj.* Having to do with, or relating to, money.

penal action *n.* A suit brought to recover a statutory penalty as punishment for an offense against the public.

penal code *n.* The body of penal law as a whole.

penal institution *n.* Any jail or other place of confinement including work camps, jails, reformatories, penitentiaries, and correctional institutions.

penal law *n.* Statute enacted to proscribe a certain offense against the public at large or against another person; imposing a penalty for violation of same.

penalties *n.* **1** Punishment in the form of fines or prison terms imposed on wrongdoers. Although normally applied in criminal cases, there are some cases of civil misdeeds for which a penalty (as distinct from a **remedy**) may be imposed. **2** Damages imposed by a contract for failing to meet a certain obligation, such as completion by the agreed-upon date.

penalty clause *n.* A provision in a contract that stipulates an excessive pecuniary charge against a defaulting party. Courts do not generally enforce such a clause, but will enforce liquidated damage clauses when they represent a legitimate approximation of actual damages. See also **damages** (*liquidated damages*).

pendente lite *n. Latin.* While the lawsuit is pending; contingent on the outcome of the legal action or litigation. See also **lis pendens.**

pendent jurisdiction See **jurisdiction.**

penitentiary *n.* A penal institution that is intended for long-term confinement of convicted criminals. See also **jail.**

pen register *n.* A device that records dialed telephone numbers. Pen registers have been deemed by federal authorities to be beyond the scope of wiretapping restrictions, because they do not intercept, hear, or monitor conversations. Some legislatures, however have ruled that their citizens are entitled to a higher degree of privacy.

peonage *n.* Involuntary and illegal servitude to pay off a debt. Forbidden by the Thirteenth Amendment to the United States Constitution.

per annum *adv. Latin.* By or through the year; yearly or annually; calculated one year at a time; at annual intervals.

per autre vie *Latin/French.* "For the life of another," term often used in bequeathing a right (but not title) in property.

per capita *adj. Latin.* By or through the head. According to the head count, or number of individuals; that is, divided equally among everyone involved.

per curiam *adv. Latin.* By the court. See **opinion.**

per diem *adv. Latin.* By or through the day. Daily pay or daily expense allowance.

peremptory *adj.* Final; conclusive; positive; incontrovertible. In a jury selection, each side is permitted a certain number of peremptory challenges for which no explanation is necessary. A peremptory trial date may be set so as to assure a speedy trial.

peremptory challenge See **challenge.**

peremptory plea See **plea.**

peremptory writ *n. Archaic.* A common law document directing the sheriff to assure the defendant's appearance in court, as long as the plaintiff has presented the former with security for the prosecution. In current practice, the peremptory writ has been replaced by the **summons.**

perfect (a lien) *v.* to take certain actions or follow certain procedures required by law in order to create a security interest that is enforceable.

perfected *adj.* A claim is said to be perfected if all steps required to put a claim right, or in final conformity with statutes, have been taken, and the litigant can proceed to an appellate court.

performance *n.* **1** The successful fulfillment of a contractual obligation. **2.** May be a promise of future payment in exchange for a contractual obligation's being done.

part performance. Partial fulfillment of obligations under a contract.

performance clause. A distinct section or provision of a legal document or piece of legislation.

specific performance. The requirement of performance of obligations as stated in the terms of an agreement, according to the exact requirements, on theory that compensation in damages would be inadequate to give recipient of the performance the "benefit of the bargain." Generally required in situations of unique services or goods.

peril *n.* Risk of exposure to injury or damage, such as that protected against in an insurance policy. See also **insurance.**

periodic tenancy See **tenancy.**

perjury *n.* The criminal offense of making false statements under oath, especially in a legal document or during a legal proceeding.

permanent injunction See **injunction.**

permission *n.* An authorization or license to do something; being allowed.

permissive counterclaim See **counterclaim**.

permissive joinder See **joinder**.

permissive waste See **waste**.

perpetuity See **in perpetuity**.

per quod *adj./adv. Latin*. Whereby. Having meaning only by reference to outside facts, such as on proof of injury or some sort of compensable damages. The opposite of **per se**.

per se *adj./adv. Latin*. By or through itself. Standing alone; on its own merits; without need for reference to outside facts. The opposite of **per quod**.

person *n*. An entity, such as an individual, or, under law, an incorporated group with certain legal rights and responsibilities; a human being; the live body of a human being. See also **natural person**.

personal holding company See **company**.

personal judgment See **judgment**.

personal notice See **notice**.

personal property *n*. Property that is movable, unlike real estate or things attached to the real estate. However, things attached to real estate may be considered as personal property, also known as personalty, if they can be relocated without doing irrevocable damage—a shed, perhaps, or even a mobile home. Personal property encompasses tangible and intangible non-real property.

personal recognizance See **release on own recognizance**.

personal representative *n*. A person whose job it is to manage the affairs of another under authority of a power of attorney, or due to the death, incompe-tency, or infancy of the principal party, as in the **executor** of a will or **guardian ad litem**.

personal service *n*. Actual delivery of a document into the hands of the person for whom it is intended; a delivery of some salable service of manual or intellectual endeavor without charge, as a favor.

personalty See **personal property**.

per stirpes *adj./adv. Latin*. By or through roots and stocks. A proportional division of the estate among beneficiaries according to the share of descent from their deceased ancestor. Essentially, each beneficiary gets shares of stock in the estate based upon the closeness of relationship to the deceased. Distinct from **per capita**.

persuasion burden See **burden**.

petition *n*. A formal written request for something to be done or not to be done, delivered to a court or other official body.

petitioner *n*. The person presenting a petition to a court or other body in order to institute an equity hearing or to appeal from a judgment. The opponent in such a proceeding is known as the **respondent**.

petit *adj. French*. Little, minor. Also spelled petty.

petit jury See **jury**.

petit larceny *n*. Originally distinguished from **grand larceny** as a matter of degree. A theft of something valued at 12 pence or less was considered petty larceny, and the death penalty was not invoked. Today, the amount differentiating between petty and **grand larceny** is in dollars and varies from state to state. See also **larceny** and **grand larceny**.

petty jury   See **jury.**

petty larceny   *n.* See **petit (petty) larceny.**

picketing   *n.* A common practice in labor disputes, in which employees patrol with signs on their fronts and backs (sandwich signs) or on wooden stakes held over their shoulders. Peaceful picketing is protected as free expression, except where considered a threat to public safety or when spreading false propaganda.

piercing the corporate veil *v.* Charging normally immune corporate officers, shareholders, and so on with personal liability for the corporation's wrongdoing. See also **corporate** (*corporate veil*).

pimp   *v. Slang.* See **pander** and **prostitution.**

piracy   *n.* **1** Robbery, kidnapping, or other criminal activity at sea. **2** Hijacking. **3** Illegal and unauthorized copying or distributing materials protected under copyright, trademark, or patent law. See also **infringement.**

plagiarism   *n.* Copying or stealing someone else's words or ideas and claiming or presenting them as if they were your own. See also **infringement.**

plain error (rule)   See **error.**

plain meaning (rule)   *n.* A rule that states if a written provision is in writing and appears on reading to be unambiguous, its meaning must be determined from the writing itself without resorting to outside evidence.

plaintiff   *n.* The party in a civil law case who brings the action in a court of law. See also **defendant.**

> *plaintiff in error. Archaic.* See **appellant.**

plain view   *n.* The exception to the requirement for a search warrant to protect one's rights against unreasonable search and seizure. If an officer has legal justification for being in a place and she spots something that is clearly suspect or proscribed, that object may be seized and introduced in a courtroom proceeding. Similarly, if the officer overhears something because it was uttered out loud so that it was overheard by an officer using normal hearing senses, that may be testified to by the officer. Additionally, use of a flashlight to make it easier to spot an object is acceptable, because it is a usual thing to do. Use of an X-ray machine, on the other hand, is unusual and, therefore, not permissible without a warrant.

plat   *n.* A small map showing the location of a piece of property in the context of adjoining lots, roads, and landmarks; a small piece of land. Also known as plot.

plea   *n.* **1** An accused person's formal reply to a charge in a criminal court, the choices being **guilty, not guilty,** and **nolo contendere** (no contest). **2** An answer in an equity case telling why a suit should be barred, delayed, or dismissed. **3** A pleading.

> *affirmative plea.* One intent on establishing a fact not in the bill that, if established, negates the merit of the complainant's case.

> *dilatory plea.* One that contests the grounds of a plaintiff's case, other than its merits, such as wrong jurisdiction, wrong defendant, or other defects in the procedure.

> *double plea.* One having two or more distinct and independent grounds of complaint for the same issue and requiring each one of those grounds to be answered separately.

peremptory plea. One directly responding to the particulars of the plaintiff's charges.

plea in abatement. A dilatory plea objecting to the time, method or place of the plaintiff's assertion, but not addressing any of that assertion's underlying merits.

plea bargaining *n.* A negotiation between prosecutor and defendant in a criminal case in an attempt to reach a mutually satisfactory middle ground and, therefore, obviate the need for a trial. Usually it consists of the defendant's pleading guilty to a lesser charge in exchange for a lesser sentence than he might receive had he been convicted on the original charge(s).

plead *v.* To make a plea of "guilty" or "not guilty" in court in response to a criminal charge; to file a pleading; to answer a plaintiff's **common law** declaration.

pleadings *n.* Formal, written declaration in legal form of logical statements setting forth the facts of the plaintiff's allegations or the defendant's responses, and or the reasons why each party believes that she is in the right (that is, the grounds).

amended pleading. One submitted to the court later than the original pleadings, correcting or adding to them.

defective pleading. One that either in form or substance fails to meet minimum standards of sufficiency or accuracy.

pleading in the alternative. One in which there are two or more independent claims or defenses that are not necessarily consistent, such as negligently inflicting pain and suffering, and intentionally causing property damage.

supplemental pleading. One that asserts a claim or defense based on events that occurred after the original pleading was filed, or which corrects defects in the original pleadings.

pleading the Fifth Amendment See **self-incrimination, privilege against.**

pledge *n.* an item of property given as security for a debt or performance.

plurality opinion See **opinion.**

pocket veto *n.* Under the United States Constitution, if the president does not sign a congressionally passed bill within ten days after receiving it, the bill becomes law, even without his or her signature. However, if the president neither signs nor vetoes the bill and Congress adjourns within that ten-day period, the legislation will become law only if the president signs it. Therefore, by not signing it, the bill is effectively killed.

point of law *n.* An individual legal issue or proposition at the heart of a case.

reserved point of law. A holding of a difficult legal issue that the judge holds in abeyance so that further testimony in the case may proceed.

police power *n.* The inherent power and obligation of a state government or sovereign, usually delegated in part to municipalities, to make whatever laws are appropriate and necessary to maintain public safety and security, morality, health, and propriety, which can neither be surrendered by the legislature nor transferred **in toto** away from the state. Such power is conferred by the Tenth Amendment to the United States Constitution, and is subject to and bound by considerations of due process.

polling the jury *v.* After a jury's verdict has been rendered, asking each individual member of a jury to confirm his or her vote, in order to ascertain unanimity, if requested by the defense.

poll tax *n.* A per capita tax of a fixed amount charged each person to register to vote, or to vote. Such a charge is prohibited in federal elections by the Twenty-Fourth Amendment to the United States Constitution. State laws requiring such fees have been ruled to violate the equal protection clause of the Fourteenth Amendment.

polygamy *n.* The condition of having more than a single spouse at one time.

pornography *n.* Media or photographs showing erotic or sexual behavior in a way designed to cause sexual arousal. Pornography is protected by the free speech provision of the First Amendment to the United States Constitution, unless it is found to be obscene. See also **obscenity.**

portfolio *n.* The total of the securities (consisting of stocks, bonds, certificates of deposit, and so on) held by an individual at any one time.

positive law *n.* The body of laws that have been enacted in a particular community and that are upheld by the courts of that community, as distinct from **natural law.**

positivism *n.* The view that true knowledge comes from studying observable traits and actions rather than through reasoning or speculating.

posse See **in posse.**

posse comitatus *n. Latin.* Power of the county. **1** A sheriff may summon citizens to assist him in making an arrest; hence posse in the traditional Old West sense. **2** A federal statute prohibiting the Army and Air Force from direct participation in civilian law-enforcement activities.

possession *n.* Exercising dominion over property; having custody and control of property. See also **custody** and **ownership.**

actual possession. Immediate physical control, and, therefore, occupancy, of real property.

adverse possession. See **adverse possession.**

constructive possession. Having the power and intention of exercising control and dominion of real property, but lacking actual presence on or direct control of same.

criminal possession. Unlawful possession of proscribed articles, such as drugs, assault weapons, and so on, or being in possession of something that individual is proscribed from possessing.

hostile possession. See **hostile possession.**

notorious possession. See **notorious possession.**

peaceable possession. See **peaceable possession.**

possessory action *n.* A lawsuit undertaken to gain physical possession of a premises or other real property, but not to take title to it. A possessory action may be instituted to evict a tenant who overstays a lease's term, or who is behind in payments.

possessory interest *n.* The right to control a property and to exclude others for the present, exercised by one who is not necessarily the owner. A current or future exclusive right to possession and use of a property.

possibility *n.* The chance of something's happening, regardless of whether or not it actually occurs; a contingent interest in property, whether real or personal.

possibility of reverter *n.* A future interest retained by a grantor of an estate so that the grantee's right to the estate would terminate and pass back to the grantor, should a certain pre-specified event or act actually occur.

post *v. Latin.* After. After in time, order, or position; behind. See also **ante.**

post-conviction relief proceedings *n.* Federal or state procedure whereby a convicted criminal can request that a conviction or sentence be corrected or vacated. Also called **PCR actions.**

post facto See **ex post facto.**

Post hoc ergo propter hoc *Latin.* After this; therefore because of this. An illogical notion that because one thing occurred after another, it must have been caused by the first thing.

posthumous child *n.* Child born after death of one of its parents.

posting *n.* A form of substitute process service by which the document is displayed in a prominent place, in order to assure public notice. It is usually used as a last resort, when all other attempts at service have failed. A method of publishing an ordinance by affixing it to the courthouse door.

post mortem *adv./n. Latin.* After death. Generally used to refer to the examination of a corpse by the coroner to ascertain the cause of death.

postnuptial agreement *n.* An agreement between a husband and wife stating the rights of each party in the event of the other's death, or in the case of a divorce, generally made at a time when neither eventuality is deemed to be imminent.

pot *n. Slang.* Marijuana. See also **controlled substance.**

pourover *n.* A statement in a will directing that certain money or property should be placed into an already existing trust.

power, enumerated See **enumerated power.**

power, implied See **implied power.**

power, inherent See **inherent power.**

power of appointment *n.* A donee's power, once authorized by the donor, to name the beneficiaries of the donor's property or income. The donee may not select anyone other than him- or herself. The donor may create this power by deed or by will, and it may be vested in any adult individual, or the donor may reserve the power for his or her self.

power of attorney *n.* **1** A written instrument whereby someone is granted the right to perform certain acts as the agent of the grantor; that is, acting in the grantor's behalf. **2** The actual authority granted in this way.

practice **1** *n.* The rules and procedures that cover all aspects of the proceedings of a court of law. **2** *n.* A law practice. **3** *v.* The practice of law. **4** *n.* a habit.

praecipe *n. Latin.* **1** Command, order. A written order or request to the clerk of the court. **2** A written court order commanding a party to do something or to show cause why it has not been already done.

prayer *n.* A request attached to the end of a pleading asking for specific damages or relief to which the plaintiff believes he is entitled.

preamble *n.* An opening statement in a document that declares the document's purpose. It is commonly found at the beginning of a constitution, statute, or other legal document.

precatory *adj.* Expressing a desire for, requesting, or advising action, but usually in a nonbinding way, such as, "it is my desire and wish to . . . ." Precatory words are often used in wills and similar documents.

precedent *adj.* Something that came before, hence preceded the event currently in question, such as a previously decided case. It may serve as a model for the interpretation of a law, or disposition as a case.

preclusion of issue See **estoppel.**

preemption *n.* **1** In law, the doctrine coming from the Supremacy Clause of the United States Constitution asserting that in legislation on the same subject, federal legislation takes supremacy over state or local laws. **2** The right to buy something before anybody else. **3** An earlier seizure of some property, real or personal.

preemptive right *n.* The right to the first opportunity to claim land subject to being preempted; the right of existing shareholders in a corporation to have the first opportunity to buy new shares when issued.

preferred stock *n.* Stock that has a higher value than common stock in terms of deriving dividends or income.

preference *n.* A debtor's transferring of property to a creditor in advance of filing a bankruptcy petition, so that the creditor receives more than would have been received under bankruptcy, to the detriment of other creditors.

prejudice *n.* A leaning toward one side in a lawsuit; an opinion held favoring one side without having heard the case; a predisposition or bias. See also **dismissal** (*dismissal with prejudice*) and (*dismissal without prejudice*).

preliminary hearing *n.* A criminal hearing, usually before a magistrate, to determine whether there is enough evidence to issue an indictment against a person or to warrant that person's being held in custody.

preliminary injunction See **injunction.**

premeditation *n.* An intention to act in a certain manner prior to so acting, as in "premeditated murder," meaning the act of killing after contemplation and intent to do so.

premise *n.* A prior statement upon which a conclusion is deduced.

premises *n.* **1** Property and the structures that are on that property. **2** Preliminary statements in a document upon which later ones are predicated.

premium *n.* **1** Money paid to an insurer in exchange for coverage. **2** Money paid by a buyer for an option to buy stock or property. **3** A reward for a job after it has been done.

premium, unearned *n.* Insurance, portion collected that must be returned to insured if policy is cancelled.

prenuptial agreement *n.* An agreement made before marriage by two people intending to marry, in order to set forth the issues of property rights and support in the case of divorce or death. See also **postnuptial agreement.**

preponderance *n.* Superiority in importance, influence, or weight.

preponderance of the evidence *n.* A more convincing amount of evidence than the other side has; the general standard for finding for one side in a civil case; enough proof to convince the judge that something is more likely to have occurred than not to have occurred.

prescription *n.* The role that the passage of time plays in the making and ending of certain rights. A way to acquire an easement on or in real property belonging to another by occupying it continuously for a prescribed period of time. See also **adverse possession.**

prescriptive easement   See **easement.**

presentence hearing   *n.* A proceeding following a criminal conviction at which a jury or judge examines all particulars relevant to the criminal and his or her offense, before passing sentence.

presentence hearing report   *n.* A report usually prepared by the probation department enumerating the convicted person's prior criminal record, aand educational, family, employment, and social background; intended to assist the court at the pre-sentence hearing.

presentment   *n.* **1** A formal written document of accusation returned by a grand jury on its own, without the prosecutor's having submitted a prior request for indictment. It is signed by all members of the grand jury, as distinct from an **indictment,** which is signed only by the foreman. Presentments are obsolete in federal courts.   **2** The production of a formal negotiable document, such as a promissory note, for payment.   **3** The delivery to a court of a formal document about a legal matter to be dealt with.

present sense impression   *n.* A person's impression of an event either while or immediately after its occurrence. Such impression is admissible evidence, even if it is hearsay.

presumption   *n.* A legal assumption that something is a fact based upon another proven fact or set thereof. The presumption is given sufficient weight, once established, that an even greater amount of evidence to the contrary would be needed in order to contravene it. It has the effect of shifting the burden of proof or that of producing evidence to the opposing party. See **inference.**

conclusive (non-rebuttable) presumption. A presumption that no amount of evidence or argument is strong enough to overcome.

rebuttable presumption. A presumption that is strong enough to make a **prima facie** case, but that is subject to being overcome by the presentation of stronger evidence to the contrary.

presumption of innocence   *n.* A basic tenet of criminal law that a person is to be presumed to be innocent until he is proven guilty beyond a reasonable doubt. The burden of proving the person guilty falls completely on the justice system, with the accused bearing no burden of proving his or her innocence. The presumption of innocence is not a determination of innocence, but rather a placing of the burden of proof entirely upon the justice system.

presumptive evidence   *n.* Evidence that is treated as sufficient for a guilty verdict unless contradicted and outweighed by presentation of rebuttal evidence. See also **presumption.**

pretermitted heir   *n.* An heir who was born after a decedent's will was drafted, but before the death of same. Because that heir was not alive for and is as a result unmentioned by the will, she generally would take nothing under the will; however, most states have laws allowing a pretermitted heir of the decedent to take whatever a child's share would have been had the decedent died **intestate.**

pre-trial conference   *n.* An informal conference among opposing attorneys and the judge in which the issues are narrowly spelled out, and that, in civil cases, allows the judge to encourage both parties toward reaching a settlement.

pre-trial detention   *n.* The detaining of an accused person in a criminal case before the trial has taken place, either because of a failure to post bail or due to denial of release under a pre-trial detention statute.

pre-trial discovery See **disclosure** and **discovery.**

prevailing party See **party.**

prevarication *n.* A lie; deceitful or dishonest behavior; equivocation.

preventive detention *n.* A confinement of an accused person pending trial, under terms of a statute authorizing denial of bail to defendants charged with having committed certain offenses and/or are considered to be a danger to themselves or to the public at large.

price discrimination *n.* The illegal charging of different prices to different persons for the identical or substantially similar goods or services. A violation of the **Sherman Antitrust Act,** price discrimination is also specifically addressed by the **Clayton Act.**

price fixing *n.* Artificially setting prices at a certain level, in exception to the workings of a free market, or conspiring to do same. The test is whether such actions or agreements restrain free traders' ability to sell according to those traders' judgment.

> *horizontal price fixing.* Price fixing by competitors on the same level, such as all supermarkets selling cereal for the same price.

> *vertical price fixing.* Price fixing between or among parties at different levels of distribution, such as manufacturers and distributors trying to control retail price.

priest-penitent privilege *n.* Disclosures made to clergy members while in active practice of their clerical duties as spiritual advisors are protected from disclosure. Some states have broadened this privilege to include marriage counselors as well as those giving counsel for other difficulties.

prima facie *adv. Latin.* At first sight. Not in need of further support to establish credibility or existence; obvious, unless disproved.

prima facie case *n.* A case supported by at least the minimal amount of evidence needed to meet the requirement for trying it; adequate to be able to avoid a directed verdict or a motion to dismiss.

primary liability See **liability.**

primogeniture *n. Latin.* First born. An ancient rule of descent by which the firstborn son inherits all the property of his deceased father, usually to the exclusion of all his siblings. The purpose of primogeniture was to keep the estate (real property), the ownership of which implied power, from being subdivided into smaller and smaller parcels of land.

principal **1** *adj.* Of greatest importance. **2** *n.* One who authorizes another to act in his or her behalf as an agent; any person involved in the commission of a criminal act.

> *disclosed.* A principal whose identity is shared by his or her agent with the third party.

> *principal in the first degree.* The actual perpetrator of a crime.

> *principal in the second degree.* Someone who assists in some way the principal in the first degree.

> *undisclosed.* A principal whose identity is kept secret by his agent. Both the undisclosed principal and the authorized agent are liable for fulfilling the provisions of a contract.

prior inconsistent statement *n.* A witness's statement made out of court that differs from his or her testimony in court. Even though the prior statement may have been **hearsay,** it may be used for purposes of impeaching the witness.

priority *n.* A condition of being higher in rank, or degree, or having occurred at an earlier time; taking precedence, especially a creditor's right to receive payment from a debtor before others are paid; the initiating court's exercising the jurisdiction in a case in which more than one court is involved.

prior restraint *n.* An unconstitutional prohibition in advance of a publication or communication before such communication or publication occurred. Prior restraint violated the First Amendment of the United States Constitution, except in cases of obscenity, defamation, or its representing "a clear and present danger" (Oliver Wendall Holmes, Jr.), and even in such cases, it is rarely upheld.

prison *n.* See **penal institution, jail,** and **penitentiary.**

privacy, right of *n.* The right to be left alone, generally derived from federal statutes assuring the right to be free from unwarranted publicity. It is usually recognized as being inherent in the right to liberty.

private corporation See **corporation.**

private necessity *n.* A necessity that includes only the personal interest of the defendant and, therefore, confers only a limited privilege or justification.

private nuisance See **nuisance.**

privilege *n.* An advantage that is not enjoyed by everyone; a special exemption, immunity, or legal right granted to a person or a class of persons; an exception.

privileged communications See **communication.**

privileges and immunities The phrase used in Fourteenth Amendment to the United States Constitution describing rights that citizens have that derive from the existence of the federal government, and include but are not limited to the right to travel, the right to vote in federal elections, the right to discuss national legislation, and immunity of the citizens of any state to be discriminated against by the laws of another state.

privity *n.* A legally recognized relationship of interest of two parties, be it in a transaction, a piece of property, or a proceeding.

> *horizontal privity.* The legal relationship between two parties in a distribution chain who are on equal level, as between two consumers. See also *vertical privity.*

> *privity of contract.* The relationship between the two parties to a contract that confers a right to take action on the contract; largely abrogated by enactment of warranty laws, permitting suits by users of products despite lack of privity with manufacturers.

> *privity of estate.* A joint or successive relationship to a property involving transfer of possession by contract, judgment, or descent, as between landlord and tenant, or life tenant and remainderman.

> *vertical privity.* **1** The legal relationship between links in a product's distribution chain. **2** The privity between a person who signs a contract containing a restrictive clause and the person acquiring the property that is so restricted.

privy *n.* Persons having a mutual interest in the same thing or who are connected by some relation other than contract.

probable cause *n.* A necessary element of a legitimate arrest or legal search and seizure; a reasonable ground to believe that someone is committing or has committed an offense. It must amount to more than just suspicion, but need not rise to the level of evidence justifying conviction, according to Fourth Amendment to the United States Constitution.

probate *n.* A judicial procedure by which a will or other instrument is ruled to be valid according to legal requirements; the proving of the validity of a will or such to the court.

probation *n.* A procedure following conviction that permits the party found guilty to be released without doing prison time, subject to conditions that are placed upon him or her by the court. Violation of any of those conditions can lead to probation being revoked and the person being remanded to confinement.

probative *adj.* Tending to persuade one or to prove that a certain proposition or allegation is true. Relevant evidence may be excluded by a court if its probative value is outweighed by the threat of prejudicing a matter unfairly.

pro bono publico *adj./adv. Latin.* For the public good. Used to refer to the taking of cases by attorneys without expectation of compensation. Also called **pro bono.**

procedural due process See **due process.**

procedure *n.* A specific course of action; the machinery by which a suit is carried on; the mechanics of the legal process; written rules for legal proceedings, whether criminal or civil, codified in rule books such as the *Federal Rules of Civil Procedure.*

civil procedure. A procedure to determine the rights of the parties, as distinguished from a *criminal procedure.*

criminal procedure. The process by which the government imposes penalties for criminal behavior through the devices of arrest, trial, and punishment of the convicted criminal.

proceeds *n.* Money or a thing of value that derives from a sale.

proceeding *n.* The orderly sequence of events that constitute the progression of a lawsuit or judicial procedure from the time of commencement, through all acts and occurrences, until and including the execution of the final judgment.

collateral proceeding. **1** One brought to deal with an issue not directly germane to the issue. **2** One instituted for the purpose of modifying the result of a judgment while not nullifying it.

informal proceeding. See **informal proceeding.**

summary proceeding. See **summary proceeding.**

process *n.* **1** A summons in writing to compel the appearance or response of a person before a court; the proceedings in a civil or a criminal case; the procedure by which a disobedient or recalcitrant defendant is made to plead. **2** Patent law, the method used to produce a thing or result.

abuse of process. Improper use of **process** after it has been issued; the wrong is not in the obtaining of process, but in the manner in which it is used.

procuring cause *n.* Proximate cause.

produce *v.* To provide or put forward.

Request to produce. Method of written **discovery** used to obtain documents or things from opposing party.

product See **work product.**

product liability *n.* The legal obligation of a manufacturer to pay financial compensation for any harm caused by a product brought to market to a consumer who had the right to expect that the product was safe to use as bought; a similar obligation of one who sells such a product.

production *n.* Response to a request to produce in which items requested are put forth or given to opposing party.

professional association See **corporation.**

proffer *v.* A preliminary offering, specifically with regard to testimony or evidence, a preview of what will be said or shown. Also known as an offer of proof.

profit *n.* The amount of money received for goods and services minus the amount spent on same; excess revenue. See also **profit à prendre.**

profit à prendre *n. French.* Profit to take. The right to take minerals, soil, trees, animals, or the like from the land of another.

pro forma *adj. Latin.* For form. **1** Done as a formality, rather than because of conviction, in order to make possible further proceedings. **2** In accounting procedures, done in advance to provide a what-if statement, predict results, or to convince. For example, a balance sheet showing combined figures of two companies in case of a merger.

progressive tax *n.* A tax that increases in rate as the amount of money being taxed increases; for example, $20,000 is taxed at 5 percent, $20,001 to $45,000 is taxed at 10 percent, and so on.

pro hac vice *Latin.* For this one purpose or occasion. The allowing of something not usually allowed, usually referring to an attorney who normally could not practice in a certain jurisdiction, but is allowed to just for one case.

prohibition *n.* **1** A statute or order forbidding a particular action. **2** The time from 1920 to 1933 when alcoholic beverages were banned by the Eighteenth Amendment (which was repealed by the Twenty-First Amendment) to the United States Constitution.

prolixity *n.* Any unnecessary or superfluous language or facts in evidence or in pleadings.

promise *n.* An avowal to do something or to refrain from doing something, conveyed in such a way as to assure another that it will be done, and that can be considered binding.

> *gratuitous promise.* A promise made without expectation of compensation; one not supported by consideration.

> *illusory promise.* An agreement cloaked in terms that make it appear to be a promise, but not actually committing anything to anybody; for example, "I'll back you up as long as it's in my interest to do so." The person who made that promise is not obligated to do anything.

promisee *n.* The person to whom a promise is made, he who is to receive the benefit of a promise.

promisor *n.* The person making a promise to another, the one who is to perform under the terms of the promise.

promissory estoppel *n.* Principle that one who has brought about certain actions or expectations by another because of promises made shall be estopped from acting or failing to act in contravention of his promises.

promissory note See **note.**

proof *n.* An establishment by evidence of the truth or falseness of an alleged fact; evidence upon which a court's judicial ruling is based.

> *burden of proof.* The responsibility placed on one party to bring forward evidence in support of his cause; as to a plaintiff (in a civil case) or a prosecutor (in a criminal case), the requirement of bringing forth sufficient evidence to support a finding in favor of plaintiff or the state.

> *standard of proof.* Level of proof required to sustain certain actions; varying levels of proof required include "beyond a reasonable doubt" (criminal cases), "by a preponderance of the evidence" (most civil cases), "clear and convincing evidence" (certain civil and some criminal cases, including fraud).

proof of loss *n.* Evidence given by an insured to insurer to support claim, both as to fact of loss having occurred, and as to amount of the loss.

proper See **Necessary and Proper Clause.**

proper lookout *n.* The obligation of the driver of a vehicle to be cautious so as not to hit another vehicle or a pedestrian.

proper party See **party.**

property *n.* All of the rights of ownership, including the rights of possession, to enjoy, to use, and to dispose of a chattel or a piece of land.

> *common property.* Property held jointly by two or or more persons, or property that belongs to all citizens. See also **community property.**

> *incorporeal property.* Property without tangible value, but that represents something of value, such as a stock certificate, which is just a piece of paper, but which indicates ownership of stock. Something of value.

> *intangible property.* Property that has no physical existence, such as stock options or goodwill.

> *intellectual property.* Property having to do with patents or trademarks.

> *personal property.* See **personal property.**

> *public property.* Community or state owned property that is not restricted to use by an individual or a select few, and over which the state or community has dominion and control.

> *real property.* Land, real estate.

> *tangible property.* Property with physical form and extent.

proponent *n.* Party advancing a cause or position.

proprietary *adj.* Held by a single particular person. Trade secret laws hold that the person who developed information or knowledge has ownership and property rights to her/his proprietary material. That right is usually protected by contract rather than by patent.

pro rata *adj. Latin.* According to the rate; in proportion. If a lawyer charges $100 per hour, and she works a quarter of an hour, her pro rata fee would be $100/4, or $25.

pro se *adj/adv. Latin.* For himself; on one's own behalf; on one's own. Characterization of one who represents himself/herself in an action without the assistance of an attorney at law and who acts as his/her own attorney of record.

prosecution *n.* A pursuing of a lawsuit or a criminal trial; the party pursuing a criminal prosecution; the carrying out of any activity or plan.

prosecutor   *n.* The person or persons who prepare for and conduct the state's case in a criminal trial; the state's attorney, district attorney, or in the case of a federal case, the United States Attorney.

prosecutorial discretion   *n.* A prosecuting attorney's option to make choices with regard to charges, plea bargaining, sentence recommendation, and so on.

prosecutorial misconduct   *n.* An illegal act or failing to act, on the part of a prosecutor, especially an attempt to sway the jury to wrongly convict a defendant or to impose a harsher than appropriate punishment.

prospective   *adj.* Effective in the future. Newly enacted laws and constitutional decisions are almost always applied prospectively.

prospectus   *n.* Written document issued by corporation, describing shares of stock and offering same for sale.

prostitution   *n.* **1** Engaging in sexual activity for compensation.   **2** Lowering in value, dignity, class, and so on.

pro tanto   *adj./adv. Latin.* To such extreme; as far as it goes; for just so much. Often, a partial payment made for invoking **eminent domain.**

protect   *v.* To keep safe; to preserve something that already exists, as in protecting trade and protecting consumers.

protective custody   *n.* State-mandated confinement of an individual to protect the person being harmed by self or others.

protective order   *n.* A court order intended to protect a party from annoyance, undue burden, or expense due to an abuse of the legal system; a restraining order.

pro tempore   *adj./adv./n. Latin.* For the time being. A temporary position or appointment. Also called **pro tem.**

protest   *n.* A formal objection to something that is, will be, or has been done.

provisional remedy   See **remedy.**

proviso   *n.* A condition or limitation that may determine the applicability of a document to certain conditions or persons.

proximate cause   See **cause.**

proxy   *n.* **1** One who receives the authority to speak for or act for another. A proxy is often allowed to vote in place of a corporation's stockholder(s) at a periodic meeting.   **2** The authority itself.

prudent   *adj.* Cautious or judicious in manner and/or actions.

prurient   *adj.* Characterized by shameful or inordinate sexual arousal or extraordinary sexual urges. See also **obscene.**

psychotherapist-patient privilege   *n.* The same as **priest-penitent privilege** but applying to the relationship between a mental health giver in the practice of counseling and a patient.

publication   **1** *v.* Announcing or declaring to the public; the distribution of a book, pamphlet, or other work to the public. **2** *n.* in libel, the act of communication of the libelous matter.

public corporation   See **corporation.**

public defender   *n.* An attorney hired by the government for the purpose of defending anyone who is accused of a crime but who is unable to afford to hire an attorney. The right to such a defense is guaranteed by the Sixth and Fourteenth Amendments to the United States Constitution.

public domain *n.* Government-owned land; all publications, processes, and inventions that are not protected by patent or copyright.

public figure *n.* A person who is famous or notorious or who has willingly become involved with a public issue or controversy,

public interest *n.* The people's general welfare and well being; something in which the populace as a whole has a stake.

public necessity *n.* A complete justification for a normally unacceptable act, if it were the lesser of two evils and done in the public's interest. See also **public interest.**

public nuisance See **nuisance.**

public property See **property.**

public purpose *n.* A governmental action or direction that purports to benefit the populace as a whole.

public utility *n.* A company such as an electric company or gas company, the nature of which is to be a monopoly in a particular region. Because no free-market forces can exist in this situation, governmental regulation of such companies is the norm.

publish *n.* To make generally known to the public; to make known to people who might or would have not known without the person's having so acted.

puffing *n.* Extravagant claims made by sellers to try to attract buyers for their wares. Such talk cannot be legally construed to be a guarantee or be used as the grounds for charging fraud.

punishment *n.* Sanctions such as fine, confinement, or loss of rights to property administered to a person convicted of a crime.

pur autre vie See **per autre vie.**

purchase *n.* The acquiring of property in exchange for money or other valuable consideration. See also **descent** and **distribution.**

purchase money security interest See **security interest.**

purchaser *n.* One who receives property in exchange for money or valuable consideration.

> *bona fide purchaser.* One who purchases property for value, without notice of any defects in title.

pure plea See **plea.**

purge(ing) contempt See **contempt.**

pursuit of happiness *n.* An inalienable right enumerated in the Declaration of Independence, in addition to life and liberty; the right to pursue any legal activity as long as it does not infringe on the rights of others.

purview *n.* The main part of a statute, as distinguished from its preamble or post script; scope; area of operation.

putative *adj.* Supposed rather than real; believed; reputed.

puts and calls *n.* Stock market terms; a "put" is a privilege of delivery or nondelivery of the subject matter of a sale; a "call" is the privilege as it relates to calling for or not calling for it.

pyramiding *n.* An illegal scheme in which paper profits are used to finance the purchase of additional investments, or the offering of the opportunity to a participant to be paid for the chance to introduce new persons to the scheme who will each pay for the opportunity to introduce new persons, and so on.

Q

Q *abbr.* The abbreviation used in trial transcripts and depositions to mark each question asked.

QDRO *abbr.* See **qualified domestic relations order.**

quaere *v. Latin.* To query or inquire. Used in law textbooks to indicate that a point was dubious or questionable.

qualified disclaimer *n.* A disclaimer stating that the taxpayer has no interest, for federal unified estate tax purposes, in the disclaimed property.

qualified domestic relations order *n.* Any decree, judgment, or order that recognizes the right of one person (the alternate payee) to participate either totally or partially in the pension of another (the participant). The alternate payee must be a dependent child, spouse, or former spouse of the participant. This is an exception to the **ERISA** rule, proscribing the assignment of plan benefits. Abbreviated **QDRO.**

quantum *Latin.* An amount; the necessary or desired portion; the required or needed amount or share.

quantum meruit *Latin.* Equitable formula for determining how much to award to one who has provided goods or services to another who has not paid, based on the reasonable value of the goods or services; the equitable principle that one who has received the benefit of a bargain should not be permitted to be unjustly enriched.

quantum valebant *Latin.* **1** The reasonable worth of goods or services, used to compute fair and reasonable damages; the market value. **2** A common-law action of assumpsit for items sold and delivered, in order to recover proper and appropriate payment for same.

quare clausum fregit *Latin.* An early form of trespass onto someone else's land, whether or not that land actually had a physical fence around it. The plaintiff would argue that because the defendant had broken the boundary "with force and arms," the former was due damages.

quash *v.* **1** To suppress a legal document, particularly a subpoena, for reasons based on defect in manner of **service** or for other procedural or substantive reasons that invalidate the document; to void or terminate; to vacate a judicial decision. **2** To suppress, as in quashing an uprising or revolt.

quasi *Latin.* Alike in some sense, but not in actuality; resembling something but not really being it; nearly; almost like.

quasi contracts. See **contract.**

quasi criminal. A proceeding similar in nature to a criminal trial in that the defendant, if he loses, will be subject to penalties such as fine, loss of job, or confinement, yet it is not a criminal trial presided over by a judge. A parole hearing or a probation hearing are two examples of such.

quasi in rem. See **in rem.**

question, federal See **federal question.**

question, leading See **leading question.**

question of fact *n.* An issue in dispute that is left to the jury to resolve, because it is not clearly covered by any law. A judge then rules on what the law says must be done. Questions of fact are usually decided in lower courts rather than on appeal. See also **fact-finder.**

question of law *n.* The legal significance of the question of fact; a disputed legal question, left to a judge to determine. Appellate courts usually make their determinations based upon questions of law rather than questions of fact.

quia timet *n. Latin.* A legal remedy sought in an equity court to enjoin someone from doing an anticipated damage. Such a remedy may be granted if the petitioner can show imminent and irreparable harm would be done.

quid pro quo *n. Latin.* Something exchanged for another thing of approximately equal value, not necessarily in a monetary sense.

quiet enjoyment *n.* To have the undisturbed use or possession of something, particularly conveyed or leased property. Often expressed in a lease by a covenant of quiet enjoyment. See also **eviction.**

quit *v.* to leave or surrender possession.

qui tam *Latin.* An action that grants the plaintiff a portion of the recovered penalty and gives the rest of it to the state. The plaintiff is said to be suing for the state as well as his or herself.

quitclaim *n.* A formal renouncement of one's right to or interest in something. See also **deed.**

quitclaim deed *n.* An instrument which transfers all of the right, title and interest that the conveyor has in a piece of property, but with no warranty or assurances that the conveyor has good and legal title; risk of liens or encumbrances pass to the transferee.

quorum *n.* The number of persons who must be present in a group for official action to be taken, e.g., a "quorum" of the board of directors must be present in order to take a vote; the number of individuals constituting a quorum may vary from body to body.

quotation *n.* **1** A passage, from an authority, that is quoted, cited, and attributed to its source. **2** The statement of the price of a stock or other financial instrument.

quotient verdict *n.* An improper verdict that a jury may arrive at by taking the arithmetic mean of what each juror believes to be an appropriate award.

quo warranto *Latin.* **1** A common law writ inquiring into the authority by which a public official claims his/her office. **2** A state action with the intent of revoking the charter of a corporation that has abused or for a long period failed to exercise its franchise.

R

Racketeer Influenced and Corrupt Organizations Act *n.* This law, enacted in 1970, is designed to fight activity by organized crime and to preserve the integrity of the interstate and international marketplace by investigating and prosecuting individuals conspiring to participate or actually participating in racketeering. Note that it has no force in intrastate commerce. Abbreviated **RICO.** See also **racketeering.**

racketeering *n.* A system of organized criminal extortion of money or favors from businesses through the use of violence, intimidating, or other illegal means; a pattern of illegal activity carried out by a criminal group or syndicate, including but not limited to fraud, murder, extortion, and bribery. See also **bribe, bribery, extort, extortion,** and **fraud.**

raised check See **check.**

ransom **1** *n.* The money paid to secure the release of a person held captive, whether as a result of having been kidnapped or captured in some other way; the release of a captured person in exchange for money or other consideration. **2** *v.* To gain the release of a captive by paying the price demanded; to hold a person captive and insist on payment as the condition of release.

rape **1** *n.* In common law, the felony of a man having illegal sexual intercourse with a woman other than his wife, by force or with threat of violence and against her will; unlawful sexual act with an unwilling other, and usually involving threat of violence. **2** *v.* to commit the act of forcible sexual intercourse.

> *date rape.* Rape committed by the victim's escort to a social event, also known as acquaintance rape or relationship rape.

> *statutory rape.* Sexual intercourse with an individual who is a minor or under the age of consent (today, usually 18), by an adult. Neither consent of the minor, nor ignorance of the minor's age, can be used as a defense.

rap sheet *n. Slang.* A person's criminal record.

ratable **1** *n.* Taxable property; a ratable distribution is a **pro rata** share of the assets of a bankruptcy. **2** *adj.* Capable of being appraised or apportioned.

rate *n.* A fixed or stated price for a specified unit of a commodity or service, such as $2 per pound or $9 per hour; a percentage of an amount, such as 5 percent interest on capital; a relative or proportional value.

ratification *n.* Affirmation or approval; adoption of an action that was done on one's behalf and treating that action as if it had been authorized by that person before the fact of it having been done. By ratifying an act or action, a person becomes responsible for the consequences of that act or action. Ratification by a two-thirds vote of Congress is needed to propose a constitutional amendment, which must then be ratified by three fourths of the states for it to take effect.

ratify *v.* To affirm or approve, usually after the fact.

ratiocination *n.* Reasoning; the process of exact, rational, reasoning something through.

ratio decidende *adj. Latin.* The reason for deciding. The rule of law or principle on which the court's decision is based. See also **obiter dicta.**

rational basis test *n.* A principle of analysis under the due process or the equal protection clause, which may be used to either uphold or void a law based upon the law's serving to reasonably attain some legitimate governmental objective. If violation of a specific right is charged, such as a restriction based upon color, religion, and so on, the law must be tested by **strict scrutiny,** a more stringent test.

ravish *v.* To take by force or seize is the literal meaning of the word. It is generally synonymous with *rape.* Traditionally, an indictment for rape demanded inclusion of the word ravished, which implied use of force and or violence by the man and resistance by the female.

real estate *n.* Land and any permanent structures attached thereto; any interest in same. See also **real property.**

real evidence *n.* Objects produced for inspection at trial. See also **evidence.**

realization *n.* A transformation of non-monetary assets into cash; a transaction such as a property sale that impacts upon the taxpayer's wealth to the extent that it may trigger the imposition of an income tax. If the tax is, in fact, imposed, the transaction is said to be recognized. See also **recognition.**

real party in interest See **party.**

real property *n.* Land, including whatever is attached to its surface, such as buildings, trees, and so on; everything beneath its surface, such as minerals; and the air space above it. This is distinct from **personal property,** which is movable. See also **chattel** and **property.**

reapportionment *n.* The altering of the boundaries of a legislative district in order to reflect shifts in population distribution. See also **gerrymandering.**

reargument *n.* The bringing of a court's attention to some substantive principle that was overlooked or misrepresented during the initial arguments before that court, usually occurring before the court reaches its decision. See also **rehearing.**

reasonable *adj.* A standard for what is fair and appropriate under usual and ordinary circumstances; that which is according to reason; the way a rational and just person would have acted.

reasonable care See **care.**

reasonable diligence See **diligence.**

reasonable doubt *n.* The amount of doubt that would cause one to believe that the defendant might not actually be guilty of the charged offense(s). "Beyond a reasonable doubt" is the amount of certainty that a juror must have in order to find a criminal defendant guilty as charged. See also **moral certainty** and **preponderance of the evidence.**

reasonable man (or **person**) *n.* An imaginary person who is used as the legal measuring stick against which to determine whether or not a defendant exercised appropriate caution in an undertaking, or whether he exhibited negligence by not taking the precautions that the hypothetical reasonable person may have taken under the given circumstances, or by doing something that a reasonable person would not have done.

reasonable time *n.* The subjectively determined amount of time that should be needed to complete what a contract requires to be done; how long the **Uniform Commercial Code** provides for an offer or goods to be accepted or rejected by a buyer or for substitute goods to be provided by the seller before one or the other becomes in default.

rebuttable presumption See **presumption.**

rebuttal evidence See **evidence.**

rebutter *n.* Someone who rebuts; a common law defendant's pleading in response to the plaintiff's **surrejoinder.**

recall *n.* **1** A removal of a public official from office by means of a popular vote to prematurely end his or her term of service. **2** A product manufacturer's requesting the public to return faulty products for replacement or repair, required by the Consumer Safety Act.

receivables See **account receivable.**

receiver *n.* **1** A disinterested party chosen by a corporation or by a court to collect and protect property that is the subject of diverse claims. A receiver is often appointed in proceedings concerning insolvency. **2** In criminal law, a receiver is one who accepts or obtains possession of goods that are known to be stolen, and as such is in turn a violator of the law. See also **liquidate** and **fence.**

receivership *n.* The situation of being in the control of a receiver; functioning as a corporate- or court-appointed receiver; the proceeding at which a receiver is appointed by the court. See also **bankruptcy.**

receiving stolen property See **receiver** and **fence.**

recidivist *n.* One who commits a second (or higher numbered) crime; a repeat offender; a habitual criminal. Such a person is usually subject to extended confinement under habitual criminal statutes. See also **criminal.**

reciprocal agreement *n.* Obligations assumed and imposed by two parties as mutual and conditional upon the other party assuming same obgliations.

reciprocal wills *n.* Wills prepared and signed close in time, with mutual and interchangeable bequests, generally between spouses.

reciprocity *n.* An agreement or relationship between states, or localities, where special advantages are bestowed upon citizens of A by B in exchange for similar advantages being bestowed on citizens of B by A. For example, State A may allow attorneys who are properly licensed in State B to become licensed in State A without taking a bar examination, if State B affords the same privilege to lawyers who are properly licensed in State A.

recital *n.* Formal statement(s) in a written document that sets forth certain facts that form a basis or reason for the agreement or transaction which follows; generally prefaced with the term "whereas," as in "Whereas, the parties intend by this agreement to set forth their agreement to divide all their marital property in anticipation of divorce."

reckless disregard *n.* An act of proceeding to do something with a conscious awareness of danger, while ignoring any potential consequences of so doing. Reckless disregard, while not necessarily suggesting an intent to cause harm, is a harsher condition than ordinary negligence. Proving a defendant's "reckless disregard for the truth" is the standard for success of a plaintiff in a suit for libel.

recognition *n.* Acknowledgement that something was authorized to be done; the acknowledgement of someone's or something's rank or status, especially the diplomatic recognition of another country; a subjecting to income tax, under the federal income tax laws. See also **realization.**

recognizance *n.* A bond made to a court, and recorded, of an obligation to do something, which if the person so bound fails to do will require the payment of a preset sum of money. Most often, a recognizance is in the form of a bail bond that guarantees an unimprisoned criminal defendant's appearance for trial. See also **bail, bond,** and **release on own recognizance.**

recognizance, one's own See **release on own recognizance.**

record **1** *n.* A documentation of things past in writing; often the exact history of a legal proceeding; information stored in electronic form on some medium such as computer drive, CD, or DVD; the official transcript of a trial or proceeding that contains its word-by-word documentation. **2** *v.* the act of filing a document with a court or official office, as in "to record a deed."

> *record on appeal.* A presentation to an appellate court of all the testimony and items introduced into evidence in the lower court, plus the compiled pleadings, briefs, motions, and other papers filed with the inferior court.

> *record, public.* Any document affecting real property, such as a deed or a mortgage concerning land within a particular jurisdiction of the government keeping that record.

record date *n.* The date by which a corporate shareholder must be registered in order to be eligible to receive dividends or to vote on company business.

recording acts *n.* Statutes that affect the recording of deeds or other interests in real property. They are designed to protect bona fide owners from previous unrecorded interests.

record owner *n.* The owner of real property and stocks, bonds, and other financial instruments as shown by public records.

recoupment *n.* A recovery of expenses; a reduction or withholding for legitimate reasons, of part or all of an owed amount; a defendant's right to have part of the plaintiff's claim reduced as the result of a breach of contract by same in the course of the same deal.

recourse *n.* A course of action for enforcing a claim; the right of the holder of a note to demand full payment of that note if the terms are not fully honored; the right to be repaid from the borrower's or cosigner's personal assets in excess of the collateral.

recover *v.* To get back the full or an equivalent amount; to obtain through a legal judgment; to be awarded damages.

recovery *n.* The getting back of something that was taken away; the amount awarded by a decree or judgment; the establishment by a court of a right to something by decree or judgment of a court.

recusal *n.* A judge's removing him- or herself from a trial or hearing, because of bias, prejudice, or an interest in the matter being decided.

recuse *v.* To remove as a judge from a trial or hearing, because of bias, prejudice, or an interest in the matter being decided; to object to or challenge the qualifications of a judge to hear a case due to a possible conflict of interest.

redemption *n.* A reclaiming or rebuying something by virtue of paying off a debt or settling some other predetermined condition of ownership; a buying back of its outstanding stock by a corporate entity; the right of a debtor to buy back property from someone who bought it at a creditor-initiated forced sale.

red herring *n.* A topic that may or may not have general significance, factual or legal, but that is of absolutely no relevance to the question or matter at hand.

re-direct examination   See **examination.**

redlining   *n.* An unlawful discrimination in granting credit practiced by some financial institutions, based upon the prospective borrower's living in a so-called "undesirable" or "bad" neighborhood.

redress   *n.* Relief, restitution, or damages.; a way of seeking remedy once the statute of limitations has expired. See also **relief, remedy, recovery,** and **restitution.**

reductio ad absurdum   *n.*   *Latin.* Reduction to the absurd. In logic, disproving an argument by demonstrating that it leads to a ridiculous conclusion.

reentry   *n.* The resumption of possession of a parcel of land by one who had formerly possessed it and who reserved the right to resume same when the new holder released it; the right of a landlord to repossess a leased premises after a tenant has defaulted on the terms of its lease.

referee   *n.* A quasijudicial master appointed by a court to assist with a specific matter, and who in certain jurisdictions is permitted to take testimony and determine factual issues that, eventually, are reported back to the court for judgment. See also **master.**

referendum   *n.* A passing of responsibility for a piece of legislation, a constitutional amendment or some other public issue to the public at large to vote upon; the vote in such an issue. See also **initiative.**

reformation   *n.* A rewriting of a deed or contract that does not express what was actually agreed upon, only when it can be demonstrated in a clear and convincing manner that a mutual mistake was made. There will be no rewriting if the mistake was made by one party only, unless it was caused by the other party's

fraud. Reformation is considered to be an equitable remedy.

refusal   *n.* Rejection of goods or denial of services to which a person is entitled; not completing a contract by either nonacceptance or nonpayment for goods or services; a chance to accept or reject something before any one else is offered that chance; the privilege of being afforded such a chance, also known as the **right of first refusal.**

register   *v.* To formally enter in a public list (as in register to vote); to make a record of (the defense registered an objection); to file a stock with the Securities and Exchange Commission, which is required before it can be offered for sale.

registered (coupon) bond   *n.* A long-term, interest-bearing instrument, in the form of a certificate, issued to the public by a corporate or governmental entity as a way to borrow money and registered on the books of the issuer. The obligor promises to repay the money on or before a specific date and makes regular interest payments until then. The owner of the bond is not a stockholder and has no ownership interest in the entity, but is only a creditor and the debt is often secured by a lien on the entity's property. Interest is paid by redeeming a coupon. See also **bond** and **debenture.**

registered   representative   *n.*   A trained securities salesperson authorized to take orders for securities from the general public and paid a commission on what she sells. After six months or more of training and after having passed tests prepared by the National Association and Securities Dealers and the New York Stock Exchange, that person is registered with the various stock exchanges, and licensed by the state(s) in which she plans to do business.

registered trademark *n.* A mark filed in the United States Patent and Trademark Office, with a precise description of the mark, including drawing or photograph if appropriate; a registered trademark confers upon its owner the sole right of use, with protection against infringements or use by others.

registrar *n.* An official record keeper, such as the one who at a university keeps the academic records, or the agent of a corporation who records and keeps records of the names of stock and bond holders.

regulation *n.* A rule issued by an administrative agency or a local governmental body prescribing conditions or authorizations that must be followed by the public or by public utilities; the process of controlling by restrictions or rules.

regulatory offense *n.* A crime that is not inherently wrong, but that is illegal because it is prohibited by legislation. Some examples of regulatory offenses are exceeding the speed limit; public intoxication; and hunting, fishing, or driving without the appropriate license. Also known as a statutory offense. See also **crime.**

rehabilitation *n.* A restoration of reputation and character, the term has many context-sensitive meanings. In penology, it is the process of improving the inmate's character so he will become a productive member of society. At a trial, it is the restoration of a witness's credibility after it has been impeached under cross examination. In the context of bankruptcy, it is restoring a corporation's solvency by satisfying the creditors' claims with future earnings, so that the corporation may continue to do business. See also **mitigating circumstance.**

rehearing *n.* A second hearing or retrial before the same court that already ruled to reconsider the issue on the grounds that there was an error or omission during the first time around. The pleadings and evidence already introduced in the first trial will remain in evidence.

rejoinder *n.* A pleading in common law, made by the defendant to answer a **replication** by the plaintiff.

relation back *n.* The principle that an act committed at a later time is considered as having occurred at the time of an earlier event; a judge's application of that principle.

relative *n.* A person who is akin to another by virtue of blood; that is a blood relation, such as sister, brother, aunt, uncle, parent, child, and so on.

relator *n.* Individual who reports or gives information upon whose word certain legal documents may be given.

release *n.* **1** Freeing from an obligation or commitment. **2** Liberating one from a duty or claim that she could have been held legally liable for. **3** Surrendering of a right or title. **4** A written permission to publish or to quote in print, given to a newspaper or book publisher by the quote's legal owner. **5** A discharge from custody, confinement, or imprisonment, whether with certain provisos or unconditionally.

release on own recognizance *n.* A pretrial release of an arrested person without bail, on that person's promise to appear for trial when it is appropriate to do so. Abbreviated **ROR.**

relevancy *n.* A test regarding the admissibility of evidence into a court of law, based upon the logical relationship of the prospective evidence and the fact that it is intended to establish.

reliance   *n.* Dependence; trust; confidence in the support of someone or something.

> *detrimental reliance.* The relying by one party on the representations of another to the detriment of the first party's position or welfare. It may be a cause for bringing an action for recovery of damages due to fraud. See **estoppel.**

reliction   *n.* A gradual shifting of a river's course, causing it to withdraw from its banks and/or to lower its level. The newly created dry land, if the retreat is permanent, becomes the property of the owner of the adjoining property; the changing of a property's boundary line by the erosion of land by a river or stream. See also **accretion, avulsion,** and **dereliction.**

relief   *n.* **1** Assistance or help given to those who are in need; especially financial assistance provided by the state. **2** The benefit or redress awarded to a claimant by a court, or claimed in a court, especially that which is equitable in nature, such as an injunction against future harm, as distinct from monetary **damages.**

relinquishment   *n.* Abandonment of a right or thing. See also **abstention.**

remainder   *n.* The part of a decedent's estate that is not otherwise specifically bequeathed in a will; a future interest vested in a third person, and intended to occur after the termination of the preceding estate(s). For instance if a grant is made "to Bob for life, and then to Erica," Erica's interest upon the death of Bob is the remainder.

> *contingent (executory) remainder.* A remainder given to a person only if certain conditions are met; one given to a person not yet born; or one left to a living person whose identity is yet to be determined.

> *vested remainder.* One going to a person in existence and without preceding condition for immediate possession, but then passed along to another. In the preceding example, Erica has a vested remainder upon the death of Bob.

remainderman   *n.* One who holds an interest in a remainder, whether contingent or vested, and who will become its possessor at some future time.

remand   *v.* **1** To send back for further consideration; an appeals court may remand a case back to the lower court for further action or for a new trial; **2** To send a prisoner back to custody after denying a plea for bail.

remedy   *n.* The way a right is enforced or an injury is redressed—most commonly by imposition of monetary damages.

> *extraordinary remedy.* A type of remedy that is not usually available, but that is used when it is shown that it is necessary in order to preserve one's rights. **Writs of mandamus, prohibition,** and **habeas corpus** are examples of such.

> *provisional remedy.* A temporary remedy that is incidental to a regular legal proceeding, but that is needed to preserve the claimant's rights or to keep same from suffering irreparable harm pending the action's conclusion. Temporary restraining orders, injunctions, attachment, or appointment of receivers are examples of provisional remedies.

remedy, mutuality of   See **mutuality of remedy.**

remitter   *n.* **1** The principle by which a person holding two titles to property and enters upon it by the lesser, or more defective, title is restored to the earlier or better title.   **2** Someone who sends a payment to another.

remittitur *n. Latin.* It is sent back. A court's order that reduces what it deems to be excessive damages awarded by a jury; the process by which the court proposes to reduce or actually reduces damages without the jury's consent. See also **additur.**

remote cause See **cause.**

removal *n.* **1** An altering or moving of a person or thing from one location to another. **2** The taking of an action from a state court and transferring it to a federal court. **3** A petition made by a defendant to have a case moved from one court to another, usually as in the second definition.

render *v.* To formally announce a verdict, either by announcing it in court or by filing a memorandum with the clerk; to deliver or transmit; to pay (render an account); to provide (render a service).

renounce *v.* To formally give up title to; to abandon (renounce title); to decline recognition of (renounce one's duty to serve).

rent *n.* Compensation (usually monetary) paid for the occupancy or use of (usually real) property.

renunciation *n.* Abandonment of a right, whether open or tacit, without transferring it to someone else; in criminal law, the total voluntary abandonment of a criminal activity before it is committed with the purpose of foiling that activity.

reorganization **1** *n.* In bankruptcy, the restructuring of a business that permits the continuation of the business even after partial discharge of debts. **2** *n.* In tax law, a corporate restructuring that involves merger with another corporation, or acquisition of one corporation by another. **3** *v.* The act of organizing in a new fashion.

repeal **1** *n.* The annullment of an existing law by the enactment of a new law. If the new law declares the old law to be revoked, the repeal is express. If the new law has provisions that contradict the old law so that both cannot logically exist together, the new law takes precedence and the repeal is implied. **2** *v.* The act of annulling a law.

replevin *n.* An action taken to recover wrongfully taken property, rather than recovering only the value of that property from the defendant; a court order authorizing the return of the plaintiff's wrongfully taken property.

replevy *v.* The recovery of goods pursuant to a writ of **replevin;** to get delivery of goods that had been kept from the rightful owner; to recover chattels as a result of replevin.

replication *n.* The plaintiff's or complainant's reply to the defendant's plea or answer.

reply **1** *n.* A plaintiff's response to a defendant's answer or counterclaim in a civil case; a plaintiff's response (with the court's permission) to a charge from a third party; in common law, the answer of the plaintiff to the answer or pleading of the defendant; the reply may be followed by a rejoinder by the defendant. **2** *v.* the act of responding to a **pleading** of an opposing party.

reporter See **court reporter.**

reports *n.* Formal written or vocal presentations of facts; written records of a court proceeding prepared by the court reporter and filed with the clerk; bound volumes of judicial decisions by a certain court or group thereof.

representation *n.* A statement of fact made with the purpose of getting someone to become party to a transaction or contract. See also **misrepresentation.**

representative *n.* Agent; someone who is authorized to act in place of and on behalf of someone else, by that other person for some special purpose. A representative is entitled to certain rights based upon her or his status, including the right to bargain on behalf of employees, or to discovery of trial preparation materials. See also **personal representative** and **registered representative.**

reprieve *n.* A temporary suspension of a criminal sentence (usually the death penalty) for a certain period of time, usually for the purpose of examining new information or permitting an appeal to take place. A reprieve cannot prevent the ultimate carrying out of the judgment. See also **clemency, commutation, pardon,** and **executive clemency.**

republication *n.* An affirmative action to publish anew an instrument, such as a will, that had been previously revoked or repudiated. The revocation of a subsequent will cannot revive an earlier one without such an affirmation or use of a **codicil.**

repudiation *n.* Words or actions of a party to a contract that indicate the intention of that person to fail to carry out the contract in the future; a threat to breach a contract.

reputation evidence *n.* Same as character evidence; see **evidence.**

requirements contract See **contract.**

res *n. Latin.* The thing. The subject of the matter—that is, an action concerning an object or property, rather than a person,; the status of individuals.

rescind *v.* To cancel a contract, whether unilaterally or by mutual agreement and restore both parties to **status quo ante** (the positions they would have been in if the contract had never existed). See also **rescission.**

rescission *n.* The termination of a contract unilaterally by a party for substantive legal reasons, such as the failure of the other party to perform its obligations; or, the mutual termination of a contract, with the result that both parties are restored to the **status quo ante** (see also **rescind**); a remedy that one may seek in a court of equity that results in a termination of the contract as though it had never existed.

rescript *n.* Written order by a judge explaining to a court clerk how to dispose of a case; the written direction of an appellate court to a lower one to enter a decree in accordance with the direction.

rescue *n.* The aiding of someone who is in immediate and serious peril; the unlawful release (usually by force) of a person who is legally imprisoned or under arrest.

rescue doctrine *n.* The principle in torts that a wrongdoer who endangers a person by negligence is liable for any injuries sustained by someone who acted reasonably in attempting to rescue the endangered person. See also **Good Samaritan doctrine.**

reservation *n.* A right held back or given to the grantor, such as some right, profit, or interest in the estate or property that is being granted; a delayed decision by a court or other body on a point of law; a preservation of the right to dispute a point of contract by a party nevertheless performing same (such as, performing under reservation). See also **under protest.**

reserve *n.* An amount of money or assets set aside against future unrealized risks; monies set aside by insurance companies to pay losses that have not yet been asserted or finalized.

reserved point *n.* See **point of law.**

res gestae *n. Latin.* Things done. Either the events at issue or other things, such as utterances, that are contemporaneous with the res gestae; spontaneous statements or exclamations made by the participants, perpetrators, victims, or onlookers at or immediately following the event, be it criminal or the subject of litigation. As present-sense impressions, they are excluded from the **hearsay** rule. See **excited utterance.**

residence *n.* A place of abode with some permanence; residence requires bodily presence and is distinct from **domicile,** which requires both bodily presence and intent to make it one's home. A person may have many places of residence, but only one domicile; a house or apartment; the place where a corporation does business, or is registered to do business. See also **domicile.**

resident *n.* One who lives in a particular place. A resident is not necessarily a citizen.

resident alien See **alien.**

residual *adj.* A leftover; remainder; a residue.

residuary *adj.* Relating to a residual.

residuary clause *n.* A clause in a will that gives all the remainder of the estate, once the specific bequests and devises are taken care of, to one or more of the beneficiaries.

residuary estate See **estate.**

residuary legacy *n.* The remaining estate after all claims against the estate and specific legacies, except those authorized by the **residuary clause,** have been satisfied.

residuum *n.* What remains after something has been taken away; residue.

res ipsa loquitur *n. Latin.* The thing speaks for itself. An evidentiary rule in torts that the very fact that an accident occurred is enough to provide a prima facie case of negligent behavior. Rear-ending another automobile is an example, showing failure to maintain a safe distance on the part of the rear-ender.

resisting arrest *n.* Physically opposing or obstructing a police officer who is attempting to make a legal arrest. The resistance is deemed to be an assault and battery upon the arresting officer, and in no case can be regarded as self defense.

res judicata *n. Latin.* A thing decided. A doctrine whereby the court's decision is binding upon the parties in any and all subsequent litigation concerning the same case. In effect, it bars the litigants from seeking to take the same case to another court in hopes of a different outcome, or of raising new issues that were not raised at the first trial.

respite *n.* A delay or postponement of a sentence, or one granted to a jury or court for further consideration or deliberation. In all cases, it is temporary.

respondeat superior *n. Latin.* Let the superior respond. The doctrine that an employer is held liable for all wrongful acts or any harm caused by an employee or agent acting within the scope of his employment or duties. See also **scope of employment.**

respondent *n.* The party against whom a civil complaint is brought; the defendant in an equity case, as well as the person who is the subject of an appeal.

responsibility *n.* The liability for an act and the obligation to repair any damage caused by that act; in criminal law, a person's mental capacity to understand and answer in court for her or his actions; guilt. See also **competent** and **capacity.**

Restatement *n.* A treatise by the American Law Institutes that attempts to describe general common law, incorporating its growth as the result of various legal decisions. Restatements have been issued in relation to agency, conflict of laws, contracts, foreign relations, judgments, restitution, security, torts, trusts, and unfair competition. Although frequently cited in cases and commentaries, restatements are not binding on the courts.

restitution *n.* A making good for loss, damages, or injury, by **indemnify**ing the damaged party; return or restoring something to its lawful owner. Useful in both torts and contract law, restitution is sometimes used in criminal law as a condition of probation.

restraining order *n.* A temporary restraining order **(T.R.O.);** a restraining order is always temporary, because it is ordered without a hearing. This distinguishes it from an **injunction.** A court order issued to prevent a family member or other party from harassing, threatening, harming, seizing the property of, and sometimes even approaching or having any kind of contact with another; a court order issued to temporarily prevent a transfer of property, pending a hearing.

restraint *n.* Limitation or confinement as in constraint on free assembly; forbearance; a holding back or prohibiting from doing something.

restraint, judicial See **judicial restraint.**

restraint on alienation *n.* A restriction on a person's right to transfer or to sell real property, usually contained in a deed, and stating that should the grantee attempt to violate the condition, the land would pass back to the estate of the grantor or to some other party. It may restrict how the person may dispose of the land, prohibiting its being sold to a particular person or group, or of its being sold in a certain way, such as at auction; a trust provision that does the preceding.

Restriction Fragment Length Polymorphism *n.* The older and more discriminating form of DNA testing. Restriction Fragment Length Polymorphism is a process that breaks DNA strands into tiny fragments at specific points on the DNA chain. Also known as HLA DQ Alpha, or simply DQ Alpha. Abbreviated **RFLP.** See also **PCR** and **DNA.**

restrictive indorsement See **indorsement.**

resulting trust See **trust.**

resulting use *n.* A use of real property brought about by implication and remaining with the conveyor when nothing of value is given in exchange by the grantee.

retainer *n.* A sum of money paid in advance to a professional in order to secure services in a particular case; a client's authorization for a lawyer's representation in a case. See also **attorney's fees.**

retaliatory eviction See **eviction.**

retire *v.* Applying to drafts, to redeem by paying out a sum of money; to withdraw from the market by buying back; a voluntary leaving of public office, or other form of employment; a leaving the courtroom by the **jury** to consider the case, or by the **judge** to her chambers.

retirement *n.* The voluntary termination of employment upon reaching a certain age. See **retire.**

retraction *n.* The act of taking back or withdrawing (a statement, a plea, an accusation, or a condition of a contract); the withdrawing or taking back of a renunciation. See also **renunciation.**

retreat (duty to), rule   *n.* A doctrine in criminal law found in some jurisdictions requiring that, unless at home, at his or her place of business, or in a situation where the assailant is a person the victim is attempting to arrest, the victim in a murderous assault must attempt to retreat safely rather than resorting to using deadly force in self-defense. In tort law, failure to exercise retreat may result in liability's being attached to the party who could have retreated.

retrial   *n.* A new trial of an already litigated issue by the same court for some substantive reason, such as a recognition of procedural errors in the first trial, that made it unfair or improper. See also **mistrial.**

retroactive   *adj.* Referring to a law, a ruling, and so on affecting matters that occurred beforehand; affecting past happenings. See also **prospective.**

retroactive law   *n.* A statute that treats with facts or occurrences something that took place before the statute was enacted. While unusual, a retroactive law is only unconstitutional if it impairs vested rights, interferes with obligations under contracts (such as creating new obligations or attaching new disabilities), has the effect of an **ex post facto** law or **bill of attainder,** or is prohibited by the United States Constitution. Certain decisions granting new rights to criminal defendants under constitutional law have been given full retroactive effect. While others have been held to be effective only from the time of enactment forward. See also **ex post facto** and **bill of attainder.**

retrospective   See **retroactive.**

return   *n.* **1** An officer of the court's bringing back a court-issued document, such as a writ, and reporting how the officer had done or why he had not done what that document had ordered.   **2** An income tax return.

rev. rul.   *abbr.* See **revenue ruling.**

revenue   *n.* Synonymous with income, derived from whatever source(s); that which comes back as a return on an investment. See also **income.**

revenue bill   See **bill.**

revenue procedure   See **revenue ruling.**

revenue ruling   *n.* A published decision by the IRS, printed in the Internal Revenue Bulletin, dictating how the federal tax code applies to a particular situation. Unlike *private rulings,* taxpayers may rely upon revenue rulings to calculate the tax consequences for them in similar situations.

> *private ruling.* An IRS determination of tax consequences of a certain transaction issued to and at the request of a private taxpayer only, and may not be relied upon by taxpayers at large.

> *revenue procedure.* An official IRS statement spelling out the administrative practices used by the IRS. For example, methods for obtaining a private ruling are often spelled out. Abbreviated **rev. proc.**

reversal   *n.* The setting aside or overturning of a lower court's decision by an appellate court; a turning around of the short-term market price trend of a security, either from downward to upward, or the other way around.

reverse discrimination   *n.* A term used to refer to the exclusion of a member of a majority class not commonly discriminated against, to compensate for the traditional discrimination against a minority member. For example, management positions traditionally filled by members of the white race would be filled by African Americans, Asians, or Hispanics to the exclusion of any white candidates, even if the latter had seniority or were better qualified by reason of education, expertise, or temperament. It has been contended that such treatment, broadly known as affirmative action, is in violation of the equal protection clause of the Fourteenth Amendment of the United States Constitution, as well as Title VII of the Civil Rights Act of 1964.

reversible error   See **error.**

reversion *n.* A future interest in land created by operation of law by a conveyance of property for a specified period of time without transfer of title to said land. Upon expiration of the period of the lease, the land reverts to the lease grantor or his or her heirs. Additionally, reversion may refer to the part of an estate that the grantor retains upon conveyance of the rest of it. See also **remainder** and **reservation.**

reverter   See **possibility of reverter.**

revest *v.* To vest anew; to return title to the possession of the original proprietor or of the donor.

review *n.* A judicial reexamination of a court's proceedings, or a reconsideration by the same court of its earlier decision. The term is often used to describe an appellate court's examination of a lower court's proceeding. See also **judicial review.**

revised statutes *n.* Laws that have been changed, altered, amended, or reenacted by a legislative body. A reenactment is generally thought of as having the effect of a repeal and replacement of the former law.

revival *n.* A reinstitution of a former will or deed that had been revoked by virtue of a later document. Of course, that later document must be destroyed or cancelled. Although some jurisdictions automatically recognize the earlier will upon the cancellation of the later

one, most jurisdictions require its republication or some other affirmation.

revocable *n.* Capable of being abrogated at the discretion of the maker. See also **revocation.**

revocation *n.* An annulment or withdrawal of a conferred power or of a statute; a withdrawal of an offer by the one doing the offering; invalidation by the testator of a will, either by superseding it with a new one, or by destroying it.

revolving credit *n.* A renewable line of credit over a certain period of time, usually synonymous with credit card account. The borrowed amount is repaid to a merchant or bank over a length of time in installments, consisting of part principal and part interest. Generally, the amount of interest a creditor can charge is limited by state **usury** laws. Often more expensive than other forms of credit.

rev. stat.   See **revised statutes.**

RFLP *abbr.*   See   **Restriction Fragment Length Polymorphism.**

RICO *abbr.* See **Racketeer Influenced and Corrupt Organizations Act.**

rider *n.* An addition or change to a written document by way of a supplemental writing; for example, a rider to an insurance policy may modify or expand the conditions of the original policy, or may change amounts of coverage, or may delete certain risks.

right *n.* What is proper and correct under the law, ethics, and/or moral code; something owed a person because of a just claim; a protected and recognized interest; a negotiable option to buy a new issue of stock at less than market pricing; a claim or interest in tangible or intangible things.

right of entry. The right to go upon land or into a dwelling.

right of redemption. The right to reclaim property previously sold or encumbered, by paying full value plus any interest and costs.

right of way. The right of one vehicle to pass before another, as in "the car to the right at a four-way stop sign has the right of way"; the right to pass over the property of another, see **easement;** a piece of land upon which a railroad may construct its tracks.

riparian rights. As to owners of land adjacent to waterways, the right to use of the water, the soil under the water, and its neighboring land structures, such as banks. Generally refers to the right of a property owner whose land includes a natural waterway to use that portion of the waterway as may pass through his land, in whatever way the property owner chooses to.

right of action *n.* The right to bring a particular case before a court; a legally enforceable right. See also **cause of action** and **claim for relief.**

right of election *n.* A spousal right to elect to receive the gifts bequeathed by the deceased's will, or to instead elect to receive a share of the estate as put forth by statute. Also known as widow's election. See also **dower.**

right of first refusal See **refusal.**

right of privacy See **privacy, right of.**

right of subscription See **subscription rights.**

right to counsel *n.* The right of a criminal defendant to be represented by a court-appointed attorney if the defendant cannot afford to hire one. This is a constitutional right guaranteed by the Sixth Amendment.

right to die *n.* The right of a terminally ill person to refuse to have her or his life extended by artificial or heroic means and often called passive euthanasia; the withdrawal of feeding tubes and other artificial means of life support from a terminally ill person. See also **advance directive.**

right-to-know act *n.* A federal law (augmented by some state statutes) that requires businesses that produce hazardous materials to inform the community in which it manufactures or stores those materials, and the employees who may handle them, about the possible hazards.

right to remain silent *n.* This right must be given to a suspect in a criminal case before interrogation begins. It grows out of the Fifth Amendment's guarantee against self-incrimination, which coupled with the Sixth Amendment's **right to counsel** give us the **Miranda rule.** Once informed of these rights, the subject has the option of waiving them.

right to work laws *n.* A law in many states preventing arrangements between labor and management to require that a person must join a union in order to be employed by the business. See also **open shop.**

ripe for judgment *n.* The time when a case has proceeded no further than, but far enough, for all the facts to have been developed to the point where an intelligent judgment should be able to be reached.

ripeness doctrine *n.* The requirement that a case be **ripe for judgment** before a court will decide the controversy.

risk *n.* **1** Peril, danger, the chance of loss or injury. **2** Liability for injury, loss, or damage, by statute placed upon the manufacturer rather than the consumer, should it happen from normal use of a product.

risk management *n.* The process of assessing risk and acting in such a manner, or prescribing policies and procedures, so as to avoid or minimize loss associated with such risk.

risk of loss *n.* A financial risk of being responsible for destruction or damage or the inability to locate property that a party may get stuck with when a transfer of property is occurring. According to the **Uniform Commercial Code,** the risk is borne by the seller until some contractual event occurs, at which point the risk shifts to the buyer. The phrase is also used in insurance contracts to denote the hazards that are covered by the insurance policy.

robbery *n.* The illegal stealing or taking of another's property from that person or another by violence or by threat of violence; aggravated larceny. The personal threat of violence and implicit fear on the part of the victim are essential in order to distinguish robbery from **burglary.**

>   *armed robbery.* Robbery committed by a felon carrying a dangerous weapon, whether or not that weapon is actually used or even shown. The crime is tried as any robbery would be in most states, but the weapon serves to bump up the severity of the crime.

ROR *abbr.* See **release on own recognizance.**

Roth IRA *n.* A special form of individual retirement account, in which contributions are not tax deductible when made, but that compensates by making the gains distributable tax free upon the owner's reaching age 70½. See also **individual retirement account** and **Keogh Plan.**

royalty *n.* **1** A payment made to the creator of an intellectual property (author, inventor, and so on) for each copy of the property that is sold. **2** A share of the profit derived from real property that is reserved for the owner in exchange for granting a lessee, who is going to mine or drill the mineral rights on that land.

R.S. *abbr.* See **revised statutes.**

rule *n.* An established or prescribed standard for action; an authoritative principal; the general norm for conduct in a specific kind of situation; a principle, standard, or regulation that governs the internal workings of a court or an agency.

rule *v.* **1** To exercise control; for example, Diane's parents rule with an iron fist. **2** Deciding a legal point or question; for example, the judge ruled the question was admissible.

rule against perpetuities *n.* The common law principle that prohibits granting of an estate that will not vest within 21 years of that granting, that is, within 21 years of the death of the person who created the interest. Its purpose is to limit the amount of time that title to a property could be suspended and thereby keep the property from becoming available in the market.

rule in Shelley's Case *n.* This rule governing property dates from 1324 and states that if a property is bequeathed to a person and a remainder to his heirs, the remainder is considered to belong to the person named in the bequeathal so that the person has a fee simple absolute. See also **fee simple.**

rule in Wild's Case *n.* A property law rule of construction that considers a property granted to A and A's children as a **fee tail** if A has no children as of the effective date of the grant, but as a **joint tenancy** if A does have children at that time.

rule of capture *n.* **1** Acquiring the ownership of property where there previously was no ownership; thereby, any wild animals captured belong to the person who captures them, regardless of whose property they were upon previously. **2** If the recipient of property displays an intent to take full control of that property and not just pass it on to another, that person captures full rights to that property including the ability to pass it on to his or her heirs.

rule of law *n.* A substantive legal principle; the prevailing of regular power rather than arbitrary power; the principle that all citizens are subject to the judicial decisions in their states as well as those of the courts of the United States, and that such decisions are the result of constitutional principles.

running with the land *adj.* Description of any right or responsibility which passes with the transfer of land, often with reference to easements or covenants. For example, where one driveway serves as an entrance to two homes, but is owned by only one of the homeowners, the right to use the driveway may be considered to "run with the land" upon sale of the home to another party.

S

salable *n.* In such a condition as to be appropriate for sale in the marketplace for the ordinary selling price, legal to sell, and free from any noticeable flaws. Same as **merchantable.**

salary, fixed *n.* An agreed-upon amount of money in exchange for services that may be set at a fixed hourly rate, but that is usually figured on a yearly basis and does not vary with the amount of goods the employer sells. See also **commission.**

sale *n.* A transfer of property or title thereto in exchange for a sum of money; the agreement or contract by which such a transfer takes place. A sale requires a free offer in exchange for a freely agreed-upon purchase price between two individuals who are competent to contract with each other, and who have mutually agreed to the deal. An actual exchange or promised exchange of money is required. Finally, the object, parcel, or title being sold must be capable of being transferred by the seller.

> *conditional sale.* A sale subject to certain events occurring, for example, a transaction to sell one's home, conditioned upon the sale by buyer of his own home. Also known as contingent sale.

> *sheriff's sale.* A forced sale of property for which full payment has not been made; proceeds of such sale are remitted to the creditor in full or partial satisfaction of the debt.

> *tax sale.* A forced sale of assets of a taxpayer to satisfy tax obligations that have not been paid.

sale on approval *n.* A transaction (usually involving goods) in which the buyer is permitted to use goods for a period, and then return them if they do not meet the buyer's needs or expectation, even though the goods are not defective. If the goods were delivered for resale, the transaction is a sale and return or a **consignment.**

sale or exchange *n.* A tax law phrase describing a voluntary exchange of property for other property as distinct from a gift or a contribution, and for which a federally taxable gain or loss may attach.

sales tax *n.* A percent of the consumer-paid sales price of certain goods in certain states and municipalities.

salvage *n.* In general, it is the value of a piece of equipment or other property after it has been functionally rendered useless for the purpose for which it was intended. In the case of a totally wrecked automobile, for example, it is the depreciated value of whatever usable parts that can be resold in used condition, plus the value per pound of the remaining scrap metal; in maritime law it's compensation for a service voluntarily given to a vessel in peril that removes it from danger by the sea; in insurance law, the first definition applies, with the proviso that the amount of salvage is deducted from what is paid to the insured.

salvage value *n.* An asset's **value** after it has become useless to the owner. It is often figured through some means of **depreciation** and must be subtracted from the **basis.**

sanction **1** *n.* A penalty imposed for violating accepted social norms. A sanction may be **civil** or **criminal** in nature. Criminal sanctions are either fine, imprisonment, or both. **2** *n.* Authorization and/or approval by someone in a position of authority; for example,   **3** *v.* the act of imposing a penalty.

sandbagging   *n.* A practice by a trial lawyer of noticing but not mentioning a possible error during a trial in hopes of using it as a basis for appeal if the court fails to correct it. Because objections must be made in a timely manner, sandbagging usually doesn't keep the issue alive.

sane   *n.* The condition of having a sound and rational mind; being mentally healthy and having the ability to distinguish right from wrong. In all jurisdictions, being sane is presumed, and it is up to the defense to prove the contrary to be true. Synonymous with sanity. See also **insanity** and **insanity defense.**

> *sanity hearing.*   **1** An examination of one's mental competency to see whether one is mentally equipped to stand trial.   **2** A court proceeding, held to determine whether a person's mental health dictates institutionalization.

satisfaction   *n.* A giving of something in order to release oneself from, or to satisfy, some outstanding obligation, be it legal or moral. Satisfaction requires the giving of one thing for another and should be distinguished from **performance,** which requires only the promising to give something. Also, payment in full, done to fulfill a contractual obligation or debt.

savings and loan association   See **bank.**

savings bank   See **bank.**

saving clause   *n.* A provision in a statute or contract that if any clause is determined to be unenforceable, the remainder of the statute or contract will remain intact and enforceable.

scalping   **1** *n.* The sale of something (especially a ticket for a popular show or sporting event) at a price far in excess of its face value and usually just before the event's beginning; the buying of a security by someone with inside knowledge, such as a broker, before recommending that security for purchase to his/her client(s). Both the foregoing are considered unethical, and the first is illegal in many jurisdictions.   **2** *v.* The act of selling items at a price far in excess of face value.

scandalous matter   *n.* Immoral or indecent content; in legal pleadings, content that is impertinent or highly irrelevant and therefore subject to being stricken as improper.

scienter   *n. Latin.* Knowingly. **1** A knowledge beforehand of the consequences of an action or failure to act that makes a person legally responsible for those consequences. Such advance knowledge may make the person subject to civil or criminal punishment.   **2** An intention to deceive or defraud (usually applied to stock fraud). See also **knowing** and **mens rea.**

scope of authority   *n.* In the law of agency, whatever amount of authority an agent has been delegated or might reasonably be expected to be delegated in order to carry out his/her principal's business. See also **respondeat superior** and **scope of employment.**

scope of employment   *n.* The complete range of activities an employee might reasonably be expected to perform while carrying out the business of the employer.

S corporation   See **corporation.**

scrip dividend   See **dividend.**

scrivener   *n.* A writer; refers to a professional drafter of contracts or other legal documents. It is also applied to someone who is an agent for another and who, for a fee, manages that person's money, property, and/or securities. Term used commonly in Europe.

scrivener's error   *n.* Mistake by preparer of a document that results in intent of the parties being thwarted; basis for not enforcing the document or reforming it. See **mutual mistake.**

seal   **1** *n.* In common law, an impression in wax, wafer, or other substance put on a document and attesting to its authenticity; a similar impression placed over the edge of an envelope, its unbroken condition indicating that the envelope is unopened, hence its contents are untampered with. A corporation's seal is at times called a common seal.   **2** *v.* the act of placing an impression upon an envelope or document to designate that it is undisturbed, the act of closing.

sealed instrument   *n.* A document that has been signed and to which a seal has been affixed. Under common law and by some statutes, that is recognized as convincing evidence that the obligation on the signer is binding. The Uniform Commercial Code holds that laws applying to sealed instruments are not valid with regard to the sale of goods or negotiable papers. See also **contract.**

sealing of records   *n.* The customary closing of criminal records of youthful offenders, mandated in some states by law, so that they can be viewed only by persons obtaining a court order to do so; the same as the first definition with regard to certain other cases. See also **expungement of record.**

search   **1** *n.* A police examination of a person's physical body, property, abode, or other area where the person would have an expectation of privacy, in order to find incriminating evidence. For a search to be legal, there must be probable cause, because the Fourth Amendment to the United States Constitution prohibits unreasonable search and seizure.   **2** *v.* To look for, as in the case of looking for evidence. See also **frisk.**

search and seizure   *n.* The same as **search,** with the added provision of retention of any contraband or evidence of criminal activity that is found. Generally, a **warrant** is required, and the scope of that warrant will be very limited, due to Fourth Amendment constraints. There are, however, certain circumstances in which a warrant is not needed, including seizure of abandoned items, a hidden weapon, or contraband items that are in plain view.

search engine   *n.* An online tool that permits a researcher to type in keywords and returns a selection of Internet sources for information on that keyword (known as hits). There are two main search engines for legal research, and both are based upon subscription for fees: **Lexis** and **Westlaw.**

search of title   See **title search.**

search warrant   *n.* A written order by a judge authorizing the examination of a specified place and the seizing of evidence found there. See also **warrant.**

seasonable   *adj.* In a timely manner; within the time agreed upon; within a reasonable amount of time.

seasonably   *adv.* Used synonymously with reasonably.

S.E.C.   See **Securities and Exchange Commission.**

secondary   *adj.* Subordinate; not of primary importance; subsequent.

secondary boycott   See **boycott.**

secondary distribution   *n.* An organized offering of a block of stock by a large share holder of a stock that has already been issued, typically by corporate founders or major investors.

secondary liability   See **liability.**

second-degree   See **murder** and **principal.**

secretary   *n.* An officer of a corporation charged with responsibility for keeping records and taking minutes.

secrets of trade   *n.* See **trade secrets.**

section   *n.* A definable portion of a town, county, or other geographic region; a land unit equal to one square mile.

secured creditor   *n.* A **creditor** who is holding security in the form of a lien sufficient to cover the amount that the **debtor** owes, as in a security interest in an automobile by the lender that financed its purchase.

secured transaction   *n.* Any business transaction involving the title to property as collateral for the borrowing of money.

securities   *n.* Stocks, bonds, and the like; any instrument of secured indebtedness or of a right to participate in the profits or assets of a profit making concern. Traditionally, securities have been a major area of investment and speculation by individuals and banks.

securities acts   *n.* A federal or state law governing the issuance, registration, offering, and trading of securities in order to protect the public by assuring against fraudulent practices.

Securities Act of 1933   *n.* A federal law governing mainly the issuance, registration, and distribution of securities by the issuer. The objective of the act is to give full disclosure of all facts related to the security being offered, so that potential investors are able to make informed decisions about whether or not to invest.

Securities and Exchange Commission   *n.* The federal administrative agency established by the **Securities Exchange Act of 1934,** in order to supervise and regulate the issuing and trading of securities and to eliminate fraudulent or unfair practices. It is a regulating agency and is not judicial in nature, although it may pursue judicial remedies in federal court. Abbreviated **SEC.**

Securities Exchange Act of 1934   *n.* A federal law designed to regulate post-issuance trading of securities by regulating security brokers and exchanges. State regulations are allowed to continue to govern intrastate transactions, as long as they do not conflict with the federal law. The act established the **Securities and Exchange Commission.**

security   *n.* **1** Safety; the condition of being protected against harm. **2** Collateral given or promised to guarantee the repayment of a debt.   **3** A document that is evidence of ownership in a corporation (for example, a **stock** or **share**), or a creditor's being owed money by a corporation or government (for example, a **bond**).

security deposit   *n.* Money held by a landlord to ensure that the tenant abides by the lease agreement and does no damage to the property above normal-use wear. It is a fund from which the landlord may draw to make repairs, if necessary, upon termination of the lease; any pledge of property or money of a debtor to acquire an obligation. See also **obligation.**

security interest   *n.* An interest in property created by the operation of law or by agreement to repay a loan; a lien on personal property created by an agreement.

purchase-money security interest. Interest taken by the collateral's seller, such as an automobile. It is a purchase-money security interest, created by a bank, allowing one to pay off the cost of a car on an installment basis while enjoying its use. The bank retains the title until the full amount (along with interest) has been paid.

sedition   *n.* An activity or communication aimed at overthrowing governmental authority. Sedition acts were passed in the United States as early as 1798 and as recently as World War I. The United States Supreme Court ruled in 1919 that communications urging sedition could only be punished if there was a clear and present danger. Otherwise, it was a contradiction of the First Amendment's guarantee of free speech.

seisin   *n.* Ownership of land; used in early British law, because ownership of the land belonged to the sovereign. It referred to the person in possession of a freehold estate. See also **covenant.**

seizure   *n.* The act of confiscating a person's property by legal process; a forcible taking of property into custody by a court.

self-dealing   *n.* Participating in a transaction for one's own personal benefit rather than for the one owed a fiduciary duty; for example, a trustee using property held in trust for her own benefit. Many states have laws prohibiting such action, and there are federal statutes that do so under certain circumstances.

self defense   *adj.* Description of actions taken to protect oneself, as in a shooting of a perpetrator by a police officer upon whom the perpetrator has pulled a gun.

self-executing   *adj.* That which takes effect without further action, as with a statute or court order.

self-help   *n.* A person's attempt to remedy a wrong perceived done to him by that person's own actions, rather than through the legal system. Under the Uniform Commercial Code, a creditor may take possession of a debtor's collateral upon default, if it can be done without breaching the peace.

self-incrimination, privilege against   *n.* A privilege granted by the Fifth Amendment to the United States Constitution, which bars the federal government from forcing a criminal defendant to give testimony against him- or herself. Through the due process clause of Fourteenth Amendment, this privilege has become applicable to state proceedings, whether criminal or civil, and is often referred to simply as, "pleading the Fifth." The rule does not apply to self-incrimination by non-testimonial means; therefore, the individual is not protected against fingerprinting or DNA evidence being compelled.

seller   *n.* A vendor; one who sells or initiates contracts to sell goods; the one who transfers property as a result of a sales contract.

senile dementia   See **senility.**

senility   *n.* A mental feebleness or insanity that results from old age and is both incurable and progressive. A person so afflicted is not capable of entering into a binding contract or of executing a will. See also **competent** and **incompetent.**

sentence   **1** *n.* The pronouncement of punishment by a court following a criminal defendant having been found guilty of a crime.   **2** *v.* The handing down of a term of punishment by a court.

cumulative sentences. See **consecutive sentences.**

concurrent sentences. Two or more periods of incarceration time that are to be served simultaneously. Concurrent sentences have the effect of being a single period of confinement, with the longer one being the limit; for example, a person sentenced to serve concurrent sentences of ten and twelve years concurrently will serve a maximum of twelve years.

conditional discharge sentence. The person is given no confinement, as long as she performs or does not perform certain specified acts. Failure to follow sentencing provisions may result in confinement after a hearing. See also **probation.**

consecutive sentences. Two or more periods of incarceration time that are to be served in succession. Consecutive sentences have the effect of being the sum of the periods of confinement named, so a person sentenced to serve consecutive sentences of ten and twelve years will serve a maximum of twenty-two years.

deferred sentence. A sentence that will not be imposed unless the defendant fails to fulfill the conditions of **probation.**

determinate sentence. A sentence of confinement for a specific length of time rather than for an unspecified period.

extended sentence. An infliction of a more severe period of confinement than is normal for an offense because the perpetrator is a repeat or habitual offender, or where there is a perception that the offender represents a continuing danger to society.

indeterminate sentence. A sentence of an unspecified duration, such as from 10 to 25 years, or one that a parole board can reduce after the statutory minimum has been served.

mandatory sentence. A sentence spelled out by law and over which the judge has no discretionary power to tailor to the person being sentenced.

split sentence. A sentence in which there is enough of a period of confinement to give the wrongdoer a taste of imprisonment, followed by a period of probation, with the second usually being the longer part of the term.

suspended sentence. See **conditional discharge sentence.**

separable   *adj.* Capable of being split or divided into its component parts.

separable controversy   *n.* A claim that is independent from, and capable of being separated out from the other claims in a lawsuit. It is used most often if a part of a larger suit can stand alone as a suit in a federal court, in which case, the whole suit is statutorily removable to a federal court.

separate but equal   *n.* The once-argued doctrine that all races are treated fairly when substantially equal facilities are made available to all, even though the races—meaning especially African Americans and Caucasians—are restricted to separate facilities. It was the argument of segregationists during the civil-rights controversy in the 1950s and '60s and was ultimately ruled to be in violation of the equal protection clause of the Fourteenth Amendment. The doctrine was established in *Plessy v. Ferguson* (1896) and overturned in *Brown v. Board of Education* (1954). It was found that separate is inherently unequal, and that segregation of whites from blacks in schools created a sense of inferiority that tended to impede educational and mental development of African-American children.

separation   *n.* **1** The condition of a husband and wife who remain married but who live apart, whether by mutual agreement or by decree of a court. See also **divorce. 2** Termination of an employment contact.

separation agreement *n.* A written agreement between husband and wife in contemplation of divorce detailing how their property is to divided, how alimony or child support is to be paid and in what amount by whom to the other, and custodial arrangements for children. Such a paper is legally enforceable and may have income-tax implications if the couple has physically separate domiciles.

separation of powers *n.* The separation of the power of the states from that of the federal government and the division of the federal government into three branches (executive, legislative, and judicial), each of which has specific powers upon which neither of the others can usurp. These checks and balances are given large credit for the prevention of a tyrant ever seizing power in this country.

sequester *v.* To isolate or keep apart from all others, as in sequestering certain funds or sequestering a jury. See also **sequestration**.

sequestration *n.* **1** The isolation of a trial jury in the custody of the court for the duration of a trial in order to prevent tampering or their hearing outside testimony; keeping witnesses apart from one another and outside the courtroom; **2** the placement of an item or monies in dispute with an independent party pending resolution of litigation between two making claim to the item or monies.

serial bond See **bond**.

seriatim *adv. Latin.* In sequence. Successively; in successive order, one by one; in due order; sequentially, one at a time.

series bond See **bond**.

servant *n.* One who is employed to work under the immediate control and instruction of the employer.

serve *v.* **1** To deliver a legal document, especially a process or notice; to present a legal notice or subpoena to a person as required by law. **2** To spend time in the armed forces or in some uniformed service (police, fire, and so on). See also **service**.

service *n.* **1** The formal delivery of a subpoena, writ, or other legal notice or process. **2** The doing of something useful or helpful for another individual or for a company in exchange for a fee. **3** The time spent in the military, as in, "in the service of one's country."

> *service by publication.* A publication of a notice in a newspaper or other publication in lieu of personal service. In some jurisdictions, the mailing of the news clipping to the last known address of the person is required.

> *substituted service by.* A presenting of service to a recognized agent of the party or by mailing notice to that party or any other way permitted by law other than personal service.

services of process *n.* A communication of the court papers or process to the defendant in a timely manner, so that the defendant has the opportunity to prepare a defense and to appear and state his/her case.

servient *adj.* Denoting an estate subject to an easement or servitude. See also **estate** and **easement**.

servient estate See **estate** and **easement**.

servitude *n.* **1** A right to use another's property without ownership. See **easement, license, profit**. **2** A condition of enforced compulsory service.

servitude, equitable *n.* An easement by necessity. See **easement**.

session *n.* The number of hours within a day that a given body is performing its duties; a meeting of a court or a legislative body for the purpose of performing its business.

session laws *n.* A bound volume of the statutes enacted by a legislative body during a single annual or biennial session; a collection of all of those aforementioned statutes.

set-aside *n.* Something, such as an amount of money, that is reserved for some particular later use.

set aside *v.* To void or annul a judicial decision, order, and so on, usually on a motion to set aside by the party that is affected detrimentally and based upon some irregularity in the original proceeding.

setback *n.* The minimum distance from the property line to where a structure may be built, as regulated by zoning statutes or restrictions in the deeds in various locales. Meant to keep houses from being built so close to each other that they cut off the light to and ventilation from a neighbor's home. Setback also applies to how close a structure may be built to a road.

setoff *n.* A counterclaim against the plaintiff by the defendant arising from a cause of action other than that she is being sued for; a reduction in the amount of a settlement by the amount the debtor is owed by the creditor. See also **counterclaim** and **cross-claim.**

settlement *n.* An agreement achieved between the adversaries before judgment in a trial, or before the trial begins, thereby obviating the need for it; completed payment of a debt or contractual obligation; a closing on a house; the completion by the executor of an estate of its distribution.

settlor *n.* Someone who creates a trust by making a settlement of property, real or personal. See also **donor** and **trustor.**

severable contract See **contract.**

severable statute *n.* A law with parts that are independent of one another, such that each part is capable of enforcement even if remaining part or parts are stricken or found unconstitutional.

several *adj.* More than one but fewer than many (said of persons, places, or things); separate or distinct, but not requisitely independent (said of liability); various or differing (said of things). See also **joint and several liability.**

severalty *n.* A condition of individuality in the holding of land. A tenant in severalty is the exclusive holder of the land for the duration of his or her estate, as distinct from holding a **joint tenancy.**

severance *n.* **1** A severing or cutting off; in criminal law the process of bringing a particular charge out of many so that only one issue, or a few closely related ones, is before the jury at a time, while reserving the right to bring other charges later; the separating of the claims of two or more parties for any of a number of reasons; the ending of a **joint tenancy.** **2** The removal of something attached to real property, such as crops or minerals, so that it becomes personal property instead of a part of the land.

sex offender *n.* A person convicted of a sexual offense, such as rape, sexual assault, or lewdness. Some states require sexual offenders to be registered for life. Sexual activity between consenting adults of the same sex is an offense in certain states.

sexual abuse See **abuse.**

sexual assault *n.* See **assault.**

sexual harassment *n.* A harassment of a sexual nature, usually in one's place of employment. See also **harassment.**

sham **1** *n.* A counterfeit; something that is not what it seems or appears to be; a fake; a person pretending to be something or someone other than who she really is. **2** *adj.* Deceitful or dishonest.

sham pleading *n.* A civil pleading that appears to have merit, but for which no supporting facts exist, and that has brought for no purpose but to vex or to harass the defendant.

sham transaction See **transaction.**

share *n.* A certain predetermined portion—for example, each partner's share of the expenses; one of many equal parts of a joint-stock company or corporation.

share *v.* To split something up into portions; to enjoy or participate in a certain right, privilege, and so on.

share and share alike *v.* To take equal parts.

share certificate *n.* A document evincing stock ownership.

shareholder *n.* A person who owns one or more shares of stock in a joint-stock company or a corporation. Synonymous with stockholder.

Shelley's Case, rule in See **rule in Shelley's Case.**

Sherman Antitrust Act *n.* The definitive antitrust statute, passed by Congress in 1890, that prohibits monopolies or unreasonable combinations of companies to restrict or in any way control interstate commerce. Specifically outlawed is two or more persons engaging in monopolistic practices, such as price fixing, although it does not outlaw

price-fixing per se. It was amended in 1914 by the **Clayton Act,** which outlaws interlocking directorates and deals with acquisitions that aim to restrain or eliminate competition.

shield laws *n.* **1** A law that protects journalists from being compelled to reveal confidential sources. **2** A law limiting or prohibiting the introduction of evidence about the previous sexual activities of the victim in sexual assault and rape cases.

shifting the burden of proof *n.* Removing the burden of proof from one party, which has presented a prima facie case, and shifting it to the other side to rebut that case. See also **burden** and **burden of proof.**

shifting use *n.* Of real property, the conferring of legal ownership of property to another, with the expectation of grantor that he will continue to have full use and enjoyment of the property.

shipment contract See **tender.**

shop *n.* A place of business or employment; a factory, office, or other business establishment. A shop may be open, closed, or union.

> *closed shop.* A shop where working conditions are covered by a collective bargaining agreement between management and a labor union. Union membership is required as a condition of working there.

> *open shop.* A shop where union membership is not a precondition of employment. Union members and nonunion members may work side by side.

> *union shop.* A shop in which all workers are members of a union. Nonunion members may be allowed to work there, provided that they agree to join the union.

show cause order See **order.**

show up *n.* An identification procedure that takes place before a trial and at which a witness to or victim of a crime meets face to face with the suspect. It differs from a **lineup** in that it is a direct confrontation, one-on-one.

sidebar *n.* A position at the side of the judge's bench where the attorneys and judge can confer during a trial, out of the hearing of the witness or the jury; the conference alluded to in; such conferences are recorded by the court stenographer, and become part of the trial record for use at appeal; an afterthought or side topic in a book or article that is set off apart from the main text or is in some other way distinguished from the main text or article. Also spelled side-bar.

sight draft See **draft.**

signature *n.* A person's mark or name, handwritten by that person or at the direction of the person for purposes of authentication of a document. It may also be a facsimile signature, affixed by a special machine at the owner's order, or a unique digital code that is necessary for e-commerce.

silent partner *n.* An investor in a business who takes a share of the profits, but who plays no active role in the day-by-day activity of that business. It is not unusual for a silent partner's name to be kept off the public record.

silver platter doctrine *n.* In criminal law, this was a doctrine that a federal court could introduce illegally or improperly state-seized evidence, as long as federal officers had played no role in obtaining it. The doctrine was declared unconstitutional in 1960 (*Elkins v. United States*).

simple *adj.* **1** In criminal law, uncomplicated by aggravating circumstances. See also **aggravated** and **mitigating cir-**

cumstance. **2** In property law, inheritable by the heirs of the owner without reservation; in contract law, not under seal. See also **sealed instrument.**

simple contract See **simple.**

simpliciter *adv. Latin.* Simple. In a direct or summary manner; without condition; summarily; **per se.**

Simultaneous Death Act *n.* A Uniform Simultaneous Death Act is a uniform law suggested in 1940, revised in 1993, and subsequently adopted by almost every state, whereby if two persons who are mutual beneficiaries die within 120 hours of each other, each is presumed to have died before the other, so that half the property of each passes to the estate of the other.

sine die *Latin.* Without day. With no day being assigned for the next meeting or for resumption of meeting.

sine qua non *n. Latin.* Without which not. Something that is indispensable and upon which something else relies.

sinking fund *n.* A fund with regular deposits made to it that is kept to pay off corporate or governmental debt.

skiptracing *n.* The locating of missing persons, such as heirs, witnesses, assets, debtors, or stockholders, usually performed by a special skiptracing agency or by a private detective.

S.L. *abbr.* Session laws or statute laws. See also **session laws.**

slander *n.* Falsely spoken words that tend to damage another person's reputation; defamation. The truth of such words is an absolute defense against slander. Unlike libel, unless the slander is defamatory **per se,** damages caused by slander must be proven by the plaintiff. See also **libel.**

slander per quod. A form of slander that does not qualify as slander per se, thereby requiring the plaintiff to prove special damages.

slander per se. A form of slander that need not be proven to qualify for damage, because its meaning is apparent on the face of the statement and involves moral turpitude, a sexually transmitted disease, conduct adversely impacting one's profession or business, or lack of chastity (especially when applied to women).

slander of goods *n.* A false statement, written or oral, that casts doubt on a person's ownership of property. See also **bait and switch** and **disparagement.**

slight care See **care.**

slight negligence *n.* Failure to exercise great care that an extraordinarily attentive person would have exercised. See also **negligence.**

slip opinion *n.* A single judicial decision that is published as an individual paper following its issuance and in advance of its being incorporated into a volume of decisions. It is, unlike an unpublished opinion, ordinarily citable as precedent. See also **advance sheets** and **reports.**

small claims court See **court.**

social guest *n.* A holder of a bare license. See also **license.**

Social Security *n.* A federal program established by the Social Security Act in 1935 in response to the Great Depression, it is a form of universal insurance contributed to by all workers and administered by the Social Security Administration that distributes benefits to retired workers when they be come eligible, by virtue of age or disability,

and to survivors. The act also gives assistance in the form of aid to families with dependent children.

sodomy *n.* Anal or oral copulation between two persons, especially when they are of the same sex; oral or anal copulation between a human and a non-human. See also **buggery, bestiality** and **crime.**

solemnity of contract *n.* A concept that it is all right for two people to enter into a contract for anything they wish to, and as long as the proper formalities are observed and no defenses exist against it, that contract is enforceable and should be respected.

sole proprietorship *n.* A business that is carried on by a single person and that is not a corporation or a trust. It differs from a corporation in that the business is not a separate entity, and its taxes are paid directly by the proprietor.

solicitation *n.* A request or petition intended to obtain something; criminally urging, advising, or ordering someone to commit a crime; offering to pay for sex or requesting money in exchange for sex; an attempt to increase the number of one's actual or potential clientele.

solicitor *n.* In England, the lawyer who prepares a case for the trial lawyer (known as the **barrister**) and who settles cases out of court. One who attempts to get business or contributions from others; an agent or representative who conducts business on behalf of someone else; the foremost officer of the law in a municipality or a state; an **Attorney General.** In some jurisdictions, the prosecuting attorney.

solicitor(s) general *n.* The number-two legal officer in a government, outranked only by the **Attorney General.** Especially the chief trial attorney for the executive branch of the government.

solvency *n.* The ability to pay one's debts as they come due or as they mature. Implied is the ownership of property of adequate value to secure those debts, should the need arise. See also **insolvency.**

sound *adj.* In good health, both physically and mentally (sound of body and mind); marketable (property); undamaged, form taken by a document, as in "the complaint sounds in negligence."

sovereign *n.* A person, state, or group that is preeminent and independent of the will of others; the ruler of an autocratic state. See also **sovereignty.**

sovereign immunity See **immunity.**

sovereignty *n.* Supreme dominion or authority; the total and supreme power of an independent state.

special appearance See **appearance.**

special demurrer See **demurrer.**

special indorsement See **indorsement.**

special master See **master.**

special power of appointment See **power of appointment.**

special prosecutor See **prosecutor.**

special traverse See **traverse.**

specialty *n.* Unique property, such as a church, that is not marketable under the principle of eminent domain. See **contract.**

specie *n.* Money that has an intrinsic value, such as silver or gold coins, minted in different denominations and in different degrees of fineness, and usually displaying government markings.

specific bequest See **bequest.**

specific denial See **denial.**

specific intent See **intent.**

specific legacy See **legacy.**

specific performance *n.* An equitable court-ordered remedy that mandates precise fulfillment of a legal or contractual obligation, when pecuniary damages would be inappropriate or inadequate, such as in the sale of a rare article or a unique piece of real estate. The decree of specific performance requires that the person so directed perform as directed or face imprisonment.

speech, freedom of See **freedom of speech.**

speedy trial *n.* Guaranteed by the Sixth Amendment to the United States Constitution, a trial conducted without arbitrary and vexatious delays, begun promptly and conducted with reasonable expedience.

spending power *n.* The power granted to a government body to spend money, especially the power of Congress to spend money in order to provide for the defense of the United States and to promote the general welfare. Since 1936, that power has been expanded to include Social Security, environmental crises, and other concerns, such as desegregation and affirmative action.

spendthrift trust *n.* Trust benefiting an individual who is financially irresponsible; grantor of the trust may establish limitations on use of money to pay debts, or may provide for direct payment to creditors, completely bypassing the beneficiary. Some states permit a spendthrift trust to state as part of its terms that creditors may not invade the trust to satisfy the debts of the beneficiary.

split gift See **gift.**

split sentence See **sentence.**

splitting a cause of action *n.* Pursuing a cause piecemeal by bringing an action for only part of a claim, while reserving another part or other parts for separate lawsuits. The practice has been long deemed impermissible.

spoliation *n.* **1** The intentional destruction, mutilation, concealment, or alteration of (usually documentary) evidence. If proven, spoliation may help to establish that the evidence was detrimental to the party responsible for it. **2** Pillaging or destroying real or personal property by violence. **3** The taking of a profit or other gain that properly should go to another.

spousal immunity *n.* The doctrine that spouses cannot sue one another for personal injury; abrogated in many states.

spousal privilege *n.* The right to not disclose confidential marital communications; may be asserted as a basis for not answering a question under oath.

springing use *n.* A use that comes to one with the occurrence of some future event; for example, B has a springing use in A's estate, which will pass to her when she marries A.

stakeholder *n.* A disinterested party who is entrusted to withhold contested money or property while the arguments are being adjudicated or worked out; the third party who is holding the stakes in a wager between two or more parties; a person with an interest in a business or enterprise of some sort, but is not necessarily an owner.

stalking *n.* A form of harassment generally comprised of repeated persistent following with no legitimate reason and with the intention of harming, or so as to arouse anxiety or fear of harm in the person being followed. Stalking may also take the form of harassing telephone calls, computer communications, letter-writing, etc. See also **cyberstalking** and **harassment.**

standard deduction See **deduction.**

standard of care *n.* The degree of prudence that a **reasonable man** (or **person**) may be expected to exercise when caring for something. See also **care** and **negligence.**

standing *n.* A party's legal right to challenge the conduct of another party in a legal proceeding. In order to have standing in a federal court, a litigant must show that 1) the conduct being challenged caused the party real injury, and 2) the concern the litigant is seeking to have protected is within the scope of interests intended to be regulated by the statute or other guarantee in question.

standing mute *n.* A defendant's refusing to enter a plea in a criminal trial, which is treated as if it were a pleading of not guilty; raising no objections.

stare decisis *n. Latin.* To stand by what was decided. The doctrine of common law under which courts follow the earlier judicial decisions made on the same points of litigation; following precedent. Stare decisis is not inviolable, but precedent will be overturned only for good cause. The doctrine, however, is essentially useless in constitutional law. See also **precedent** and **res judicata.**

state action *n.* Any action taken by a government, especially an intrusion on one's civil rights by a governmental agency, or a requirement that can be enforced only through governmental action, such as correcting a policy of sexual or racial discrimination that requires judicial action to enforce.

statement *n.* A declaration of fact or an allegation by a witness; a piece of sworn testimony. See also **closing statement, evidence,** and **opening statement.**

status crime See **crime.**

status quo *n. Latin.* The situation as it currently exists.

status quo ante *n. Latin.* The situation as it existed before. As things were before whatever happened or is being discussed took place. For example, status quo ante bellum is the situation as it existed before the war.

statute *n.* A law that has been enacted by a legislative body.

statute of frauds *n.* A statutory requirement that certain contracts must be written and signed to be enforceable, most often applicable to contracts for real estate and contracts whose purpose spans more than one year.

> *part performance.* Exception to statute of frauds; if all or part of the goods have been delivered and accepted, or all or part of the purchase price has been paid, no written evidence is needed.

statute of limitations *n.* Law governing time permitted for filing various types of lawsuits, differing from state to state and as to type of matters; for example, states' statutes of limitations for filing a negligence action may vary from one to three years, a claim for breach of contract may have a statutory limit of some other amount of time; in all cases, statutes of limitations are specifically set forth and are strictly enforced; failure to comply by even one day will result in dismissal of lawsuit.

statute of repose *n.* A statute barring a suit a fixed number of years after the defendant had acted (usually by designing or manufacturing an item), even if the injury suffered by the plaintiff occurred after the period had lapsed.

statutory construction *n.* The process by which courts interpret the meaning of statutes, or the actual process or act of interpreting a statute's meaning. See **construction.**

statutory offense See **crime.**

statutory rape See **rape.**

stay *n.* A judicial order forbidding or holding in abeyance some action until some particular event occurs, or until the court lifts the stay. A single justice of the United States Supreme Court has the power to stay an injunction's being enforced pending an appeal to the full Court. See also **injunction** and **restraining order.**

> *stay of execution.* A procedure to prevent the carrying out of a judgment for a specified period of time; in the case of death penalty, an order from a higher court or executive branch of a state to halt the execution, usually pending further appeals.

stipulation *n.* A factual condition or requirement incorporated as a term of a contract; an agreement between opposing parties as to a procedure, as in a "stipulation to extend time to respond," or a fact, as in "a stipulation as to liability." A stipulation made by a party to a pending court case or made by the party's lawyer with respect to the case is always binding.

stirps *n. Latin.* A branch of a family or of the family tree. See also **per stirpes.**

stock See **securities.**

stolen property *n.* Property obtained by larceny, by stealing, by robbing, by theft; something unlawfully taken from its rightful owner.

stop and frisk   *n.* A police action to momentarily detain and search the body of a person. Under judicial interpretation of the Fourth Amendment to the United States Constitution, such a search may be conducted only under circumstances where the officer believes that the person is armed and dangerous to the officer's person, or that the person has just committed or is about to commit an unlawful act.

straight-line method   *n.* A method for figuring depreciation of an asset by subtracting the anticipated salvage value, and then dividing the remainder by the estimated number of years of its usefulness.

straw person (or **man**)   *n.* A third party used as a temporary transferee in order to allow the principal parties to accomplish a transfer that might not be directly allowable.

strict construction   See **construction.**

strict liability   See **liability.**

strict scrutiny   *n.* The standard used to determine whether a classification of a group of persons (such as a racial group) or a fundamental right (such as the right to vote) violates due process and equal protection rights under the United States Constitution. Strict scrutiny is used to establish whether there is a compelling need that justifies the law being enacted. See also **compelling interest test.**

strike   *n.* **1** An organized stoppage of labor by employees in order to compel the employer to meet their demands.   **2** The dismissal of a prospective juror from the panel, whether for cause or peremptorily.   **3** A negative mark on one's record (as in, three strikes and you're out).

strike suit   *n.* A suit brought without legitimate claim (usually by a shareholder in the name of the company) in hopes of an inflated settlement.

sua sponte   **1** *v.* Regarding a judge or court, to raise an issue or take an action independently of any request or suggestion made by the parties or lawyers;   **2** *adj.* Description of action taken by court in absence of any party urging such action to be taken.

subcontractor   See **contractor.**

subdivision   *n.* A reduction in area of a piece of land by dividing it up into two or more smaller parcels.

subjacent support   *n.* In property law, the support of the surface of the land by the earth's underlying strata. See also **lateral support.**

subject matter   *n.* Whatever is in dispute; the actual cause of the law suit; the issue about which a right or obligation has been asserted or denied.

subject matter jurisdiction   See **jurisdiction.**

subject to open   *n.* Used to describe the future interests in real estate or in a trust when the number of persons in that class is liable or likely to change over time.

sub judice   *adv. Latin.* Under a judge. A case that is before the bar for determination, rather than one being settled out of court.

sublease   *n.* A lease held by a lessee who has, in turn, leased part or all of the leased property to another sublessee; the original lease may require approval by landlord before subleasing.

sublet   *v.* The act of transferring one's lease to another, generally with all rights and obligations passing to the sublessee.

submit   *v.* To give in to the will or authority of another; to agree to allow mediators or arbitrators to settle a dispute.

subordination *n.* A giving of lower ranking, class, or priority to one claim or debt with respect to another claim or debt.

suborn *v.* To cause a person to do an illegal or immoral act, especially in a secretive or underhanded fashion; to cause a person to perjure his or herself; to get perjured testimony from someone.

subornation of perjury *n.* The crime of inducing or persuading a person to commit perjury; sometimes shortened to simply the first word of the phrase.

subpoena **1** *n. Latin.* Under penalty. A writ issued by a court commanding a person to appear, with penalties that attach for failure to comply. **2** *v.* The act of sending a subpoena to a witness or other person to secure his attendance and testimony at trial or other proceeding (such as deposition); generally, subpoenas are obtained and sent out by the lawyers, rather than directly by the court.

subpoena ad testificandum. The most common type of subpoena, ordering a witness to testify.

subpoena duces tecum. Issued at the request of one of the parties to a lawsuit, ordering a witness to appear and bring relevant documents to the hearing.

subrogation *n.* **1** A paying of or an assumption of the debt of one person by another. **2** The passing of rights from one party to another by virtue of the second's assumption of a debt on behalf of the first party; **3** In insurance, the right of an insurer to recover from a third party all amounts paid out on behalf of its insured.

subscription rights *n.* The contractual right of a shareholder in a corporation to buy additional shares of stock of the same kind that she currently holds if and when such are issued by the corporation, before that stock is offered to the general public. See also **preemptive right.**

subsidiary See **corporation.**

sub silentio *Latin.* Under silence. Without notice being taken. If a case is decided against precedent, the newer case is said to have over-ruled the previous decision sub silentio.

substantial capacity test *n.* A test established by the Model Penal Code for the **insanity defense,** including elements of the McNaughten rules and the test of irresistible impulse by allowing the court to consider both awareness of wrongdoing and involuntary compulsion. Since 1984, many jurisdictions, including federal courts, have stiffened the rules due to the acquittal by reason of insanity of attempted presidential assassin John Hinkley.

substantial compliance See **substantial performance (compliance).**

substantial performance (compliance) *n.* A doctrine in equity that if a good faith attempt was made to perform the requirements of a contract, but failed to exactly meet the specifics, and if the essential aim of the contract has been met, the agreement will still be considered as having been completed. Minimal damages for the impreciseness may be permitted by the court. See also **performance.**

substantive due process See **due process.**

substantive law *n.* The law that governs the merits of a matter or transaction, as opposed to procedural law; for instance, laws relating to manslaughter are "substantive," while laws pertaining to speedy trial, use of confessions, etc., are procedural.

substituted basis   See **basis.**

substituted service   See **service.**

substitution   *n.* The selection of an individual or a thing to take the place of another; the process of one thing taking another's place or one person acting in lieu of another.

succession   *n.* The taking over of a previous official's office, rank, or duties by a new person; the process by which a decedent's property or rights passes to the inheritors thereof, under the laws of descent and distribution. See also **descent.**

> *intestate succession.* State laws governing inheritance of property belonging to individual who dies without a will.

successor   *n.* A person who takes over the rank, office, duties, or privileges of another; a corporation that through merger, buy-out, or other means acquires the duties, stock, rights, and debts of another corporation, known as the predecessor.

sue out   *v.* To petition a court and to obtain the issuance of a court order or a writ of some sort.

sufferance   See **tenancy.**

sufficient consideration   See **consideration.**

suicide   *n.* The voluntary and intentional act of taking one's own life. It was a felony under common law, but is somewhat murky in today's criminal courts. There is also no unanimity on whether either assisted suicide or attempted suicide are criminal acts.

suicide, assisted   *n.* An intentional providing of a person with the medical knowledge or the means to commit suicide. Synonymous with **euthanasia.** Split among states as to whether legal or illegal.

suicide, attempted   *n.* An unsuccessful try at taking one's own life. There is also no unanimity as to whether this is a criminal act.

sui generis   *Latin.* Of its own kind. Unique; of its own particular type; in a class of its own.

sui juris   *Latin.* Of one's own right. Used to describe one who is no longer a dependent; having reached majority and having full civil and social rights. See also **emancipation** and **incompetency.**

suit   *n.* Any proceeding brought by one or more parties against another one or more parties in a court of law. See also **action** and **litigation.**

> *class suit.* See **action.**

suitor   *n.* A plaintiff or petitioner in a lawsuit; the party that brings the suit; a person or a corporation seeking to take over another company.

sum certain   *n.* Any fixed, settled-upon, precise amount. It may be a commercial instrument with a fixed amount specified on its face. See also **liquidated damages** and **unliquidated.**

summary judgment   See **motion for summary judgment.**

summary proceeding   *n.* A proceeding in a lower court, usually as to a minor offense or claim, generally fast-tracked. Although certain legal rights are overlooked or minimized during a summary proceeding, the rights to notice and to be heard are preserved.

summons   *n.* A written notice for a person to appear before a court under penalty of having a judgment entered against that person for failing to appear; a written notice to a person to appear for jury duty; a written notice to appear in court to testify as a witness in a case. Synonymous with **subpoena.**

sunshine laws *n.* Statutes that require governmental and municipal bodies to conduct public proceedings, and to submit records to examination by the public.

superior court See **court.**

supersedeas *n. Latin.* You shall forbear or desist. A writ suspending or staying a proceeding in order to maintain the status quo, pending appeal. It usually stays a creditor's taking possession of property pursuant to a lower court's ruling.

superseding cause See **cause.**

suppress *v.* To end, prohibit, or keep something from being known, heard, discussed, or seen.

suppression of evidence *n.* A trial judge's preclusion of evidence that was obtained in an unlawful manner; the withholding of evidence by the prosecution in a criminal trial when such evidence might be helpful to the defense

supra *adv. Latin.* Above; superior to.

Supremacy Clause *n.* The clause in United States Constitution's Article VI, stating that all laws made furthering the Constitution and all treaties made under the authority of the United States are the "supreme law of the land." Chief Justice John Marshall interpreted the clause to mean that the states may not interfere with the functioning of the federal government and that federal law prevails over an inconsistent state law.

supreme court See **court.**

Supreme Court of the United States See **court.**

supreme judicial court *n.* The highest state court in Maine and Massachusetts.

surcharge **1** *v.* To impose an additional cost or burden (usually exces-

sive). **2** *n.* A court fine imposed on a fiduciary for failure of duty.

surety *n.* The person immediately responsible for the debt of another, in the event that the principal fails to meet his responsibility.

surrebuttal *n.* A rebuttal by the defendant to the plaintiff's rebuttal; in trials, the order of presentation is: plaintiff's case, the defense, plaintiff's rebuttal, defendant's surrebuttal.

surrejoinder *n.* A rejoinder by the plaintiff to the rejoinder by the defendant (in common law pleadings). See **replication.**

surrender *n.* Delivery into the possession of another, such as vacating of property by the tenant before the lease has terminated so that the landlord may consider termination to have occurred; the giving up of a claim or a right; yielding to the control or power of another; the return of an estate to the one who has a reversion so as to merge the estate into a larger one.

surrogate *n.* A person appointed in place of another, especially a judicial officer who administers things concerning incompetents or decedents, and in certain instances, adoptions; any stand-in.

surrogate mother *n.* A woman who bears a child for a couple that is unable to have children. Upon the child's birth, the surrogate mother gives up all rights and responsibilities to the child. Surrogate parenting contracts were in earlier times held to be illegal under laws that forbade selling of babies; still strictly regulated.

surrogate parent *n.* One who stands in the place of a child's parent, but who is not that parent. Either by virtue of voluntary or court-appointed status, that person assumes all rights, duties and responsibilities of the child's parent.

surrogate's court   *n.* Synonymous with probate court. See **court.**

surtax   See **tax.**

surveillance   *n.* A legal investigative process entailing a close observing or listening to a person in effort to gather evidentiary information about the commission of a crime, or lesser improper behavior (as with surveillance of wayward spouse in domestic relations proceedings). Wiretapping, eavesdropping, shadowing, tailing, and electronic observation are all examples of this law-enforcement technique.

survival statute   *n.* A statute that permits survivors to seek damages for claims that the decedent would have had, but for his death, as with a claim for pain and suffering between time of injury and death; the claim becomes an asset of the **estate**.

survivorship   *n.* The right whereby someone who has an interest in a property becomes entitled to the entire property by virtue of outliving all others with an interest in that property. It is one of the features of **joint tenancy.** Also, the condition of the one person out of two or more to remain alive after the others die.

suspect   **1** *n.* A person believed to have committed a crime and who is, therefore, being investigated by the police. **2** *v.* Having a slight belief or a vague idea but not a knowledge that something happened or that someone did something.

suspect classification   *n.* A classification by racial group, national origin, sex, or citizenship, subject to strict scrutiny.

suspended sentence   See **sentence.**

sustain   *v.* To support or adequately maintain over a long period of time; (in court) to uphold; to rule in favor of; to corroborate. See also **overrule.**

symbolic speech   A form of speech that expresses an idea or emotion without use of words, such as burning one's draft card, bra, or flag, or picketing. Such activities are protected by the First Amendment to the United States Constitution.

syndicate   **1** *n.* A group of corporations that band together for a single enterprise that each alone would be unwilling or incapable of performing. For example, it took a syndicate of motor vehicle makers and aircraft companies to produce America's warplanes of World War II. In the negative sense it is used to denote organized crime. **2** *v.* To organize into a syndicate or to sell shares in.

T

tacit *adj.* Something implied but not actually named, for example, there was a tacit understanding that if she testified against her co-conspirator, she would not have to spend any time in prison.

tacking *n.* An adding together of consecutive times of occupation or possession by different persons, and treating those periods as a single continuous one, especially the uniting of consecutive terms of land possession by persons other than its owner in order to establish a continuous period of **adverse possession** for the required statutory period, so as to establish ownership. See also **adverse possession**.

tail See **fee tail.**

tail, estate in See **fee tail.**

tainted evidence See **fruit of the poisonous tree.**

takeover (bid) *n.* An attempt to assume control or management of a corporation by another corporation, generally by purchase of all outstanding stock.

taking the Fifth *v. Slang.* Allusion to a person asserting his right under the Fifth Amendment to the United States Constitution to not give testimony or produce evidence that might be self-incriminating. See also **self-incrimination, privilege against.**

tangible *adj.* **1** Exhibiting physical, touchable form; capable of being perceived by sight and by touch. **2** Comprehensible to the human mind.

tangible property See **property.**

target *n.* The focus of an investigation, as in grand jury target; in corporate law, the focus of a takeover bid.

target corporation See **corporation.**

target letter *n.* Correspondence sent to one who is scheduled to testify before a grand jury, so as to provide background or comment on subject of investigation.

tariff *n.* **1** Term is most frequently used to refer to a customs duty imposed on imported and exported merchandise. See also **customs.** **2** A public document that enumerates the services offered by a public utility or carrier (freight company), along with the rates charged for those services.

> *Gatt (General Agreement on Tariffs and Trade).* The 1977 international agreement, signed by all of the major industrial nations and most other nations of the world, the purpose of which was to promote expansion of trade by eliminating tariffs and other trade impediments and by establishing certain regulations promoting fairness. It has since been superseded by the establishment of the World Trade Organization.

tax **1** *n.* A charge assessed on an individual or on property for the purpose of supporting the functioning of the government. Such charges may be imposed on sale of property or goods, imports, exports, wages and income, privileges, and just about anything else that one can think of. Although usually thought of as being monetary in nature, it is not necessarily so. **2** *v.* The act of imposing a charge upon individuals or property by a government or other taxing authority; to strain or place weight upon.

abatement of taxes. See **abate.**

ad valorem tax. Latin. In proportion to its value; a proportional tax imposed upon something's value, rather than on its quantity (especially on real property).

alternative minimum tax. A flat tax originally imposed upon corporations or individuals with high incomes in the event that they wrote off all their income through use of deductions, credits, and contributions. It was enacted to make sure that these parties paid at least some income tax, but it also can affect middle-income families.

capital gains tax. See **gain.**

estate tax. A tax imposed on the property of a decedent that diminishes the value of the total estate to the inheritor. See also *inheritance tax.*

estimated tax. A quarterly amount paid by persons whose income is not subject to witholding tax, in anticipation of what that person's income tax liability will be come April 15 of the following year.

flat tax. A tax that remains a constant percentage regardless of the size of the amount being taxed. Most state sales taxes are flat taxes.

gift tax. See **gift tax.**

hidden tax. See **hidden tax.**

income tax. See **income tax.**

inheritance tax. A tax imposed upon the inheritor of property, sometimes known as a succession tax. There is no federal inheritance tax, but many states have statutes imposing such taxes. See also *estate tax.*

poll tax. See **poll tax.**

progressive tax. See **progressive tax.**

property tax. An *ad valorem tax* upon (usually) real property, usually imposed by states and municipalities in order to support local and state services, such as schooling and policing.

regressive tax. A tax that creates a greater burden on those less well off than on those with a higher income. The structure of most sales taxes make them regressive in nature. See also **progressive tax.**

sales tax. A tax on the selling price of goods and some services levied by some states and some municipalities. Those goods and services taxed varies from state to state, as does the rate of taxation. The tax is usually a fixed percentage of the price and is tacked onto that price. See also *flat tax.*

surtax. An amount tacked onto an already taxed article, or onto the tax itself; a surcharge. See also **surcharge.**

transfer tax. Same as an *estate tax.*

unified estate and gift tax. A federal law that imposes a tax on the net worth of an estate and on gifts of and above a certain amount. Both estates and lifetime gifts are treated the same way, with the transferror being responsible for the payment of the tax, but with the responsibility passing to the transferee in the event that the former fails to pay it. Also known as the unified transfer tax.

use tax. A tax imposed by some jurisdictions on goods bought outside that jurisdiction, and so not subject to that jurisdiction's sales tax. It is usally set at the same rate as the sales tax and is meant to discourage shopping outside the jurisdiction. See also *sales tax.*

value added tax. A tax imposed at each step in the production or construction of a manufactured good based upon the difference between the cost of producing the item and its selling price. Abbreviated **V.A.T.**

witholding tax. The amount of income tax that is witheld from the paychecks of employees and sent directly to the government by the employer. It is counted as a credit toward that individual's tax liability when tax returns are filed.

taxable *adj.* Something that is subject to being taxed, such as property or earned income; the amount or portion on which a tax is assessed.

taxable estate See **estate.**

taxable gift *n.* The part of a gift that, after allowable deductions are made, is subjected to the **unified estate and gift tax.**

taxable income See **income.**

tax avoidance *n.* The act of taking advantage of legal tax-planning opportunities and shelters in order to minimize one's income tax liability. See also **tax evasion,** which is not legal.

tax benefit doctrine *n.* The principle that if a loss was suffered in a previous year and taken as an income reduction for tax purposes, and an insurance reimbursement for that loss is received in the current year, that reimbursement must be counted as part of gross income for the current year, at least in the amount of the reduction previously taken.

tax court *n.* **1** The United States tax court. **2** A court in some states that hears appeals in non-federal cases and that has the power to modify assessments, valuations, tax classification, or appeals.

tax court, United States *n.* An appellate court to which taxpayers may appeal adverse IRS decisions and levies. Created in 1942, it replaced the Board of Tax Appeals.

tax credit *n.* An amount counted directly dollar-for-dollar to reduce one's tax liability, rather than a reduction in gross income. See also **tax deduction.**

investment tax credit. A credit allowed for investments in personal property that is exclusively used for business or is income-producing (applicable through tax years before 1986).

tax deduction *n.* A reduction in gross income in order to reduce one's income tax liability. It is worth a percentage of what a tax credit is worth. See **deduction.** See also **tax credit.**

tax evasion *n.* This term is generally used to designate criminal tax fraud, in which the taxpayer intentionally and deliberately understates her income or overstates her deductions and/or credits for the purpose of underpayment of tax liability. Contrast tax **avoidance,** the legal minimization of tax liability by aggressive interpretation of tax law.

tax exempt *adj.* Not subject to tax. This term is usually descriptive of interest on municipal and state government bonds, which (since 1913) have been exempt from federal income taxes. This is viewed as a form of federal revenue sharing.

tax lien *n.* Encumbrance placed upon property or assets following nonpayment of taxes.

taxpayer *n.* The one who bears the tax liability for any particular transaction. Even though a partnership may receive income, each individual partner is liable for the taxes on that income.

tax-preference items *n.* Those articles that, even though taken as deductions or credits on one's tax return, must nonetheless be considered when computing the taxpayer's **alternative minimum tax.**

tax rate *n.* A percentage of net income used to compute one's income tax liability. Currently, there are three brackets for computing federal income tax. The percentage one pays increases, as income increases, enough to move one from one bracket into a higher one of those three. See also **tax.**

tax return *n.* A form issued by the federal government, many state governments, and some municipalities on which a person reports income, deductions, exemptions, and credits and then uses those figures to calculate income-tax liability.

tax shelter *n.* A transaction or investment by which a taxpayer shelters some or all income from tax liability because of tax credits or applicable deductions. Abuses of tax shelters resulted in extensive reform of the Internal Revenue Code, restricting loss from a business or an investment to only the capital that is at risk. This greatly reduced the availability of tax shelters.

temporary *adj.* Something that will last for only a limited period of time; transitory. Temporary is meaningless with regard to the duration of the length of time that it will last; however, it is used to designate absence of permanence.

temporary restraining order See **restraining order.**

tenancy *n.* **1** The occupancy or possession of land under the terms of a lease; an interest in real estate by virtue of a leasehold. **2** The period of such occupancy or possession. **3** Tenancy in

general is any right to hold property, but in a more limited sense it is holding that property in subordination to someone else's title, as in a landlord-tenant relationship. The many types of tenancy include the following:

cotenancy. An occupancy or possession held by two or more persons who have **unity of possession.** See also **unities.**

holdover tenancy. See *tenancy at sufference.*

joint tenancy. A tenancy with two or more tenants having identical interests and who take over simultaneously by the same instrument and having the same right of possession, along with the right of survivorship to the share of the other. In some states, that must be expressly conveyed. See also **unities.**

periodic tenancy. A tenancy that automatically continues for repeated consecutive periods of time, be it month to month or year to year, unless notice of termination is given at the end of a period. This is typified in a metropolitan apartment building's lease.

tenancy at sufference (holdover tenancy). This tenancy arises when one who had lawful possession of property remains wrongfully and continues to occupy that property after her legal term has expired. This usually takes the form of a *periodic tenancy* or a *tenancy at will.* See also **holdover.**

tenancy at will. A tenancy where no formal terms for rent or duration exist, but the person holds possession with the landlord's consent. This type of tenancy may be terminated by either tenant or landlord upon fair notice being given.

tenancy by the entirety. The joint ownership of property by husband

and wife when a single instrument conveys the property to both; an indivisible interest in real property held by a married couple.

tenancy for a term. A tenancy whose duration is specified in days, weeks, months, or years from its creation.

tenant *n.* **1** The possessor or occupier of land by virtue of any kind of title or right. See **tenancy.** **2** One who pays rent in order to temporarily occupy or possess someone else's land under the terms of a lease or similar document. See **lessee.**

life tenant. a person with the right to use property for life, with no ability to bequeath same to own heirs.

tenantable repair *n.* A repair that is necessary to render a premises fit for current human habitation. See **habitability.**

tender *n.* **1** An unconditional offer of performance in order to satisfy a debt. It may be offered to save the party making the tender from a penalty for nonpayment or lack of performance. On the other hand, if the other party should refuse the tender without a justifiable reason, that party may be placed in default. **2** Something offered in order to settle a debt or obligation. **3** An offer put forward in hope of acceptance. **4** Something that serves as a means of payment, such as banknotes or coin (as in, legal tender).

tender of delivery. The placement by a seller at the disposal of the buyer, that is, arranging delivery of those paid for goods in a timely manner.

tender offer *n.* A corporate law offer to buy all shares of a corporation's stock up to a certain number by shareholders at a fixed price (usually higher than market value) within a certain period of time. Tender offers are usually precur-

sors to corporate takeover moves. The Williams Act of 1968 was passed by Congress to regulate tender offers so that shareholders can make an informed decision about whether or not to tender their shares for sale.

tenement *n.* **1** Any building, structure, or house attached to the land. **2** Any property held by freehold. **3** A building used as a residence. See also **tenement house.**

dominant tenement. Property that carries with it the right to use part of an adjoining property.

servient tenement. Property that contains features used by occupier of adjoining property, as with an easement.

tenement house *n.* An apartment building, especially a dilapidated low-rent building that meets, at best, minimal conditions of sanitation and safety.

tenure *n.* **1** An ancient hierarchical system of land possession or holding in subordination to a superior. **2** The status afforded teachers and professors, long considered a cornerstone of academic freedom of protection against dismissal without adequate cause. **3** A general legal protection of a long-term relationship, such as employment.

tenurial ownership See **tenure.**

terminable interest *n.* An interest in property that will end upon the passage of time, the occurrence of an event, or the failure of an event to occur. It applies to a class of property that usually does not qualify for a marital deduction under the federal estate and gift tax regulations.

term of art *n. Slang.* A word specific to a specific discipline and having a special meaning within that discipline other than what it is understood to mean in common usage. For example, in computer jargon, "to burn" is to record a CD, and "to rip" is to record a DVD.

territorial court   *n.* A court created by Congress under Article IV of the Constitution of the United States that endows Congress with the power to make rules and regulations respecting the territory or other property of the United States.

territorial jurisdiction   *n.* The geographical area over which a government or governmental subdivision has power.

territorial waters   *n.* All inland waterways and all waters on a country's coastline within three geographical miles of that coastline.

terrorism   *n.* The threat or actual use of violence in order to intimidate or create panic, especially when utilized as a means of attempting to influence political conduct.

testacy   *n.* The condition of having left or leaving a valid will at the time of one's death, rather than intestacy. See also **intestate.**

testament   *n.* A document disposing of a person's personal property upon his or her death, distinct from a will, which is a **devise** of real estate.

testamentary capacity   See **capacity.**

testamentary intent   *n.* A testator's intention that a document should function as his last will and testament, the determination of which is up to probate court. See also **testator (testatrix).**

testamentary trust   See **trust.**

testator (testatrix)   *n.* One who makes a will, especially one who dies and leaves a will. Because testator has come to be applied to both sexes, the use of the feminine testatrix has become obsolete. See also **intestate, testacy,** and **testament.**

test case (action)   See **case.**

testify   *v.* **1** To tell a court what pertinent information to a case one has, while under oath, and while the defendant is present.   **2** To bear witness.

testimonial immunity   See **immunity.**

testimony   *n.* Statements made by competent witnesses, who have been sworn in at a trial or deposition or in an affidavit. Although frequently used synonymously with **evidence,** the latter is the broader term and encompasses both testimony and physical evidence.

> *expert testimony.* Testimony given by an individual with special qualifications or credentials that enable him to provide information to the factfinder to assist with resolving the ultimate facts in issue. Also known as "opinion testimony," because, as opposed to "fact witnesses," expert witnesses are permitted to give their opinions.

theft   *n.* **1** Larceny; the unlawful expropriation of someone else's property with the intent of keeping it from its rightful owner.   **2** In its broadest sense, any example or act of stealing, which includes burglary, embezzlement, false pretenses, fraud, and larceny. While larceny is generally categorized as petty or grand depending on the value of the goods taken, theft is generally categorized by the type of property stolen.

> *identity theft.* The misappropriation of another's confidential and personal information such that the one taking such data can use such information to pass as the other by submission of credit documents, forging of identification cards, etc.

theocracy   *n.* **1** A country or state whose government derives its power directly from God or another divine spirit.   **2** A country or state in which government powers are vested in the clergy.

third party *n.* Someone who is not a party to a lawsuit, agreement, or other interaction, but is in some way involved or affected by it; someone other than the principles to an agreement or a lawsuit.

third-party beneficiary See **beneficiary.**

third-party plaintiff *n.* A defendant who files a pleading attempting to bring a third party into the lawsuit. See also **action** and **complaint.**

threat *n.* A declaring of one's intention to cause harm or loss to another's person or property or to limit one's freedom to act in a lawful voluntary manner (a threat to kidnap). A threat may be made by innuendo or suggestion, as well as by explicit language, and may be the basis of criminal or civil liability. Mere words, however, have been held not to constitute an assault. See also **coercion, extortion,** and **fighting words.**

three-strikes law *n.* This type of law has been enacted in about half the states and is a statute that requires a person convicted of a third felony get an extended sentence, often lifetime imprisonment.

thrift institution *n.* A catch-all term that includes savings banks and savings and loan associations. See also **bank.**

tide land *n.* Land that is between the extremes of the normal high and low tides, and which is covered by high tide, but exposed at low tide. The limit of tideland is usually set at the arithmetic mean high tide. See also **avulsion** and **reliction.**

time *n.* A measure of continuity, or duration. **2** A certain point in a given duration when something is said to have occurred. **3** *Slang.* The period of incarceration of a convicted criminal. See also **reasonable time.**

time draft See **draft.**

time is of the essence *n.* Contractual provision that requires prompt and timely fulfillment of obligations under the contract; failure to complete performance under time constraints set forth in the document may constitute a breach. Example: "Time is of the essence in the completion of this contract."

timeshare **1** *n.* A form of joint ownership of property under which as many as 52 owners, either singly or severally, receives the use of the property, condominium, or other property for a specified period each year, such as one or more weeks. The term is also used to refer to the shared use of computer equipment. **2** *v.* To occupy by time-sharing.

title *n.* Ownership; the legal right to possess and to dispose of property. See also **ownership, possession, tenancy.** **2** Legal evidence of a person's right of ownership of property; a deed or similar instrument that evidences ownership.

adverse title. A title that has been acquired as a result of **adverse possession.**

bad title. A title that cannot legally convey the applicable property to a new owner, usually because of one or more conflicting claims to that property. An *unmarketable title* is not necessarily a bad title, but a bad title is always an unmarketable one.

clear title. **1** A title that is free from any burdens, such as encumbrances or other limitations. **2** A marketable title. See *marketable title.*

defective title. See *bad title.*

equitable title. A title indicating that its holder has a favorable interest in the property and entitles its holder to acquire formal title to it.

good title. A title that is legally in effect and is valid. See also *clear title* and *marketable title.*

marketable title. A title that would be acceptable to a reasonable buyer, in that it appears to cover all the property that the seller is offering and it lacks any defect or limitation.

paramount title. A title that supersedes any and all other titles or claims against the same property. It signifies immediate right to possession and may be the basis for eviction of a tenant.

unmarketable title. A title that a reasonable buyer would fail to accept, due to pending litigation or some other unresolved conflicts over the property.

title insurance *n.* Insurance taken at time of purchasing property to protect against defects in chain of title.

title search *n.* A search of the public records to determine the status of a title, including any encumbrances, liens, mortgages, and future interests affecting the property. Doing a title search is the way in which the chain of title is established. Normally, a title search is conducted by a real estate attorney or by a title company at the request of a prospective buyer or mortgagee.

title theory *n.* A property-law doctrine that a mortgage transfers title to a property to the mortgagee, who holds it until the mortgage has been paid off, at which time title passes to the mortgagor. Only a few American states have adopted this theory, and they are known as title states or title theory jurisdictions. Compare **lien theory,** applicable in most jurisdictions, which provides that a mortgagee of property holds only a lien, not title, to the property until such time as the mortgage is fully paid, at which time the lien is removed.

toll *v.* **1** To bar, or take away; to defeat. **2** To stop from running (said of a statutory period of time). **3** To charge for the use of another's property, hence toll roads, toll bridges, and so on.

tort *n.* **1** A private or civil wrong for which a remedy may be sought, usually in the form of monetary damages; a breach of duty that exists under societal expectations regarding interaction among equals in a transaction, rather than arising from a specific contract. **2** The branch of the legal system or legal code that deals with such wrongs.

Tort Claims Act *n.* A law passed by the federal government and by most state governments waiving sovereign immunity from liability in torts for injury or loss of property. The Federal Tort Claims Act of 1946 confers exclusive jurisdiction on the United States District courts to hear claims against the federal government.

tortfeasor *n.* A person who commits a tort; a wrongdoer.

tortious *adj.* Being a tort; wrongful; in the nature of a tort.

total *adj.* **1** Complete; entire; undivided. **2** Absolute; supreme.

total disability *n.* As interpreted in the insurance industry, the inability of a person to perform the needed duties of the occupation for which he is qualified by training or experience. Total helplessness or absolute physical disability is not requisite for being classified as totally disabled.

totality of the circumstances test *n.* A test originally formulated to evaluate whether a defendant's constitutional rights were violated in the eliciting of a confession. It concentrates on looking at all the circumstances surrounding the alleged violation rather than only one or two aspects, as had been the case before. It had been used as a measure of whether a defendant's privilege against self incrimination had been violated, but since the advent of the **Miranda rule** (1966), that use has become obsolete. It is now used to determine whether a defendant consented to a warrantless search, and whether probable cause exists for the issuing of a search warrant.

total loss *n.* An insurance contract concept that is said to exist if property is destroyed to the extent as to be no longer useful for the purpose for which it was intended, or that renders it useless and of no value to its owner.

to wit *adv. Archaic.* That is to say; namely. Sometimes spelled "to-wit," or "towit."

tract index *n.* An index usually kept in the county recorder's office and listing each parcel of land according to its location, along with all transactions involving it. See also **abstract of title** and **chain of title.**

trademark *n.* **1** Any phrase, name, word, or graphic logo used by one manufacturer or marketer to distinguish its products from those of all others. A trademark's main purpose is to assure the genuineness of an article, and it is roughly equivalent to a commercial signature. For a trademark to be eligible for federal protection, it must be distinctive, attached to a product that is actually marketed, and registered with the United States Patent and Trademark Office. **2** The body of law that is concerned with how businesses uniquely differentiate their products.

tradename *n.* The name under which a company or person does business. Note that a tradename (or commercial name) applies to a business and its good will, as distinct from a **trademark,** which applies only to a marketable commodity.

trade secrets *n.* Formulas, devices, or other manufacturing or business pattern, and so on that are kept confidential in order to continue an advantage over the competition. Whatever the secrets are, they are not protected by patent, so their owner holds no formal protection. Once a trade secret is leaked or discovered by analysis, the discoverer is free to use it to his or her own advantage.

trade usage See **usage of trade.**

traditionary evidence *n.* Statements of fact based on longstanding tradition and reputation derived from a deceased person. It may be used to prove ancient boundaries, ancestry, or similar facts, especially when there are no living witnesses to testify to something.

transaction *n.* **1** An act of carrying out some form of business between two persons. **2** A business agreement or exchange. **3** Any activity in which two or more persons are involved.

> *closed transaction.* A transaction that is complete, so that the actual realized gain may be calculated for tax purposes.

> *open transaction.* A transaction in which all the events have not yet occurred, and so the computation of taxes on that transaction is not yet possible.

> *sham transaction.* A transaction that will be disregarded for tax purposes because it has no real substance.

transactional immunity See **immunity.**

transaction or occurrence test *n.* test used under federal law to determine whether a particular claim should have been filed as a **counterclaim** and will be barred from future filing as a separate claim. The four separate suggested tests are: 1) Are factual and legal claims raised by claim and counterclaim really the same? 2) Would a later suit be barred by **res judicata** if it weren't for the compulsory counterclaim rule? 3) Will essentially the same evidence support or refute both the plaintiff's claim and the counterclaim? 4) Are claim and counterclaim largely related?

transcript   *n.* A certified copy of the proceedings that occurred in a court or at a deposition, usually prepared by the court reporter from notes made during the proceeding. It is most frequently used at appeal hearings when the court's proceedings are checked for errors.

transfer   **1** *n.* Any and every method of removing something from one person or place to another; specifically, the handing over of possession or control of assets or title. Transfer may be affected by assignment, by delivery, by indorsement, and by operation of law.   **2** *v.* the act of handing over possession or control.

transfer agent   *n.* An individual or business that keeps a record of all shareholders in a corporation by name, address, and number of shares owned. Not every stock transaction results in a transfer, because a considerable share of most issues is held in the street name in order to support margin or for the owner's convenience. See also **registrar.**

transferred intent   *n.* A doctrine in both criminal and tort law that holds that if one intends to harm Party A, but accidentally (or for some other reason) harms Party B, the harm will be treated as if Party B were the intended victim. This is a legal fiction designed to bring about the desired outcome, which is for the person to be held responsible for and prosecuted for an act of intent, and is most frequently applied in cases where there is a homicide involved.

transportation   *n.* **1** The movement by a carrier of either people, goods, or products from one location to another.   **2** A

kind of criminal punishment, whereby a convicted criminal is sent out of the country to an offshore penal colony for a specified period of time. See also **deport** and **deportation.**

traveler's check   *n.* An instrument with a monetary face value that can be redeemed at locations other than one's own financial institution. Generally accepted in all countries, a traveler's check must be countersigned in presence of one who is accepting the traveler's check as payment.

traverse   *n.* A pleading in common law denying an allegation of fact in an adversary's pleading or contesting that the adversary lacked adequate knowledge to make such an allegation in the first place. See also **denial.**

> *general traverse.* A flat denial of all of the allegations in the pleadings of one's adversary.

> *special traverse.* A denial of one alleged fact that is not absolute, but that seeks to explain it away or qualify it by virtue of special circumstances, such as an inducement that can be verified.

treason   *n.* An attempt to overthrow the government of the state or nation to which one owes allegiance, by making war against that government or by giving material support to the enemies of that government. In order to be convicted of treason, a person must confess in open court or there must be testimony to overt acts by two witnesses. See also **sedition.**

treasure trove   *n. French.* Treasure found. Valuables found, secreted in the ground or other hiding place, usually gold or silver, that is of unknown ownership. The finder of such, under common law, is afforded title to the treasure trove against all except the actual owner.

treasury *n.* The branch of any government or corporation that is in charge of its financial dealings. See also **Treasury Department, United States.**

treasury bill *n.* A short-term promissory note issued by the federal government with a maturity of 3 months, 6 months, or one year. Treasury bills are sold at a discounted rate and attain full face value upon maturity. See also **treasury bond** and **treasury note.**

treasury bond *n.* A long-term promissory note issued by the United States government for terms of 10 to 30 years and backed by the full faith of the United States government. Because they are considered to be risk-free, they carry the lowest taxable yield of any bonds. They are sold at a discounted rate and attain full face value upon maturity. See also **treasury bill** and **treasury note.**

Treasury Department, United States *n.* The United States Treasury Department's basic functions are to develop and propose national and international monetary policies, and to serve as the financial agent of the government to collect taxes, manage the public debt, disburse funds, mint coins, and print currency. As part of the executive branch of government, it is also responsible for enforcing certain laws. Toward that end, the Treasury Department includes the Bureau of Alcohol, Tobacco, and Firearms (ATF), the United States Customs Service, the Internal Revenue Service (IRS), and the Secret Service.

treasury note *n.* An intermediate-term promissory note issued by the federal government for a period of two to five years. As with all other debt instruments of the federal government, they carry no risk, and so pay the lowest interest rate of all instruments of similar term. See also **treasury bill** and **treasury bond.**

treasury securities *n.* A security issued by governmental unit.

treasury stock *n.* Shares of stock issued by a corporation, and then repurchased by it.

treaty *n.* An agreement or compact between two or more sovereign nations for the benefit of those nations. In the case of the United States, that agreement must address external interests of the country, as distinguished from those of a purely internal kind. The president of the United States has the sole power to make treaties with the advice and consent of the Senate. Individual states are prohibited from making treaties, and once a treaty is ratified by the Senate, it becomes binding on all of the states under the supremacy clause. See also **treaty clause.**

treaty clause *n.* The provision of the United State Constitution that vests the power to make treaties in the President with the advice and consent of the Senate, and a concurrence of two-thirds of that body.

treble damages See **damages.**

trespass **1** *n.* An illegal act committed against another's person or property; especially entering upon another's land without the owner's permission. **2** *n.* In common law, a legal suit for injuries resulting from an instance of the first definition. **3** *v.* To enter upon property without permission, either actual or constructive.

trespass on the case. A common-law precursor to today's negligence, nuisance, and business torts, it was a suit to remedy injury to person or property not resulting directly from the defendant's conduct but a later consequence of same.

trespass quare clausem fregit. See **quare clausem fregit.**

trespass vi et armis. Latin. With force and arms. An immediate injury, such as an assault to another's person or property, accompanied by force or violence.

trespasser　*n.* One who, without permission of the owner or privileges, enters onto another's property intentionally. Under tort law, such a person is owed no consideration by the landowner for any ills that may befall him or her. See also **invitee.**

trial　*n.* **1** A formal judicial examination of issues of law or fact between parties by a court with jurisdiction in such cases.　**2** A formal adversarial proceeding to hear evidence and decide legal issues and claims. Trials are covered by established rules of courtroom procedure as well as rules of evidence.

> *bench trial.* A trial held in front of a judge, but without the presence of a jury. Both parties must waive their constitutional rights to a trial by jury. The judge then gets to decide matters of fact as well as matters of law.

> *trial by jury.* See **jury trial.**

> *trial de novo.* A new trial, usually ordered by an appellate court that retries both matters of fact and law and proceeds as if the original trial had never taken place. See also **mistrial** and **retrial.**

trial court　See **court.**

tribunal　*n.* **1** An officer or body with the authority to pronounce judgment on a matter based upon the evidence.　**2** A court or other judicial body.　**3** The bench or seat where the judge sits while presiding over a hearing or trial.

tripartite　*adj.* Composed of or having three parts; divided into three parts or elements.

T.R.O.　*abbr.* Temporary restraining order. See **restraining order.**

trover　*n.* A common-law tort action to recover damages for personal property that was wrongly converted or for recovery of actual possession of that property. See also **detinue** and **replevin.**

true bill　See **bill.**

trust　*n.* Property that is held by one party, the **trustee,** for the benefit of another, the **beneficiary.** The one who supplied the property or consideration for the trust is the **settlor.** Trust also encompasses any relationship in which one acts as a **fiduciary** or **guardian** for another.

> *blind trust.* A trust whereby the settlor places all financial interests under the control of an independent trustee for a period of time, most often in order to avoid the appearance of a conflict of interest.

> *constructive (involuntary) trust.* A trust that is imposed by a court against one who has acquired property by wrongful means, in order to prevent the holder of that property's being unjustly enriched and for the benefit of the rightful owner. No fiduciary relationship is created by this type of trust.

> *discretionary trust.* A trust in which the settlor has granted the trustee the discretion to pay to the beneficiary as much of the income or principal as the trustee sees fit. This is the type of trust most often used in estate planning.

> *express (direct) trust.* A trust set up with an affirmative expression by the settlor (usually in writing) of the purpose of the trust. This is an ordinary trust as distinct from a resulting or constructive one.

> *fixed investment trust.* See **nondiscretionary trust.**

generation skipping trust. A trust set up to transfer property to a beneficiary more than one generation removed from the settlor, such as a grandchild.

grantor trust. In this type of trust, the settlor retains so much control over the property in trust and/or its income that the settlor is responsible for taxes on that property.

inter vivos trust. A trust created and takes effect during the lifetime of the grantor.

pourover trust. An intervivos trust that receives money from another trust or other source or that distributes receipts to another trust.

precatory trust. Trusts created by a will by use of precatory words such as "wish" or some other entreaty rather than specific direction. See also **precatory.**

resulting trust. A trust brought about by law when the circumstances in which property is transferred that suggest that it was not the intention of the transferor to give beneficial interest in the property to the transferee.

testamentary trust. A trust created by a will and that comes into existence upon the death of the grantor.

Totten trust. A bank account created by the depositor in trust for another. It is often used to name a successor to an account without the need to write a will. It is also fully revocable.

voting trust. The combination of voting rights among a group of stockholders to exert a higher degree of influence or control within the corporation, or to bring about a specific result.

trust company *n.* A financial organization that specializes in providing services such as acting as a trustee, fiduciary, or agent for individuals and companies. Trust companies typically provide transfer agents to administer funds and manage investments. Trust companies are regulated by the government and often provide banking services.

trustee *n.* Someone who holds title in trust for the benefit of another person and who owes fiduciary responsibility to that beneficiary. Also used loosely to refer to anyone acting as guardian or fiduciary with respect to another person.

> *bankruptcy trustee.* A court officer appointed by a judge or elected by creditors to act as the representative of a bankruptcy estate.

trustor *n.* The person who created the trust, also known as the **donor** or the **grantor,** but most frequently called the **settlor.**

truth *n.* A completely accurate account of the facts; an affirmative defense in a suit for defamation.

Truth-in-Lending Act *n.* A federal statute that requires commercial lenders to provide accurate information relating to the cost of borrowing, in language that a normally intelligent person could be expected to understand. Lenders must furnish the dollar amount of the interest charges, as well as the annual rate of interest. Borrowers pledging real property as collateral must be given a three-day cooling-off period, during which they may change their minds.

try *v.* To judiciously examine both sides of a dispute and to come to an equitable solution by virtue of a trial.

try title   *n.* Submitting the legitimacy of the title to property to the scrutiny of a court.

turntable doctrine   See **attractive nuisance doctrine.**

turpitude   See **moral turpitude.**

tying arrangement   *n.* An antitrust practice of one seller agreeing to sell one product or service to a buyer only if the buyer agrees to buy another product or service. Such an arrangement may be deemed illegal under the **Sherman Antitrust Act.**

U

U3C See **Uniform Consumer Credit Code.**

UCC See **Uniform Commercial Code.**

UCCC See **Uniform Consumer Credit Code.**

ultimate facts See **fact.**

ultimatum *n.* The final offer in negotiating an agreement, carrying with it the implication that if it is not accepted, bargaining will cease.

ultra vires *adj. Latin.* In excess of, or outside of powers; that which is beyond a corporation's or an agency's authorized power. A corporation's ultra vires activity may lead to its forfeiting its charter of incorporation.

unavoidable accident *n.* See **accident.**

unclean hands *n.* The doctrine that a party seeking damages or redress in a suit cannot have done anything illegal or dishonest himself in the transaction with which the suit is concerned; an equitable principle stemming from the concept that one who has done wrong should not recover from another who may also have done wrong. See also **clean hands.**

unconditional discharge *n.* **1** A release from a debt with no further obligations to fulfill. **2** A release from confinement without the requirement of spending time on parole.

unconscionable *adj.* So harmful to the interests of one of the parties to an agreement or contract as to make that paper unenforceable and, therefore, null and void.

unconstitutional *adj.* In conflict with the letter or intent of the United States Constitution. When a statute is found to be unconstitutional, all obligations arising from it are unlawful, and no person can be held accountable for having failed to live up to his or her obligations under that statute, nor is the statute enforceable.

uncontrollable impulse *n.* An impulse so overwhelming that it cannot be resisted. See also **irresistible impulse test** and **insanity.**

under protest *n.* Complying with an obligation while asserting an objection to the obligation. For instance, when paying a disputed debt, the payor may note that it is being paid "under protest," thereby preserving any claim he may have for subsequent repayment.

under the influence See **driving while intoxicated.**

undisclosed principal See **principal.**

undue influence *n.* A persuasive power sufficient to sway the free will of a donor or testator. Such influence constitutes just cause for a court to nullify a will or invalidate a donor's gift. A contract may not be binding if one party has undue influence over the other; for example, one between an employer and an employee or between a priest and a penitent.

unethical *adj.* Not in accordance with the moral standards customarily followed in a business or professional relationship. See also **conflict of interest** and **Model Rules of Professional Conduct.**

unfair competition *n.* Misrepresenting the reputation, name, or good will of a company or person as that of another;

untrue or misleading advertising that causes a consumer to be misled; unethical business practices. Unfair competition is a **tort** and a **fraud,** for which legal remedy and redress may be sought.

unfair labor practice   *n.* An act of an employer against an employee that has been prohibited under the National Labor Relations Act, particularly those relating to an employee's efforts to form or join a union, or the refusal of an employer to collectively bargain with a group of employees or their representatives.

unfit   *adj.* In products law, not qualified or unsuitable for a particular use or purpose.

unfit parent   *n.* A parent with suspect morality, or one who may engage in illegal or excessively unhealthy habits, such as habitual drinking to the point of inebriation, or use of illicit drugs.

unified estate and gift tax   *n.* A tax imposed on property transfer, especially by inheritance, by will, or as a gift. The federal tax laws treat lifetime gifts and death gifts equally. Sometimes referred to as the federal transfer tax or the unified transfer tax.

Uniform Commercial Code   *n.* A law governing the sale of goods, commodities, and bank transactions. With some modifications, this law has been adopted by all 50 states and in the District of Columbia and the U.S. Virgin Islands.

Uniform Consumer Credit Code   *n.* One of several uniform codes that states may or may not adopt. It was intended to give consumers a better understanding of all aspects of credit transactions and to help encourage sound consumer credit practices. Also known as U.C.C.C., U3C, and UCCC.

Uniform Gifts to Minors Act   *n.* A law adopted by every state that creates a method for setting up a trust as a gift to minors. The gift is made by setting up a trust in the name of the custodian or registering the property in the name of the custodian "as custodian for . . . ." The statute also sets forth the terms under which the custodian may make withdrawals to be used for the benefit of the minor. Unless otherwise specified by the donor, the custody of the trust goes to the minor upon reaching age 18. Otherwise, custody passes at age 21.

uniform laws   *n.* An unofficial set of laws proposed for all states to adopt as written, for the purpose of their being more uniformity of laws from state to state. Uniform laws have been put forth by Commissioners on Uniform State Laws. Some of the uniform laws have been adopted by a few states only, after making minor or major changes, while others have been universally adopted, e.g. Uniform Child Custody and Jurisdiction Act; Uniform Power of Attorney Act; Uniform Anatomical Donations Act; and Uniform Arbitration Act.

unilateral   *adj.* Literally, one-sided; relating to only one of two or more people or things.

unilateral contract   See **contract.**

unilateral mistake   See **mistake.**

union shop   *n.* A place of employment that hires only unionized workers.

United States Attorney   *n.* An attorney appointed by the President of the United States to plead the United States government's case in civil and criminal cases in a federal district court. A United States attorney works under the direction of the Attorney General of the United States; each federal judicial district has one United States Attorney, with an office composed of multiple Assistant United States Attorneys. See also **district attorney.**

United States Claims Court See **court.**

United States Code *n.* The official, bound codification of federal law; this multi-volume set is issued anew every six years and updated by supplements in the intervening years. The supplement is called the United States Code Congressional and Administrative News.

United States courts See **court.**

United States magistrate *n.* Appointed by U.S. district court judges, U.S. magistrates are judicial officials with broad powers to conduct pre-trial hearings and conferences in both civil and criminal cases. With consent of the parties, Magistrate Judges may preside over trials in civil cases as well as criminal misdemeanor cases.

unities *n.* A legal fiction left over from common law—a creation of a unity for joint tenancy or ownership. The four unities are interest, possession, time, and title. See also **joint tenancy.**

> *unity of interest.* Requires that each and every joint tenant's interests are identical in kind, breadth, and time.

> *unity of possession.* The necessity that each joint tenant must be entitled to possess the whole property in its entirety.

> *unity of time.* The necessity that all joint tenants' individual interests must vest simultaneously.

> *unity of title.* Requires that all joint tenants acquire their interests by means of a single document.

universal agent *n.* One who by mutual consent is authorized to carry out all business of every kind for another.

unjust enrichment *n.* **1** The keeping of a benefit bestowed or performed by another without offering appropriate compensation, in circumstances where compensation is appropriate. **2** A benefit conferred by another and neither intended as a gift nor legally appropriate, for which the recipient must make restitution or payment. **3** The portion of the law that treats unjustifiable enrichment of either of the foregoing types.

unlawful *adj.* **1** Not authorized by law; illegal. **2** Punishable under criminal law. **3** Characterized by moral corruption.

unlawful act *n.* Behavior that is not authorized by law; commission of or participation in an activity that violates criminal or civil law.

unlawful assembly See **assembly.**

unlawful detainer See **detainer.**

unlawful entry *n.* An entering onto someone's property without that person's consent, by force or fraudulent pretense. Unlawful entry is distinct from **burglary,** which entails the breaking and entering into someone's dwelling with criminal intent.

unlawful force *n.* Power or violence that is directed against a person without that person's consent. Such an act is punishable as an offense or actionable tort.

unliquidated *adj.* Not previously determined or specified (left to be determined by the court).

unreasonable *adj.* **1** Not determined by reason; capricious; arbitrary; irrational. **2** Unsupported by a valid exception to requirements of a warrant; for example, unreasonable search and seizure.

unreasonable search and seizure *n.* An inspection or examination without legal authority (warrant) of a person's self, papers, or belongings, with a hope toward recovering stolen or illicit property or gathering incriminating evidence to be used against that person; the actual taking of that property into possession. Both the Sixth and Fourteenth Amendments to the United States Constitution protect individuals from unreasonable search and seizure.

upzoning See **zoning.**

usage of trade *n.* A trade practice that is so common in a particular region or vocation that an expectation of its being followed in a given transaction is justified; a usual and customary practice or set of practices connected with a particular type of business or trade; for example, in mortgage loan transactions it is customary for the borrower to pay for an appraisal of the value of the property.

use *n.* **1** The right to enjoy the benefits derived from ownership of property, both real and personal. **2** A habitual practice, such as drug use. **3** A purpose or an end served; for example, a screwdriver's use is tightening or loosening screws. **4** The purpose for which something is adapted; for example, neighbors complaining of the owner's use of the building to give trumpet lessons.

useful life *n.* An estimation of the amount of time that exhaustible property will generate income. It is used to calculate depreciation and amortization.

use immunity See **immunity.**

usurious contract *n.* A contract that imposes an illegally high interest rate on the repayment of a debt. See also **usury** and **loan-sharking.**

usury *n.* **1** *Archaic.* Charging interest on borrowed money. **2** The charging of an illegally high rate of return, typical of a loan shark. **3** An illegally high interest rate.

utility *n.* **1** Some society-benefiting quality. **2** The ability to form some function. **3** A business that forms an essential public service and that is often government regulated, such as a public-service utility, electric company, and so on.

utter **1** *adj.* Total, complete, absolute. **2** *v.* To speak or publish. **3** *v.* To use a forged check or instrument; to put it into circulation, as opposed to just creating the forged document.

ux. See **uxor.**

uxor *n. Latin.* Wife.

V

vacate *v.* **1** To set aside or make void; to nullify; to vacate a judgment. **2** To physically leave, as in "to vacate the building. See also **abandonment** and **overrule.**

vagrancy *n.* A vague, poorly delineated set of minor offenses (dating from the downfall of feudalism in England, when there was an acute shortage of laborers), such as being in a condition of unemployment, wandering from place to place with no apparent purpose, and having no visible means of support. More recently, the police have utilized vagrancy statutes for arresting persons thought to have committed a crime, when lack of probable cause for the person's arrest is lacking. Vagrancy statutes have not been well received by the courts, due to their abuse, and have often been declared unconstitutional due to their **vagueness,** and their ignoring of **due process.**

vagueness See **void for vagueness.**

valid *adj.* **1** Legally binding, such as a valid agreement. **2** Having merit, as in, "given the facts presented in this case, it is valid to conclude that she did what she was charged with having done."

valuable consideration See **consideration.**

value *n.* **1** What something is worth in monetary terms, or in money; a thing's market worth. **2** The usefulness or desirability of something. **3** Adequate contractual consideration. See also **fair market value.**

value-added tax See **tax.**

vandalism *n.* Deliberate defacing or destruction of property; ignorant defacing of anything beautiful or treasured, such as a work of art, architecture, or a valued building. Ignorance or malice is usually inferred.

variance *n.* **1** A discrepancy between two documents or statements that should agree; especially in a criminal trial, a disparity between what is alleged in the charges and what is presented at trial as proof. **2** In zoning law, an exception to a specified zoning regulation that may be granted by a zoning board or authority; for example, reducing the number of required parking spaces for a business below the number set forth in zoning regulations as being required for a business of that size or type.

vend *v.* To sell for money or other valuable consideration. (The term is not usually used to refer to real property, although its other forms, **vendor** and **vendee,** are.)

vendee *n.* A purchaser, especially in a contract to purchase real estate; a buyer.

vendor *n.* The person selling, especially in the case of real property. The term **seller** is more frequently used when referring to transactions involving personal property.

> *vendor's lien.* A lien on real property held by the seller until the purchaer has made full payment.

venire *n. Latin.* A panel of jury duty selectees, from among whom the actual jury will be chosen.

> *venire de novo.* A calling of a new jury panel for the purpose of holding a second trial, in cases where a first trial has failed to render a verdict.

venue   *n.* Usually, the locality within which the trial or suit will take place, as sometimes there may be several places where **jurisdiction** could be established. Venue is often a matter of convenience to the parties in a civil suit. In a criminal suit, where it may be difficult to empanel an impartial jury (due to extensive publicity or other considerations), a change of venue may be sought. See also **forum nonconveniens.**

veracity   *n.* **1** Honesty; credibility; truthfulness, as in, "the witness's previous criminal record brings into question his veracity." **2** The accuracy of an account of an event.

verdict   *n.* The conclusion of a jury, or of a judge in a non-jury case, of what the facts are or were. A verdict, being a finding of fact, is different from a **judgment** or a judicial decision. The trial court may choose to accept or to disregard the verdict in determining judgment.

> *compromise verdict.* A verdict achieved by some juror giving in on one of his or her misgivings in exchange for another juror's doing the same, in order to avoid a deadlock or extended period of deliberation. Such an exchange, although considered improper, happens often.

> *general verdict.* A verdict that simply declares which side wins, without finding any special facts to be true.

> *partial verdict.* A verdict in a criminal case that finds the defendant guilty of some charges but innocent of others.

> *quotient verdict.* An improper verdict in a damage case, whereby the jurors find the arithmetic mean of what they think are appropriate damages; that is, the total of what each juror believes should be awarded, divided by the number of jurors to arrive at the amount of the award.

> *special verdict.* A jury verdict that sets forth findings on the merits of each factual issue posed by the court, then used by the court in applying the law to the facts that were found to have merit. When applied in a criminal case, where the judge directs the jury to render special verdicts on specific charges in a case, such action has been declared to be unconstitutional, as the defendant is entitled to a general verdict.

verification   *n.* A statement attesting to the truth, correctness, or authenticity of the things avowed in a written statement; an **affidavit** attached to a written statement affirming its truthfulness.

vertical price fixing   See **price fixing.**

vertical privity   See **privity.**

vested   *n.* An unconditional right of current or future enjoyment of title to and actual possession of property, whether personal or real. See also **contingent.**

> *vested estate.* See **estate.**

> *vested interest.* A current right or title to possess a thing, even though the actual possession may not take place until sometime in the future.

> *vested remainder.* A property in the estate of a deceased that is limited to a certain specified person, whose enjoyment of same may be deferred to some future time.

veto   **1** *n.* The power of one branch of government to prohibit a certain action by another; for example, the chief executive's right to refuse to sign a legislature-passed bill into law. **2** *v.* The act of refusing or canceling the act of another or the passage of a law.

pocket veto. As to a chief executive of a governmental body, such as the President of the United States, the failure to approve a proposed legislative act, thereby resulting in the proposed law not being passed, and therefore "vetoed."

vexatious litigation   *n.* A civil suit that can be shown to have been brought maliciously and in the absence of reasonable cause. See **malicious prosecution.**

vicarious   *adj.* Suffered, performed, or experienced by one person as a substitute for another; indirect; in surrogate.

vicarious liability   See **liability.**

vice crimes   *n.* Activities that are made illegal because they offend the moral standards of the community banning them. Gambling, pornography, and prostitution are the big three of vice crimes in most states and communities.

vicinage   *n.* The vicinity or neighborhood in which a criminal activity has been perpetrated, or in which a trial is being held; the community from which the jurors are being called.

videlicet   See **viz.**

view   *n.* **1** An unobstructed look out of the windows of a dwelling.   **2** An urban encumbrance prohibiting the building of anything that would obstruct a person's view from his or her window.   **3** A jury's trip to a crime scene or other location thought necessary to see the physical particulars of the case before it that might not be capable of being observed in the courtroom.   **4** A lineup. See also **lineup.**

violation   *n.* **1** A breaking of the law; an infraction; a transgression.   **2** The act of breaching the law; contravening a duty or right.   **3** An offense against the public welfare.

violation of probation   See **probation.**

violence   *n.* The use of physical force, especially physical force utilized with malice and/or the attempt to harm someone. Some courts have ruled that in labor disputes, violence includes picketing with false information on the placards, in an attempt to harm a business.

vir   *n. Latin.* Man.

virtual representation   *n.* A bringing of an action on behalf of a party or parties unnamed, as in the case of a class action where a number of people have an interest similar to the named party, and upon whom the court's judgment will be binding. It is often preferable to have a **guardian ad litem** appointed to protect the interests of the nonparties.

visitation rights   *n.* The right of the non-custodial parent, granted by the divorce or family court, to visit with the child on some sort of scheduled or regular basis.

vis major   *n. Latin.* A superior force; the term is used in civil cases to denote an act of God. A loss vis major results from natural causes, such as a hurricane, tornado, or earthquake, and without the intervention of human beings. It is a loss that could not have been prevented by diligence or by having taken precautions. See also **force majeure.**

vitiate   *v.* **1** To interfere with; to impair; to render null and void; to cause to have no effect.   **2** To invalidate either partially or completely.   **3** To corrupt morally.

viz.   *abbr. Latin.* Namely; to wit; that is to say. Used to elaborate on what has already been said in more particular or precise language.

voice exemplar   *n.* A sample of one's voice for the purpose of comparing to the actual person's voice, or a recording of same, used for identification.

void   *n.* Of no legal effect; empty; unenforceable; those provisions having no effect whatsoever.

voidable   *n.* Able to be later voided or nullified; a valid act that may achieve what its purpose was until its fatal flaw is discovered or takes effect and causes it to be voided. For example, a minor may enter into an agreement with a book club and not buy the number of books she contracts to. When the book club tries to recover the remaining part of the contract, the minor repudiates it and it becomes void, because a minor may not make a valid contract.

> *voidable preference.* Bankruptcy term referring to a payment or transfer made by the debtor to a creditor within a certain period of time before declaration of bankruptcy is made, to the disadvantage of other creditors seeking a share of remaining assets of the debtor; such payments may be set aside.

void for vagueness   *n.* When it becomes necessary for a person of average intelligence to guess at the meaning of a law or how that law is to be applied, the statute is constitutionally void for vagueness. A criminal statute may be vague for how it is to be applied, to whom it applies, what conduct is forbidden, or what the punishment is for violating it.

voir dire   *n. French.* Literally to see, to speak; hence, idiomatically, to speak the truth. The usual reference is to an examination by the attorneys and/or the court of prospective jurors to determine whether reasons exist that might dis- qualify them or cause their selection to be challenged, other than peremptorily. During a trial, a *voir dire* examination refers to one outside the hearing of the jury concerning some issue of fact or law that requires the court to rule.

volenti non fit injuria   *n. Latin.* The volunteer suffers no wrong; a person cannot usually sue for damages when he consented in the first place to whatever it was that caused the damages.

voluntary appearance   See **appearance.**

voluntary manslaughter   *n.* An act of murder reduced to a charge of manslaughter due to extenuating circumstances, such as diminished capacity or being provoked in the heat of passion.

voluntary waste   See **waste.**

voting   *n.* The casting of ballots to decide an issue; usually used to refer to the casting of votes in order to elect officials or to decide a question on the ballot.

> *voting trust.* Entrustment by a group of stockholders in a corporation of their votes to a trustee, who shall be empowered to act on their behalf, without the stockholders retaining control to direct the trustee's actions.

voting right   *n.* **1** In corporate law, the right of a shareholder to cast a vote in the election of corporate officers and to vote at meetings to decide corporate policy or transactions. **2** In constitutional law, the right to vote may not be denied to an individual based on race, sex, color, or previous condition of servitude. In addition, in federal elections it is not permissible to charge a poll tax.

Voting Rights Act *n.* A federal law passed in 1965 that states that no voting qualification, prerequisite, or standard practice or procedure shall be imposed or implied by any state or political subdivision to deny or abridge the right of any citizen of the United States to vote because of race or color. Specifically proscribed by the law is use of intimidation. In 1973, the act was expanded to prohibit restrictions based on literacy or education.

W

W-2 form   *n.* A federal tax form, copies of which are provided by the employer to employees and to the IRS, stating total earnings; federal, state, and municipal taxes withheld; FICA taxes; and various other deductions including contributions to retirement accounts, unemployment insurance (in some states), and health insurance (in certain states).

W-4 form   *n.* A federal tax form, on which the employee indicates the number of personal exemptions she will be claiming so that the employer can calculate the amount of federal income tax to be withheld from that employee's paycheck.

wage   *n.* The payment to an employee, usually based on hours worked or quantity of goods or services produced.

wager   *n.* **1** Money or other consideration put at risk on a gamble, a bet, or some other uncertain occurrence. **2** Money promised if a certain event should occur.

waiting period   *n.* The amount of time that must pass before a right is given, as, for example, registration of a handgun, or grant of a marriage license; in insurance policies, the period of time during which a policyholder must wait before starting to collect benefits, e.g., as with a 90 day wait after disability commences before disability benefits will start to be paid by the insurance company.

waive   *v.* **1** To voluntarily give up, abandon, or surrender a right, privilege or claim. Usually, a right may only be waived if the person so doing has full knowledge of what the consequences might be.   **2** To abstain from insisting on a formality, such as an extradition hearing prior to extradition.

waiver   *n.* **1** A voluntary relinquishing of a right or privilege. Although a waiver may result from an explicit surrender or by circumstances, courts frown on accepting waivers of constitutional rights. The party waiving a right must have knowledge of that right and the informed intention of surrendering it. **2** The paper by which a person surrenders his or her rights; for example, when the courier delivered the package, the recipient may sign a waiver relieving the former of any further responsibility.

>*express waiver.* A deliberate and voluntary waiver.

>*implied waiver.* A waiver of certain rights based upon the action of the waiving party. For example, if a person tells a courier he does not care what condition a package is in as long as it arrives by a certain time, that person has waived the right to require the courier to treat the parcel with the normally expected care.

>*prospective waiver.* A waiver of something that may occur in the future; for example, the right to participate in an award from a future, anticipated law suit. Prospective waivers are often deemed to be unenforceable, as the party giving up a right cannot, by definition, know the parameters of what is being given up.

want of consideration   *n.* The lack of consideration in exchange for goods or services, may form the basis for a contract to be unenforceable. See also **consideration.**

want of prosecution   *n.* The failure of a litigant to pursue a case in a timely manner, sometimes resulting in dismissal of the case.

wanton   *adj.* Reckless; extremely careless; acting with utter disregard for others; implies conduct that is beyond mere negligence. In criminal law, malicious or malevolent intent.

ward   *n.* **1** A person for whom a guardian has legal responsibility, or one over whose property a guardian has responsibility. Title to legal property remains with the ward, although he or she may not enter into any contracts involving same.   **2** A division of a town for electoral or educational purposes.

wardship   *n.* **1** The position of guardian usually, but not necessarily, over a minor.   **2** The situation or condition of being a ward.

warrant   *n.* **1** An order in writing from a competent authority instructing that a certain act be carried out.   **2** In commercial and property law, a warrant also refers to a guarantee that a property being sold or transferred meets certain specified criteria.

> *arrest warrant.* A court order directing that a certain person be taken into custody by the sheriff or other law officer and made to appear before the court to answer a complaint, or for some other reason.

> *bench warrant.* An arrest warrant issued specifically by a judge for a person who has failed to appear before a court after previously having been summoned to do so, or who has been indicted for an offense or found to be in contempt of court.

> *death warrant.* A warrant issued by a governor or other person with authority, commanding that a prisoner under sentence of death be put to death at a certain time and in a certain manner.

> *general warrant.* A warrant used by the government to search a described premises and seize any proscribed substances not described in the warrant. This type of warrant has been held unconstitutional by the Supreme Court as violating the Fourth Amendment of the United States Constitution, except in cases where the seized items are in plain sight.

> *stock warrant.* A certificate entitling the bearer to buy a certain number of shares of stock at a specified time for a set price.

warranty   *n.* The attesting of one party to a contract to the other of reliable facts so that the second party does not need to ascertain such facts for him or herself. Such assurance carries with it a promise to indemnify the second party for any loss should the particulars of the warranty prove not to be factual. Such a warranty may be express or implied.

> *express warranty.* A warranty created by the specific words of the warrantor promising the purchaser of goods that the merchandise being sold possesses or lacks certain qualities.

> *implied warranty.* A warranty arising from the existence of certain laws governing the conditions under which a certain thing may be transferred, rather than from the words of the seller.

> *limited warranty.* Warranty limited as to period of time or scope, e.g., a warranty for an automobile may be for only certain components of the car, or for a specified number of miles or months.

> *warranty of fitness for a certain purpose.* A warranty that the merchandise is suited for use for the special purpose for which the buyer is acquiring it, rather than merely fit for general use.

warranty of habitability. A landlord's promise that from the start of the lease there are no hidden difficulties or defects that might affect the use of the premises for residential purposes, and that the premises will remain habitable for the lease's duration.

warranty of merchantability. An implied guarantee on the part of a merchant that the merchandise he sells is suitable for the general purpose that it is sold. For example, if the merchant sells house paint, it is implied that that paint will adhere to walls.

warranty deed   See **deed**.

waste *n.* Permanent harm done to real property by a person or persons in legal possession of that property (such as a tenant), such that the property's value to its actual owner or future inheritor is diminished. The legal possession part is critical in distinguishing waste from trespass.

ameliorating waste. An unauthorized physical change of an occupied structure by a tenant that, while technically waste, actually increases the value of the property, such as tearing out old carpeting and putting in new, better quality carpeting. Such an act is rarely considered grounds for liability.

equitable waste. Damage done by a lifelong tenant who normally would be unchallengeable, but who may be enjoined by the court using the standard of variance from what a prudent man would do with his own property.

hazardous waste. By-product of certain industries or activities, determined to be of unusually dangerous nature, e.g., radioactive waste, generally subject to special rules of disposable and/or recycling.

permissive waste. Damage done by a tenant's failure to make reasonable repairs that he might normally be expected to see to, such as allowing water to accumulate in a leaky basement over the course of years.

voluntary waste. Damage directly caused to the property by a voluntary act of the tenant, such as filling in drainage ditches or punching a hole in the roof.

wasting property *n.* Ownership, right to, or interest in a wasting asset.

wasting asset. An asset that will be consumed through normal use, such as the gold in a gold mine, oil in an oil well, or a copyright.

weapon *n.* An implement used or designed to be used to kill or injure a person. See also **gun-control law**.

concealed weapon. A weapon that is carried by someone but is not visible to the ordinary observer's eye.

dangerous weapon. An implement or device that is capable of causing serious bodily harm or death; not to be confused with a deadly weapon. A dangerous weapon *may* be deadly; a deadly weapon *must* be dangerous.

deadly weapon. Any firearm or other device (crossbow, longbow, bomb, grenade, and so on), substance (poison), or material (dagger, cutlass), that, when used in the manner it was intended to be used, will be likely to cause death.

weight of the evidence *n.* The relative value of the total evidence presented by one side of a judicial proceeding when compared to the evidence presented by the other. The phrase refers to the persuasiveness of the testimony of witnesses and the physical evidence combined. See also **burden of proof**.

Westlaw *n.* An online legal research service for legal and law-related materials and services, including searches of United States and international legal materials, federal and state statutes, and legal periodicals; maintained by the West Group of Thomson Learning, Inc.

white-collar crime *n.* A phrase denoting a variety of nonviolent crimes and commercial offenses committed by business people, public officials, and con artists. Consumer fraud, bribery, stock manipulation, and embezzlement are among the improprieties in this category.

wilful See **willful.**

will *n.* **1** Desire, intent, choice, as in, "she exercised her own free will." **2** A document spelling out what is to be done with the person's (testator's) belongings after she has died. Such document has no force while the person is alive and may be altered or revoked at any time, but becomes applicable at the time of the testator's death to whatever the conditions of the estate are at the time of death. The difference between a **deed** and a will is that a deed passes an interest upon delivery, while a will is effective only on death.

estate at will. The right of a grantee to use and possess land by mutual agreement (or will) with the grantor; the right to use the property terminates when the will of either party ends.

holographic will. See **holographic will.**

joint and mutual will. One will executed by two or more persons with reciprocating provisions of consideration of each to the other.

joint will. A single will signed by two or more persons but that is not necessarily reciprocating or mutual.

last will and testament. Phrase commonly used to refer to the latest (most recent) instrument directing the disposition of the personal property of the signer(s).

mutual wills. See **reciprocal will.**

nuncupative will. An oral will dictated by the testator just before death, before a certain number of witnesses (depending on state law), and put in written form after death; generally invalid in most states.

willful *adj.* **1** In civil law, intentional, voluntary, knowing; distinguished from accidental, but not necessarily malicious. **2** In criminal law, an act done stubbornly or with an evil intent.

winding up *v.* The process of dissolving a partnership or corporation by collecting all assets and outstanding income, satisfying all the creditors claims, and distributing whatever remains (the net assets). These may be distributed as cash or in kind, first to preferred stockholders, if any, and then to remaining shareholders, if any, pro rata. Winding up is in anticipation of a company's dissolution. See also **liquidate.**

wiretap **1** *n.* The listening in of any wire or oral communication by use of electronic or mechanical means; generally illegal where both parties to the communication are unaware of the wiretap. Unauthorized use or possession of wiretap devices is prohibited under state and federal law. **2** *v.* The act of placing an electronic device to listen in on oral communications. See also **bugging,** and **pen register.**

withholding *n.* **1** The portion of earned wages that an employer deducts to cover income tax purposes and forwards to the government. **2** The process by which the employer makes the deduction. See also **W-2 form** and **W-4 form.**

withholding tax See **tax.**

witness **1** *n.* A person who gives testimony under oath and penalty of perjury in a court of law **2** *v.* To observe the execution of a legal document and to authenticate it by affixing one's name to it.

adverse witness. See **hostile witness.**

character witness. One who testifies to the reputation of another as a reliable, reputable member of the community. Character witnesses may be used to support or impugn the testimony of a key party.

expert witness. See **expert.**

hostile witness. One whose adverse relationship to a party may prejudice his or her testimony against that party. A person declared to be a hostile witness may be asked leading questions and may be cross-examined by the party who called him or her.

lay witness. A witness other than an expert witness.

material witness. A witness called to testify about an important or essential matter, or a matter having a logical and necessary connection to the facts under consideration.

w.o.p. See **want of prosecution.**

words of limitation *n.* Words in a deed or will that are conventional, but non-literal. As an example, the phrase, "to B and her heirs," by longstanding convention of property laws, gives an interest in land to B, but nothing to her heirs.

words of purchase *n.* Language in a deed or will conveying to whom the grant is going. The words designate the nature of the estate granted, for example, "to B and his heirs" might be interpreted the grant goes to B, and then to his heirs as long as the family line exists.

workhouse *n.* A jail for criminals who have committed minor offenses and who will not be serving lengthy terms.

work product *n.* That work done for a client by an attorney representing the client and generally considered protected from discovery. It includes statements written and spoken, as well as tactics, opinions, and thoughts that are protected by the attorney-client privilege.

work release program *n.* A program allowing a prisoner to voluntarily participate in a training program away from the prison, or to work at a paying job in the community, while continuing to serve as a prisoner at a penal institution. State prisoners in such a program may not be involuntarily removed from that program without due process showing that he or she is a threat to the community. See also **halfway house.**

worth *n.* **1** The value of something, expressed in monetary terms; all of a thing's qualities that make it useful and valuable, expressed in terms of a medium of exchange. **2** The total monetary value of a person. **3** The sentimental value of something; emotional value.

writ *n.* The written order of a court in the name of the state or other legal authority ordering the person addressed to either do something or restrain from doing something.

writ of assistance *n.* **1** *Archaic.* One of the most hated abuses of common law in colonial America, it was a general warrant for an officer of the crown to search wherever he pleased for goods imported without paying British tariffs. They were greatly abused and led to the constitutional ban against unreasonable search and seizure. **2** In current practice, a writ of assistance is a remedy for the transfer of property when the title has been previously decided by a proceeding, and is issued to enforce the prior judgment or decree.

writ of certiorari   See **certiorari.**

writ of error   *n.* An order from an appellate court to a lower one to deliver a case's records for the purpose of reviewing them.

writ of habeas corpus   See **habeas corpus.**

writ of mandamus   See **mandamus.**

writ of possession   See **writ of assistance.**

writ, peremptory   See **peremptory writ.**

written instrument   *n.* Anything expressed in writing; a contract or agreement contained in the writing. Many statutes are required to be expressed in writing in order for them to take effect.

wrong   **1** *n.* A violation of another person's legal rights; an illegal act.   **2** *v.* To violate another person's rights or to do harm. See also **tort.**

wrongful act   *n.* Any act that will damage the rights of another, unless it is done in the exercise of another equal or superior right. For that reason, the scope of wrongful acts is not limited to illegal acts, but includes acts that are immoral, anti social, or libel to result in a civil suit.

wrongful-birth action   *n.* A legal suit brought by parents against a doctor who failed to inform them of the risks of having a child with prospective birth defects. See also **wrongful-life action.**

wrongful conduct   See **wrongful act.**

wrongful-death action   *n.* A lawsuit brought alleging damages from a wrongful act, default, or negligent behavior that resulted in the aforementioned's demise. Such action may be brought by the executor or administrator of the decedent's estate, as well as his or her surviving family, claiming deprivation of economic benefit that would have been had in the way of income or services had the decedent survived. Wrongful-death laws are different from **survival statutes,** which provide for legal action to sue for mental anguish, medical expenses, pain and suffering, or lost wages springing from the act leading to the death. Both statutes, however, circumvent the common law rule that death extinguishes civil law suits. There is a wrongful death statute in every state in the United States.

wrongful-life action   *n.* A legal action on behalf of a child with birth defects, alleging that the parents would not have conceived the child or would have aborted the fetus if the doctor-defendant had informed them of the congenital defects to be expected, in order to avoid the pain and suffering resulting from the child's defects. Most jurisdictions reject these actions.

wrongful-pregnancy action   *n.* A lawsuit brought against a doctor by a parent for damages resulting from a pregnancy after a failed procedure to sterilize.

XYZ

yellow dog contract *n.* A document required of an employee by the employer, as a condition of employment, in which the employee promises not to join a labor union, with penalty for breach being the termination of employment. Federal laws, including the National Labor Relations Act, have made such contracts illegal.

yield **1** *v.* To let go of or forego something **2** *n.* The monetary return from an investment.

x *n.* A mark or indication utilized as a signature by an illiterate person who is unable to sign his or her name.

year and a day rule *n.* The rule of common law that in order for **homicide** to have been committed, the victim's death must occur within a year and a day after the act that allegedly caused it.

years, estate for *n.* An interest in land for a specific and predetermined period of time.

zoning *n.* The creation by a legislature of geographical sectors within a municipality or other geographical entity, in which different uses of or activities upon property are permitted or forbidden.

Part II

APPENDICES

Abbreviations

AAA American Arbitration Association. A national organization that promotes the use of arbitration to resolve commercial and labor disputes. It also maintains a panel of arbitrators for those who wish to utilize their services.

AALS Association of American Law Schools. A national organization of law schools that have each graduated at least three classes of students and have offered instruction for at least five years.

ABA American Bar Association. The largest national organization of lawyers, it promotes improvements and reform in the administration of justice and in the provision of legal services to the public.

ACLU American Civil Liberties Union. A national organization of lawyers and others who are interested in enforcing and preserving the individual rights and civil liberties guaranteed by the federal and state constitutions.

ADA Americans with Disabilities Act. Federal law enacted in 1990 to protect individuals with physical or mental disabilities from intentional or unintentional discrimination in housing, employment, education, access to public services, etc.

ADEA Age Discrimination in Employment Act. Federal statute that protects most employees between 40 and 70 years of age from age discrimination in the workforce. Other federal and local laws provide other protections against age discrimination in such areas as housing.

ADR Alternative dispute resolution. Formal methods of settling disputes other than by court action, collectively referred to as alternative dispute resolution or ADR.

aff'd Affirmed.

aff'g Affirming.

A.G. Attorney General. The chief legal officer of the United States or of a state, who advises the federal or state government on legal matters, represents the federal or state government in litigation, and heads the United States Department of Justice or a state's legal department.

a.k.a. Also known as. Phrase used before a list of names used by a specific individual in order to avoid confusion about the person's true identity or by others when referring to the individual.

ALI American Law Institute. A national organization of attorneys, judges, and legal scholars who seek to promote consistency, clarity, and simplification in the law through such projects as the Restatements of the Law and the Model Penal Code.

ALJ Administration law judge.

AMEX American Stock Exchange. The second largest stock exchange in the United States. Located in New York City, it frequently engages in the trading of stock of small or new companies because of its less rigid listing requirements.

AMT Alternative minimum tax. A flat tax originally imposed upon corporations or individuals with high incomes in the event that they wrote off all their income through use of deductions, credits, and contributions. It was enacted to make sure that these parties paid at least some income tax, but it also can affect middle-income families.

APA Administrative Procedure Act. A federal statute governing the rule-making and administrative proceedings of federal administrative agencies by providing guidelines for rule-making and adjudicative hearings, judicial review, and public access. Most states have similar statutes governing their state administrative agencies.

APR Annual percentage rate.

ASE See **AMEX**

AWOL Absent without leave. The act of being away from one's military duties or post without permission but with no intent of deserting.

BAC Blood alcohol content. The amount of alcohol in an individual's bloodstream expressed as a percentage of the total composition of one's blood. The percentage is used to determine whether the person is legally drunk, especially in regard to laws prohibiting the driving of vehicles while under the influence of alcohol.

B and E (or B & E) Breaking and entering. Two of the elements constituting the crime of burglary. Under the common law, forcible entry into a building (however slight) without permission used to be required, but many state laws now only require one to enter (for example, through an unlocked door or open window) or remain on the premises (for example, hiding in a closet until no one else is left in the building) without authorization.

BFOQ Bona fide occupational qualification. Employment practices that would constitute discrimination as to certain individuals of a particular religion, gender, national origin, or age range (but not race or color) when the otherwise illegal discrimination is a bona fide qualification that is reasonably necessary for the normal performance of the duties of that particular occupation. For example, a designer of women's clothes by necessity is permitted to hire only female models to show off new designs. Such practices are not illegal under federal law. In addition, religious organizations and schools are allowed to hire only members of that religion even if religion is not a bona fide occupational qualification for that position (such as the requirement that all teachers in a parochial school be Catholic, even though they teach subjects that do not require Catholic background).

BFP Bona fide purchaser. One who receives property in exchange for money or valuable consideration.

B/L Bill of lading. A document issued by a carrier or by a shipper's agent that identifies the goods received for shipment, where the goods are to be delivered, and who is entitled to receive the shipment.

C & F Cost and freight. Both the initials and phrase are used in offers and contracts for the sale of goods to indicate that the quoted price includes the cost of the freight to a named destination as well as the cost of the goods.

C.D. Certificate of deposit. **1** A certificate from a bank acknowledging the receipt of money and a promise to repay it at a specified time and with interest determined at a specified rate. **2** A bank document evidencing a time deposit.

cert. From *Latin* certiorari. To be more fully informed. A writ issued at the discretion of an appellate court directing a lower court to certify and deliver the record of a case that is not appealable **as of right** to the appellate court for possible review. See also **appeal** and **writ of error.**

cf. Compare. In legal citation, a direction to the reader to review a cited authority in which an explanatory or an analogous (but supportive) proposition might be found.

> *but cf.* In legal citation, a direction to the reader to review a cited authority in which a analogous (but contradictory) proposition might be found.

C.F. See **C & F**

C.F.I. See **C.I.F.**

C.I.F. Cost, insurance, and freight. Phrase used in an offer or a contract for the sale of goods indicating that the quoted price includes the combined cost of the goods, insurance, and the freight to a named destination.

C.F.R. Code of Federal Regulations. The official annual compilation of all regulations and rules promulgated during the previous year by the agencies of the United States government, combined with all the previously issued regulations and rules of those agencies that are still in effect.

C.J. **1** Chief justice. **2** Chief judge. **3** Circuit judge. **4** Corpus juris

C.J.S. Corpus Juris Secundum. An authoritative legal encyclopedia that provides general background knowledge of the law with footnoted citation to relevant case law.

CLE Continuing legal education. **1** The training available to lawyers, usually through seminars, to continue their legal education, hone their skills, and keep up with the latest developments within a particular area of the law. **2** The industry of the providers of seminars, books, and other materials designed to provide such training to lawyers.

COBRA Consolidated Omnibus Budget Reconciliation Act of 1985. A federal statute requiring employers who provide a group health insurance plan for their employees to continue providing coverage to an employee for 18 months following termination or firing, or to a spouse of an employee in the event of divorce, for a period of 36 months following the entry of the divorce decree, provided that the spouse was covered by the employee's health insurance during the marriage. Obligation for payment of the health insurance premium is borne by the terminated employee or, in the event of divorce, by the party designated in the divorce papers, but in no event by the employer.

corp. Corporation. An entity, usually a business, created by a legislative act or by individuals who have agreed upon and filed articles of incorporation with the state government. Ownership in the corporation is typically represented by shares of stock. Furthermore, a corporation is legally recognized as an artificial person whose existence is separate and distinct from that of its shareholders who are not personally responsible for the corporation's acts and debts. As an artificial person, a corporation has the power to acquire, own, and convey property, to sue and be sued, and such other powers of a natural person that the law may confer upon it.

d/b/a Doing business as, identifying an individual's trade name; for example, John James d/b/a James Productions.

DUI See **DWI.**

DWI Driving while intoxicated. The criminal law offense of operating a vehicle after having drunk an amount of alcohol sufficient to raise one's blood alcohol content above a legal limit, commonly referred to by the acronym DWI. Also known as driving under the influence (DUI), which, in some jurisdictions means that the driver had a lower level of intoxication than DWI, but was still impaired. In some jurisdictions, the term driving while impaired is used.

e.g. From the Latin, *exempli gratia,* meaning, for example.

ERISA Employee Retirement Income Security Act of 1974. Federal legislation enacted in 1974 that sets forth rules for employee benefit plans.

et al. From *Latin* et alii or et alia. And others; typically used in the caption of court documents following the first named party, to signify that more than one individual is aligned on one side of the case.

ex. *Latin.* Previous, from.

FOIA Freedom of Information Act. A federal law that allows individuals and organizations to compel the federal government to release copies of documents it might not otherwise choose to disclose.

GAAP Generally accepted accounting principles. Standards adopted by the accounting profession for the form and content of financial statements

GAAS Generally accepted auditing standards. Standards adopted by the accounting profession governing the audit of corporations and organizations.

GATT General Agreement on Tariffs and Trade. An international agreement governing imports and exports; predecessor to the World Trade Organization.

HLA test Human-leukocyte-antigen test. A paternity test utilizing genetic material.

ICC Interstate Commerce Commission. A federal agency, no longer in existence today, that regulated interstate carriers.

id. *Latin.* Like ibid., indicates that a citation is identical to the immediate past one.

i.f.p. From *Latin* in forma pauperis. In litigation, to proceed as an indigent.

IRA Individual retirement account. A tax-deferred retirement account established by federal law. The portion of annual income contributed to the account is not taxed until it is drawn out after retirement age.

IRC Internal Revenue Code. Contains the current federal tax laws and is located in Title 26 of the United States Code.

IRS Internal Revenue Service. A federal government agency charged with the collection of income taxes.

J. Judge or justice.

J.D. Juris Doctor. The law degree conferred by most American law schools.

JJ. Judges or justices.

j.n.o.v. From *Latin* judgment non obstante veridicto. Judgment notwithstanding the verdict. In rare cases, a judge may enter a judgment in favor of one party despite a jury's award against that party; generally in cases where the evidence was such that no reasonable jury could have come to the determination that it did.

J.P. Justice of the peace. A local official, not necessarily an attorney or judge, with jurisdiction over limited matters such as performing weddings or resolving minor civil or criminal complaints.

L.J. Law journal.

L.L.B. The law degree formerly granted by American law schools, most of which now confer the J.D. degree.

LLC Limited liability company. An entity that blends features of a corporation and a partnership, but is neither; owners are called "members" and may consist of one or more individuals, corporations, or even other LLCs. Members have some of the same protection as stockholders in a corporation, especially, no personal liability.

L.L.M. Master of Laws degree.

LMRA Labor Management Relations Act. A 1947 federal law designed to protect employers, employees and the public. It governs union activities and provides an arbitration mechanism for strikes that cause national emergencies.

MACRS Modified Accelerated Cost Recovery System. An accounting approach for the rapid depreciation of assets.

m.o. Modus operandi. *Latin.* A method of operating.

NASDAQ National Association of Security Dealers Automated Quotation system. An automated national stock exchange.

n.b. *Latin.* Nota bene; used to emphasize or call notice to something.

NLRA National Labor Relations Act. A federal law governing certain labor issues and creating the National Labor Relations Board.

NLRB National Labor Relations Board. A federal labor agency that oversees union elections and other labor issues.

NSF A banking term meaning "not sufficient funds."

NSF check. Not sufficient funds check. A check that a drawee bank may not pay because the drawer has insufficient funds on deposit to cover it when it is presented for payment.

NYSE New York Stock Exchange. A national exchange operated by an association of securities firms based in New York City.

OSHA Occupational Safety and Health Administration. An agency of the federal government established by Act of Congress in 1970 that creates and enforces rules governing the safety of workers in the workplace. The agency routinely inspects workplaces and issues citations for businesses that are in violation of its standards. The agency is a part of the Department of Labor.

P.A. Professional association.

pat. pending A designation attached to a product while the Patent Office is considering the patent application. Such a designation imparts no protection against infringement unless the actual patent is eventually granted.

P.C. Personal computer; politically correct; probable cause; professional corporation; and protective custody.

PCR Stands for polymerase chain reaction, the newest (at this writing) method of DNA analysis. Using PCR technique, it is possible to analyze a biological specimen that is one-tenth the size of that required for the older RFLP method. It also gives quicker results, but the analysis is not as discriminating as RFLP.

PCR actions Post-conviction relief proceedings. Federal or state procedure whereby a convicted criminal can request that a conviction or sentence be corrected or vacated.

P.D. Police department; also public defender.

PSA Property settlement agreement.

Q The abbreviation used in trial transcripts and depositions to mark each question asked.

QDRO Qualified domestic relations order. Any decree, judgment, or order that recognizes the right of one person (the alternate payee) to participate either totally or partially in the pension of another (the participant). The alternate payee must be a dependent child, spouse, or former spouse of the participant. This is an exception to the ERISA rule, proscribing the assignment of plan benefits.

rev. proc. Revenue procedure. An official IRS statement spelling out the administrative practices used by the IRS. For example, methods for obtaining a private ruling are often spelled out.

rev. stat. Revised statutes. Laws that have been changed, altered, amended, or reenacted by a legislative body. A reenactment is generally thought of as having the effect of a repeal and replacement of the former law.

RFLP Restriction Fragment Length Polymorphism. The older and more discriminating form of DNA testing. Restriction Fragment Length Polymorphism is a process that breaks DNA strands into tiny fragments at specific points on the DNA chain. Also known as HLA DQ Alpha, or simply DQ Alpha.

RICO Racketeer Influenced and Corrupt Organizations Act. This law, enacted in 1970, is designed to fight activity by organized crime and to preserve the integrity of the interstate and international marketplace by investigating and prosecuting individuals conspiring to participate or actually participating in racketeering. Note that it has no force in intrastate commerce.

ROR Release on own recognizance. A pretrial release of an arrested person without bail, on that person's promise to appear for trial when it is appropriate to do so.

R.S. Revised statutes. Laws that have been changed, altered, amended, or reenacted by a legislative body. A reenactment is generally thought of as having the effect of a repeal and replacement of the former law.

S.E.C. Securities and Exchange Commission. The federal administrative agency established by the Securities Exchange Act of 1934, in order to supervise and regulate the issuing and trading of securities and to eliminate fraudulent or unfair practices. It is a regulating agency and is not judicial in nature, although it may pursue judicial remedies in federal court.

S.L. Session laws or statute laws. See also session laws. A bound volume of the statutes enacted by a legislative body during a single annual or biennial session; a collection of all of those aforementioned statutes.

T.R.O. Temporary restraining order. A restraining order is always temporary, because it is ordered without a hearing. This distinguishes it from an injunction. A court order issued to prevent a family member or other party from harassing, threatening, harming, seizing the property of, and sometimes even approaching or having any kind of contact with another; a court order issued to temporarily prevent a transfer of property, pending a hearing.

U3C See **UCC**

UCC Uniform Commercial Code. A law governing the sale of goods, commodities, and bank transactions. With some modifications, this law has been adopted by all 50 states and in the District of Columbia and the U.S. Virgin Islands.

UCCC See **UCC**

value-added tax A tax imposed at each step in the production or construction of a manufactured good based upon the difference between the cost of producing the item and its selling price.

viz. From *Latin* videlicit. Namely; to wit; that is to say. Used to elaborate on what has already been said in more particular or precise language.

w.o.p. Want of prosecution. The lack of consideration in exchange for goods or services; may form the basis for a contract to be unenforceable.

Foreign Words and Phrases

ab initio *adv. Latin.* "From the first act." From the beginning; back to one's creation or inception.

actus reus *n. Latin.* "Criminal act" or "guilty act." The voluntary and wrongful act or omission that constitutes the physical components of a crime. Because a person cannot be punished for bad thoughts alone, there can be no criminal liability without actus reus.

ad damnum *n. Latin.* "To the damage." The amount of money sought as damages by the plaintiff in a civil action.

additur *n. Latin.* "It is added to." A trial court's order to increase the damages awarded by a jury. It is done to prevent the plaintiff from appealing on the grounds that inadequate damages were awarded, but the court cannot issue the order without the defendant's consent. The term may also refer to the increase itself, the procedure by which it is done, and the court's power to issue the order.

ad hoc *adj. Latin.* "For this; for a particular purpose." For example, ad hoc committees are often created to accomplish a particular purpose.

ad hominem *adj. Latin.* "To the person." Appealing to personal prejudices instead of reason; attacking one's character rather than his arguments.

ad litem *Latin.* "For the suit." For the purposes of, or pending, the particular lawsuit.

ad testificandum *Latin.* "For testifying." See **subpoena** (*subpoena ad testificandum*). See also **habeas corpus.**

ad valorem *Latin.* "In proportion to its value."

> *ad valorem tax.* A proportional tax imposed upon something's value,

rather than on its quantity (especially on real property).

a fortiori *adv. Latin.* "By the stronger (reason)." To draw an inference that when one proposition is true, then a second proposition must also be true, especially if the second is included in the first. For example, if a 19 year old is legally an adult, then a 20 year old is, too.

alter ego *n. Latin.* "The other self." A doctrine allowing a court to ignore the limited personal liability of a person who acts in a corporate capacity and impose personal liability for the corporation's wrongful acts when it is shown that the individual was using the corporation to conduct personal business and that there was no real separation between the individual's and the corporation's identity. See also **corporate** (*corporate veil*).

a mensa et thoro *Latin.* "From board and hearth."

> *divorce a mensa et thoro.* (*Archaic. Latin*) Divorce from bed and board. A proceeding, current in Britain until the 19th century, that resulted in the parties remaining married but living separately. The term is still used in a few jurisdictions.

amicus curiae *n. Latin.* "Friend of the court." One who is not a party to an action but petitions the court or is invited by the court to provide information or submit her views because she has a strong interest in the case at hand or a perspective that may not be adequately presented by the parties.

animus *adj. Latin.* "Purposefully; intentionally." **1** Animosity; hostility; ill will; strong dislike; hate. **2** The animating thought, intention, or purpose of an act.

ante *Latin.* "Before." Before in time, order, or position; in front of. See also **post.**

a posteriori *adv. Latin.* "From what comes after." Inductive; empirical; reasoning or the ascertaining of truth by actual experience or observation. See also **a priori.**

a priori *adv. Latin.* "From what is before." Deductive reasoning or the ascertaining of truth by proceeding from an assumption to its logical conclusion rather than by actual experience or observation. For example, one who walks by a store when its alarm is sounding and sees that its window is broken can deduce that a burglary has occurred without having watched the burglars commit the actual crime.

arguendo *adv. Latin.* "In arguing." **1** Hypothetically; for the purpose or sake of argument. A term used to assume a fact without waiving the right to question it later on. For example, a defense attorney may state to the judge: "Assuming arguendo that the defendant committed the crime, the statute of limitations prevents the state from prosecuting him for it." **2** During the course of an argument or a conversation. For example, "Mr. Smith mentioned arguendo that his client had three prior convictions."

assumpsit *n. Latin.* "He undertook." **1** An enforceable promise or undertaking that is not under seal. **2** An action for expectation damages caused by the breach of a promise or a contract not under seal.

autre or auter *French.* "Other, another." See also **estate.**

autrefois acquit *French.* "Formerly acquitted." A plea by a person indicted for a crime for which he or she had previously been tried and acquitted. See also **double jeopardy** and **autrefois convict.**

autrefois convict *French.* "Formerly convicted." A plea by a person indicted for a crime for which he or she had previously been tried and convicted. See also **double jeopardy** and **autrefois acquit.**

autre (or auter) vie *n. French.* "Another's life." See **estate.**

a vinculo matrimonii *Latin.* "From the bond of marriage."

> *divorce a vinculo matrimonii. (Latin)* Common law, meaning, "from the bonds of marriage"; a form of divorce based on grounds that pre-existed the marriage, which resulted in a legal fiction that the marriage never existed (with the result that any children of the marriage are then considered illegitimate).

bona fide *adj./adv. Latin.* "In good faith." Acting, being, carried out, or made in good faith; authentic; genuine; sincere.

casus omissus *n. Latin.* "Case omitted." A legal issue or situation not governed by statutory or administrative law or by the terms of a contract. The resolution of any legal dispute arising from such an issue or situation is governed by the case law or, if it is a case of first impression, by whatever guidance the court finds in the common law.

causa *Latin.* "Case, cause." See **cause.**

causa mortis *Latin.* "Because of death." Something done or made by a person in anticipation of his own imminent death. See also **gift.**

causa proxima *Latin.* "The nearest cause." See also **cause.**

causa sine qua non *Latin.* "A cause without which not." Same as but-for cause. See **cause.**

caveat *n. Latin.* "Let him or her beware." **1** An admonition, caution, or warning. **2** A formal notice or warning given by a party to a judge or other court officer concerning his or her behavior and requesting a suspension of the proceeding until the merits of the notice or warning are determined. **3** A formal notice to a court or public official that the notifier has an interest in a matter or property and requests the suspension of some procedure or proceeding concerning the matter or property until the notifier is given a hearing.

caveat emptor *n. Latin.* "Let the buyer beware." The legal principle that, unless the quality of a product is guaranteed in a warranty, the buyer purchases the product as it is and cannot hold another liable for any defects. Statutes and court decisions concerning products liability and implied warranties have substantially altered this rule.

certiorari *n. Latin.* "To be more fully informed." A writ issued at the discretion of an appellate court directing a lower court to certify and deliver the record of a case that is not appealable **as of right** to the appellate court for possible review. See also **appeal** and **writ of error.**

cognovit *n. Latin.* "He has conceded." An acknowledgment of a debt or liability in the form of the debtor's written consent to a judgment taken against the debtor by the creditor, if a particular event does or does not occur.

corpus *n. Latin.* "Body." **1** The main body, mass, or part of something. **2** A collection of things that, when together, can be considered or regarded as a single thing (such as a collection of writing by an author). **3** The capital or principal sum (as opposed to income or interest). **4** The property or subject matter of a trust.

corpus delicti *n. Latin.* "Body of the crime." The objective evidence that there has been an injury (physical or otherwise) or loss and that it was caused by the criminal act of some person or thing.

corpus juris *n. Latin.* "Body of law." The law in general, especially when compiled, codified, and published in a single text or in a series consisting of a collection of individual laws. Abbreviated c.j.

cy pres *French.* "As near as." The equitable doctrine that a deed or will whose terms cannot be carried out may be modified by a court so that the intent of the instrument's maker can be fulfilled as closely as possible.

dehors *French.* "Outside" or "beyond the bounds of," as in matters that are dehors the trial record or the pages of a written agreement.

del credere *adj. Italian.* "Of belief or trust." Used in connection with agents who guarantee the good faith or financial capability of the persons or entities on whose behalf they act. See also **agent.**

delict *n.* From the Latin *delictum,* "an offense." A breach of criminal or civil law.

duces tecum *Latin.* "To bring along." A type of **subpoena** that requires a witness to bring specified documents when he or she appears in court or for a **deposition.**

ejusdem generis *Latin.* "Of the same category." A legal principle stating that a general phrase following a list of specific items refers to an item of the same type as those in the list.

en banc *adj/adv. French.* "On the bench." Of appeals courts, before a full court, with all judges present. Federal appeals are typically heard by a panel of three judges, but may be reheard by the full circuit court of appeals sitting en banc.

eo instante *Latin.* "At that moment."

eo nomine *Latin.* "In the name of."

ergo *conj., adv. Latin.* "Therefore."

et al. *abbr. Latin.* "And others"; typically used in the caption of court documents following the first named party, to signify that more than one individual is aligned on one side of the case.

ex. *Latin.* "Previous, from."

ex parte *adv. Latin.* "In behalf of." A judge's action in conducting a hearing or conference with one party only, without notice to the other party; typically improper, except under the limited circumstances in which a party is seeking a temporary restraining order and alleging that notice to the adverse party will result in the destruction of evidence or other illegal action. Also used as an adverb, such as, "the judge conducted the hearing ex parte". It also refers to a party's attempts to make such contact with the judge.

ex post facto *adv. Latin.* "After the fact."

factum *n. Latin.* "Fact." A fact or an action.

force majeure *n. French.* "Greater force"; a natural or human-induced disaster that causes a contract to fail of performance.

forum conveniens *Latin.* "Suitable forum." Litigation: the most appropriate court for the resolution of a particular dispute.

forum nonconveniens *Latin.* "Unsuitable forum." Litigation: the doctrine that a court may decline jurisdiction of a case, based on factors such as residence of the parties, thus allowing or causing another more convenient court to take the case.

habeas corpus *Latin.* "You have the body." In criminal procedure, a process to challenge the detention of a prisoner; frequently used as a way to attack a conviction in federal court when state appeals have been exhausted.

ibid. *abbr. Latin.* (*ibedem.* "In the same place"). When citing a work, indicates that the citation is to the same volume and page as the previous citation.

id. *abbr. Latin.* (*idem.* "The same.") Like **ibid.**, indicates that a citation is identical to the immediate past one.

ignorantia juris non excusat *Latin.* "Ignorance of the law is no excuse"; typically refers to criminal charges, in which such ignorance is not a cognizable defense.

in absentia *Latin.* "In the absence of."

in camera *Latin.* "In a chamber." In the judge's chambers; implying a private, closed, or informal hearing or conference before the judge.

in delicto *Latin.* "In the wrong."

in extremis *Latin.* "In extremity." Upon the point of dying.

in forma pauperis *Latin.* "In the manner of a pauper." In litigation, to proceed as an indigent.

infra *adj./adv. Latin.* "Below." See below; referring to the placement of a particular citation or assertion in a text.

in futuro *adv. Latin.* "In the future."

in limine   *adv. Latin.* "At the outset."

> *motion in limine.* A **motion** to limit the evidence that will be submitted to the jury, by excluding matters that are not relevant, are prejudicial, or are otherwise inadmissible under applicable rules.

in loco parentis   *Latin.* "In the place of a parent." Acting in place of a parent.

innuendo   *n. Latin.* "By nodding to" or "by hinting." **1** An indirect or suggestive remark, usually a disparagement of someone. **2** A section in a **libel** pleading explaining the plaintiff's construction of the defendant's allegedly libelous utterances.

in pais   *French.* "In the country." *Archaic.* Outside of court.

in pari delicto   *Latin.* "At equal fault."

in pari materia   *Latin.* "In the same matter." On the same topic or pertaining to the same subject matter.

in personam   *adj. Latin.* "Against the person." Pertaining to a person or personal rights or interests, as opposed to **in rem**.

in posse   *Latin.* "In possibility." Latent; not currently in existence.

in praesenti   *Latin.* "Currently; at present."

in re   *Latin.* "In regard to." Used in the title of cases involving an interest in property.

in rem   *adj. Latin.* "Against a thing." Pertaining to a thing or to property. Litigation in rem (as opposed to **in personam**) determines the respective rights to property that has been brought before the court.

> *quasi in rem.* A type of case initiated by the seizure of property that is within the court's jurisdiction, as a step toward obtaining monetary damages against an individual who is outside the jurisdiction of the court.

inter alia   *adv. Latin.* "Among others."

in terrorem   *adj./adv. Latin.* "In terror." A characteristic marked by threat or warning.

> *in terrorem clause.* A provision in a contract or will that warns a beneficiary or party not to engage in certain behavior, by providing a prospective penalty for such behavior.

inter se   *Latin.* "Among themselves."

inter vivos   *adj. Latin.* "Between the living." A conveyance of property between living parties and not by bequest.

in toto   *adv. Latin.* "In entirety."

ipse dixit   *Latin.* "He himself said it." Asserted but unproven.

ipso facto   *Latin.* "By the fact itself." As a matter of fact.

jurat   *n. Latin.* From *jurare,* "to swear." A certification at the bottom of an affidavit or deposition by a notary public that states the paper was signed, and thereby sworn to, in his or her presence by the individual who signed it.

jus tertii   *n. Latin.* "The right of a third party." The rights of third parties affected by a controversy or claim.

laches   *French.* "Lax; negligent." Equitable doctrine that precludes or limits relief to one who delays in acting or bringing a claim.

lex fori   *n. Latin.* "The law of the forum." Law of the jurisdiction where an action is pending.

lex loci contractus   *n. Latin.* The law of the place where a contract was signed or is to be performed.

lex loci delicti   *n. Latin.* The law of the place where a wrong was committed.

lis pendens   *n. Latin.* "A pending lawsuit." **1** A court's authority over property resulting from a pending lawsuit.   **2** A notice filed in a government office with the title documents pertaining to real property, giving notice to the public that the property is the subject of a litigation.

locus   *n. Latin.* "Place." The place or location of a thing or event.

locus delicti   *n. Latin.* "Place of the wrong." The place where a crime was committed.

locus in quo   *n. Latin.* "Place in which or where." The place where an event allegedly occurred.

malum in se   *n. Latin.* "Evil in itself." An act, such as murder, that is inherently evil or immoral.

malum prohibitum   *n. Latin.* "Prohibited evil." An act that is wrong solely because prohibited by law, as opposed to **malum in se.**

mandamus   *n. Latin.* "We command." A writ issued by a court to compel a public official (including the judge of a lesser court) to perform a task or duty.

mensa et thoro   *Latin.* "Bed and board."

mens rea   *Latin.* "Guilty mind." The defendant's guilty state of mind, as an element in proving the crime with which he or she is charged.

modus operandi   *n. Latin.* A method of operating.

nisi   *adj. Latin.* "Unless." Of an ex parte decision or ruling, that it is valid unless opposed by the adverse party.

nisi prius   *n. Latin.* "Unless before then." Refers to a court in which a jury is the ultimate finder of fact.

nolens volens   *adj./adv. Latin.* "Willing or unwilling." Willing or not.

nolo contendere   *Latin.* "I do not wish to contest."A plea available in certain jurisdictions in which a party declines to contest a charge without formally admitting guilt.

non compos mentis   *adj. Latin.* "Not of sound mind." Mentally incompetent.

non obstante veredicto   *n. Latin.* "Not withstanding the verdict." A judgment notwithstanding the verdict, in which a jury verdict is set aside by the judge as being factually or legally invalid.

> *judgment non obstante veridicto (j.n.o.v.).* Judgment notwithstanding the verdict. In rare cases, a judge may enter a judgment in favor of one party despite a jury's award against that party; generally in cases where the evidence was such that no reasonable jury could have come to the determination that it did.

non prosequitur   *Latin.* "He does not prosecute." A judgment against a plaintiff who has abandoned the case.

non sequitur   *n. Latin.* "It does not follow." A conclusion or a statement that does not logically follow from what preceded it.

noscitur a sociis   *Latin.* "It is known by its associates." A rule of interpretation that states that the meaning of unclear language in a contract or other legal document should be construed in light of the language surrounding it.

nudum pactum   *n. Latin.* "Bare agreement." A bare or scant agreement that is not enforceable because **consideration** is lacking.

nunc pro tunc   *adj. Latin.* "Now for then." Of an order or decision, that it has a retroactive effect.

obiter dicta   *Latin.* "By the way . . . ." A passing statement reached in a court opinion that is irrelevant to the outcome of the case. See also **dictum.**

oyez   *v. French.* Literally, "hear!" An exclamation used to bring a court to order, or to gain attention for an official proclamation to be publicly made. A customary greeting uttered by a court bailiff to signify that court is in session.

parens patriae   *n. Latin.* "Parent of his [or her] country." The state, in its role of provider of protection to people unable to care for themselves; a doctrine giving the government standing to sue on behalf of a citizen who is unable to pursue an action due to a legal disability.

pari delicto   *adj. Latin.* Equally at fault.

pari materia   *adj. Latin.* Of equal matter, on the same subject.

pendente lite   *adv. Latin.* "While the action is pending." While the lawsuit is pending; contingent on the outcome of the legal action or litigation. See also **lis pendens.**

per annum   *adv. Latin.* "By or through the year"; yearly or annually; calculated one year at a time; at annual intervals.

per autre vie   *Latin/French.* "For the life of another," term often used in bequeathing a right (but not title) in property.

per capita   *adj. Latin.* "By or through the head." According to the head count, or number of individuals; that is, divided equally among everyone involved.

per curiam   *adv. Latin.* "By the court." See **opinion.**

per diem   *n. Latin.* "By or through the day." Daily pay or daily expense allowance.

per quod   *adj./adv. Latin.* "Whereby." Having meaning only by reference to outside facts, such as on proof of injury or some sort of compensable damages. The opposite of **per se.**

> *slander per quod.* A form of slander that does not qualify as slander per se, thereby requiring the plaintiff to prove special damages.

per se   *adj./adv. Latin.* "By or through itself." Standing alone; on its own merits; without need for reference to outside facts. The opposite of **per quod.**

> *slander per se.* A form of slander that need not be proven to qualify for damage, because its meaning is apparent on the face of the statement and involves moral turpitude, a sexually transmitted disease, conduct adversely impacting one's profession or business, or lack of chastity (especially when applied to women).

per stirpes   *adj./adv. Latin.* "By or through roots and stocks." A proportional division of the estate among beneficiaries according to the share of descent from their deceased ancestor. Essentially, each beneficiary gets shares of stock in the estate based upon the closeness of relationship to the deceased. Distinct from **per capita.**

petit   *adj. French.* "Little, minor." Also spelled petty.

posse comitatus   *n. Latin.* "Power of the county."   **1** A sheriff may summon citizens to assist him in making an arrest; hence posse in the traditional Old West sense.   **2** A federal statute prohibiting the Army and Air Force from direct participation in civilian law-enforcement activities.

post *Latin.* "After." After in time, order, or position; behind. See also **ante.**

post mortem *Latin.* "After death." Generally used to refer to the examination of a corpse by the coroner to ascertain the cause of death.

praecipe *n. Latin.* "Command." **1** command, order. A written order or request to the clerk of the court **2** A written court order commanding a party to do something or to show cause why it has not been already done.

prima facie *adj. Latin.* "At first sight." Not in need of further support to establish credibility or existence; obvious, unless disproved.

> *prima facie case.* A case supported by at least the minimal amount of evidence needed to meet the requirement for trying it; adequate to be able to avoid a directed verdict or a motion to dismiss.

primogeniture *n. Latin.* "First born." An ancient rule of descent by which the firstborn son inherits all the property of his deceased father, usually to the exclusion of all his siblings. The purpose of primogeniture was to keep the estate (real property), the ownership of which implied power, from being subdivided into smaller and smaller parcels of land.

pro bono publico *Latin.* "For the public good." Used to refer to the taking of cases by attorneys without expectation of compensation. Also called **pro bono.**

profit à prendre *French.* "Profit to take." The right to take minerals, soil, trees, animals, or the like from the land of another.

pro forma *adj. Latin.* "For form." **1** Done as a formality, rather than because of conviction, in order to make possible further proceedings. **2** In accounting

procedures, done in advance to provide a what-if statement, predict results, or to convince. For example, a balance sheet showing combined figures of two companies in case of a merger.

pro hac vice *Latin.* For this one purpose or occasion. The allowing of something not usually allowed, usually referring to an attorney who normally could not practice in a certain jurisdiction, but is allowed to just for one case.

pro rata *adv. Latin.* "According to the rate"; in proportion. If a lawyer charges $100 per hour, and she works a quarter of an hour, her pro rata fee would be $100/4, or $25.

pro se *adj./adv. Latin.* "For himself"; on one's own behalf; on one's own. Characterization of one who represents himself/herself in an action without the assistance of an attorney at law and who acts as his/her own attorney of record.

pro tanto *adj./adv. Latin.* "To that extent." To such extreme; as far as it goes; for just so much. Often, a partial payment made for invoking **eminent domain.**

pro tempore *adj./adv. Latin.* "For the time being." A temporary position or appointment. Also called **pro tem.**

quaere *Latin.* "To query or inquire." Used in law textbooks to indicate that a point was dubious or questionable.

quantum *Latin.* "An amount"; the necessary or desired portion; the required or needed amount or share.

quantum meruit *Latin.* "As much as he deserved." Equitable formula for determining how much to award to one who has provided goods or services to another who has not paid, based on the reasonable value of the goods or services; the equitable principle that one who has received the benefit of a bargain should not be permitted to be unjustly enriched.

quantum valebant   *Latin.* "As much as they were worth." **1** The reasonable worth of goods or services, used to compute fair and reasonable damages; the market value.   **2** A common-law action of assumpsit for items sold and delivered, in order to recover proper and appropriate payment for same.

quare clausum fregit   *Latin.* "Why he broke the close." An early form of trespass onto someone else's land, whether or not that land actually had a physical fence around it. The plaintiff would argue that because the defendant had broken the boundary "with force and arms," the former was due damages.

quasi   *Latin.* "As if." Alike in some sense, but not in actuality; resembling something but not really being it; nearly; almost like.

quia timet   *Latin.* "Because he fears." A legal remedy sought in an equity court to enjoin someone from doing an anticipated damage. Such a remedy may be granted if the petitioner can show imminent and irreparable harm would be done.

quid pro quo   *Latin.* "What for what." Something exchanged for another thing of approximately equal value, not necessarily in a monetary sense.

qui tam   *Latin.* "Who as well . . . ." An action that, if prevailed in, grants the plaintiff a portion of the recovered penalty and gives the rest of it to the state. The plaintiff is said to be suing for the state as well as his or herself.

quo warranto   *Latin.* "By what authority." **1** A common law writ inquiring into the authority by which a public official claims his/her office.   **2** A state action with the intent of revoking the charter of a corporation that has abused or for a long period failed to exercise its franchise.

ratio decidende   *n. Latin.* "The reason for deciding." The rule of law or principle on which the court's decision is based. See also **obiter dicta.**

reductio ad absurdum   *Latin.* "Reduction to the absurd." In logic, disproving an argument by demonstrating that it leads to a ridiculous conclusion.

remittitur   *Latin.* "It is sent back." A court's order that reduces what it deems to be excessive damages awarded by a jury; the process by which the court proposes to reduce or actually reduces damages without the jury's consent. See also **additur.**

res   *n. Latin.* "The thing." The subject of the matter—that is, an action concerning an object or property, rather than a person,; the status of individuals.

res gestae   *n. Latin.* "Things done." Either the events at issue or other things, such as utterances, that are contemporaneous with the res gestae; spontaneous statements or exclamations made by the participants, perpetrators, victims, or onlookers at or immediately following the event, be it criminal or the subject of litigation. As present-sense impressions, they are excluded from the **hearsay** rule.

res ipsa loquitur   *Latin.* "The thing speaks for itself." An evidentiary rule in torts that the very fact that an accident occurred is enough to provide a prima facie case of negligent behavior. Rear-ending another automobile is an example, showing failure to maintain a safe distance on the part of the rear-ender.

res judicata *Latin.* "A thing decided." A doctrine whereby the court's decision is binding upon the parties in any and all subsequent litigation concerning the same case. In effect, it bars the litigants from seeking to take the same case to another court in hopes of a different outcome, or of raising new issues that were not raised at the first trial.

respondeat superior *Latin.* "Let the superior respond." The doctrine that an employer is held liable for all wrongful acts or any harm caused by an employee or agent acting within the scope of his employment or duties. See also **scope of employment.**

scienter *n. Latin.* "Knowingly." **1** A knowledge beforehand of the consequences of an action or failure to act that makes a person legally responsible for those consequences. Such advance knowledge may make the person subject to civil or criminal punishment. **2** An intention to deceive or defraud (usually applied to stock fraud). See also **knowing** and **mens rea.**

seriatim *Latin.* "In sequence." Successively; in successive order, one by one; in due order; sequentially, one at a time.

sine die *Latin.* "Without day." With no day being assigned for the next meeting or for resumption of meeting.

sine qua non *n. Latin.* "Without which not." Something that is indispensable and upon which something else relies.

stare decisis *n. Latin.* "To stand by what was decided." The doctrine of common law under which courts follow the earlier judicial decisions made on the same points of litigation; following precedent. Stare decisis is not inviolable, but precedent will be overturned only for good cause. The doctrine, however, is essentially useless in constitu-

tional law. See also **precedent** and **res judicata.**

status quo *n. Latin.* "The situation as it currently exists."

status quo ante *n. Latin.* "The situation as it existed before." As things were before whatever happened or is being discussed took place. For example, status quo ante bellum is the situation as it existed before the war.

stirps *n. Latin.* "Stalk; root." A branch of a family or of the family tree. See also **per stirpes.**

sua sponte *Latin.* "Of itself." regarding a judge or court, to raise an issue or take an action independently of any request or suggestion made by the parties or lawyers; *adj.* description of action taken by court in absence of any party urging such action to be taken.

sub judice *adv. Latin.* "Under a judge." A case that is before the bar for determination, rather than one being settled out of court.

subpoena **1** *n. Latin.* "Under penalty." A writ issued by a court commanding a person to appear , with penalties that attach for failure to comply. **2** *v.* the act of sending a subpoena to a witness or other person to secure his attendance and testimony at trial or other proceeding (such as deposition); generally, subpoenas are obtained and sent out by the lawyers, rather than directly by the court.

subpoena ad testificandum. The most common type of subpoena, ordering a witness to testify.

subpoena duces tecum. Issued at the request of one of the parties to a lawsuit, ordering a witness to appear and bring relevant documents to the hearing.

sub silentio *Latin.* "Under silence." Without notice being taken. If a case is decided against precedent, the newer case is said to have over-ruled the previous decision sub silentio.

sui generis *Latin.* "Of its own kind." Unique; of its own particular type; in a class of its own.

sui juris *Latin.* "Of one's own right." Used to describe one who is no longer a dependent; having reached majority and having full civil and social rights. See also **emancipation** and **incompetency.**

supersedeas *n. Latin.* "You shall forbear or desist." A writ suspending or staying a proceeding in order to maintain the status quo, pending appeal. It usually stays a creditor's taking possession of property pursuant to a lower court's ruling.

supra *Latin.* "Above"; superior to.

trespass vi et armis *Latin.* "With force and arms." An immediate injury, such as an assault to another's person or property, accompanied by force or violence.

ultra vires *Latin.* "In excess of," or outside of powers; that which is beyond a corporation's or an agency's authorized power. A corporation's ultra vires activity may lead to its forfeiting its charter of incorporation.

uxor *n. Latin.* Wife.

venire *Latin.* "To come" *n.* A panel of jury duty selectees, from among whom the actual jury will be chosen.

> *venire de novo.* A calling of a new jury panel for the purpose of holding a second trial, in cases where a first trial has failed to render a verdict.

vir *n. Latin.* Man.

vis major *n. Latin.* "A superior force"; the term is used in civil cases to denote an act of God. A loss vis major results from natural causes, such as a hurricane, tornado, or earthquake, and without the intervention of human beings. It is a loss that could not have been prevented by diligence or by having taken precautions. See also **force majeure.**

viz. *abbr.* for videlicit. *Latin.* "Namely; to wit; that is to say." Used to elaborate on what has already been said in more particular or precise language.

voir dire *n. French.* Literally "to see, to speak"; hence, idiomatically, to speak the truth. The usual reference is to an examination by the attorneys and/or the court of prospective jurors to determine whether reasons exist that might disqualify them or cause their selection to be challenged, other than peremptorily. During a trial, a *voir dire* examination refers to one outside the hearing of the jury concerning some issue of fact or law that requires the court to rule.

volenti non fit injuria *n. Latin.* "The volunteer suffers no wrong"; a person cannot usually sue for damages when he consented in the first place to whatever it was that caused the damages.

The Constitution of the United States of America, 1787

WE the people of the United States, in Order to form a more perfect Union, establish Justice, insure domestic Tranquility, provide for the common defense, promote the general Welfare, and secure the Blessings of Liberty to ourselves and our Posterity, do ordain and establish this Constitution for the United States of America.

Article I

Section 1. All legislative Powers herein granted shall be vested in a Congress of the United States, which shall consist of a Senate and House of Representatives.

Section 2. The House of Representatives shall be composed of Members chosen every second Year by the People of the several States, and the electors in each State shall have the qualifications requisite for electors of the most numerous branch of the State legislature.

No Person shall be a Representative who shall not have attained to the Age of twenty five Years, and been seven Years a citizen of the United States, and who shall not, when elected, be an Inhabitant of that State in which he shall be chosen.

Representatives and direct Taxes shall be apportioned among the several States which may be included within this Union, according to their respective Numbers, which shall be determined by adding to the whole number of free Persons, including those bound to Service for a Term of Years, and excluding Indians not taxed, three fifths of all other Persons. The actual Enumeration shall be made within three Years after the first Meeting of the Congress of the United States, and within every subsequent Term of ten Years, in such Manner as they shall by law Direct. The number of Representatives shall not exceed one for every thirty Thousand, but each State shall have at least one Representative; and until such enumeration shall be made, the State of New Hampshire shall be entitled to choose three, Massachusetts eight, Rhode Island and Providence Plantations one, Connecticut five, New York six, New Jersey four, Pennsylvania eight, Delaware one, Maryland six, Virginia ten, North Carolina five, South Carolina five, and Georgia three.

When vacancies happen in the Representation from any State, the Executive Authority thereof shall issue Writs of Election to fill such Vacancies.

The House of Representatives shall choose their Speaker and other Officers; and shall have the sole Power of Impeachment.

Section 3. The Senate of the United States shall be composed of two Senators from each State, chosen by the legislature thereof, for six Years; and each Senator shall have one Vote.

Immediately after they shall be assembled in Consequence of the first Election, they shall be divided as equally as may be into three Classes. The Seats of the Senators of the first Class shall be vacated at the expiration of the second Year, of the second Class at the expiration of the fourth Year, and of the third Class at the expiration of the sixth Year, so that one third may be chosen every second Year; and if vacancies happen by Resignation, or otherwise, during the recess of the Legislature of any State, the Executive thereof may make temporary Appointments until the next meeting of the Legislature, which shall then fill such Vacancies.

No person shall be a Senator who shall not have attained to the Age of thirty Years, and been nine Years a Citizen of the United States, and who shall not, when elected, be an Inhabitant of that State for which he shall be chosen.

The Vice-President of the United States shall be President of the Senate, but shall have no Vote, unless they be equally divided.

The Senate shall choose their other Officers, and also a President pro tempore, in the Absence of the Vice-President, or when he shall exercise the Office of President of the United States.

The Senate shall have the sole Power to try all Impeachments. When sitting for that Purpose, they shall be on Oath or Affirmation. When the President of the United States is tried, the Chief Justice shall preside: And no Person shall be convicted without the Concurrence of two thirds of the Members present.

Judgment in cases of Impeachment shall not extend further than to removal from Office, and disqualification to hold and enjoy any Office of honor, Trust or Profit under the United States: but the Party convicted shall nevertheless be liable and subject to Indictment, Trial, Judgment and Punishment, according to Law.

Section 4. The Times, Places and Manner of holding Elections for Senators and Representatives, shall be prescribed in each State by the Legislature thereof; but the Congress may at any time by Law make or alter such Regulations, except as to the Places of choosing Senators.

The Congress shall assemble at least once in every Year, and such Meeting shall be on the first Monday in December, unless they shall by law appoint a different Day.

Section 5. Each House shall be the Judge of the Elections, Returns and Qualifications of its own Members, and a Majority of each shall constitute a Quorum to do Business; but a smaller Number may adjourn from day to day, and may be authorized to compel the Attendance of absent Members, in such Manner, and under such Penalties as each House may provide.

Each house may determine the Rules of its Proceedings, punish its Members for disorderly Behavior, and, with the Concurrence of two-thirds, expel a Member.

Each house shall keep a Journal of its Proceedings, and from time to time publish the same, excepting such Parts as may in their Judgment require Secrecy; and the Yeas and Nays of the Members of either House on any question shall, at the Desire of one fifth of those Present, be entered on the Journal.

Neither House, during the Session of Congress, shall, without the Consent of the other, adjourn for more than three days, nor to any other Place than that in which the two Houses shall be sitting.

Section 6. The Senators and Representatives shall receive a Compensation for their Services, to be ascertained by Law, and paid out of the Treasury of the United States. They shall in all Cases, except Treason, Felony and Breach of the Peace, be privileged from Arrest during their Attendance at the Session of their respective Houses, and in going to and returning from the same; and for any Speech or Debate in either House, they shall not be questioned in any other Place.

No Senator or Representative shall, during the Time for which he was elected, be appointed to any civil Office under the authority of the United States, which shall have been created, or the Emoluments whereof shall have been increased during such time; and no Person holding any Office under the United States, shall be a Member of either House during his Continuance in Office.

Section 7. All Bills for raising Revenue shall originate in the House of Representatives; but the Senate may propose or concur with Amendments as on other Bills.

Every Bill which shall have passed the House of Representatives and the Senate, shall, before it become a Law, be presented to the President of the United States; If he approve he shall sign it, but if not he shall return it, with his Objections to that House in which it shall have originated, who shall enter the Objections at large on their Journal, and proceed to reconsider it. If after such Reconsideration two thirds of that house shall agree to pass the Bill, it shall be sent, together with the Objections, to the other House, by which it shall likewise be reconsidered, and if approved by two thirds of that House, it shall become a law. But in all such Cases the Votes of both Houses shall be determined by Yeas and Nays, and the Names of the Persons voting for and against the Bill shall be entered on the Journal of each House respectively. If any Bill shall not be returned by the President within ten Days (Sundays excepted) after it shall have been presented to him, the Same shall be a Law, in like Manner as if he had signed it, unless the Congress by their Adjournment prevent its Return, in which case it shall not be a Law.

Every Order, Resolution, or Vote to which the Concurrence of the Senate and House of Representatives may be necessary (except on a question of Adjournment) shall be presented to the President of the United States; and before the Same shall take Effect, shall be approved by him, or being disapproved by him, shall be repassed by two thirds of the Senate and House of Representatives, according to the Rules and Limitations prescribed in the Case of a Bill.

Section 8. The Congress shall have Power to lay and collect Taxes, Duties, Imposts and Excises, to pay the Debts and provide for the common Defense and general Welfare of the United States; but all Duties, Imposts and Excises shall be uniform throughout the United States;

To borrow Money on the credit of the United States;

To regulate Commerce with foreign Nations, and among the several States, and with the Indian Tribes;

To establish an uniform Rule of Naturalization, and uniform Laws on the subject of Bankruptcies throughout the United States;

To coin Money, regulate the Value thereof, and of foreign Coin, and fix the Standard of Weights and Measures;

To provide for the Punishment of counterfeiting the Securities and current Coin of the United States;

To establish Post Offices and Post Roads;

To promote the Progress of Science and useful Arts, by securing for limited Times to Authors and Inventors the exclusive Right to their respective Writings and Discoveries;

To constitute Tribunals inferior to the supreme Court;

To define and punish Piracies and Felonies committed on the high Seas, and Offenses against the Law of Nations;

To declare War, grant Letters of Marque and Reprisal, and make Rules concerning Captures on Land and Water;

To raise and support Armies, but no Appropriation of Money to that Use shall be for a longer term than two Years;

To provide and maintain a Navy;

To make Rules for the Government and Regulation of the land and naval Forces;

To provide for calling forth the Militia to execute the Laws of the Union, suppress Insurrections and repel Invasions;

To provide for organizing, arming, and disciplining, the Militia, and for governing such Part of them as may be employed in the Service of the United States, reserving to the States respectively, the Appointment of the Officers, and the Authority of training the militia according to the discipline prescribed by Congress;

To exercise exclusive Legislation in all Cases whatsoever, over such District (not exceeding ten Miles square) as may, by Cession of particular States, and the Acceptance of Congress, become the Seat of the Government of the United States, and to exercise like Authority over all Places purchased by the Consent of the Legislature of the State in which the Same shall be, for the Erection of Forts, Magazines, Arsenals, Dockyards, and other needful Buildings;—And

To make all Laws which shall be necessary and proper for carrying into Execution the foregoing Powers, and all other Powers vested by this Constitution in the Government of the United States, or in any Department or Officer thereof.

Section 9. The Migration or Importation of such Persons as any of the States now existing shall think proper to admit, shall not be prohibited by the Congress prior to the Year one thousand eight hundred and eight, but a Tax or Duty may be imposed on such Importation, not exceeding ten dollars for each Person.

The Privilege of the Writ of Habeas Corpus shall not be suspended, unless when in Cases of Rebellion or Invasion the public Safety may require it.

No Bill of Attainder or ex post facto Law shall be passed.

No Capitation, or other direct, Tax shall be laid, unless in Proportion to the Census or Enumeration herein before directed to be taken.

No Tax or Duty shall be laid on Articles exported from any State.

No Preference shall be given by any Regulation of Commerce or Revenue to the Ports of one State over those of another: nor shall Vessels bound to, or from, one State, be obliged to enter, clear, or pay Duties in another.

No Money shall be drawn from the Treasury, but in Consequence of Appropriations made by Law; and a regular Statement and Account of the Receipts and Expenditures of all public Money shall be published from time to time.

No Title of Nobility shall be granted by the United States; and no Person holding any Office of Profit or Trust under them, shall, without the Consent of the Congress, accept of any present, Emolument, Office, or Title, of any kind whatever, from any King, Prince, or foreign State.

Section 10. No State shall enter into any Treaty, Alliance, or Confederation; grant Letters of Marque and Reprisal; coin Money; emit Bills of Credit; make any Thing but gold and silver Coin a Tender in Payment of Debts; pass any Bill of Attainder, ex post facto Law, or Law impairing the Obligation of Contracts, or grant any Title of Nobility.

No State shall, without the Consent of the Congress, lay any Imposts or Duties on Imports or Exports, except what may be absolutely necessary for executing it's inspection Laws: and the net Produce of all Duties and Imposts, laid by any State on Imports or Exports, shall be for the Use of the Treasury of the United States; and all such Laws shall be subject to the Revision and Control of the Congress.

No State shall, without the Consent of Congress, lay any Duty of Tonnage, keep Troops, or Ships of War in time of Peace, enter into any Agreement or Compact with another State, or with a foreign Power, or engage in War, unless actually invaded, or in such imminent Danger as will not admit of delay.

Article II

Section 1. The executive Power shall be vested in a President of the United States of America. He shall hold his Office during the Term of four Years, and, together with the Vice President chosen for the same Term, be elected, as follows:

Each State shall appoint, in such Manner as the Legislature thereof may direct, a Number of Electors, equal to the whole Number of Senators and Representatives to which the State may be entitled in the Congress: but no Senator or Representative, or Person holding an Office of Trust or Profit under the United States, shall be appointed an Elector.

The Electors shall meet in their respective States, and vote by Ballot for two Persons, of whom one at least shall not lie an Inhabitant of the same State with themselves. And they shall make a List of all the Persons voted for, and of the Number of Votes for each; which List they shall sign and certify, and transmit sealed to the Seat of the Government of the United States, directed to the President of the Senate. The President of the Senate shall, in the Presence of the Senate and House of Representatives, open all the Certificates, and the Votes shall then be counted. The Person having the greatest Number of Votes shall be the President, if such Number be a Majority of the whole Number of Electors appointed; and if there be more than one who have such Majority, and have an equal Number of votes, then the House of Representatives shall immediately choose by Ballot one of them for President; and if no Person have a Majority, then from the five highest on the List the said House shall in like Manner choose the President. But in choosing the President, the Votes shall be taken by States, the Representation from each State having one Vote; a Quorum for this Purpose shall consist of a Member or Members from two thirds of the States, and a Majority of all the States shall be necessary to a Choice. In every Case, after the Choice of the President, the Person having the greatest Number of Votes of the Electors shall be the Vice President. But if there should remain two or more who have equal Votes, the Senate shall choose from them by Ballot the Vice President.

The Congress may determine the Time of choosing the Electors, and the Day on which they shall give their Votes; which Day shall be the same throughout the United States.

No Person except a natural born Citizen, or a Citizen of the United States, at the time of the Adoption of this Constitution, shall be eligible to the Office of President; neither shall any Person be eligible to that Office who shall not have attained to the Age of thirty five Years, and been fourteen Years a Resident within the United States.

In Case of the Removal of the President from Office, or of his Death, Resignation, or Inability to discharge the Powers and Duties of the said Office, the Same shall devolve on the Vice President, and the Congress may by Law provide for the Case of Removal, Death, Resignation or Inability, both of the President and Vice President, declaring what Officer shall then act as President, and such Officer shall act accordingly, until the Disability be removed, or a President shall be elected.

The President shall, at stated Times, receive for his Services, a Compensation, which shall neither be increased nor diminished during the Period for which he shall have been elected, and he shall not receive within that Period any other Emolument from the United States, or any of them.

Before he enter on the Execution of his Office, he shall take the following Oath or Affirmation:—"I do solemnly swear (or affirm) that I will faithfully execute the Office of President of the United States, and will to the best of my Ability, preserve, protect and defend the Constitution of the United States."

Section 2. The President shall be Commander in Chief of the Army and Navy of the United States, and of the Militia of the several States, when called into the actual Service of the United States; he may require the Opinion, in writing, of the principal Officer in each of the executive Departments, upon any Subject relating to the Duties of their respective Offices, and he shall have Power to grant Reprieves and Pardons for Offenses against the United States, except in Cases of impeachment.

He shall have Power, by and with the Advice and Consent of the Senate, to make Treaties, provided two thirds of the Senators present concur; and he shall nominate, and by and with the Advice and Consent of the Senate, shall appoint Ambassadors, other public Ministers and Consuls, Judges of the supreme Court, and all other Officers of the United States, whose Appointments are not herein otherwise provided for, and which shall be established by Law: but the Congress may by Law vest the Appointment of such inferior Officers, as they think proper, in the President alone, in the Courts of Law, or in the Heads of Departments.

The President shall have Power to fill up all Vacancies that may happen during the Recess of the Senate, by granting Commissions which shall expire at the End of their next session.

Section 3. He shall from time to time give to the Congress Information of the State of the Union, and recommend to their Consideration such Measures as he shall judge necessary and expedient; he may, on extraordinary Occasions, convene both Houses, or either of them, and in Case of Disagreement between them, with Respect to the Time of Adjournment, he may adjourn them to such Time as he shall think proper; he shall receive Ambassadors and other public Ministers; he shall take Care that the Laws be faithfully executed, and shall Commission all the Officers of the United States.

Section 4. The President, Vice President and all civil Officers of the United States, shall be removed from Office on Impeachment for, and Conviction of, Treason, Bribery, or other high Crimes and Misdemeanors.

Article III

Section 1. The judicial Power of the United States, shall be vested in one supreme Court, and in such inferior Courts as the Congress may from time to time ordain and establish. The Judges, both of the supreme and inferior Courts, shall hold their Offices during good behavior, and shall, at stated Times, receive for their Services, a Compensation, which shall not be diminished during their Continuance in Office.

Section 2. The judicial Power shall extend to all Cases, in Law and Equity, arising under this Constitution, the Laws of the United States, and Treaties made, or which shall be made, under their Authority;—to all Cases affecting Ambassadors, other public Ministers and Consuls;—to all Cases of admiralty and maritime Jurisdiction;—to Controversies to which the United States shall be a Party;—to Controversies between two or more States;—between a State and Citizens of another State;—between Citizens of different States; —between Citizens of the same State claiming Lands under Grants of different States, and between a State, or the Citizens thereof, and foreign States, Citizens or Subjects.

In all cases affecting Ambassadors, other public Ministers and Consuls, and those in which a State shall be Party, the supreme Court shall have original Jurisdiction. In all the other Cases before mentioned, the supreme Court shall have appellate Jurisdiction, both as to Law and Fact, with such Exceptions, and under such Regulations as the Congress shall make.

The Trial of all Crimes, except in Cases of Impeachment, shall be by Jury; and such Trial shall be held in the State where the said Crimes shall have been committed; but when not committed within any State, the Trial shall be at such Place or Places as the Congress may by Law have directed.

Section 3. Treason against the United States, shall consist only in levying War against them, or in adhering to their Enemies, giving them Aid and Comfort. No Person shall be convicted of Treason unless on the Testimony of two Witnesses to the same overt Act, or on Confession in open Court.

The Congress shall have power to declare the punishment of Treason, but no Attainder of Treason shall work Corruption of Blood, or Forfeiture except during the Life of the Person attainted.

Article IV

Section 1. Full Faith and Credit shall be given in each State to the public Acts, Records, and judicial Proceedings of every other State. And the Congress may by general Laws prescribe the Manner in which such Acts, Records, and Proceedings shall be proved, and the Effect thereof.

Section 2. The Citizens of each State shall be entitled to all Privileges and Immunities of Citizens in the several States.

A Person charged in any State with Treason, Felony, or other Crime, who shall flee from Justice, and be found in another State, shall on Demand of the executive Authority of the State from which he fled, be delivered up, to be removed to the State having Jurisdiction of the Crime.

No person held to Service or Labor in one State, under the Laws thereof, escaping into another, shall, in Consequence of any Law or Regulation therein, be discharged from such Service or Labor, But shall be delivered up on Claim of the Party to whom such Service or Labor may be due.

Section 3. New States may be admitted by the Congress into this Union; but no new States shall be formed or erected within the Jurisdiction of any other State; nor any State be formed by the Junction of two or more States, or Parts of States, without the Consent of the Legislatures of the States concerned as well as of the Congress.

The Congress shall have Power to dispose of and make all needful Rules and Regulations respecting the Territory or other Property belonging to the United States; and nothing in this Constitution shall be so construed as to Prejudice any Claims of the United States, or of any particular State.

Section 4. The United States shall guarantee to every State in this Union a Republican Form of Government, and shall protect each of them against Invasion; and on Application of the Legislature, or of the Executive (when the Legislature cannot be convened) against domestic Violence.

Article V

The Congress, whenever two thirds of both Houses shall deem it necessary, shall propose Amendments to this Constitution, or, on the Application of the Legislatures of two thirds of the several States, shall call a Convention for proposing Amendments, which, in either Case, shall be valid to all Intents and Purposes, as Part of this Constitution, when ratified by the Legislatures of three fourths of the several States, or by Conventions in three fourths thereof, as the one or the other Mode of Ratification may be proposed by the Congress; Provided that no Amendment which may be made prior to the Year one thousand eight hundred and eight shall in any Manner affect the first and fourth Clauses in the ninth Section of the first Article; and that no State, without its Consent, shall be deprived of its equal Suffrage in the Senate.

Article VI

All Debts contracted and Engagements entered into, before the Adoption of this Constitution, shall be as valid against the United States under this Constitution, as under the Confederation.

This Constitution, and the Laws of the United States which shall be made in Pursuance thereof; and all Treaties made, or which shall be made, under the Authority of the United States, shall be the supreme Law of the Land; and the Judges in every State shall be bound thereby, any Thing in the Constitution or Laws of any State to the Contrary notwithstanding.

The Senators and Representatives before mentioned, and the Members of the several State Legislatures, and all executive and judicial Officers, both of the United States and of the several States, shall be bound by Oath or Affirmation, to support this Constitution; but no religious Test shall ever be required as a Qualification to any Office or public Trust under the United States.

Article VII

The Ratification of the Conventions of nine States, shall be sufficient for the Establishment of this Constitution between the States so ratifying the Same.

Done in Convention by the Unanimous Consent of the States present the Seventeenth Day of September in the Year of our Lord one thousand seven hundred and eighty seven and of the Independence of the United States of America the Twelfth. In Witness whereof We have hereunto subscribed our Names,

Go. Washington—
Presid. and deputy from Virginia

New Hampshire
John Langdon
Nicholas Gilman

Massachusetts
Nathaniel Gorham
Rufus King

Connecticut
Wm. Saml. Johnson
Roger Herman

New York
Alexander Hamilton

New Jersey
Wil: Livingston
David Brearley
Wm. Paterson
Jona: Dayton

Pennsylvania
B Franklin
Thomas Mifflin
Robt Morris
Geo. Clymer
Thos FitzSimons
Jared Ingersoll
James Wilson
Gouv Morris

Delaware
Geo: Read
Gunning Bedford jun
John Dickinson
Richard Bassett
Jaco: Broom

Maryland
James Mchenry
Dan of St Thos. Jenifer
Danl Carroll

Virginia
John Blair
James Madison Jr

North Carolina
Wm. Blount
Rich'd Dobbs Spaight
Hu Williamson

South Carolina
J. Rutledge
Charles Cotesworth Pinckney
Charles Pinckney
Pierce Butler

Georgia
William Few
Abr Baldwin
Attest:
William Jackson, Secretary

Amendment I (1791)

Congress shall make no law respecting an establishment of religion, or prohibiting the free exercise thereof; or abridging the freedom of speech, or of the press; or the right of the people peaceably to assemble, and to petition the Government for a redress of grievances.

Amendment II (1791)

A well regulated Militia, being necessary to the security of a free State, the right of the people to keep and bear Arms, shall not be infringed.

Amendment III (1791)

No Soldier shall, in time of peace be quartered in any house, without the consent of the Owner, nor in time of war, but in a manner to be prescribed by law.

Amendment IV (1791)

The right of the people to be secure in their persons, houses, papers, and effects, against unreasonable searches and seizures, shall not be violated, and no Warrants shall issue, but upon probable cause, supported by Oath or affirmation, and particularly describing the place to be searched, and the persons or things to be seized.

Amendment V (1791)

No person shall be held to answer for a capital, or otherwise infamous crime, unless on a presentment or indictment of a Grand Jury, except in cases arising in the land or naval forces, or in the Militia, when in actual service in time of War or public danger; nor shall any person be subject for the same offense to be twice put in jeopardy of life or limb; nor shall be compelled in any criminal case to be a witness against himself, nor be deprived of life, liberty, or property, without due process of law; nor shall private property be taken for public use, without just compensation.

Amendment VI (1791)

In all criminal prosecutions, the accused shall enjoy the right to a speedy and public trial, by an impartial jury of the State and district wherein the crime shall have been committed, which district shall have been previously ascertained by law, and to be informed of the nature and cause of the accusation; to be confronted with the witnesses against him; to have compulsory process for obtaining witnesses in his favor, and to have the Assistance of Counsel for his defence.

Amendment VII (1791)

In Suits at common law, where the value in controversy shall exceed twenty dollars, the right of trial by jury shall be preserved, and no fact tried by a jury, shall be otherwise reexamined in any Court of the United States, than according to the rules of the common law.

Amendment VIII (1791)

Excessive bail shall not be required, nor excessive fines imposed, nor cruel and unusual punishments inflicted.

Amendment IX (1791)

The enumeration in the Constitution, of certain rights, shall not be construed to deny or disparage others retained by the people.

Amendment X (1791)

The powers not delegated to the United States by the Constitution, nor prohibited by it to the States, are reserved to the States respectively, or to the people.

Amendment XI (1795)

The Judicial power of the United States shall not be construed to extend to any suit in law or equity, commenced or prosecuted against one of the United States by Citizens of another State, or by Citizens or Subjects of any Foreign State.

Amendment XII (1804)

The Electors shall meet in their respective states, and vote by ballot for President and Vice-President, one of whom, at least, shall not be an inhabitant of the same state with themselves; they shall name in their ballots the person voted for as President, and in distinct ballots the person voted for as Vice-President, and they shall make distinct lists of all persons voted for as President, and of all persons voted for as Vice-President and of the number of votes for each, which lists they shall sign and certify, and transmit sealed to the seat of the government of the United States, directed to the President of the Senate;

The President of the Senate shall, in the presence of the Senate and House of Representatives, open all the certificates and the votes shall then be counted;

The person having the greatest Number of votes for President, shall be the President, if such number be a majority of the whole number of Electors appointed; and if no person have such majority, then from the persons having the highest numbers not exceeding three on the list of those voted for as President, the House of Representatives shall choose immediately, by ballot, the President. But in choosing the President, the votes shall be taken by states, the representation from each state having one vote; a quorum for this purpose shall consist of a member or members from two-thirds of the states, and a majority of all the states shall be necessary to a choice. And if the House of Representatives shall not choose a President whenever the right of choice shall devolve upon them, before the fourth day of March next following, then the Vice-President shall act as President, as in the case of the death or other constitutional disability of the President.

The person having the greatest number of votes as Vice-President, shall be the Vice-President, if such number be a majority of the whole number of Electors appointed, and if no person have a majority, then from the two highest numbers on the list, the Senate shall choose the Vice-President; a quorum for the purpose shall consist of two-thirds of the whole number of Senators, and a majority of the whole number shall be necessary to a choice. But no person constitutionally ineligible to the office of President shall be eligible to that of Vice-President of the United States.

Amendment XIII (1865)

Section 1. Neither slavery nor involuntary servitude, except as a punishment for crime whereof the party shall have been duly convicted, shall exist within the United States, or any place subject to their jurisdiction.

Section 2. Congress shall have power to enforce this article by appropriate legislation.

Amendment XIV (1868)

Section 1. All persons born or naturalized in the United States, and subject to the jurisdiction thereof, are citizens of the United States and of the State wherein they reside. No State shall make or enforce any law which shall abridge the privileges or immunities of citizens of the United States; nor shall any State deprive any person of life, liberty, or property, without due process of law; nor deny to any person within its jurisdiction the equal protection of the laws.

Section 2. Representatives shall be apportioned among the several States according to their respective numbers, counting the whole number of persons in each State, excluding Indians not taxed. But when the right to vote at any election for the choice of electors for President and Vice-President of the United States, Representatives in Congress, the Executive and Judicial officers of a State, or the members of the Legislature thereof, is denied to any of the male inhabitants of such State, being twenty-one years of age, and citizens of the United States, or in any way abridged, except for participation in rebellion, or other crime, the basis of representation therein shall be reduced in the proportion which the number of such male citizens shall bear to the whole number of male citizens twenty-one years of age in such State.

Section 3. No person shall be a Senator or Representative in Congress, or elector of President and Vice-President, or hold any office, civil or military, under the United States, or under any State, who, having previously taken an oath, as a member of Congress, or as an officer of the United States, or as a member of any State legislature, or as an executive or judicial officer of any State, to support the Constitution of the United States, shall have engaged in insurrection or rebellion against the same, or given aid or comfort to the enemies thereof. But Congress may by a vote of two-thirds of each House, remove such disability.

Section 4. The validity of the public debt of the United States, authorized by law, including debts incurred for payment of pensions and bounties for services in suppressing insurrection or rebellion, shall not be questioned. But neither the United States nor any State shall assume or pay any debt or obligation incurred in aid of insurrection or rebellion against the United States, or any claim for the loss or emancipation of any slave; but all such debts, obligations and claims shall be held illegal and void.

Section 5. The Congress shall have power to enforce, by appropriate legislation, the provisions of this article.

Amendment XV (1870)

Section 1. The right of citizens of the United States to vote shall not be denied or abridged by the United States or by any State on account of race, color, or previous condition of servitude.

Section 2. The Congress shall have power to enforce this article by appropriate legislation.

Amendment XVI (1913)

The Congress shall have power to lay and collect taxes on incomes, from whatever source derived, without apportionment among the several States, and without regard to any census or enumeration.

Amendment XVII (1913)

The Senate of the United States shall be composed of two Senators from each State, elected by the people thereof, for six years; and each Senator shall have one vote. The electors in each State shall have the qualifications requisite for electors of the most numerous branch of the State legislatures.

When vacancies happen in the representation of any State in the Senate, the executive authority of such State shall issue writs of election to fill such vacancies: Provided, That the legislature of any State may empower the executive thereof to make temporary appointments until the people fill the vacancies by election as the legislature may direct.

This amendment shall not be so construed as to affect the election or term of any Senator chosen before it becomes valid as part of the Constitution.

Amendment XVIII (1919)

Section 1. After one year from the ratification of this article the manufacture, sale, or transportation of intoxicating liquors within, the importation thereof into, or the exportation thereof from the United States and all territory subject to the jurisdiction thereof for beverage purposes is hereby prohibited.

Section 2. The Congress and the several States shall have concurrent power to enforce this article by appropriate legislation.

Section 3. This article shall be inoperative unless it shall have been ratified as an amendment to the Constitution by the legislatures of the several States, as provided in the Constitution, within seven years from the date of the submission hereof to the States by the Congress.

Amendment XIX (1920)

The right of citizens of the United States to vote shall not be denied or abridged by the United States or by any State on account of sex.

Congress shall have power to enforce this article by appropriate legislation.

Amendment XX (1933)

Section 1. The terms of the President and Vice President shall end at noon on the 20th day of January, and the terms of Senators and Representatives at noon on the 3d day of January, of the years in which such terms would have ended if this article had not been ratified; and the terms of their successors shall then begin.

Section 2. The Congress shall assemble at least once in every year, and such meeting shall begin at noon on the 3d day of January, unless they shall by law appoint a different day.

Section 3. If, at the time fixed for the beginning of the term of the President, the President elect shall have died, the Vice President elect shall become President. If a President shall not have been chosen before the time fixed for the beginning of his term, or if the President elect shall have failed to qualify, then the Vice President elect shall act as President until a President shall have qualified; and the Congress may by law provide for the case wherein neither a President elect nor a Vice President elect shall have qualified, declaring who shall then act as President, or the manner in which one who is to act shall be selected, and such person shall act accordingly until a President or Vice President shall have qualified.

Section 4. The Congress may by law provide for the case of the death of any of the persons from whom the House of Representatives may choose a President whenever the right of choice shall have devolved upon them, and for the case of the death of any of the persons from whom the Senate may choose a Vice President whenever the right of choice shall have devolved upon them.

Section 5. Sections 1 and 2 shall take effect on the 15th day of October following the ratification of this article.

Section 6. This article shall be inoperative unless it shall have been ratified as an amendment to the Constitution by the legislatures of three-fourths of the several States within seven years from the date of its submission.

Amendment XXI (1933)

Section 1. The eighteenth article of amendment to the Constitution of the United States is hereby repealed.

Section 2. The transportation or importation into any State, Territory, or possession of the United States for delivery or use therein of intoxicating liquors, in violation of the laws thereof, is hereby prohibited.

Section 3. The article shall be inoperative unless it shall have been ratified as an amendment to the Constitution by conventions in the several States, as provided in the Constitution, within seven years from the date of the submission hereof to the States by the Congress.

Amendment XXII (1951)

Section 1. No person shall be elected to the office of the President more than twice, and no person who has held the office of President, or acted as President, for more than two years of a term to which some other person was elected President shall be elected to the office of the President more than once. But this Article shall not apply to any person holding the office of President, when this Article was proposed by the Congress, and shall not prevent any person who may be holding the office of President, or acting as

President, during the term within which this Article becomes operative from holding the office of President or acting as President during the remainder of such term.

Section 2. This article shall be inoperative unless it shall have been ratified as an amendment to the Constitution by the legislatures of three-fourths of the several States within seven years from the date of its submission to the States by the Congress.

Amendment XXIII (1961)

Section 1. The District constituting the seat of Government of the United States shall appoint in such manner as the Congress may direct: A number of electors of President and Vice President equal to the whole number of Senators and Representatives in Congress to which the District would be entitled if it were a State, but in no event more than the least populous State; they shall be in addition to those appointed by the States, but they shall be considered, for the purposes of the election of President and Vice President, to be electors appointed by a State; and they shall meet in the District and perform such duties as provided by the twelfth article of amendment.

Section 2. The Congress shall have power to enforce this article by appropriate legislation.

Amendment XXIV (1964)

Section 1. The right of citizens of the United States to vote in any primary or other election for President or Vice President, for electors for President or Vice President, or for Senator or Representative in Congress, shall not be denied or abridged by the United States or any State by reason of failure to pay any poll tax or other tax.

Section 2. The Congress shall have power to enforce this article by appropriate legislation.

Amendment XXV (1967)

Section 1. In case of the removal of the President from office or of his death or resignation, the Vice President shall become President.

Section 2. Whenever there is a vacancy in the office of the Vice President, the President shall nominate a Vice President who shall take office upon confirmation by a majority vote of both Houses of Congress.

Section 3. Whenever the President transmits to the President pro tempore of the Senate and the Speaker of the House of Representatives his written declaration that he is unable to discharge the powers and duties of his office, and until he transmits to them a written declaration to the contrary, such powers and duties shall be discharged by the Vice President as Acting President.

Section 4. Whenever the Vice President and a majority of either the principal officers of the executive departments or of such other body as Congress may by law provide, transmit to the President pro tempore of the Senate and the Speaker of the House of Representatives their written declaration that the President is unable to discharge the powers and duties of his office, the Vice President shall immediately assume the powers and duties of the office as Acting President.

Thereafter, when the President transmits to the President pro tempore of the Senate and the Speaker of the House of Representatives his written declaration that no inability exists, he shall resume the powers and duties of his office unless the Vice President and a majority of either the principal officers of the executive department or of such other body as Congress may by law provide, transmit within four days to the President pro tempore of the Senate and the Speaker of the House of Representatives their written declaration that the President is unable to discharge the powers and duties of his office. Thereupon Congress shall decide the issue, assembling within forty eight hours for that purpose if not in session. If the Congress, within twenty one days after receipt of the latter written declaration, or, if Congress is not in session, within twenty one days after Congress is required to assemble, determines by two thirds vote of both Houses that the President is unable to discharge the powers and duties of his office, the Vice President shall continue to discharge the same as Acting President; otherwise, the President shall resume the powers and duties of his office.

Amendment XXVI (1971)

Section 1. The right of citizens of the United States, who are eighteen years of age or older, to vote shall not be denied or abridged by the United States or by any State on account of age.

Section 2. The Congress shall have power to enforce this article by appropriate legislation.

Amendment XXVII (1992)

No law, varying the compensation for the services of the Senators and Representatives, shall take effect, until an election of Representatives shall have intervened.